Canadian Small Business Kit For Dummies®, 2nd Edition

Cheat Sheet

W9-CVO-254

Ten Tips for Small Business Success

1. **Decide whether small business is right for you.** Before you dash out and start up your own business, stop and think whether you have the right stuff to be an entrepreneur. If you don't, it's better to realize that before you sink a lot of time, effort, and money into a business start-up.

2. **Learn as much as you can about running a business before you start.** Don't invest money in a business start-up without investing some time and mental activity first. Get general information about starting and carrying on a business. Find out as much as you can about your particular field of business. Then make sure you have the skills you need to run your business.

3. **Don't be a loner.** Starting up a business takes a lot of work, so get professional help — at the very least you'll need a lawyer, an accountant, and an insurance agent or broker. Also consider bringing in an associate if that will make your business stronger.

4. **Pick your product and market carefully.** You need a product or service to sell. Preferably something that customers or clients want to buy! Do pre-start-up customer research to identify a target market for the product or service and to estimate the size of the market. Don't forge ahead with a product that hardly anyone will buy from you.

5. **Make sure you have the right to use all of your brilliant ideas.** "Your" ideas may already be owned by someone else. If that's the case, you can't use them without the owner's permission. And if your ideas are really yours, you'll want to protect them so that nobody else can steal them from you.

6. **Budget for your business's first year.** Calculate carefully how much money you'll need to set up your business and run it for the first year. Then think about where you'll get the money you need. You have to be realistic about how much money you'll be able to borrow — especially if you don't own a home you can offer as security for a loan.

7. **Be profitable before being fancy.** Make sure that your business is properly housed, equipped, and staffed, but don't spend money you don't have. Work out of your home if you can. Get functional rather than top-of-the-line equipment and furniture. Don't hire a permanent employee if computer software or contract workers can do the job instead.

8. **Be prepared to be a Jack or Jill of all trades.** You'll have to wear many hats when your business is in the early stages, so you'll need the skills to do many things — such as sales, bookkeeping, and secretarial work. But know when it's time to outsource work or hire an employee, so that you can concentrate on what you do best.

9. **Have set hours of business, even if you work from home.** Having set hours makes it easier for your customers to find you when they need you. It also helps you make sure you actually work, if you're someone who tries to avoid working, or that you don't work all the time, if you're a workaholic.

10. **Satisfy your customers and satisfy yourself.** You have to satisfy your customers by providing good quality products or service. But they have to satisfy you, too, principally by paying you in full and on time. Learn how to manage your relationship with your customers so that you'll both be satisfied.

For Dummies: Bestselling Book Series for Beginners

Canadian Small Business Kit For Dummies®, 2nd Edition

Cheat Sheet

Five Great Web Sites for Setting Up a Small Business

1. **Canada Business Service Centres** (www.cbsc.org) Get government and general business information on topics such as starting a business, writing a business plan, finding financing, marketing, exporting, and being an employer. There's a CBSC for every province and territory, and they are designed for use by start-up entrepreneurs in any field.

2. **Strategis** (www.strategis.gc.ca) Search for information about specific business sectors. For each business sector there are also links to company directories, contacts, industry events, and statistics.

3. **The Yellow Pages** (www.yellowpages.ca) Look for suppliers for your business in a particular business sector and/or geographic area. Let your fingers do the walking (across your keyboard instead of through the phone book)!

4. **Thomas Net, the Thomas Register Online** (www.thomasnet.com) Track down suppliers for your business another way with this database that includes over 650,000 distributors, manufacturers, and service companies within more than 67,000 searchable categories.

5. **Royal Bank** (www.royalbank.com) Get information about many general business topics such as starting, managing, financing, and growing a business. Or use "The Big Idea," an online guide through the steps of developing a business plan.

Five Reasons Why Small Businesses Fail

1. **The business is based on an idea that only a mother could love.** A business idea may seem wonderful to the business owner, but a business needs a slightly larger market than the owner if it's going to prosper. A business won't last long if it offers a product or service that nobody wants or can afford.

2. **The business is undercapitalized.** A business with too much debt will fail, even if it's based on a great idea and is otherwise well run. The business has to make enough money to cover its loan payments as well as pay the owner. If a business doesn't repay its loans, its creditors will pull the plug.

3. **The business doesn't keep the customers happy.** A fantastic business concept and good advertising may get customers in the door — once — but it takes excellent customer service to keep customers coming back. Dissatisfied customers don't pay their bills, won't return, and won't refer other customers. Without customers (who pay) the business will fail.

4. **The business doesn't change with the times.** A business must be able to adapt — what worked in the past may not work in the future. A business that doesn't respond to the changing marketplace may find that there is no longer a market for its product or services, or that its customers have gone over to the competition.

5. **The business expands unwisely.** Some unprofitable businesses expand in the hope that doing more business will increase profits — but expanding an unprofitable business just creates a bigger unprofitable business. And a business that expands without proper planning may lose its core customers because it can no longer serve them properly, or may not generate enough new customers to cover the cost of financing the expansion.

For Dummies: Bestselling Book Series for Beginners

Canadian Small Business Kit

FOR DUMMIES®

2ND EDITION

by Margaret Kerr and JoAnn Kurtz

WILEY

John Wiley & Sons Canada, Ltd.

Canadian Small Business Kit For Dummies,® 2nd Edition

Published by
John Wiley & Sons Canada, Ltd.
6045 Freemont Boulevard
Mississauga, Ontario, L5R 4J3
www.wiley.com

Library and Archives Canada Cataloguing in Publication Data

Kerr, Margaret Helen, 1954-
    Canadian small business kit for dummies / by Margaret Kerr and
JoAnn Kurtz. — 2nd ed.

Includes index.
ISBN-13 978-0-470-83818-1

    1. Business planning — Canada. 2. New business enterprises — Canada —
Management. 3. Small business — Canada — Management. I. Kurtz, JoAnn,
1951- II. Title.

HD62.7.K47 2006   658.1'141'0971   C2006-900781-0

Printed in Canada

3 4 5 TRI 10 09 08 07

Distributed in Canada by John Wiley & Sons Canada, Ltd.

For general information on John Wiley & Sons Canada, Ltd, including all books published by Wiley Publishing, Inc., please call our warehouse, Tel 1-800-567-4797. For reseller information, including discounts and premium sales, please call our sales department, Tel 416-646-7992. For press review copies, author interviews, or other publicity information, please contact our marketing department, Tel 416-646-4584, Fax 416-236-4448.

For authorization to photocopy items for corporate, personal, or educational use, please contact in writing The Canadian Copyright Licensing Agency (Access Copyright). For an Access Copyright license, visit www.accesscopyright.ca or call toll free, 1-800-893-5777.

WILEY

About the Authors

Margaret Kerr and **JoAnn Kurtz** are lawyers, and they are also both entrepreneurs — and they have the bumps, bruises, and scars to prove it. Occasionally, they find they have a minute of free time here and there, and that's how they came to be the authors of, among other books, *Buying, Owning and Selling a Home in Canada* (now in its second edition); *Canadian Tort Law in a Nutshell* (with Laurence Olivo, also in its second edition); *Legal Research: Step by Step* (with Arlene Blatt, another one in its second edition!); *Make it Legal: What Every Canadian Entrepreneur Needs to Know About the Law;* and *Facing a Death in the Family.* They're also the authors of another excellent *For Dummies* book that's to die for — *Wills and Estates for Canadians For Dummies Planning Kit.*

Dedication

JoAnn dedicates this book to her father, George Kurtz, with love.

Margaret dedicates this book affectionately to Bree and Poppy (although they didn't offer much help).

Authors' Acknowledgments

We very much appreciate the assistance of the following people who reviewed chapters for us and gave us the benefit of their expertise: Frank Altman, Suzette Blom, Noel Courage, Krista Kehl, Michael Kerr, and Yoram Rostas. Thanks! We wouldn't have gotten it quite right without you.

We'd like to thank our editor on the first edition, Joan Whitman, and our editor on this edition, Robert Hickey; our copyeditor, Heather Ball; our project manager, Elizabeth McCurdy; and our project coordinator, Pam Vokey.

Publisher's Acknowledgments

We're proud of this book; please send us your comments at `canadapt@wiley.com`. Some of the people who helped bring this book to market include the following:

Acquisitions, Editorial, and Media Development

Associate Editor: Robert Hickey

Copy Editor: Colborne Communications

Cartoons: Rich Tennant
(`www.the5thwave.com`)

Composition

Publishing Services Director: Karen Bryan

Publishing Services Manager: Ian Koo

Project Manager: Elizabeth McCurdy

Project Coordinator: Pam Vokey

Layout and Graphics: Wiley Indianapolis Composition Services

Proofreader: Techbooks

Indexer: Belle Wong

John Wiley & Sons Canada, Ltd

   Bill Zerter, Chief Operating Officer

   Jennifer Smith, Publisher, Professional and Trade Division

Publishing and Editorial for Consumer Dummies

   Diane Graves Steele, Vice President and Publisher, Consumer Dummies

   Joyce Pepple, Acquisitions Director, Consumer Dummies

   Kristin A. Cocks, Product Development Director, Consumer Dummies

   Michael Spring, Vice President and Publisher, Travel

   Suzanne Jannetta, Editorial Director, Travel

Publishing for Technology Dummies

   Andy Cummings, Vice President and Publisher, Dummies Technology/General User

Composition Services

   Gerry Fahey, Vice President of Production Services

   Debbie Stailey, Director of Composition Services

Contents at a Glance

Introduction *1*

Part I: Launch Preparations..*7*

Chapter 1: Do You Have the Right Stuff? 9

Chapter 2: First Contact — Is There Any Business Information Out There?............29

Chapter 3: Whose Idea Is This, Anyway?...47

Chapter 4: The Void and How to Avoid It — Choosing a
Product and Customers 67

Part II: Blast Off into Business *83*

Chapter 5: A Vehicle for Your Business 85

Chapter 6: Getting Your Gear Together 103

Chapter 7: Your Business Coordinates 125

Chapter 8: Attention: Now Entering Cyberspace 143

Chapter 9: Custom-Made Business — or Off-the-Shelf?.................................161

Chapter 10: The Money-Hunter's Guide to the Galaxy 185

Chapter 11: So Long and Thanks for All the Cash...203

Part III: On Board Your Enterprise *223*

Chapter 12: Alert! Incoming Risks Detected 225

Chapter 13: Co-existing with Other Life Forms I: Customers and Clients..............245

Chapter 14: Co-existing with Other Life Forms II: Suppliers and Advisors............267

Chapter 15: Beam Up the Crew 287

Chapter 16: Tax Attacks! 309

Chapter 17: Close Encounters with Accounting 329

Part IV: What Does the Future Hold?..........................*351*

Chapter 18: Houston, We Have a Problem 353

Chapter 19: The Expanding Business Universe 373

Chapter 20: The Contracting Business Universe...393

Part V: The Part of Tens 411

Chapter 21: Ten Mottos for a Successful Small Business................................413
Chapter 22: Ten Key Documents for a Small Business 419
Chapter 23: Ten Internet Sites You May Find Useful...................................427

Appendix: What's on the CD-ROM 433

Index 439

Table of Contents

Introduction *1*

Why You Need This Book...1
How to Read This Book 1
What's in This Book 2
    Part I: Launch Preparations 2
    Part II: Blast Off into Business 2
    Part III: On Board Your Enterprise 3
    Part IV: What Does the Future Hold? 4
    Part V: The Part of Tens..4
Icons..4

Part 1: Launch Preparations *7*

Chapter 1: Do You Have the Right Stuff? 9

The Pros and the Cons 10
    The pros...10
    The cons 11
Have You Chosen Your Business Yet?..12
    Those who have a clue 13
    Those who are clueless 14
The Small Business Personality 17
    The small business personality aptitude test...............................19
Your Personality Is Charming, but You Need Great Legs Too 24
    Your personal life 24
    Your practical resources 25
    The economy and the market..26
Should You Give Up Your Day Job?...27
Can You Believe What We've Put You Through, and It's Only
    the First Chapter? 28

Chapter 2: First Contact — Is There Any Business Information
Out There? .... .29

Getting Started 30
    Canada Business Service Centres 30
    Provincial/territorial government Web sites 33
    Bank and trust company Web sites...34
    Small business or entrepreneurship centres.................................34
    Business incubators..35
Getting Information Geared to Your Specific Business 36
    Strategis 36
    Trade and professional associations 38

Pre-mission Training...39
  Skills for your particular business 39
  General business skills 40
Finding Ground Support..40
  Do you really need a lawyer? 41
  And an accountant? 41
  And an insurance agent or broker too?...................42
  Anyone else? 42
  How do you find professional help?.........................43
  Where do you turn for emotional support?.............43
Getting the Scoop on Customers and Suppliers 44
  Customers 44
  Suppliers...45

Chapter 3: Whose Idea Is This, Anyway? **47**

What a Fine Idea..47
  What's the value of an idea? 48
  Who owns an idea?...48
  How do owners protect ideas from unauthorized use? 49
Manufacturing or Selling a Product in Your Business 50
  Manufacturing or selling a product from a design..........................50
  Manufacturing a product that you've invented................................51
  Manufacturing or selling a product that someone else
    has invented 55
Using a Name or Word in Your Business...................................56
  Naming your business 57
  Selecting a name, slogan, or logo that identifies
    your business or product 58
Using Written Materials in Your Business.................................62
  Understanding copyright 62
  Using someone else's written material.....................63
  Using someone else's confidential materials..........64
  Using your own written materials..............................65
Using Pictures and Drawings in Your Business.......................65
Using Music in Your Business...66

**Chapter 4: The Void and How to Avoid It — Choosing
a Product and Customers** **67**

What Is Marketing? 68
Developing Your Product or Service with a Market in Mind 68
  Eureka! 68
  Sober second thoughts..69
  Tinker with your idea...73
Finding a Route to the Target Market 73
  Business to buyer...74
  Business to business to buyer....................................74

Pricing Your Product or Service..74
    Deciding on the minimum price you can charge.................75
    Deciding on the maximum price you can charge................76
    Setting your price..77
Finding Customers or Clients...77
    Promotion..78
    Advertising...78
    Publicity..79
    Professional help..80
    Don't get depressed..80
Now Get Out There and Sell!..80

Part II: Blast Off into Business.................................83

Chapter 5: A Vehicle for Your Business.....................85
Should You Go Alone or Take on a Co-pilot?................................85
Should You Incorporate?...86
    What are your options?...87
    What's the difference?..87
The Corporation — a Form of Business with a Life All Its Own.......88
    Understanding corporations...88
    Setting up a corporation..89
    Running a corporation...90
    Advantages of incorporation . . . at least in theory............91
    Advantages of incorporation, continued............................93
    Disadvantages of incorporation..93
Protecting Your Assets without Incorporating..............................94
Your Choices If You're the Only Owner.......................................94
    Sole proprietorship..95
    A solely owned corporation...96
Your Choices If There Are Two or More Owners............................96
    Partnership...96
    A multi-shareholder corporation.......................................99
So How Do You Choose?...100
Some Other Start-up Concerns..101
    Investigating permits, licences, and other government
      requirements..101
    Registering for payroll taxes and the GST.........................102

Chapter 6: Getting Your Gear Together.....................103
Setting Up Your Business Office..103
    Choosing between functional and fancy............................103
    Finding furniture...104
    Finding furnishings...105
    Stocking survival equipment...106

Getting low-tech hardware 107
Getting high-tech hardware...107
Getting software and services 110
Establishing a Web presence 113
Specific Equipment for Your Business 114
Buying Equipment versus Leasing Equipment..115
Buying 115
Leasing..116
Looking for help?...117
Getting Business Stationery and Printed Materials................................118
Well-managed 118
Successful 119
Putting It All Together 122

Chapter 7: Your Business Coordinates 125
Working from Home..125
Should you have a home-based business?.....................................126
Tips for working at home successfully..130
Working from Real Business Premises 133
Premises available, apply within..133
Space-sharing arrangements...134
Renting Business Premises 135
Knowing what you're looking for 135
Finding what you're looking for 136
Determining the cost of your space..137
Exploring commercial leases 137
Buying Business Premises 140

Chapter 8: Attention: Now Entering Cyberspace 143
What Is This Cyberspace Place Anyway?...143
Using the Internet in your business..144
Getting to the Internet 144
Avoiding cyberspace hazards 145
Surfing the Web on Business 145
Communicating Over the Internet 146
E-mail...146
Instant messaging..148
VoIP 149
Using the Internet to Get Access to Your Office 150
Remote access to your e-mail...151
Remote access to your data..151
Linking Up with Your Colleagues 152
Getting a Web Site of Your Own..153
Why do you need a Web site? 153
A Web server or a Web host..154
A domain name 155
What to put on your Web site..156
Attracting visitors 158

Getting Paid Online 159
    Merchant account 159
    Third party processor 159

Chapter 9: Custom-Made Business — or Off-the-Shelf? 161

Why Buy an Existing Business? 162
Where Do You Shop for a Business? 163
I'd Like to Have a Look at That One, Please 164
    Why is the owner selling the business? 164
    What is the reputation of the business? 165
    What is the reason for the success of the business? 165
    How's the neighbourhood? 165
    What do the financial statements tell you? 166
    What is the "corporate culture"? 169
I Might Be Interested . . . If the Price Is Right 170
    What's a business worth? 170
    Sources of information for valuing a business 172
Putting the Deal Together 173
    Buy assets or buy shares? 173
    Deciding between a share purchase and an asset purchase 174
    Allocation of the purchase price in an asset purchase ...176
    The dear departed — can you control the former owner? ...176
What about a Franchise? 178
    What are the advantages of a franchise? 178
    What are the disadvantages of a franchise? 179
    Finding a franchise 180
    Evaluating the franchises you find 181
    Before you sign 183
Well 183

Chapter 10: The Money-Hunter's Guide to the Galaxy 185

Your Business Needs Capital 185
Your Business Needs Operating Funds 187
    Projecting your expenses and revenues 187
    Preparing a forecast of income and expenses 188
    Projected cash flow 189
Locating Sources of Financing for a Start-Up Operation 191
    Mix-and-match financing 192
    Personal assets 192
    Love money 193
    Money borrowed from commercial lenders 193
    Micro-credit funds 197
    Credit from suppliers and clients 198
    Sale of accounts receivable 198
    Government loans and grants 199
    Arm's-length investment 199
Applying for Money 202

Chapter 11: So Long and Thanks for All the Cash **203**

Don't Panic!...203
 First reason not to panic 204
 Second reason not to panic 204
 Third reason not to panic...204
First Step 205
Filling Out an Application Form 205
Preparing a Business Plan...206
Checking Out What Goes into a Business Plan 207
 A full-scale business plan 207
 A mini business plan 208
Stating How Much You Want (Your Objective).......................................208
Describing Your Business 209
 Your product or service 209
 The goals of your business 210
 Your business within the industry..210
 Why your business can compete successfully...............................212
 Your market...212
 Your competitors..215
Explaining How Your Business Runs 216
 Business info and history...216
 Business managers..216
 Business operations..217
Supplying Financial Information 217
 Capital requirements of your business...218
 Assets and liabilities of your business 219
 Projected income and expenses of your business.........................219
 Your personal capital...219
Providing References..220
Pulling the Final Product Together 221
 Cover...221
 Executive summary...221

Part III: On Board Your Enterprise *223*

Chapter 12: Alert! Incoming Risks Detected **225**

What Kind of Trouble Can a Business Run Into?.....................................226
 Injury to others...226
 Injury to your business...227
 Injury to you and your business associates 228
Making Your Risks as Small as Possible..228
 Injury to others...228
 Injury to your business...231
 Duh..236
Getting Somebody Else to Take Over Your Risks....................................236
 Have you already got insurance? 237
 Do you really need insurance?...237

Insurance Policies 238
    Insurance in case your business causes damage......................239
    Insurance against damage to your business................................240
    Insurance to protect the people working in your business..........243

Chapter 13: Co-existing with Other Life Forms I:
Customers and Clients **245**
    Recognizing What You Want from Your Customers or Clients..............246
    Reviewing What Happens in the Usual Business Transaction 246
    Getting Your Customers in the Door 247
    Making the Sale...247
        The pitch and the close 247
        Customer service, part 1 — first impressions....................248
    Documenting Your Agreement 248
        Contracts for the sale of goods 249
        Contracts for services 251
        Speak to your lawyer 253
    Doing the Work...253
        Do the work..253
        Customer service, part 2 — happy customers....................253
        Customer service, part 3 — unhappy customers 254
    Getting Paid...255
        Planning to get paid 256
        Collecting your accounts receivable 257
        Customer service, part 4 — customer privacy 258
    Getting Repeat Business and Referrals 260
        Customer service, part 5 — the aftermath 261
    When Peaceful Coexistence Is Shattered 261
        If you get fired for no good reason.................................261
        If you really screw up...263

Chapter 14: Co-existing with Other Life Forms II:
Suppliers and Advisors **267**
    So Now You're the Customer 268
        Determining what goods and services you need 268
        Finding suppliers 269
        Choosing a supplier 270
    Establishing Credit with Your Suppliers 273
    Entering Into Contracts with Your Suppliers............................273
        Contracts for goods 274
        Contracts for services 275
        Speak to your lawyer 277
    Establishing a Good Relationship with Your Suppliers..................278
    Problems with Suppliers 279
        Try to avoid problems in the first place...........................280
        Some problems that can arise 280
        If you suffer loss or damage because of your supplier................282

Using Suppliers of Professional Services 282
   Finding professional help 283
   Entering into contracts with professional advisors.................283
   Working with professional advisors.................................285
   Dealing with problems with professional advisors...................285

Chapter 15: Beam Up the Crew **287**
   What Are You Getting Yourself Into? 287
      Paying wages...288
      Providing paid vacation and statutory holidays.................288
      Remitting money to the feds . . . and the provs................289
      Providing a safe workplace 289
      Taking responsibility for your employees' actions..............290
   Hiring an Employee..290
      Drafting a job description and qualifications 291
      Funding an employee..292
      Finding job candidates 292
      Reviewing the job applications 293
      Interviewing the most promising candidates 294
      Checking the candidates out 297
      Making an offer 298
      Don't forget the unsuccessful candidates 300
   Being an Employer 300
      Being a manager 301
      Complying with government requirements 301
      Maintaining records 302
      Establishing policies 303
   Firing an Employee 304
      Firing for just cause..304
      Firing without just cause 305
      Wrongful dismissal 305
      Human rights concerns 306
   When Your Employee Is Gone 306
   Welcome Aboard! 307

Chapter 16: Tax Attacks! **309**
   First, Review Your Troops...310
      The lone warrior...310
      Cyberhelp 311
      Battle-hardened soldiers 311
   Income Taxes 311
      What income is a business taxed on?............................312
      What is business income? 312
      What are legitimate business expenses?.........................313
      How much tax will you pay? 316
      When and how do you have to pay?...............................318
      If you've engaged in conduct unbecoming 321
      What records must you keep? 321
      What if you're audited?..322

Sales Taxes 323
    Provincial sales tax 323
    Goods and Services Tax 324
    Harmonized Sales Tax 326
Payroll Taxes...326
Business Taxes 327
We Surrender! 327

Chapter 17: Close Encounters with Accounting **329**
What's Accounting and Why Is It Important?.................................329
Close Encounter of the First Kind: Bookkeeping 330
    Saving pieces of paper 331
    Recording your transactions 331
    Sorting your income and expenses by category....................333
    Handling the bookkeeping burden 336
Inventory Accounting..338
Internal Controls 339
Close Encounter of the Second Kind:
    Preparing Financial Documents...339
    Tax and related returns 339
    Financial statements 340
Historical Financial Statements..341
    Creating financial statements 341
    The income statement 341
    The balance sheet 343
    Case Study: E.T.&T. Telecommunications Inc. 345
Cash Flow Projections 347
Close Encounter of the Third Kind: Hiring an Accountant 348
What kind of accountant? 349

Part IV: What Does the Future Hold? 351

Chapter 18: Houston, We Have a Problem **353**
No Money 354
    Your business can't make a payment that's due 354
    You've personally guaranteed a debt for your business
      and your business can't pay 357
    Your business can't pay its rent 358
    Your business can't pay a mortgage on real property 359
    Your business can't pay its taxes 360
    Your business is insolvent..360
    Bankruptcy 362
Disputes...362
    Negotiation of a settlement..363
    Alternative dispute resolution (ADR) 368
    Litigation...370

Chapter 19: The Expanding Business Universe 373

What "Doing More Business" Means 373
Don't Do More Business If 374
    Lowering expenses..375
    Raising prices...376
How Do You Find More Business?...377
    See if you can do more of the same work for existing
        customers 377
    Find more customers for the same work 379
    Do new and additional work for existing customers 380
    Find new customers for new products or services 380
How Do You Finance Your Expansion? 381
    Sale or sale and leaseback of equipment 381
    Retained earnings..381
    Equity investment 381
How Do You Manage a Bigger Business?...383
    Learning personal management techniques......................384
    Learning business management techniques......................389

Chapter 20: The Contracting Business Universe 393

Parting from Your Business May Be a Joint Venture 394
Tax Considerations When You Get Out of Business 394
    Taxation of capital gains...395
    Calculation of capital gains 395
    And now a few words in plain English 396
Selling Your Business as a Going Concern 396
    Knowing what your business is worth 396
    Finding a buyer 397
    Dealing with prospective buyers.......................................397
    Putting the deal together..398
Going Out of Business 401
    Finding buyers for your business's assets 401
    Unloading leased equipment 403
    Paying off your debts...403
    Notifying your clients or customers 403
    Notifying your suppliers..404
    Negotiating with your landlord...404
Being Put Out of Business...404
    How your secured creditors can put you out of business............405
    How your unsecured creditors can put you out of business 406
Dying to Get Out of Business...406
    Short-term planning versus long-term planning 407
    Keeping it in the family..408
    Selling to an outsider 409

Part V: The Part of Tens 411

Chapter 21: Ten Mottos for a Successful Small Business 413
Eyes on the Prize..413
We learn something new about this business every day..............414
We've even got our competitors working for us 414
We're focused on what we do best...414
We have 80/20 vision...415
We watch every penny..416
Our customer is our CEO 416
Here today, there tomorrow..416
The buck stops everywhere...417
Make haste slowly..417
Ten Expressions That Sum Up Your Feelings 417
Added Bonus! Five Personal Mottos for You...............................418

Chapter 22: Ten Key Documents for a Small Business 419
Marketing Plan..419
Partnership agreement or shareholder agreement 420
Lease for your business premises..421
Insurance policy 421
Business plan 422
Loan documents 422
Standard customer contract 423
Employment contract 424
Confidential disclosure agreement 425
Non-competition agreement 425

Chapter 23: Ten Internet Sites You May Find Useful 427
Canada Business Service Centres (www.cbsc.org)......................427
Your provincial government 428
Royal Bank (www.royalbank.com) 429
Strategis (www.strategis.gc.ca) 429
Search engines (www.yahoo.com; www.google.com)..................429
The Yellow Pages (www.yellowpages.ca)...................................430
Suppliers (www.thomasnet.com; www.strategis.gc.ca/cdncc) 430
Office supplies (www.staples.ca; www.officedepot.ca) 430
Business Development Bank of Canada (www.bdc.ca) 431
Canada Revenue Agency (www.cra.gc.ca) 431

Appendix: What's on the CD-ROM...............................433
System Requirements 433
Using the CD 434

What You'll Find on the CD 434
    Forms 435
    Software 436
Troubleshooting 437

Index 439

Introduction

• •

Starting a business: The final frontier.

Your entrepreneurial mission: To explore new products and services. To seek out new markets, new customers, and new suppliers. To boldly go into business for yourself.

And as you boldly go, who knows where you may end up? To keep from ending up lost in space, you need help setting up your business — choosing the right vehicle, charting the right course, and taking off with the right payload. This book gives you a head start on your voyage.

Why You Need This Book

Actually, we need you to buy this book. We're small businesspeople ourselves — this book is our product and you're our customer. You don't want to be responsible for fellow entrepreneurs winking out of existence, do you?

You need to buy this book for your own selfish reasons as well for as our selfish reason of making our business a success. It's common knowledge that many small businesses fail in the first year or two. And it's because the business owners are poorly prepared to go into business. They don't know the things they need to know. This book isn't long enough to tell you everything you need to know, but it's a good start.

How to Read This Book

The way to read this book is . . . carefully! You could be holding the key to your future business success in your hands.

Each chapter is self-contained, so you can pick up some information here and some information there about a topic that's of particular interest to you. But if you're really thinking of starting a business and you haven't been in business before (or you've been in business and got sucked into the black hole of ignominious failure), you should begin at the beginning and keep going until you reach the very end.

What's in This Book

This book is made up of four major sections, plus a Part of Tens. Each of the major sections covers a stage in setting up and running a new business.

Part 1: Launch Preparations

We don't want you to take flight into entrepreneurship without any idea about what you're getting into. So in this part we do a kind of prelaunch check to help you figure out whether you'll make the grade or whether you'll wash out.

In Chapter 1, we tell you what going into business for yourself is really like. It's not all coffee breaks and exciting foreign travel — that's for sure! Do you think you have the right stuff to survive and prosper as an entrepreneur? Take our questionnaire . . . if you dare. (If you don't dare, you're a wuss and you just got washed out.) In Chapter 2, we tell you how to make contact with sources of information about starting and carrying on a business, about acquiring general business skills and skills specific to your business field, and about linking up with your chosen field. We also give you some ideas on how to find experts whose help you'll need. In Chapter 3, we help you figure out what ideas you'll want use in your business — ideas such as inventions, written materials, business names, and slogans and logos — and whether you have or can get the legal right to use them. (We also tell you what can happen if you use ideas without having the right to use them.) Finally, in Chapter 4, we take you through the process of developing a product and identifying a market . . . so that you don't just set up an earthworm-flavoured chewing-gum booth in the middle of a denture clinic and wonder why your sales are so low.

Part 11: Blast Off into Business

Looks like we can't hold you back! You're determined to launch yourself into business. To make sure your launch doesn't fizzle, there are a few things you'll need.

In Chapter 5, we explain about the three forms of business organization, and how you have to choose one (or else one will choose you). What's your pleasure — sole proprietorship, partnership, or corporation? If you haven't got a clue, this chapter will help you decide what's best for you. In Chapter 6, we take you shopping for all the basic equipment your business will require. Wear a comfortable rocket-pack because we cover a lot of territory — furniture, hardware, software, domain name and Web site, business cards, and stationery. And we don't stop for ice cream or bathroom breaks. Hey, you gotta be tough if you wanna succeed in business. In Chapter 7, we help you decide where your business (and all the equipment you bought in Chapter 6) is going to be located — your home office? leased commercial space? purchased premises? We also discuss the pros and cons of each choice. In Chapter 8, we tell you how to navigate through cyberspace by using the Internet in your business. In Chapter 9, we tell you that you could have avoided the whole hassle of Chapters 6 and 7, and maybe even Chapter 8, by buying an existing business. We take you through the process of buying a business, and leave you exhausted at the end. Then we finish you off with some wise words about buying a franchise. In Chapter 10, the bills start to come in. Now you realize that Chapters 5 through 9 don't come free, and that you'll need money to start your own business. Don't panic; after we help you calculate how much you'll need, we also tip you off about where to find the money. In Chapter 11, we complete the money-hunting process by explaining how you go about asking potential lenders and investors to part with some of their cash.

Part III: On Board Your Enterprise

You're all set up and ready to leave orbit, but we'd like to tell you about just a few more things. Ackk! What was that? Probably just an incoming risk — nothing to worry about as long as you keep out of its way.

In Chapter 12, we wise you up to risk management — the art of keeping yourself and your business out of trouble. In Chapter 13, we introduce you to your customers and explain how to keep both them and yourself happy. In Chapter 14, we introduce you to your suppliers, who are often just as important to a business as its customers. And in Chapter 15, you meet your crew! (Once you've hired them, that is.) This voyage is going to be anything but lonely. By the time you learn to manage your customers, suppliers, and employees, you may be thinking wistfully of the good old days when it was just you and the entrepreneurial urge hanging around in the backyard and staring up into the night sky.

Oh-oh — red alert! You're under attack . . . by taxes. Bring up phasers to full power! In Chapter 16, we help you fight back by clueing you in about how taxes on a business work. You'll survive the tax attack, but you may wish you hadn't when we immediately bring you within firing range of the basic principles of accounting for a small business. In Chapter 17, we explain what you have to know about accounting, even if you have an accountant and a bookkeeper.

Part IV: What Does the Future Hold?

Who can say what you'll run into as you continue your voyage? We try to prepare you for the good, the bad and even the ugly in this part. In Chapter 18, we discuss a few common problems (our focus is on two areas: lack of money, and disputes) and some solutions. In Chapter 19, we offer some tips to help you steer a course to success as your business expands. And in Chapter 20, we give you the keys to the shuttlecraft in case you decide to leave the ship for some permanent R & R — or in case you have to abandon ship.

Part V: The Part of Tens

In this part, in three short and perky chapters, we offer you

- **Ten mottos for a successful small business:** So you won't have to waste your time casting about for a Meaningful Motto. In addition, each motto gives you valuable advice about how to run your business successfully!

- **Ten key documents a business needs:** We discuss them briefly here but refer you to various chapters throughout the book where we talk about them at greater length.

- **Ten Internet sites you'll find useful:** This is a quick reference guide to some sites that a small businessperson will find handy.

Icons

This icon tells you to fire up your CD drive and have a look at the great software that comes with this book, or at an electronic version of a document or table that we're talking about.

This icon draws your attention to important information you've probably already forgotten if we've told you about it before, or to information that we want you to remember in the future.

This icon suggests that we're going to say something that will make your eyes glaze over. But we use it sparingly — instead we try to make sure to cover technical points in understandable language, so you hardly know you've hit a technical bump at all.

This icon tells you to sit up and pay attention. We're telling you something that's worth acting on or keeping in mind.

This icon says that you're heading for trouble and should reconsider your flight path!

This icon is kind of self-explanatory, don't you think? We use it when we think you should consult an expert — instead of trying to do it yourself and getting into a legal tangle.

This icon is also self-explanatory. We use it to steer you toward an expert who will keep you out of financial tangles.

This icon tells you that you have work to do, to find out more information than we can tell you in this book.

Part I
Launch Preparations

The 5th Wave   By Rich Tennant

"Right here..., crimeorg.com. It says the well run small criminal concern should have no more than nine goons, six henchmen and four stooges. Right now, I think we're goon heavy."

In this part . . .

We do a kind of prelaunch check to see whether you'll make the grade . . . or wash out. We help you to figure out whether you've got the right stuff to go into business in the first place, to get information about starting and carrying on a business, and to decide what ideas you'll want to use in your business and whether you can get the legal right to use them. Finally, we take you through the process of developing a product and identifying a market.

Chapter 1

Do You Have the Right Stuff?

· ·

In This Chapter

▶ Knowing the pros and cons of becoming a small business owner

▶ Finding the right business opportunity

▶ Assessing your entrepreneurial spirit

▶ Looking at timing

▶ Reviewing your resources

▶ Eyeing the market

▶ Deciding if you should keep your day job

· ·

So you're thinking of starting your own business! Every year, lots of people get the entrepreneurial urge and start businesses. Some of those businesses become very successful. But every year lots of new businesses fail.

Business success or failure isn't the result of fate, or random chance, or (usually) acts of God. When a business does well, there are good reasons — like a great product or service, a solid marketing plan, and the owner's good management skills.

Likewise, when a business goes under, you can often identify the reasons — lack of money to get the business properly started, poor timing or location for entering the market, or a wipeout on the customer service front. Whatever the reason for a business failure, it usually boils down to this: The business owner didn't look carefully before leaping into business.

This chapter and the others in this section of the book help you think about going into business before you hit the ignition button and blast off. Think of this first section as "countdown."

The Pros and the Cons

People start up their own businesses for different reasons. One of the best reasons is that they've found a business opportunity that's just too attractive to pass up. A good reason is that they want to work for themselves rather than for someone else. A depressing — but still valid — reason is that their other job options are poor (the number of small business start-ups always rise when the economy sinks).

Whatever your reason is for wanting to become an entrepreneur, you should know that life as an entrepreneur is kind of a mixed bag. There are some great pros to running your own business, and there are also some hefty cons.

The pros

Here are some of the advantages of going into business for yourself:

✔ **You're free!** You'll have the freedom to

- Make your own decisions — you're in charge now. Only investors, customers and clients, government regulators, and so on will tell you what to do.

- Choose your own work hours — in theory, anyway. You may not be able to get away with sleeping in until noon or concentrating your productive hours around 3 a.m. But you're more likely to be able to pick up the kids from school at 3 p.m., or work out from 10 a.m. to 11 a.m., or grocery shop during normal office hours.

- Create your own work environment — surround yourself with dirty coffee cups and overflowing ashtrays if you feel like it.

✔ **You can be creative!** You can build your business from scratch following your own ideas rather than following someone else's master plan.

✔ **You'll face new challenges!** Every day. And twice as many on days that end in a *y*. You'll never be able to say that work is always the same old boring routine.

✔ **Your job will be secure . . . as long as you have a business!** Your business may fail — but no one can fire you. (You can ask yourself to resign, though.)

✔ **You'll have increased financial opportunities!** If your business is successful, you have the potential to make more than you could as an employee.

> ✔ **You'll have tax advantages!** This is especially true if your business is not incorporated (a sole proprietorship or a partnership), but it's also true in a different way if your business is incorporated (see Chapter 5).

The cons

Do you think there were enough exclamation marks in the exuberant Pros section? Bet they got you all enthused and excited about entrepreneurship. But calm down for a minute — being an entrepreneur has plenty of disadvantages, too. For some people, they outweigh the advantages. For example:

> ✔ **You may not make a lot of money.** You may make enough money to live on, but it may not come in regularly like an employment paycheque, so you'll have budgeting problems. Or you may not make enough money to live on. You may not make any money at all. You may go bankrupt and lose not only your business but most of your personal possessions as well. See Chapter 18 for comfort (or failing comfort, at least for information).

> ✔ **You lose easy and inexpensive access to employment benefits if you don't hang on to employeeship elsewhere.** These may be benefits that you have come to count on — extended health and dental benefits, disability insurance, life insurance, a pension plan, and so on.

> ✔ **You'll have to work really hard.** That is, if you want to succeed — and you won't just be working at the business your business is about. You'll also have to do stuff you may not be trained to do, such as accounting, sales, and collection work.

> ✔ **You may not have a lot of free time.** You may see less of your friends, family, and pets (even if you're working at home) and have less time for your favourite activities. It takes more than hard work; it also takes your time and commitment to get a business up and running. Don't scoff that you won't let that happen to you, at least not until you've put in hours filling out government paperwork (GST/HST for example) on a beautiful sunny day that would be perfect for, well, almost anything else. By the way, you don't get paid for your sacrificed time, either.

> ✔ **You may have to put a lot of your own money into starting up the business.** And even if you can borrow the money, unless the lender is your mother and your mother is a naive little old lady rather than a financial shark, you'll have to give personal guarantees that the money will be repaid (with interest) within a certain time. The pressure is building! For more on borrowing, see Chapter 11. By the way, not to add to the pressure or anything, but you should know that you might lose your own money or not be able to repay borrowed money because of factors beyond your control. You could get sick (and now you probably don't

have disability insurance), be flattened by a competitor, squashed by a nose-diving economy, or whacked by a partner who pulls out on you.

✔ **The buck stops here.** No excuses — it's up to you to succeed, and it's your fault if you fail. You'll have to keep on top of changes in your field, the impact of new technology, economic fluctuations. . . .

✔ **Your personal life can stick its nose into your business life in a major way.** If you and your spouse split up, your spouse may be able to claim a share of your business under equalization provisions in the family law of some provinces. You might have to sell your business or your business assets (property) to pay off your spouse.

Have You Chosen Your Business Yet?

Now that you're feeling a little more sober and businesslike about going into business, we can talk about how people choose a business to go into.

There are five main kinds of businesses:

✔ **Service:** Doing things for others, including the professions (doctors, lawyers, dentists, architects, accountants, pilots); skilled trades (plumbers, electricians, carpet installers, bookkeepers, renovators, truckers, carpenters, landscapers); and a huge range of other things for which you might need a lot of training and skill, or at least some talent and willingness. We're talking about music teachers, financial planners, real estate agents, painters, insurance brokers, management consultants, taxi drivers, travel agents, dry cleaners, caterers, event planners, hairdressers, equipment repairers, commercial printers, photographers, gardeners, snow removers . . . this list could go on.

✔ **Retail:** Selling things to the general public, such as jewellery, groceries, clothing, appliances, books, furniture, antiques and collectibles, toys, hardware, cards and knick-knacks, garden accessories, plants, cars . . . this is also a list that could go on.

✔ **Wholesale:** Buying large quantities of goods from manufacturers at a discount and selling in smaller quantities to others — usually retailers — for a higher price. For example, you could buy nails in bulk from a manufacturer and resell them to hardware stores. Wholesalers sometimes also sell to the general public, usually without the frills of a retail establishment (for example, bulk food, carpets, and clothing).

✔ **Manufacturing:** Making things from scratch — from designing and sewing baby clothes for sale through a local children's clothing store to making furniture in a workshop to manufacturing steel ingots in a mammoth industrial plant.

✔ **Extraction:** Harvesting natural resources, including agriculture, fishing, logging, and mining.

Note that e-commerce is not a new and separate kind of business — that kind of thinking is what got it into trouble in the first place and caused the dotcoms to crash. E-commerce is simply a tool for use in business.

Small businesses are most likely to concentrate in service and retail. Service, in particular, is usually the cheapest business to start up, so it attracts a lot of entrepreneurs.

Now, most people don't look at a list of the five kinds of businesses and wonder "Service or extraction? Retail or manufacturing? What best expresses my personality?" Instead, they have an idea that happens to fit into one of the five categories. At least it helps to have an idea. And some people do, but others don't.

Those who have a clue

Most people who are thinking seriously about going into business for themselves have an idea about what they want to do before they start thinking seriously. Many people, maybe even most people, get their idea from a job they've held and decide to develop a new product or service similar to a former employer's, or become a consultant in the field.

If you're going into the same field as your previous employer, be careful not to breach any confidentiality agreement or noncompetition agreement you may have entered into, and not to infringe your previous employer's copyright or trademark (see Chapter 3).

The idea may come from your skills:

✔ If you have professional training or training in a skilled trade, you can set up your own business instead of joining a firm.

✔ If you have a hobby, you may be able to expand it into a business.

✔ If you invent something, you may be able to create a business around it.

✔ If you have always wanted to start a particular kind of business, maybe now is the time.

Or you may have become aware of an excellent business opportunity. It may or may not be related to your training, or a hobby, or your "dream" business.

Or in your travels, you may have seen a good idea that hasn't hit your hometown yet. (Starbucks was once confined to one city on the West Coast, believe it or not. Years ago, one of the authors was taken from Vancouver to Seattle by a friend to try a cup of Starbucks coffee but remained oblivious to business opportunities!)

Those who are clueless

Some people are serious about going into business but haven't decided on the business yet. If you're one of these people and you're looking for ideas . . . you probably need to look further than this chapter, or even this book. So here are some suggestions about where to look for an appealing business start-up idea.

To get an idea in the first place, you can

- ✔ Look around the field in which you have work experience to see if any opportunities are waiting to be explored. Maybe you've noticed that customers would be delighted if they could get a specific product or service that no one's offering right now.

- ✔ Look around a field in which you have play experience to scope out opportunities — a few thousand people's hobby could become one person's successful business. Parlay your love of mountain climbing into an outfitting or guiding business.

- ✔ Take out your pet peeves and look them over. You may not be the only person who wishes someone would make/import/distribute a better pair of dog boots.

- ✔ Read newspapers and magazines, trade publications, and newsletters to find out what's going on in the business world at large.

- ✔ Visit trade shows, inventors' shows, conventions, or conferences to find out what's going on in a particular field.

- ✔ Go on field trips (in your own city or town or in the wide world) to see what businesses are out there and how they're doing.

- ✔ Look for government or other lists of licensing opportunities.

- ✔ Ask friends and acquaintances for ideas.

Once you have an idea, you need to evaluate it. Next, we offer some guidelines for giving the thumbs-up or thumbs-down to a business idea. Even if you've already got your idea, it's worth your while to check it out by reading the next two sections.

What to look for in a business start-up

To begin with, try to aim toward something you'll enjoy doing. Starting a business is hard enough without choosing a business that you're pretty sure you'll loathe, despite the fact that you think it could make a lot of money.

Next, look for something people want . . . as opposed to something they don't want, or that they'll have to be carefully educated to want. It should also be something they'll want tomorrow and next week as well as today — in other words, don't base your business on a product or service that's going out of use or out of style. If possible, your product or service should be something that people want often, rather than occasionally or only once in their lifetimes. In Canada, this also means a product or service that isn't completely seasonal, like skate sharpening or outdoor ice cream stands. Choose something with a good distribution and advertising system in place: For example, a product you manufacture should be one that established retailers will be happy to carry; a product you sell should be one that already benefits from a national marketing campaign by the manufacturer; a service you offer should be positioned within a network that will bring you lots of referrals.

Look for a business with a high profit margin. You'd like your direct cost of performing the work or supplying the product to be a small percentage of what you charge the client or customer. (The service industry is good for high profit margins, manufacturing and extraction aren't.)

What to avoid in a business start-up

While you're searching for a business with lots of advantages, you also have to avoid a business with too many disadvantages.

You'll probably be happier if you stay away from a business that will be immediately overwhelmed by the existing competition. If the field is competitive (as are most fields worth going into), look for a niche where you have a competitive advantage (say, because you have a lot of natural talent or you've acquired great skills and experience; or because you have exclusive manufacturing or distribution rights). Don't go head-to-head with the established players and imagine you'll knock them down!

You also don't want a business that will be overwhelmed by regulation — by the federal, provincial, or municipal government; or by the governing body of a professional or skilled trade. You'll find regulation in any type of business, but it's worse in some than in others. For example, the manufacture of food and drugs is heavily regulated by the federal government, as are telecommunications and commercial aviation. If you open a restaurant or bar, municipal food inspectors and provincial liquor inspectors will visit you fairly regularly.

You might prefer to avoid a business that will require expensive insurance from the start (this describes most of the professions, and the manufacture of products that are potentially harmful).

Unless you've got guaranteed access to a big wad of cash, you'll certainly also want to avoid a business with high start-up costs. You may think you can build a better steel mill, but you can't do it on a $25,000 loan. Consider how much you have to invest in starting up a business, or how much you can raise by borrowing. If you have almost nothing to invest and realistically don't expect anyone else will want to invest a lot in you and your business, choose a business that requires almost no initial investment (that's usually service).

Helpful hints for aimless entrepreneurs

Here are some trendy areas for business start-ups:

Become an alter-ego for people who have money but no time.

Be a concierge or rent-a-wife (do chores for individuals, like picking up dry cleaning or getting tickets to a show); a personal shopper, closet organizer, or rent-a-husband (provide handyman services); a drop-in cook (shop for ingredients, go to the client's home and spend a few hours cooking meals for the entire week); or a personal dating service operator or matchmaker.

Sell the promise of health, youth, and beauty to an aging population.

Be a personal trainer, spa service provider (massage, manicure, pedicure, makeup, facials); a plastic surgery consultant or coordinator; a tattoo artist or tattoo removal specialist, or body piercer; or a manufacturer of exercise equipment, comfortable furniture, sun-protection clothing, or sports clothing.

Be an outsource for other people's businesses.

Provide telephone surveys, market surveys, data processing, technical support, secretarial support, bookkeeping, or Web site design.

Go the eco-entrepreneur route.

Manufacture, distribute, or sell to the public ecologically sound cleaning products, recycling systems, or energy sources that are environmentally friendly or recyclable.

Provide specialty travel arrangements.

Organize seniors' tours, educational tours, eco-tours, or singles' tours.

Look after other people's kids, parents, or pets.

Provide a chauffeur service for kids (to get them to school, practices and games, after-school lessons, or appointments); offer dog walking, house sitting, child sitting (rent-a-parent), or health care coordination for the elderly; tutoring, keyboarding/typing, music lessons, computer lessons, or test preparation; or provide sports coaching, a summer camp program, party planning and preparation, or a party place.

You'll probably also want to steer clear of a business with immediate high labour needs. Paying employees isn't just a matter of cash flow (although that's pretty important). As an employer, you'll also have to deal with a lot of regulations and paperwork — such as income tax, Employment Insurance, Canada or Quebec Pension Plan, provincial workers' compensation, and occupational health and safety rules — and you may already have enough on your plate.

The Small Business Personality

Whatever your reason for wanting to go into business for yourself, and whatever the business you decide to go into, stop and check whether you have the right personality for the adventure before you decide to start. This is true whether you really want to go into business for yourself or whether you think you have no choice but to do so. And it will give you an excuse to put off figuring out your finances.

If you don't have the right stuff to run your own business, you can always pursue other options — and it's better to realize that before you sink a lot of time and effort, and maybe even money, into a business.

And if it turns out that you're not going to be the perfect entrepreneur but you're determined to go ahead anyway, then a self-assessment will tell you where your weaknesses and strengths lie and will show you where you need to work on yourself or get outside help.

An entrepreneur needs most of the following qualities — whether you were born with them, or developed them, or are about to get working on them now.

- ✔ **Self-confidence:** You have to believe in yourself and your abilities . . . whatever other people might think. You have to believe that your success will depend on the good work you know you can do and not on matters beyond your control. However, your self-confidence should be realistic and not induced by whatever weird thing they put in the coffee at your current place of work.

- ✔ **Goal-orientation:** You have to know what you want, whether it's to revolutionize a particular industry or to be home when your children return from school. However, if your main goals are money, power, and prestige, you probably need to reorient yourself toward something that's a little more attainable in the small business sector.

- ✔ **Drive to be your own boss:** The burning desire and the ability to be your own boss — if you need or even want direction about what to do next, you won't make it in your own business. You have to be able to make your own plans and carry them out.

✔ **Independence:** The ability to work independently rather than as part of a team. You've probably had propaganda pounded into your head since you were a kid that teamwork is really important, and maybe even that it's better than work done on your own. It isn't if you're an entrepreneur.

✔ **Survival skills:** The ability to survive without a social group is handy. When you start up your own business, you'll probably be working by yourself for some time. If you need people around you to chat with, or else you start to go crazy . . . then you may go crazy.

✔ **People skills:** Even though you have to be able to get along without being surrounded by people all the time, you still have to be able to get along with people. You'll be dealing directly with customers and clients, investors, suppliers, associates, and employees and you want their willing cooperation.

✔ **Determination and persistence:** You have to want to succeed, and you have to plan to succeed and keep working at succeeding. It's that "fire in the belly" stuff you hear about from people who look like they haven't slept in the past eight months. They might stop talking about fires in the belly if they took some Maalox, but then they'd be on to some other cliché like "a business needs a champion to succeed."

✔ **Self-discipline:** You can't let yourself be distracted from your work by nice weather, phone calls from family and friends, earthquakes, or wrestling matches on TV.

✔ **Reliability:** You'll build most of your important business relationships by always meaning what you say and doing what you promise.

✔ **Versatility:** You have to be prepared to do many different things in any given short period of time, probably constantly switching from task to task.

✔ **Creativity:** You have to want to do something new or something old in a new way. If copying what someone else is already doing is the best you can manage, you may not go far.

✔ **Resourcefulness:** Creativity's country cousin, resourcefulness, means being prepared to try different ways of doing things if the first way doesn't work.

✔ **Organizational talents:** You'll be plunged into chaos if you can't organize your goals, your time, or your accounts, to name just a few things.

✔ **Risk-management instincts:** You have to be able to spot risks, weigh them, and come up with a plan to steer around them or soften their impact if there's a collision.

✔ **Nerves of steel — or some other unyielding substance of your choice — when faced with a crisis:** Nerves of granite, titanium, oak, and so on are acceptable. Nerves of rubber, talc, or pasta al dente are not. Crises won't necessarily be frequent but they will occur. Don't count on gin or prescription drugs to stiffen your spine during a crisis. And you can't collapse until the crisis is over.

- ✔ **Pick-yourself-up-itiveness — a combination of optimism and grit:** You're going to have failures, some of them caused by your own mistakes, and you have to be able to see them as valuable experiences rather than as signs that you and your business are doomed.

- ✔ **Opportunism:** You need to not only recognize opportunities when they come along but also to seek them out — and even create them yourself if they're shy and tend to hide behind the furniture when looked for.

- ✔ **Success-management instincts:** You can't let yourself be bowled over or lulled by success. You have to be able to see each success as a platform on which you can build your next success.

- ✔ **Objectivity:** For a business owner, it's always reality-check time. You have to have the courage to stare down reality's throat, even when it means acknowledging your own mistakes. You also have to corner reality by getting feedback about your business and how you run it from customers and clients, suppliers, professional advisors, competitors, employees, and even your mother-in-law. Then you have to have the strength to make necessary changes.

That's a long list! And you'll also need a Zen-like calm about not having a regular paycheque. Not only will you not get a bank deposit once a month, but you won't get paid for sick days, personal days off, or days when you show up at the office but are too zonked to work.

In addition, it helps if your parents (or close relatives or close friends) are or were in business for themselves. You may have absorbed some business know-how from them, plus you may have easy access to advice.

And to finish you off, good health and physical stamina can do an entrepreneur no harm.

The small business personality aptitude test

Now that you know what an entrepreneur is supposed to look like, it's time to hold the mirror up to yourself. After years of laboratory and field research, we have created the Kerr & Kurtz Not-Particularly Standard Scale of Aptitude for Entrepreneurship and a questionnaire to peg you on the scale. Take the test now.

Scoring: Unless scoring is otherwise indicated in the question, for each (a) you choose, award yourself 0 points; for each (b), 1 point; for each (c), 2 points, and for each (d), 3 points. The total number of points you can score is 49.

1. At school, when you were urged to show team spirit and join a team or production, you

   a) enthusiastically tried out for everything because you loved working on a team or in a group;

   b) tried out for a couple of teams or productions that you really wanted to be on;

   c) tried out for something to avoid being harassed by the team spirit police;

   d) made gagging noises and said you'd rather eat bugs. (Give yourself an extra point if your answer is "none of the above," but you offered to manage one or more teams or productions on the condition that you received a percentage of any revenues.)

2. You've arranged to meet a friend to see a movie. You

   a) wouldn't hesitate to cancel at the last minute if something better came up;

   b) would show up but wouldn't worry about being on time;

   c) wouldn't worry obsessively about being on time, but if you were late you'd try to have a good excuse ready (whether true or not);

   d) would show up at exactly the appointed time, if not earlier . . . unless the friend is someone who would choose (b) — it's okay to choose realism over reliability sometimes.

3. You're preparing for a dinner party. At practically the last minute you go to the grocery store, armed with a list of necessary ingredients. Because you're in a hurry and aren't paying enough attention, you buy some wrong ingredients. In fact, they're so wrong that you won't be able to make the main course you had carefully planned. You

   a) are filled with despair at your own incompetence and stupidity, so you call up your guests and tell them the party's cancelled;

   b) serve dinner without a main course and hope no one will notice;

   c) assume everyone's coming for your company rather than your food, and replace the main course with tinned spaghetti from the back of your cupboard;

   d) create a new main course from whatever ingredients you have on hand, refuse to admit even to yourself that it tastes a little funny, and keep the wine flowing.

4. You're in your kitchen. Just as you see that a pot on the stove is about to boil over, the phone rings, the doorbell chimes, and in another room your printer starts making noises that signal a monumental paper jam. You

   a) black out from stress;

   b) answer the phone and ignore the door, the stove, and the printer;

   c) go to the door and ask whoever's there to take the pot off the stove and answer the phone while you take care of the printer;

   d) take the pot off the stove, take the phone with you as far as it will extend toward the printer, stop the printer from destroying itself, and then open the window, stick your head out, and yell "Who is it?" to the person at the door.

5. In your household, there's a dishwasher storm trooper who insists that the dishes always be loaded in a particular way. You

   a) obey the storm trooper's orders to the letter;

b) assure the storm trooper that you load the dishwasher according to the rules, but always make a point of putting some of the silverware in the wrong way up;

c) get into constant arguments with the storm trooper about the correct way to load the dishwasher;

d) are the storm trooper.

6. When a home appliance you're using for a necessary job breaks down, your reaction is to

a) head for the nearest coffee bar for a double-double Mocha Java;

b) kick the damn thing to terrorize it into working again;

c) ignore the CAUTION! OPENING THIS PANEL WILL LEAD TO RISK OF ELECTROCUTION! label, insulate yourself, and poke around in the hope you can get it going;

d) take it in for repairs, but use all your skill to negotiate a one-hour turn-around time or a free replacement while the repairs are being carried out.

7. You're driving in heavy traffic on the highway and your exit comes up very suddenly. You're not in the exit lane. You

a) quickly pull over into the exit lane without checking, working on the assumption that all other drivers are on the alert for idiots like you and will be able to react in time to avoid crashing into you;

b) go on to the next exit, even though you'll end up driving some distance out of your way;

c) quickly check the lane you want to pull into and calculate that you can change lanes without having an accident as long as you accelerate through the change instead of braking or maintaining your present speed

and as long as no one in the exit lane changes speed;

d) were already aware of traffic all around you because it's your habit to keep a 360-degree watch when driving, and you calculate that you have time to change lines safely if you slow down slightly and pull in behind the car currently beside you in the exit lane.

8. You're in a store on a major shopping spree. When you hand your credit card over to the sales clerk, he runs it through the machine and says, "Sorry, the machine isn't accepting this card, you're over your credit limit." You give the clerk a different card and it gets rejected too. You

a) abandon your purchases and flee the store, terrified you'll be arrested for a criminal offence;

b) ask, in a dignified way, if the store will put the items away for 24 hours while you get the matter straightened out — and then never return;

c) ask to use the store's phone to call up one of the credit card companies and see if you can get your limit raised;

d) offer to write a cheque, using your credit cards as ID.

9. On a shopping expedition, you find two products that are similar, except one is on "Special" and considerably less expensive than the other. You

a) buy the cheaper one because the store says it's a good deal;

b) buy the more expensive one because things that cost more must therefore be better;

c) snag a passing sales clerk and ask if he can tell you about any difference between the two products, and base your decision on that information;

(continued)

d) don't trust a salesclerk to know the product line he or she sells, so you also carefully compare the two products for quality, manufacturer's reputation, and (as applicable) fit, range of use, warranty, and so on and base your decision on all of these factors.

10. If a service person is nasty to you without provocation when you're trying to buy something you really need right now, you say,

a) "Screw you, I don't need to take this crap," and leave without making the purchase;

b) "I want to talk to your manager, buster";

c) "Hey, whatever's eating you isn't my fault, can't you be a little more pleasant?";

d) "Looks like you're having a bad day, I hope I'm not doing anything to make it worse."

11. If we asked you to drop by next Tuesday to organize a CD collection that's gone wild, you would

a) immediately call up your dental surgeon to make a Tuesday appointment for that root canal she said you needed;

b) show up, square the piles of CDs, and maybe blow some of the dust off the cases;

c) come and line up the CDs against the wall in alphabetical order;

d) arrive early, your eyes glowing with enthusiasm, sort the collection into Rock, Country, Jazz, Musical Comedy, and Classical, sort each category alphabetically by group, artist, or name of musical, and sort each release by recording date.

12. You're working on a project. The radio is playing quietly in the background. At what point are you distracted from your work?

a) As soon as you sit down to work. You immediately get up and change stations — why wait for a distraction to happen when you can distract yourself?

b) When you hear a song you really like.

c) When the news comes on, and the announcer says that police have surrounded your immediate neighbourhood because of a bomb threat.

d) When the radio suddenly explodes.

13. You make a request based on a plan you've thought out, and are refused. When you don't instantly vanish, the person to whom you made the request says, "What part of 'No' don't you understand?" Your automatic response is to

a) burst into tears;

b) apologize politely for taking up the person's time;

c) find someone else to harass;

d) explain your request again, leaving out the big words.

14. On Monday morning, you

a) look back fondly on the weekend, which you spent with your pals from work;

b) look forward to getting in to work so you can chat with your co-workers whom you haven't seen since Friday;

c) exchange civil conversation with your co-workers for a few minutes about how the weekend went;

d) politely answer "Fine, thanks" to anyone who asks, "So how was your weekend?" and then get down to business as quickly as possible.

15. One minute before you are to start an important presentation in front of several dozen people, you bend over to pick up your notes that fell on the floor, and your pants

split up the back seam. You don't have a jacket with you, your shirt isn't long enough to cover the rip, and you don't have time to look for a concealing garment. So you

a) sidle out of the building and later mail in a letter saying you quit your job;

b) persuade someone you meet while hiding out in the washroom to go and say that the presentation is cancelled;

c) enter the room, keeping your back to a wall, and deliver the presentation sitting down;

d) begin your presentation by cheerfully announcing that you've ripped out the seat of your pants. (If you would then turn around and flash your underwear at the audience, deduct a point — you've gone beyond self-confidence to exhibitionism . . . and this is especially true if you're not wearing underwear.)

16. You've been ordered to travel to another city on business. This trip is the last thing in the world you need or want at the moment, but you have no choice about going. So you go, but

a) sulk before, during, and after the trip and swear you'll make them all pay for sending you;

b) resign yourself and determine to do the best job you can;

c) look on the trip as a break from your routine — when you get back, your daily grind will seem great in comparison;

d) investigate what personally rewarding activity of your own you can work into the trip — such as a meal at a good restaurant, a visit to a museum or spa, or a reunion with an old friend.

So having taken the test, how did you do? In case you're feeling shy, we'll encourage you by telling you what we got on the test. One of us got 36, and the other got 28 and 39 (she's a Gemini and she took the test twice, once for each side of her business personality). We're not revealing which one of us got what. There have to be some cosmic mysteries, even in business.

Now for interpretation of the questionnaire. Our scoring system, as you might imagine, is completely unscientific. If you scored 48 (or 49) points, you're kind of scary. A year from now you'll probably send us a terse e-mail telling us where we got this book right and where we got it wrong, and mentioning as an afterthought that the business you started after taking our questionnaire is now worth $1.7 billion! If you scored, say, 47 to 40 points, you probably won't get around to sending us the e-mail for two years. If you scored 39 to 30 points, you've got a bit of work to do on some aspects of your business personality, but being an entrepreneur for a while should take care of that — you learn pretty quickly when your livelihood depends on it! If you scored 29 to 20 points, you've got potential — but think entrepreneurship over very carefully before you take the leap! If you scored 19 to 10 points, keep your day job. And finally, if you scored 9 to 0 points, you may actually be a small furry rodent and you should be nibbling this book, not reading it.

As for our scores, we've both run small businesses on and off for the past 20 years. Either this means we shouldn't be in business, or else it means you don't have to score high on our test to do okay in the business world. Or else it means that questionnaires don't mean very much. But everyone likes questionnaires, and this isn't a bad one as questionnaires go; it ranks somewhere between "Does Your Car Need a Tune-up?" and "Rate Your Sex Drive: From 'Not Now' to 'Ka-zow!'"

Your Personality Is Charming, but You Need Great Legs Too

The questionnaire may have given you confidence that you're cut out for the business world. But we haven't finished with you yet.

Even if you're a potential paragon of entrepreneurship, before you roll your dice, you should also think about

- Whether your personal life will allow you to take the entrepreneurial plunge right now
- Whether you have the practical resources to go into the particular business you have your heart set on
- Whether this is a good time (for economic and market reasons) for anyone to go into this particular business

Your personal life

What's going on in your personal life right now? Starting a small business makes more sense at some times than at others.

- Do you need a steady income right now — maybe because you have small children and your spouse has given up paid employment to stay home with them, or because you have debts to repay?
- Do you need a steady and conventional lifestyle right now because all hell is breaking loose in the rest of your life?
- Do you need to be physically present in your home more (maybe because you want to be able to spend time with your young children after school or you have to look after a frail elderly parent), so a home-based business makes more sense than working outside your home?

✔ Do you have some money to throw around right now, perhaps from an inheritance or a buyout package from your employer?

✔ Would you have trouble raising the necessary cash to start a business — say, because you've just gone bankrupt?

 If you have a spouse, or someone who depends on your income or companionship, ask him or her to list the pros and cons of your going into business for yourself right now — from his or her own point of view. You might as well get it all out in the open.

Your practical resources

Do you really have what it takes to start this business? It's better to ask yourself now, before you invest time, money, and effort and maybe pass up other work or opportunities for which you're better suited.

For starters, if you go into any business, you'll have to

✔ Find customers; identify customer needs; develop new product and service ideas; decide on prices; and develop promotional strategies. (This is marketing.)

✔ Persuade customers to buy. (This is sales.)

✔ Do good work so customers will (a) be more likely to pay you and (b) come back to you. (This is commitment to excellence.)

✔ Enter into contracts to buy and provide goods and services — you need to know what has to go into the contract, even if you don't draft it yourself. (This is business law.)

✔ Have a working knowledge of the law so you don't break it and it doesn't break you (for example, you need to know about different kinds of taxes and levies, nondiscrimination in providing goods and services or in hiring, breach of the *Competition Act* in your advertising, arrest of shoplifters). (This is hair-raising.)

✔ Understand the financial side of your business and keep proper accounts (payable and receivable), collect and pay taxes, borrow money, manage cash flow, handle credit, and create and stick to a budget. (This is accounting and money management.)

✔ Keep track of the product or service you provide or sell (if it's a service, you provide your time) and purchase supplies and materials on time. (This is inventory management.)

✔ Buy and use a computer and software. (This is computer literacy.)

- ✔ Get money owed to you by deadbeat customers and clients. (This is collections.)

- ✔ Eventually hire, supervise, train, motivate, and evaluate employees. (This is human resources management.)

If you don't have these skills, you'll have to fill in the blanks. We give you some ideas about that in Chapter 2. (Don't get into a funk! You may be surprised at how many of the skills you've already acquired through courses at school, jobs you've held, participation in clubs or organizations, and even just from running your own life.)

You'll also need a set of skills to run the particular kind of business you have in mind. Ask yourself these questions:

- ✔ **Do I need particular skills, talents, years of experience, expertise, or connections to succeed in this business?** Or, in some cases, do I need all this just to get my foot in the door of this business?

- ✔ **Is this business heavily regulated?** Do I need particular education, training, or other official qualifications before I start? Do I need government approval that may not be automatic?

- ✔ **Is this business expensive?** Do I need a lot of money to get set up? (For example, will it cost a lot to develop the product or service, to manufacture the product, or to find customers or develop a distribution system?)

If you don't know the answers to these questions, you need to do your homework. Speak to people who are already in this business, read trade papers or publications about the business, or contact government offices and professional or trade associations. We'll help you out with some of this in Chapter 2.

The economy and the market

Your personal life and practical resources may be in just the right shape for you to start your own business, but the business world will chew up and spit out a navel-gazer. You also need to look at the economy generally, and at the market for your proposed product or service in particular. If the economy's tanking, it's probably not the right time to launch a luxury business . . . but it may be exactly the right time to start a business that will appeal to penny-pinchers. If the market for your product is jammed with competitors or if demand has started to dry up, you're headed for trouble if you decide to stay on course. But if the market is just about to expand in a big way, it could be that you've hit on a surefire success.

Hey, kids, try this at home!

Once you have a good idea of what you need to get into and run the business of your choice, here's an exercise for you to do if you want to put off doing really useful work for a while. First, write a job description for starting this business. What education, background, and skills are required to do the job now and as it grows? What experience would be useful? What personal characteristics should the owner have? Be objective. Forget that you're the only person to whom you're going to offer the job.

Then apply for the job by writing your own *curriculum vitae* (CV).

✔ Detail your formal education.

✔ List the jobs you've held and tasks you performed in those jobs. (You can include jobs that aren't normally considered paid employment, such as running a household.)

✔ List the skills you've acquired through formal education and training, jobs, and personal interests and activities (hobbies, sports, membership in organizations, and so on) and through life experience.

✔ Finish up with your character by listing your strengths and weaknesses.

Compare your CV with the job description. Are you up to the job? Would you hire yourself? If you think the job applicant is on kind of shaky ground, maybe you're heading into the wrong business.

But don't despair. If you don't qualify for the job yet, ask yourself what reasonable steps you could take to improve your qualifications. Maybe you can get some needed training or experience, even as you start to set up the business.

Should You Give Up Your Day Job?

Last but not least, should you start a business and keep your day job (if you've got one)?

Conventional wisdom says that you shouldn't give up your day job until absolutely necessary (that's the point when you have to devote the time to your business or give it up) or until you don't need a day job (that's the point when you're making a living from your business). Conventional wisdom also urges entrepreneurs not to go it alone until they've saved up about six months' salary. That's a good joke! It would take most of us a lifetime to save six months' salary, unless we were offered a fantastic buyout package.

Even if you're dying to tell your current employer "I quit!" ask yourself the following questions:

✔ **Do you have to have the money from employment?** Even if your business turns out to be a success, there will probably be an early period when you don't have much, or even any, income.

✔ **Do you want to keep your employment contacts?** The business you're starting might be something your employer or fellow employees could assist or patronize.

✔ **Do you have the time to hold down a job and start a business (and still have time to eat and sleep)?**

✔ **Would starting your own business and keeping your day job be problematic because of**

- Your employer's requirement (in your employment contract) that you not carry on any kind of a competing business while you're an employee?

- Your employer's requirement (in your employment contract) that you put your full effort toward your employment work?

- Suspicious superiors and co-workers who would assume you were goofing off by focusing on your own business instead of doing what you were paid to do?

✔ **Do you want to be able to fall back on your day job if your business venture doesn't work out?** Remember, if you quit to start a business, you might not get hired back.

Can You Believe What We've Put You Through, and It's Only the First Chapter?

No wonder most people don't look before they leap into business! By the time you finish looking, you're too exhausted to start a business. And we've got lots more work for you to do in the following chapters. This could be why they say you need good health and stamina to be an entrepreneur.

Chapter 2

First Contact — Is There Any Business Information Out There?

In This Chapter

▶ Searching for information

▶ Getting information about business in general

▶ Investigating your own field

▶ Building your skill set with education

▶ Finding experts to help you

▶ Looking for potential customers and suppliers

*A*re you really alone in the business universe? Or is there intelligent business information out there, waiting just beyond the limits of your vision, wondering whether you've evolved the technical capability to tap into it?

In this chapter, we'll tell you how to launch a probe to collect data about the following areas:

✔ Starting and carrying on a business

✔ Acquiring general business skills

✔ Acquiring skills for your chosen business field

✔ Choosing potential customers and suppliers

We'll also help you line up a team of experts, at the very least a lawyer, an accountant, and an insurance agent. You'll need their help to get your business off the ground.

Getting Started

Space is infinite. Information seems to be too. There are galaxies of information about business out there. How do you zero in on the information that's useful to you?

The first step is to get general information about starting and carrying on a business. Our advice is to find a fairly comprehensive and self-contained start-to-finish source, such as a book — hey, this book is a great choice! — or a business resource centre, or a Web site. You've already got the book, so below are our suggestions for resource centres and Web sites. We'll start with the superstars, the Canada Business Service Centres, but we'll also tell you about provincial and private-sector resources.

Canada Business Service Centres

The Canada Business Service Centres (CBSCs) provide access to both government and general business information. Both start-up entrepreneurs and established, small- to medium-sized businesses in any field can use them. Every province and territory has a CBSC.

Taking a look at the services offered by CBSCs

The CBSCs provide information on government services, programs, and regulations pertaining to business. Each centre also has an extensive and up-to-date reference collection of general business information from government and non-government sources — topics include starting a business, writing a business plan, finding financing, marketing, exporting, and being an employer. The Centres have information officers to help you navigate your way through all this information.

In addition, you can get products, services, publications, and referrals to experts. Here are some examples of the products the CBSCs provide:

- **Interactive Business Planner:** This software helps you work online to prepare a business plan.

- **Business Start-up Assistant:** This Web site contains business start-up information from the federal and provincial governments and other sources.

- **Online Small Business Workshop:** This Internet-based workshop gives information and techniques for developing your business idea, getting started, marketing and financing a new business, and improving an existing small business.

✔ **Info-Guides:** These free guides on different topics provide brief overviews of services and programs.

✔ **"How-to" Guides:** These guides provide information about the potential licence, permit, and registration requirements for specific types of businesses.

✔ **Fact Sheets:** These fact sheets contain information about starting and running a business and are available online.

✔ **Business Information System:** This searchable database contains more than 1,000 documents that describe business-related services and programs of the federal and provincial governments and other Canada Business partners. Each provincial/territorial Centre has a similar collection of information about provincial/territorial programs. Business Information System documents are available free of charge.

Some of the CBSCs also offer low-cost seminars and workshops on a variety of business topics.

Getting access to CBSC services

You can get in touch with your provincial or territorial CBSC in five different ways:

✔ **Telephone:** You can call the CBSCs' toll-free telecentres and listen to pre-recorded messages dealing with frequently asked questions on business topics, or you can speak to a business information officer who will direct you to the best sources of information or refer you to programs and services relevant to your business situation.

✔ **Web site:** The Canada Business Web site (www.cbsc.org) contains information about business-related programs and services of federal and provincial agencies, and provides links to the Web sites of the individual provincial/territorial CBSCs. Though each provincial Web site is individual, they all contain information on such topics as

- Starting up a business

- Financing a business

- Choosing a business location

- Franchises

- Market research

- Legal issues in business

- Becoming an employer

- Buying a business

- Provincial and municipal licensing

- Programs and services offered by the federal and provincial/territorial governments

Some of the CBSC sites also provide information about and online registration for business workshops and seminars, as well as links to other useful Web sites.

✔ **E-mail:** You can send questions to the CBSC via e-mail from the Web site.

✔ **"Talk To Us!" service:** This service, available in Alberta, British Columbia, Manitoba, New Brunswick, Newfoundland and Labrador, Nova Scotia, Ontario, Prince Edward Island, Quebec, Saskatchewan, and Yukon, allows you to connect immediately by voice to a business information officer (at vweb.cbsc.org/english/forms/na/talktous.jsp) who will search the Internet with you for the information you need.

✔ **A visit in person:** At the offices of your provincial/territorial CBSC, you can use the resource materials on your own or with the help of a business information officer. The CBSCs also have arrangements with existing business service organizations in communities across Canada to provide CBSC information. Contact your provincial/territorial CBSC for the location nearest you.

CBSC locations and contacts

Alberta

The Business Link, Business Service Centre, Suite 100, 10237 104 Street NW, Edmonton, AB T5J 1B1; phone 780-422-7722 or 1-800-272-9675, fax 780-422-0055; Web site www.cbsc.org/alberta.

British Columbia

Small Business BC, 601 West Cordova Street, Vancouver, BC V6B 1G1; phone 604-775-5525 or 1-800-667-2272 (BC only), fax 604-775-5520, TTY: 711; e-mail askus@smallbusinessbc.ca, Web site www.sb.gov.bc.ca.

Manitoba

Canada/Manitoba Business Service Centre, 250–240 Graham Avenue, P.O. Box 2609, Winnipeg, MB R3C 4B3; phone 204-984-2272 or 1-800-665-2019, fax 204-983-3852, TTY 1-800-457-8466; e-mail Manitoba@cbsc.ic.gc.ca, Web site www.cbsc.org/manitoba.

New Brunswick

Canada/New Brunswick Business Service Centre, 570 Queen Street, Fredericton, NB E3B 6Z6; phone 506-444-6140 or 1-800-668-1010 (Atlantic only), fax 506-444-6172, TTY 506-444-6166 or 1-800-887-6550; e-mail cbscnb@cbsc.ic.gc.ca, Web site www.cbsc.org/nb.

Newfoundland and Labrador

Canada/Newfoundland and Labrador Business Service Centre, 90 O'Leary Avenue, P.O. Box 8687, Station A, St. John's, NL A1B 3T1; phone 709-772-6022 or 1-800-668-1010 (Atlantic only), fax 709-772-6090, TTY 1-800-457-8466; e-mail info@cbsc.ic.gc.ca, Web site www.cbsc.org/nf.

Nova Scotia

Canada/Nova Scotia Business Service Centre, 1575 Brunswick Street, Halifax, NS B3J 2G1; phone 902-426-8604 or 1-800-668-1010 (Atlantic only), fax 902-426-6530, TTY: (902) 426-4188 or 1-800-797-4188; e-mail Halifax@cbsc.ic.gc.ca, Web site www.cbsc.org/ns.

Ontario

Canada-Ontario Business Service Centre; phone 416-775-3456 or 1-800-567-2345 (Ontario only), TTY 1-800-457-8466; e-mail ontaro@cbsc.ic.gc.ca, Web site www.cbsc.org/ontario.

Prince Edward Island

Canada/Prince Edward Island Business Service Centre, 75 Fitzroy Street, P.O. Box 40, Charlotte-town, PE C1A 7K2; phone 902-368-0771 or 1-800-668-1010 (Atlantic only), fax: 902-566-7377; e-mail: pei@cbsc.ic.gc.ca, Web site www.cbsc.org/pe.

Quebec

Info entreprises, 380 St-Antoine West, local 6000, Montreal, QC H2Y 3X7; phone 514-496-INFO (4636) or 1-800-322-INFO (4636), fax 1-888-417-0442, TTY: 1-800-457-8466; Web site www.infoentrepreneurs.org.

Saskatchewan

Business Infosource, Canada-Saskatchewan Business Service Centre, 2–345 Third Avenue South, Saskatoon, SK S7K 1M6, phone 306-956-2323 or 1-800-667-4374, fax: 306-956-2328, TTY 1-800-457-8466; e-mail Saskatchewan@cbsc.ic.gc.ca, Web site www.cbsc.org/sask.

Northwest Territories

Canada/NWT Business Service Centre, P.O. Box 1320, 7th Floor, 5201 Fiftieth Avenue, Yellowknife, NT X1A 3S9; phone 867-873-7958 or 1-800-661-0599, fax: 867-873-0573, TTY 1-800-457-8466; e-mail yel@cbsc.ic.gc.ca, Web site www.cbsc.org/nwt.

Nunavut

Canada-Nunavut Business Service Centre, Inuksugait Plaza, P.O. Box 1000, Station 1198, Iqaluit, NU X0A 0H0, phone 867-975-7860 or 1-877-499-5199, fax 867-975-7885 or 1-877-499-5299; e-mail cnbsc@gov.nu.ca, Web site www.cbsc.org/nunavut.

Yukon

Canada-Yukon Business Service Centre, Suite 101, 307 Jarvis Street, Whitehorse, YT Y1A 2H3, phone 867-633-6257 or 1-800-661-0543, fax 867-667-2001, TTY 1-800-457-8466; e-mail Yukon@cbsc.ic.gc.ca, Web site www.cbsc.org/yukon.

Provincial/territorial government Web sites

Each provincial and territorial government maintains a Web site. Some of the provincial sites contain good general business information that you can use to get started.

For example, the Nova Scotia site contains a "Business Room" page with links to publications on starting, operating, and growing your business. The Manitoba site contains a "Business" page with links to information about starting, financing, operating, and selling or closing a business. The Ontario government site is particularly helpful. Its "Business" page contains links to many useful sources, including a Portable Document Format (PDF) booklet entitled "Your Guide to Small Business."

Provincial government Web sites

Alberta	`www.gov.ab.ca`	Ontario	`www.gov.on.ca`
British Columbia	`www.gov.bc.ca`	Prince Edward Island	`www.gov.pe.ca`
Manitoba	`www.gov.mb.ca`		
New Brunswick	`www.gov.nb.ca`	Quebec	`www.gouv.qu.ca`
Nova Scotia	`www.gov.ns.ca`	Saskatchewan	`www.gov.sk.ca`

Bank and trust company Web sites

The major banks' and trust companies' Web sites have information about the products and services they provide to small businesses. Some have information about general business topics as well. For example, the Bank of Montreal site (`www.bmo.com`) contains the "Business Coach Series," with links to PDF brochures and worksheets on a variety of business finance topics.

The Royal Bank Web site (`www.royalbank.com`) is particularly good because it contains information about many general business topics such as starting a business, expanding a business, and business succession. It also has pages for women entrepreneurs and young entrepreneurs. In addition, the Royal Bank Web site gives you access to the "Big Idea," an online guide through the steps of developing a business plan, including sample business plans for several different types of businesses.

Small business or entrepreneurship centres

A number of small business or entrepreneurship centres provide support and training to start-up and small businesses, for example:

✔ **Ontario Small Business Enterprise Centres:** These Ontario government centres are located throughout the province and provide support to start-up and small enterprises during their first five years of operation. They offer a wide variety of support resources, including consultations with qualified business consultants, workshops and seminars, and mentoring and networking opportunities. Visit `www.ontariocanada.com/ontcan/en/expanding/ex_sm-bus-ent-ctrs.jsp` for more information.

- ✔ **Centre for Entrepreneurship Education & Development Incorporated (CEED):** This Nova Scotia not-for-profit society is devoted to helping people discover and use entrepreneurship as a vehicle to become self-reliant. Its services include technical assistance, entrepreneurship consulting, and entrepreneurship courses. CEED's Web site (www.ceed.info) has more information.

- ✔ **The Asper Centre for Entrepreneurship:** The University of Manitoba's I.H. Asper School of Business operates this Centre. Its role is to support young entrepreneurs in the province of Manitoba through a combination of education, contact with the business community, and practical experience.

- ✔ **Centre of Entrepreneurship:** Centennial College's School of Continuing Education & Corporate Training operates this Centre in Toronto. It offers a thirty-day New Business Starter Program, designed to provide entrepreneurs with the basic principles and practices of business, along with the skills needed to market, operate, and control a business. Visit www.centreofentrepreneurship.ca to find out more.

Business incubators

A business incubator is a business-mentoring facility that nurtures small- and medium-sized businesses during the start-up period. Business incubators provide management assistance, education, technical and business support services, and financial advice. They may also provide flexible rental space and flexible leases.

There are approximately 1,000 business incubators in North America, with about 150 of them in Canada, located throughout the country. The vast majority of Canadian business incubators are non-profit and sponsored by government, economic development organizations, and academic institutions. Some examples of business incubators are

- ✔ **Toronto Business Development Centre:** Started by Toronto, Ontario's Economic Development Corporation (TEDCO).

- ✔ **Northern Alberta Business Incubator:** Created by and located in the city of St. Albert, Alberta.

- ✔ **CDEM Business Incubator:** Run by the Economic Development Council for Manitoba Bilingual Municipalities and located in St. Boniface, Manitoba.

- ✔ **Enterprise UNB:** Co-sponsored by the University of New Brunswick and the Research and Productivity Council and located in Fredericton, New Brunswick.

The business incubator process usually has three stages:

- **Pre-incubation:** Applicants are screened for ability and compatibility with the business incubator's goals and may be referred for business skills training.

- **Incubation:** The business becomes a tenant of the business incubator and has access to the incubator's services for about three years.

- **Graduation:** The business moves into the community.

For more information about business incubators in Canada, contact the Canadian Association of Business Incubators (www.cabi.ca).

Getting Information Geared to Your Specific Business

After you've learned about starting and carrying on a business in general, you can find out more about your field of business in particular. For example, you might want to know these facts:

- What skills you need for this business

- What government regulations apply to this business

- How much it will cost to run this kind of business

- What the demand is for the goods or services you'll be supplying

- Who the likely customers are for the goods and services you'll be providing

- What the competition is like for this type of business

- What supplies and equipment you require for this type of business

You need a good gateway into the sector you're interested in. Here are our recommendations.

Strategis

Strategis (www.strategis.ic.gc.ca) is an Industry Canada Web site. The site contains 2 million electronic documents and more than 50,000 links to related business sites.

Avoid getting lost in cyberspace

The Internet is the best way to get your hands on the information you need. You can find what you're looking for on the Internet reasonably easily — once! What seems to be remarkably hard is finding the same information a second time.

We can't tell you how many times we've found a wonderful site on the Web — just to have it vanish into a black hole when we decide to return for a bit more information. We can never remember the Web site address or re-create the search that got us there. Don't let that happen to you. Here are some tips:

✔ Make a note of the Web address of any site that seems useful. Bookmark the site, and your Web browser will store the address for

you. But be warned that Web sites often move — sometimes without leaving a forwarding address.

✔ Mark your trail. If you found a site through a Web search, make a note of the keywords you used. Also, make a note of the search engine! The same keywords on a different search engine may not turn up the site you're looking for. Not all sites turn up in all search engines. And the same site may be locatable with different keywords in different search engines.

✔ Print anything useful. If you find information, print it or save it to a file. Then you won't have to go looking for it again.

The site will be particularly useful to you at this stage because it contains information on a wide variety of businesses, organized by sector. Each type of business has its own page, with additional pages on a number of subtopics. The subtopics vary for each business category but include things such as the following:

✔ **Company directories:** With links to lists of Canadian companies carrying on business in the field

✔ **Contacts:** With links to major trade associations in the field and a list of Industry Canada contacts

✔ **Electronic business:** With links to various information about e-business and e-commerce

✔ **Events:** With links to major trade shows in the field

✔ **Regulations and standards:** With links to relevant government regulations and standards organizations

✔ **Related sites:** With links to relevant economic statistics, trade and investment information, labour unions, licences, legislation, trade periodicals, and research and technology information

  ✔ **Statistics, analysis, and industry profiles:** With links to North American Industry Classification definitions and to selected Canadian statistics on topics such as the Canadian market, imports, and exports

  ✔ **Trade and investment:** With links to relevant international trade agreements and export information

Trade and professional associations

Trade and professional associations are another great source of information about particular fields of business. There are thousands of associations in North America, many of them based in the United States. Whatever your field of business, the odds are that an association exists. A good association will give you access to industry-specific information. Most associations maintain a Web site, setting out the services the association provides and membership information.

The Internet is the best way to track down the trade or professional associations in your field. Use a Web directory such as Yahoo! (www.yahoo.com). You can get a list of sites, using their categories by following the links through Business to Trade Associations. Or you can use the search feature or a search engine such as Google (www.google.com) by typing in the name of the specific field you're interested in plus the word **association**, for example **giftware association**. If you use Yahoo! Canada's site (www.yahoo.ca or www.ca.yahoo.com) or Google's Canada site (www.google.ca), you can restrict your search to Canadian sites only. You can also get information about associations on the Strategis Web site by following the Contact links for your business field.

Trade and professional journals

Many trade and professional associations publish journals or newsletters with current information about the field. They also contain ads for equipment and supplies used by that kind of business, and some list business opportunities (businesses for sale, partners wanted, premises for lease, equipment for sale, and so on).

Workshops and seminars

Many trade and professional associations hold seminars and workshops on topics of specific interest to members. Some offer courses leading to a designation or certification in the field.

Trade shows

Most trade associations hold an industry-wide trade show at least once a year. They are good places to make contacts in the industry and learn about the latest trends in the field.

Pre-mission Training

Once you've researched your chosen business field, you may realize that you need some training before you can pilot your business. You may need skills specific to your chosen business field (such as how to frame a picture if you're going into the framing business, or how to mediate if you're going into family counselling), or you may want to pick up some general business skills and knowledge such as simple bookkeeping, basic computer skills, or how to prepare a business plan.

When people think of education, they usually think of universities, community colleges, career colleges, vocational schools, and boards of education. But in fact, many different places offer business education and skills training. You may be able to pick up the skills you need from a trade association, a Canada Business Service Centre, or the little place in your local mall that teaches keyboarding. In fact, you may want to avoid many of the educational institutions, since they often offer certificate or diploma programs more suited to people looking for a job, rather than individual courses focused on the specific skills an entrepreneur needs.

Where you go to get your training will depend on the kind of skill you're trying to acquire.

Skills for your particular business

You may be able to pick up the special skills required for your particular business in a day, a weekend, or a week. On the other hand, you may have to have a certificate or diploma in the field that will take months or years to get.

You may be able to find out not only what skills you need, but also where to get them from Strategis or from the relevant trade or professional association. Or you can use a Web directory such as Yahoo! Canada (www.yahoo.ca) to get a list of places that offer the training you need. Follow the links through Education to Career and Vocational Training to Career Specific Training, and then follow the links to your own field. Or you can use the search feature or a search engine such as Google (www.google.ca) by typing in the name of the specific field you're interested in and the word **education** or **training**.

If you're not required to have a diploma or certificate offered by a university or community college, you may want to consider programs offered by privately run career colleges or vocational schools. These programs tend to be shorter in duration than university and community college programs, but be warned — these courses are usually more expensive, sometimes much more expensive!

The trade or professional association in your field may offer short workshops or seminars on individual topics of interest to you as well as complete training programs designed specifically for your field.

General business skills

To acquire in-depth business skills, you can enroll in *degree,* or *diploma,* or *certificate* programs offered by colleges and universities. These programs run over the course of a year, or from two to three years. You probably won't be able to take one course of interest to you without taking another course as a prerequisite or without signing on for the entire program.

If you want to acquire some business skills as quickly as possible, look for *continuing education* courses offered by your local university. For example, the University of Toronto (www.learn.utoronto.ca) offers courses (usually with classes held once a week for about three months) in a wide variety of business-related areas, including Accounting Fundamentals, Business, Business Law, Business Management, Business Strategy, A Conceptual Overview of E-Business Technologies, Marketing: An Introduction, Strategies for a Web Presence, Taxation for Canadian Business, and Solving Conflict in the Workplace. The University of Calgary (www.ucalgary.ca/cted) has seminars on numerous topics, including Time Management, Accounting for the Non-Accountant, Essentials of Customer Service, Writing Skills for Business, Marketing on a Budget, and Creative Negotiating.

Your local board of education may offer courses in business skills as part of its continuing education program, and you should have no problem enrolling in individual courses rather than in programs. Classes will probably be scheduled once a week over several months.

You may also be able to find weekend workshops or evening seminars offered by your trade or professional association, or through your provincial Canada Business Service Centre.

Finding Ground Support

Planning a business start-up takes a lot of work. But you don't have to fly all by yourself. You can and should get professional help with many of the tasks involved. At the very least, you'll need a lawyer, an accountant, and an insurance agent or broker. We offer suggestions for other professionals you might find useful.

Do you really need a lawyer?

Do you really need a lawyer? Yes, you do. That's because almost everything that happens in the business world has legal implications. A lawyer can help you navigate through every stage of your business odyssey.

When you're setting up your business, a lawyer can

- Help you decide whether or not to incorporate (see Chapter 5)
- Help you form a corporation or partnership (see Chapter 5)
- Review start-up documents such as loan agreements (see Chapter 10), leases (see Chapter 7), and franchise agreements (see Chapter 9)
- Draft standard forms for contracts to use in your business (see Chapters 13, 14, and 15)

Once you're in business, a lawyer can be of further assistance by

- Helping you negotiate contracts (see Chapters 10, 13, 14, 15, and 19)
- Giving you advice about hiring and firing employees (see Chapter 15)
- Helping you collect your unpaid accounts (see Chapter 13)
- Acting for you in a lawsuit if you sue or are sued (see Chapter 18)

Even if you decide to get out of the business, you'll still need a lawyer to help you sell it, or give it to your children, or wind it up (see Chapter 20).

And an accountant?

An accountant, too? Afraid so. In Canada, anyone can call himself or herself an accountant. What you want is a professional accountant — a chartered accountant, certified general accountant, or certified management accountant. Professional accountants are licensed and regulated.

You'll probably need an accountant to help you

- Buy an existing business (see Chapter 9)
- Set up a bookkeeping system (see Chapter 17)
- Prepare budgets and cash-flow statements (see Chapters 11 and 16)
- Prepare financial statements (see Chapter 17)
- Prepare your income tax returns (see Chapter 16)
- Deal with the Canada Revenue Agency (CRA) from time to time (see Chapter 16)

And an insurance agent or broker too?

You'll need insurance for your business, including

- ✔ Property insurance to cover loss or damage to your business property
- ✔ Business interruption insurance to cover your loss of earnings if your business premises are damaged
- ✔ General liability insurance to cover claims made if you cause injury to a customer, supplier, or innocent bystander
- ✔ Key person insurance to tide over your business in case you, a partner, or an important employee dies or becomes disabled

We tell you more about insurance in Chapter 12.

An insurance agent (a person who deals with and sells the policies of only one insurance company) or insurance broker (a person who deals with and sells the policies of several insurance companies) can give you advice about what kind of insurance you need and how much. Both agents and brokers are regulated and licensed by provincial governments.

Anyone else?

Depending on the nature of your business, you may also want help from (in no particular order)

- ✔ **A business evaluator:** To help you decide on the value of a business you are thinking of buying
- ✔ **An advertising firm and/or a media relations firm:** To help you get the word out about your business
- ✔ **A marketing consultant:** To help you identify the market for your product or service and determine how best to reach that market
- ✔ **An interior designer:** To help you set up your business premises attractively
- ✔ **A graphic designer:** To help you design a business logo, your business cards, and letterhead
- ✔ **A computer systems consultant:** To help you choose and set up your computer equipment and choose and install your software
- ✔ **A Web site designer:** To help you create a great Web site for you business
- ✔ **A management consultant:** To help you polish your management skills

✔ **A human resources specialist (also known as a headhunter):** To help you hire staff

✔ **Business coaches:** To help you do various things such as acquire presentation skills, get pointers on power dressing, pick up business etiquette, and even improve your table manners (for those four-fork lunches with potential investors and customers)

How do you find professional help?

Whatever kind of help you're looking for, you want to find someone who has experience in small business matters, someone with whom you'll feel comfortable, and someone who will charge you a reasonable fee.

Before you hire a professional, you should take these steps:

1. **Get recommendations:** Ask your friends, relatives, or business associates for names of good people.

2. **Investigate:** Call each recommended person's office to find out more about his or her area of expertise, experience with business start-ups, fees, and location (if the person doesn't make client calls but expects you to come to him or her).

3. **Interview:** Meet the top two or three candidates in person. You want not only more information than you collected in Step 2, but also to see how you react to each individual personally.

Where do you turn for emotional support?

Even though you're going it alone in the business universe, you may want to seek out the companionship of fellow travellers with whom you can share your experiences and from whom you can get advice. Whatever demographic group you fall into, you'll likely find a business organization for you. These organizations provide opportunities to network and get advice geared to your demographic.

Here's a sampling:

✔ **The Young Entrepreneurs Association:** A volunteer, non-profit organization whose mandate is to support business owners 35 years of age and under (www.yea.ca)

✔ **Canadian Association of Women Executives & Entrepreneurs:** An organization that provides networking, support, mentoring, and professional development to businesswomen at all stages of their careers (www.cawee.net)

 ✔ **Canadian Council for Aboriginal Business:** A national, no-profit organization that promotes the full participation of Aboriginal individuals in
   the Canadian economy (www.ccab.com)

 ✔ **Canadian Gay & Lesbian Chamber of Commerce:** An organization
   designed to improve opportunities for gay, lesbian, bisexual, transgen-
   der, transsexual, two-spirited, and intersex owned/operated/friendly
   businesses (www.cglcc.ca)

Getting the Scoop on Customers and Suppliers

You don't need a satellite surveillance system to investigate your potential
customers and suppliers. (Although, these days you can probably get satellite surveillance if you want it.) All kinds of information is floating around — a
lot of it produced by the customers and suppliers themselves. You just need
to know how to tap into it.

Customers

This early stage is a good time to do some research to help you figure out
who your customers will be and what you'll have to do to persuade them to
buy what you have to sell. (We tell you more about marketing your goods
and services in Chapter 4.)

Who will your customers be?

We've already told you about the Strategis Web site and that it has a separate
page for each of many business sectors. For many of the sectors, you'll find
a subheading entitled Business Support and Financing that will link you to
pages with distribution information. For example, the Furniture sector page
has links for business furniture to lists of principal buying groups, wholesalers, and retailers and for residential furniture to major chain retailers,
buying groups, and department stores, as well as information on selling to
government.

What can you find out about your potential customers?

If your prospective customers are businesses or government, you'll probably
be able to learn a great deal without having to get up from your computer.

If you hope to sell your goods or services to the government of Canada, go to the Web site for Business Access Canada, formerly Contracts Canada, (www.contractscanada.gc.ca). Business Access Canada is an inter-department initiative involving 31 participating federal departments and agencies, designed to simplify access to federal government purchasing information. The site contains information, for suppliers who want to do business with the federal government, about how the government does its buying.

If you hope to sell your goods or services to a provincial government, find out if the province has a centralized purchasing department that handles purchases of goods and services on behalf of various government departments. Examples are the Purchasing Commission in British Columbia or the Purchasing Branch of the Saskatchewan Property Management Corporation. Search the provincial Web site for a page on procurement or purchasing.

In addition, there are bidding services that provide information on tenders being sought by the federal and provincial governments and by the municipal, academic, school, and hospital sectors. Examples are BIDS (www.bids.ca) and MERX (www.merx.com).

If you hope to sell your goods or services to another business, find out as much as you can about the business. If it has a Web site, visit it. Large purchasers such as retail chains may provide information to prospective suppliers. For example, Wal-Mart provides a Supplier Proposal Packet and Supplier Standards on its Web site. Even if the business you're targeting is not quite that helpful, you can still pick up information about the business's operations and needs that will help you fine-tune your sales pitch to the business.

Suppliers

As you research your particular type of business, you'll get a sense of the equipment and supplies you need to get set up. (See Chapter 6 for general advice on equipping your business.) You can then search the Internet for suppliers of that kind of equipment and supplies. The Web sites of major and many minor suppliers have online catalogues that include specifications, pricing, and shipping information. Some major suppliers offer consultants to help you choose the right equipment for your business.

Chapter 3

Whose Idea Is This, Anyway?

In This Chapter

▶ Thinking about business ideas

▶ Learning that ideas can have (possessive) owners

▶ Understanding how to protect your ideas

▶ Using your own business idea without fear that someone else will make off with it

▶ Using someone else's idea in your business without getting whacked with a lawsuit

The more you think about your business-to-be, the more clearly it will take shape in your mind. You've got notions about a product you want to manufacture or sell, a name or slogan to identify the business, information you'll include in an instruction manual, a favourite quotation you'll use on your Web site, a cartoon you'll incorporate into presentations or your newsletter, background music you'll play on the phone when you put clients on hold, and customer lists you can get your hands on. Some of these notions may just be whims, but others may be fundamental to the business.

Stop just a minute! You could be about to run into severe turbulence as you daydream your way through the stratosphere. These ideas you're having may already be owned by someone else. If that's the case, you can't use them without the owner's permission. And if they're your own original ideas, you'll want to make sure that nobody else can pirate them.

What a Fine Idea

Why are we getting all shook up about your ideas for your business? An idea's just an idea; it's not a gold mine or an expensive piece of equipment, right? Right, it's an idea. . . . Wrong; it's not "just" an idea. Many ideas are commercially valuable, and the owner of a valuable idea may go to great lengths to prevent anyone else from using it. And you may need to go to great lengths to keep someone else from stealing an idea out from under your nose — and making off with an important asset of your business.

What's the value of an idea?

Need some convincing that an idea can have immense value? What do you think the word-ideas and music-ideas combined into the song "Yesterday" are worth? What about the chemical formula-idea for the drug Viagra? What about the name-idea for Coca-Cola, or the logo-idea for Nike? If you tried to buy any of these ideas, they'd cost you millions of dollars.

Of course, lots of ideas have no commercial value. The chemical formula for a drug that doesn't work (or worse, causes harm to a person who takes it) doesn't have much value; neither does the crawling worm logo for Fred and Mike's Pizzeria and Fish Bait Stand. The value of an idea is linked to its ability to sell products. An idea that sells a lot of products is very valuable; an idea that sells few products is not.

Who owns an idea?

The general rule is that only the *owner* of an idea (or someone with whom the owner has a legal agreement) can legally use the idea. So before you decide to use an idea in your business, you need to know who the owner is. Only the owner can give permission to use the idea. If the owner isn't you (or nobody), you can get into hot water if you use the idea without permission.

Even if you personally came up with an original idea, you're not necessarily the owner. The owner of an idea could be the creator, the person who had the idea first; or it could be someone who hired the creator to have ideas; or it could be someone who bought ownership of the idea from its original owner.

Creator versus owner

If the creator was working independently when the idea sprang from his or her brain, the creator usually owns the idea.

Excuse me, may I please use your idea?

Permission to use an idea is given in the form of a licence agreement negotiated between the owner and the user. Licence agreements are usually long and incomprehensible legal documents. One of the long and incomprehensible clauses in the document says that in exchange for the right to use the idea, the user will pay the owner an upfront fee plus a royalty. A royalty is a percentage of the money made from the use of the idea. If the creator or other owner has sold or otherwise transferred the idea by legal agreement (assignment) to someone else — such as a business that wants the idea — then the other party to the agreement owns the idea.

If the creator was hired for the purpose of creating an idea, the person who hired the creator owns the idea (even if there's no written agreement to this effect).

If the creator created the idea in the course of his or her employment, the idea normally belongs to the employer (unless there's a prior agreement between the employer and the employee-creator that the creator rather than the employer owns the idea).

Ownerless ideas

Some ideas are orphans — they no longer have an owner. An idea without an owner is said to be in the *public domain*, which means that anyone can use it freely. An idea moves into the public domain once its legal protection expires (ideas are protected only for a limited number of years; more about that further on in this chapter) or, for certain kinds of ideas, if the idea has been made public before it got the right legal protection.

Beethoven's symphonies and Shakespeare's plays, for example, are in the public domain. Anyone can publish them or perform them because legal protection ended years ago. Similarly, the drug penicillin is in the public domain (and can be manufactured as a "generic drug") because legal protection for the drug formula has ended. Sometimes the creator of an idea accidentally or deliberately puts the idea into the public domain by making the idea public without first arranging for protection. This could happen, for example, if the creator of a drug published the chemical formula in a journal of chemistry without first applying for patent protection (we talk about patents later in this chapter).

How do owners protect ideas from unauthorized use?

The bottom line is that there are only two real ways for an owner to protect an idea. One is to keep the idea secret — if nobody else knows about the idea, then nobody else can use it. The other way is to sue the pants off anybody who uses the idea without permission. So when we talk about *protection,* it turns out that we mainly mean "the exclusive right to sue anybody else who uses the idea." (The lawsuit is for infringement. Sounds kind of floppy and nasty, doesn't it? Now imagine how it would feel to be called an infringer.) This exclusive right to sue comes with official ownership of an idea. Official ownership of ideas is given through different methods. They include copyright, industrial design registration, patent, and trademark. We could talk to you like lawyers about each of these things — but you don't want a course on intellectual property (that's what lawyers call this field — IP for short). You just want to know what you can do and what you can't do. So that's what we're going to tell you. Unfortunately, to do this we have to take you through an asteroid field of intellectual property law . . . but maybe it won't cause you permanent damage if you turn on your force shields and zip through quickly.

Manufacturing or Selling a Product in Your Business

If you want to set up a business to manufacture or sell a product, you can't just fire up the assembly line and start churning out the product or go out and take orders. You have to make sure you have the right to make or sell the product in the country in the first place.

Manufacturing or selling a product from a design

If you've found or created a design for a product you want to manufacture, there are two different problems you could run into if you just go ahead and start manufacturing. One is that someone else already may have registered that same design as an industrial design and so can prevent you from manufacturing and distributing your product. The other is that if you've come up with an original design, another manufacturer who sees your product on the market might think it looks pretty good and might start making and selling something very similar (maybe at a lower price). To prevent that, you need to register your design as an industrial design.

An *industrial design* is an original artistic shape, or pattern, or ornamentation that is to be applied to a mass-produced useful article. (The design itself is not supposed to be useful, only ornamental.) Industrial design registration protects the right to mass-produce — produce more than 50 copies of — a designed article. If a design has not been registered, anyone can imitate it and sell it, and the owner of the design has no legal means of stopping them. But if a design has been registered, the owner can sue anyone who makes or sells a product with the design, and force them to stop making or selling it.

Industrial design protection isn't automatic; it's short-lived and it isn't renewable indefinitely. Protection has to be bought country by country. In Canada, registration protects the design for a maximum period of 10 years. In the United States, a design patent protects the design for 14 years.

For more information about industrial design, see the Canadian Intellectual Property Office (CIPO) Web site: www.cipo.gc.ca. If you're interested in manufacturing or distributing a product in the United States, see the United States Patent and Trademark Office (USPTO) Web site: www.uspto.gov. Some other countries have Web sites, such as the United Kingdom Patent Office site: www.patent.gov.uk/index.htm.

A product from your own design

If you decide to register your design before you get into the manufacturing process, the first thing to do is to check whether your design is new and original, or whether something very similar already has industrial design protection. At the moment, this can't be done through the Internet. In Canada, a search has to be conducted at CIPO's Client Service Centre in Gatineau, Quebec. For assistance with an industrial design application, go to an intellectual property lawyer. The process of registering your design takes from six months to a year. You have to apply no more than one year after your design has been made public.

Form 3-1 on the CD-ROM is the CIPO Application for the Registration of an Industrial Design.

After your design is registered, you can mark it with a D followed by your name as owner. If you have registered your design, you can sue anyone who produces your design to force them to stop. If you've registered and marked your design, you can sue to stop another user, and you can also get financial compensation for the harm they've caused you.

A product from someone else's design

If the design you want to use has been protected in a country, you need the owner's permission to manufacture or sell the product in that country. You may be able to tell if a product is protected: for example, if the product is marked. Since industrial design protection doesn't last very long, the protection may have expired. The only way of being sure about the status of protection is to do a search in that country's industrial design office.

Manufacturing a product that you've invented

Suppose your business isn't going to manufacture or sell a product with just a new look. Suppose it's going to manufacture a product that's new, period — something that you've dreamed up that hasn't been made before. In this case, you're manufacturing an invention.

In Canada, *inventions* include any kind of product (and that extends to a machine for making a product, or a chemical formula, or even a non-human life form such as a genetically modified mouse) and also an improvement on a product. In the United States, in addition to products and improvements, inventions can include a business method or a surgical method. For examples of inventions, all you have to do is look around you — computer hardware and software, appliances, machines and machine parts, the shampoo you use, prescription and over-the-counter drugs, DNA sequences — you're surrounded by inventions wherever you go.

If you don't arrange to protect your invention before you start telling the neighbours about it, you're letting your invention slip into the public domain. Once it's in the public domain, anybody who can figure out the invention can make it and sell it — without your permission and certainly without paying you anything.

You can protect an invention in two different ways: by secrecy or by patent.

Should you keep your invention secret?

You don't have to get patent protection for an invention if you think you can keep others from using (and making money from) your invention by keeping it a secret (Coca-Cola, for example, has never patented its recipe for Coke Classic). This kind of secret is known as a *trade secret*.

However, a secret that's totally and completely secret isn't going to be all that useful to a business. The secret has to be used in some way in order to generate revenue. It may be possible for the owner of the secret to use it without revealing it to anyone else, but in most cases the secret eventually has to be shared if it's going to be used. For example, the owner of a secret recipe for a soft drink will eventually have to tell various people what the recipe is — an investor, a chemist who will scale the recipe up for mass production, or a manufacturer who will produce the drink according to specifications.

The trick to manufacturing a product using a trade secret is to keep the secret reasonably safe. Here are some tips for keeping things under wraps:

✔ If you're going to tell your secret to anyone (including employees and outsiders), first get an agreement with them in writing that this is confidential information that belongs to you and that they cannot reveal it to others or use it themselves without your written permission.

✔ Form 3-2 on the CD-ROM is a confidentiality agreement that may work for you. (Or it may not. You should consult with your own lawyer before telling your valuable secrets to anyone.) Stamp any document relating to your secret with the word "CONFIDENTIAL." But don't tell the secret to anyone who doesn't actually need to know it in order to carry out his or her job.

✔ Keep your secret physically safe — lock confidential documents in a drawer or a safe when you're not using them. Keep your office doors locked when you're not in the office, and don't allow anyone to poke around, even when you're there.

If your secret gets out anyway, you can try locking the barn door after the horse is stolen. If you had a confidentiality agreement with the person who made off with your secret, you can sue the person and ask the courts to prevent the person from using or revealing the information any further, or you can ask for money damages to compensate you for losses you've suffered.

But even if you keep your secret safe from the people you work with, once your product is in the marketplace, competitors will be able to look at it and try to duplicate it. If they succeed, then they can just go ahead and use the idea — you can't stop them or get any money from them.

Should you patent your invention?

If you *patent* an invention, you give up your exclusive knowledge of how the invention works in exchange for an exclusive right to make money from the invention for a period of years.

Maybe the first question to ask in this section should be "*Can* you patent your invention?" You can't if the invention hasn't been "reduced to practice" yet. (Essentially, this means that the invention hasn't been described through written text and pictures in such a way that a skilled person reading the description can re-create the invention. The description of the invention forms the main part of a patent application.) You also can't patent if someone beat you to the draw and has already patented it — you can't patent the exact same thing that's already patented — even if you invented it without knowing anything about the patent or the other inventor's work. You can, however, patent an improvement on the patented invention.

Even if no one has already patented your invention, a patent will be granted only for an invention that meets the test of "novelty, utility, and ingenuity." The invention has to be something new — something that hasn't been seen before (in many countries this means something that has never been made public before, although in Canada and the United States it can have been publicly disclosed by the inventor no more than one year before the patent application is filed), something useful, and something that wasn't obvious to a skilled person in the field.

Now that we've dealt with "can you" a bit, let's go back to "should you." Patent protection is not automatic in Canada or anywhere else. In fact, it involves a long and expensive process, and at the end of it there's no guarantee that a patent will be granted. The entire process, from filing a patent application to receiving a patent, takes at least two years and can quite easily take five or six years, or more. If a patent is granted, patent protection can extend back to the date the application was *published* (made public by the patent office as part of the application process). If you see a product marked *patent pending,* it means that an application has been filed, but the patent had not yet been granted when the product was marked. If a patent is not granted, the invention never had any protection at any time. And once your patent application is published by the patent office, everyone in the world will be able to see how your invention works.

An invention has patent protection only in the country where a patent has been granted. A patent application has to be made in every country where the owner of the invention wants protection. In Canada, most invention owners file an application in Canada or the United States first, and then file in a few additional countries (often including countries in the European Union or East Asia). Once the deadline for filing a patent in a country has passed, the invention is in the public domain in that country, even though it's protected elsewhere against use without the owner's permission.

The cost of getting patent protection is high. Getting a patent in the United States alone might cost up to $20,000 (Canadian) in patent lawyers' fees and filing fees. Getting a patent in additional countries might cost $10,000 to $15,000 per country — or more. So in total, getting a patent in the United States and a handful of other countries can cost about $100,000. Even well-heeled corporations balk at doing widespread patenting. It's worthwhile to patent only in a country where there's a big market and a good chance of making lots of money from the invention. (Think at least twice, and preferably three or four times, about spending money to patent something that will be obsolete in a couple of years, as is often the case with computer software or fad products.) If you personally don't have the money to patent your invention, you may be able to interest an investor in paying the bill if your invention is potentially worth a lot. In return, the investor will almost certainly want part ownership of the patent and a guaranteed share of any revenues that flow from the patent.

After you go to all the trouble of getting a patent, patent protection doesn't last very long — only 20 years from the date the patent application was first filed! But once you've got a patent, you can sue anyone who manufactures or sells your patented product in the country. Except that . . . sometimes you can be forced to let someone else use your patent. In some countries, you may be required to license the invention to a local manufacturer.

For more information about patents, you can visit the following Web sites: the Canadian Intellectual Property Office (CIPO) at www.cipo.gc.ca; the United States Patent Office (USPTO) at www.uspto.gov; and the European Patent Office (EPO) at www.european-patent-office.org.

Manufacturing or selling a product that someone else has invented

Not everybody has a great new idea for a product, and that may include you. But the fact that you don't have your own idea doesn't necessarily mean you can't manufacture or sell the product of your choice. Many inventors and patent owners are very keen to find someone who will manufacture or distribute their product.

Using someone else's patent

If you want to use an invention that is under patent in the country where you're going to manufacture and sell it, you have to get the permission of the patent owner if you don't want to run the risk of being sued. If a product is subject to patent protection, there may be the words "patent" or "patent pending" on it somewhere. Or you can do a patent search if you don't have the product itself at hand.

Once you've located the patent owner, you can start negotiating for use of the invention. If the owner is willing to let you use it, the owner will want you to pay an initial fee and/or a royalty on sales of the product in return.

If the invention is patented (or patent pending) in one or more countries, but a patent application was not filed in the country where you want to make or market it, you don't need the owner's permission. You can just go ahead and do your thing. The published patent application should contain all the information that you'll need to make the invention. So you can search for the patent in the patent office of the country where the patent was registered. (Canadian, U.S., and European Union patents are available through online databases. See the Web site addresses in the "Should you patent your invention?" section earlier.) The Canadian Patent Database, at `http://patents1.ic.gc.ca/intro-e.html`, provides access to over 75 years of patent descriptions and images, and allows you to search, retrieve, and study more than 1,500,000 patent documents.

You can also just go ahead if the patent protection has expired. Again, you'll want to search for the patent in the country's patent office to make sure that the patent really has expired and to get the specifications of the invention. And you might be wise to approach the patent owner for a discussion anyway; the owner may have some information that would be of value to you about making or marketing the product, and might provide it in exchange for a payment of some kind.

Using someone else's unpatented invention

If an invention is in the public domain, anyone can use it. It's in the public domain, for example, if it's been published in a journal or been presented at a conference or trade show before the owner applied for patent protection (although in Canada and the United States an inventor has a year after publishing or presenting an invention to file for patent protection); or if patent protection has expired.

But what if the invention isn't patented but it's not exactly in the public domain either? In other words, what if it's somebody else's trade secret?

Theoretically, you could use someone else's trade secret under the following conditions:

✔ You're not an employee of the owner of the trade secret. Unless you're an industrial spy, the place you'll most likely acquire trade secrets is from your own employer — and employees have a legal duty not to use their employer's trade secrets even if they haven't signed a confidentiality agreement. (We tell you about confidentiality agreements under the heading "Should you keep your invention secret?" earlier in this chapter.)

✔ You're not an ex-employee of the owner of the trade secret who picked up the trade secret during your employment. If you removed or copied documents containing information about the secret, you could probably be charged with theft. If you held a senior management position with the employer, there's a good chance you had a legal duty of faithfulness to the employer and you could be sued for breach of fiduciary duty if you use the secret for your own gain.

✔ You were never an employee of the owner of the trade secret and you didn't sign a confidentiality agreement with the owner saying that you wouldn't use or reveal the secret; or, if you did sign such an agreement, it has expired (typically confidentiality agreements last for a limited period of time, say five or ten years).

Using a Name or Word in Your Business

The manufacture and sale of products are a couple of places where you can get into trouble when you're starting up a business, but they're not the only ones. Something as apparently minor as a name or word you want to use in your business can cause you major headaches.

A name or word could get mixed up in your business in a number of ways. You might want a name for the business, or you might want to use a catchy word or phrase to identify your product or service, or you might want a domain name for your business's Web site. But woe betide you if you jump in without thinking and use a name that somebody else already owns.

Naming your business

An incorporated business has a corporate name. That's the business's legal name and it's taken at the time of incorporation. It can be a name made up of words, or it can be a "number name." (For more on incorporating a business, see Chapter 5.)

A business that isn't incorporated can be carried on under the name of its owner(s) — the sole proprietor or the partners. (For more on starting an unincorporated business, see Chapter 5.)

An incorporated or unincorporated business can also be carried on under a trade name, which is kind of like an alias.

When it comes to naming a business, you can have problems not just with someone who's already using the name, but also with the government authorities who register names . . . and who've made up a slew of rules about acceptable names.

Choosing a corporate name

The authorities that incorporate businesses (the federal and the provincial governments) all have rules about choosing a word name. Check them out in the Business Corporation Act of your province if you're incorporating provincially, or the *Canada Business Corporation Act* if you're incorporating federally. One of the numerous rules is that the name has to include the word *Incorporated,* or *Inc.,* or *Corporation,* or *Corp.,* or *Limited,* or *Ltd.* But even if the name you choose meets all the rules, the incorporation authorities won't allow another business to take a name that is "confusingly similar" to the name of an existing corporation.

Before you try to register a corporate word name, you have to search a registry of names to make sure the name you want isn't already taken or isn't confusingly similar to another name. In Canada, this involves paying to have a NUANS search done, and there are various companies that will do the search for you. (On the Internet, you can locate these companies by searching the acronym "NUANS.") For federal incorporations only, you have the option of ordering your own NUANS report in real-time from the NUANS "Do it yourself" Real-Time System (RTS). (See www.nuans.com/nuansinfo_en/faq_en.htm#rts-str for more information.)

There are a lot of businesses out there and only so many great business names. Most of the great names you've thought of are probably already in use. Many business owners get tired of searching for a name that will be allowed by the authorities and just incorporate with a *number name.* Every corporation is assigned a number at the time of incorporation. (The incorporator doesn't get to choose it like a lucky lottery number; it's just the next available number in sequence, as if you took a ticket at the meat counter or the passport office.) This number, when combined with the name of the incorporating jurisdiction and the word *Limited,* is the corporation's number name — such as "123456 Ontario Limited" or "654321 Canada Ltd."

Choosing a trade name

An incorporated or unincorporated business can carry on business under a trade name. A trade name can be any word or phrase the business owner likes (although an unincorporated business can't use a word like *Inc.,* or *Ltd.,* or *Corporation* in its trade name, because only corporations can use those words). However, someone else may own the trade name already and be able to prevent others from using confusingly similar names. In some cases, a trade name has actually been trademarked by another business and the trademark owner can sue to prevent others from using the name (there's more about trademarks a little later on).

Selecting a name, slogan, or logo that identifies your business or product

Maybe you want to generate some excitement around your business by giving your product a neat-o name or attaching a cool logo to it.

A *trademark* is a distinctive word, or phrase, or symbol, or design (or a combination of some or all of these) that is marked on a business's goods or displayed with its services. The trademark identifies the business's goods and services in the mind of the consumer (and that's why confusingly similar trademarks are a problem). A trademark usually appears on packaging or in advertisements, accompanied by ® (for registered trademark) or MD (*marque déposée* = registered trademark), or by TM (trademark), or SM (service mark), or MC (*marque de commerce*). For example, "Bell Mobility" is a trademark of Bell Canada, "Windows" is a trademark of Microsoft Corp., "The Document Company" is a trademark of Xerox Corporation, and a tiny little polo player is a trademark of Ralph Lauren.

For more information about trademarks, see the Canadian Intellectual Property Office Web site at www.cipo.gc.ca and the United States Patent and Trademark Office Web site at www.uspto.gov/main/trademarks.htm.

Choosing a trademark

Telling you what you *can't* choose as a trademark is easier than telling you what you *can* choose. Visit the Canadian Intellectual Property Office (CIPO) Web site for more information, but generally you cannot trademark

- ✔ **A person's name (not even your own)** — although there's an exception if you can show that the name has become linked in the public mind with certain products or services (think McDonald's and Ralph Lauren).

- ✔ **Words that are simply descriptive** — such as "hot" soup or "soothing" lotion

- ✔ **A geographical name** — such as "Atlantic" cod

- ✔ **A business's name** — unless the name is used to identify the business's products or services (for example, "Xerox" is a trademark of the Xerox Corporation, and "Microsoft" is a trademark of Microsoft Corp.)

You definitely can't trademark words or symbols that are confusingly similar to someone else's existing trademark. There are also other rules about choosing a trademark; as we said, visit the CIPO Web site for more information.

Before you choose a trademark, you should search the Canadian trademark database on the Internet to see whether a trademark that's the same or similar is already registered. (It's similar if it has a slightly different spelling, sounds the same when pronounced, or has the words in different order.) If you're planning on doing business in the United States, search the U.S. trademark database on the United States Patent and Trademark Web site too. You might want to get a lawyer familiar with trademarks, or a trademark agent, to do the search for you. If you're thinking of doing business in other countries, you probably won't be able to do the search by Internet; you'll have to get the help of a trademark agent.

If you search trademark databases and find nothing, you could still run into an unregistered trademark. A trademark owner doesn't have to register the trademark in order to have the right to prevent another business from using it in the geographical area where the owner does business. It's harder to find out about unregistered trademarks, but you could try the following:

- ✔ Search the Internet for domain names that are the same as or very similar to the word or phrase you want to use, and check to see where the business associated with the domain name is located.

- ✔ Search business name registers — NUANS for Canada or ThomasNet, (www.thomasnet.com) for the United States — for similar names and the location of the business.

- ✔ Search in your local telephone book if you're feeling very low-tech (or the telephone book for any area where you want to do business — available at some public libraries or, if you're feeling higher-tech, on the Internet at http://canada411.yellowpages.ca/search Business.do) for business names. If the companies are in the phone book, you can assume they do business in the neighbourhood.

Protecting your trademark

To become the owner of a trademark, a business simply has to be the first to use it. Then it's protected as the business's trademark in the geographical areas where it's in use.

You can register a trademark for more complete protection. If an owner registers a trademark in a country, then it's protected throughout that country for a specified period of time (15 years in Canada, for example; 10 years in the United States). Once registered, a trademark can be renewed as many times as you want. A registered trademark is stronger than an unregistered trademark.

If your trademark is registered in a country, you can sue a competitor anywhere in that country to make the competitor stop using your trademark. A court will give a registered trademark much more protection than it will give to an unregistered trademark. If your trademark is not registered, you can sue only a competitor who's using your trademark in the particular geographical area(s) where you do business.

To register a trademark, you have to file an application for registration with the country's trademarks office. In Canada, the registration fee is a few hundred dollars. (If you use a trademark agent, you'll have to pay his or her fees as well.) You have to file a new trademark application in each country where you want protection.

Form 3-3 on the CD-ROM is the CIPO Application for Registration of a Proposed Trademark. Form 3-4 on the CD-ROM is the CIPO Application for Registration of a Trademark in Use in Canada.

Using someone else's trademark

The fact that someone already owns the trademark you want doesn't necessarily mean you can't use it.

If you're going to use the trademark in relation to a completely different product, you will probably be able to use it. So, if you find someone is already using the term or logo you'd like to use, ask yourself these questions:

- ✔ Is the trademark well known and owned by a business that has lots of money to sue you?

- ✔ Will your goods or services compete with the goods or services being sold, or even simply registered, under the trademark in use? (For example, are both of the businesses selling sports equipment, or is one selling sports equipment and the other musical instruments?)

- ✔ Will your use of the trademark confuse customers, even though your goods or services are not competing directly with those of the trademark owner? (Will people think an ad for your product is an ad for the trademark owner's product, or vice versa?)

If the answer to any of these questions is yes, you should probably look for another trademark — unless you currently receive so little mail that you'd look forward to getting a chilly letter from the trademark owner's lawyers.

You can also use someone else's trademark if they are not using it in the geographical area in which you plan to use it, as long as they haven't registered it with the federal government. (If the trademark is registered, the owner doesn't have to use it to get protection.)

Or you can arrange with the trademark owner for permission to use the trademark. For example, if you're a franchisee, you can use the franchisor's trademark. The trademark is one of the most important things the franchisee gets under the franchise agreement. (For more about franchises, see Chapter 9.) Even without a franchise agreement, it's possible to arrange to manufacture or sell a product under licence from the owner of the trademark and to display the trademark on the product. (Disney, for example, licenses lots of businesses to sell things with the Disney trademark.)

Registering an Internet domain name

If you're starting up a Web site to go with your business, you want a name for it. You can register pretty well any domain name you like, as long as it's not the same as an existing domain name. But once you've registered a domain name, you could run into trouble if it's the same as or confusingly similar (either deliberately or accidentally similar) to another business's trademark. You could be forced by the owner of the trademark to stop using your domain name.

For example, the authors once had the domain name `www.kerr-and-kurtz.com`. We knew it was unlikely that someone would come after us for trademark infringement. And if we were infringing on the trademark of the Kerr & Kurtz Diamond Mine, we wanted to meet the owners anyway. (You can never tell where a smile and a wave across a courtroom might lead these days.) But if our names were Margaret McDonald and JoAnn Burger, we might be in for a rough ride if we chose the domain name of `www.mcdonald-burger.com`. No one would confuse our Web site with that of McDonald's the fast-food chain — but McDonald's might still prefer that we use a different name, and it would cost us a lot of money to argue with them.

Choosing a domain name

Before you choose a distinctive domain name, you should check whether your name is going to be the same as or confusingly similar to another business's trademark or name or trade name. The Internet Corporation for Assigned Names and Numbers (ICANN) can get shirty with anyone who registers a domain name in bad faith (this is called "cybersquatting" and "cyberpiracy"). ICANN has the power to cancel a domain name registration if a complainant can prove that the domain name was registered for the purpose of trying to sell the name to the complainant or a competitor of the complainant, or to keep the complainant from using a trademark as a domain name, or to disrupt a competitor's business, or to confuse Internet users and attract them to the registrant's site, rather than the complainant's, for commercial gain. See `www.icann.org`. You can also have a look at `www.resolutioncanada.ca/`, the Web site for a Toronto-based company that specializes in resolving disputes over domain names in the dot-ca domain.

Using someone else's domain name

If you want to use a domain name that someone else is already using, see if you can buy it from the owner. Check for contact information on their Web site. If there isn't any, you may be able to find contact information by going to `www.register.com` and typing in the domain name. You can also find Web sites where people offer to sell their domain names (try `www.greatdomains.com` or `register.com`).

For more information about domain names see Chapter 8.

Using Written Materials in Your Business

Unless you and your customers and suppliers have all entered the post- post-modern commercial age and are conducting business entirely by cell phone and videophone, your business will probably use some written materials.

Understanding copyright

Written materials are protected by *copyright*. Copyright is the exclusive right to copy or reproduce, publish, translate, adapt, or perform a work. Copyrightable works include books, articles, manuals, plays, screenplays, scripts, scores, and computer software programs. They don't have to be printed (typeset) or published to be copyrighted. They can be written by hand, or they can be virtual text on the Internet.

There is no copyright in facts or ideas. That means that the actual information contained in a written or otherwise recorded document is not protected. It's really the way that the information is expressed that is protected. Copyright also does not protect a name, character, or slogan you might want to associate with your business (these are protectable by trademark — we talk about trademarks earlier in this chapter).

Copyright is automatic. Once text is written, copyright exists. And it exists not only in Canada but also in nearly every country in the world. Almost all countries have signed one of the several international copyright treaties littering the landscape. (If you wish, however, you can register a copyright with the federal government.)

Form 3-5 on the CD-ROM is the CIPO Application for Registration of a Copyright.

Copyright also lasts a long time — at least 50 years from the date of creation or performance, and often more than twice that long. (Exactly how long depends on what the copyrighted material is and the circumstances of its creation.)

You may be wondering why copyright is so easy to get, and free, and lasts so long, when a patent is hell to get, costs the earth, and lasts for the blink of an eye. Invention owners all wonder exactly the same thing — and nobody seems to have a good answer at the moment.

For more information about copyright, see the Web site of the Canadian Intellectual Property Office at www.cipo.gc.ca. You can also go to the Web site of the United States Copyright Office at www.copyright.gov or the Web site of the World Intellectual Property Organization at www.wipo.int/portal/index.html.en.

Using someone else's written material

If you want to reproduce software — for example, if you want to make and distribute copies of someone else's computer program as part of your business activities — you have to get the copyright owner's permission. Software is very easy and cheap to reproduce, so it's no wonder that the world is full of pirated software. Don't confuse "easy and cheap" with "legal."

If you want to reprint text from a book, or manual, or screenplay, or newspaper article, or Web site rant in a document you distribute or on your own Web site, again you have to get permission from the copyright owner. To find the copyright owner, start by searching the National Library of Canada (www.collectionscanada.ca/amicus/index-e.html) or the Library of Congress (www.loc.gov) to find an author's publisher(s); or do an Internet search under the author's name to find the author's or publisher's Web site. You can also contact organizations of creators or publishers (you can find links to them at www.accesscopyright.ca/resources.asp?a=36).

You may not need permission

You don't always need permission to use a copyrighted work. "Fair dealing" allows you to use another's work for purposes such as criticism, review, or news reporting. (That's why a newspaper doesn't have to get permission to quote a passage from a book that it's reviewing.)

So you may be able to quote in your newsletter or on your Web site a short passage that someone else has written, as long as you identify the source of the quotation and credit the author. But fair dealing is quite a limited exception, so don't try to push it too far.

Even if you have permission to use copyrighted material, you can't use the material in a way that interferes with the original creator's "moral rights" in the work. So you have to mention the creator's name in connection with the material, and you can't mess around with the material without the creator's permission. For example, if you have the right to use someone's love poem, you can't change the words and turn it into a jingle for transmission repairs.

If all you want to do is photocopy materials to distribute to potential or actual clients or customers or others, contact Access Copyright, the Canadian Copyright Licensing Agency, for permission. It's a not-for-profit collective that administers Canadian creators' and publishers' reproduction rights, and it also represents foreign creators and publishers through agreements with similar organizations in other countries including the United States, Great Britain, Australia, and France. See Access Copyright's Web site at www.accesscopy right.ca.

Using someone else's confidential materials

You may have come into contact with materials at your (perhaps former) place of employment that could be quite useful in your new business. We're not talking about government publications or the phone book. We're talking about materials that are valuable to the business and that the business wants to keep confidential. Can you make use of an employer's or former employer's materials in your own business — without getting permission?

When you leave an employer, or you stay but start up your own business on the side, you can't take away copies of confidential documents such as customer lists, market reports, and financial projections. That's theft, and the company could sue you or possibly even have you charged criminally.

After employment ends, unless you've signed a written agreement with your employer that you won't compete with the employer or won't use the employer's confidential information for your own gain, an employer would probably have difficulty preventing you from using information (as opposed to documents or other property) you picked up as an employee. For example, a former sales manager who knows the names of customers can approach them to pitch her own business. But beware if you held a fairly high management position with your former employer! If you use your employer's confidential information — such as information about a great business opportunity — to start up your own business, you could be sued for "breach of fiduciary duty."

Using your own written materials

Before you use copyrighted work that you think is your own, check it out. If you created the work as an employee, it probably belongs to your employer, and you can't use it without the employer's permission. The same is true if you were hired to create the work (for example, if you were commissioned to provide a report or manual). If the work is definitely your own, then you can go ahead and use it as you like.

Using Pictures and Drawings in Your Business

Pictures and drawings are subject to copyright just like written works. Copyright also covers film or video, paintings, sculpture, maps, photographs, and designs. So if you want to use someone else's picture or drawing for business purposes, you'll have to get the copyright owner's permission.

Clip art

Many Internet Web sites offer access to "clip art." (To find some, just type **clip art** into a search engine.) For most commercial purposes, you don't have to ask special permission to use clip art, and you can download and use an image instantly. You should check the terms of use set out on the Web site, however, to find out what you can and can't do with the clip art.

If you're just looking for something to liven up your business stationery or a newsletter or presentation, you can easily find pictures and cartoons that you can license with a minimum amount of effort and trouble. On the Internet you'll find sites that offer licences to use cartoons (such as *New Yorker* cartoons, at www.cartoonbank.com) and photographs (for example, at www.corbis.com).

You can also find drawings and pictures that you can use without special permission and without paying a licence fee. See the "Clip art" sidebar.

Using Music in Your Business

If you're not actually in the music business, you might think that you're not going to use music in your business and you might skip this section. But suppose you want to make public use of musical works that you choose — suppose you want to play a tape of classical music in your restaurant during dining hours, or have pop music or Christmas music in your retail store, or have a karaoke night at your bar, or play rap on your telephone when customers are on hold, or run a jazz theme when someone enters your Web site, or blast a rock 'n' roll song out at the beginning of a presentation, or have background music in your radio or TV ad, or hire a group to play hits from the '70s in front of your store during a street festival?

Music is also subject to copyright, and that applies not only to the composer. So what if Mozart has been dead for hundreds of years and his music is in the public domain? The orchestra that recorded his works ten years ago isn't dead, and the orchestra expects to be paid royalties for the use of the performance.

If you want to use music publicly for a business purpose, contact SOCAN (The Society of Composers, Authors and Music Publishers of Canada). SOCAN can give you the right to use or present performances of copyright-protected music in a public setting. SOCAN can get you rights not only to Canadian music, but also, through its agreements with similar foreign organizations, to music from all over the world. See the SOCAN Web site at www.socan.ca.

Chapter 4

The Void and How to Avoid It — Choosing a Product and Customers

. . . .

In This Chapter

▶ Finding out exactly what marketing involves

▶ Developing, pricing, and distributing a product or service

▶ Helping potential customers and clients find you

▶ Selling a product or service

. . . .

*T*he void of space . . . unimaginably vast areas that are deathly cold and devoid of life and matter. But the void of space isn't nearly as dangerous to your new business as a void in the marketplace. You'll be in big trouble if you offer a product or service that not a soul wants, or that your chosen customer group is not interested in. Then your business will just drift forever in frozen silent emptiness.

But you can avoid the void. You can navigate around it if you understand the marketing process.

Marketing is a big subject, and we're taking just one chapter in this book to look at it. So we encourage you to find out more by reading two very good books on this subject, *Small Business Marketing For Dummies* by Barbara Findlay Schenck and *Marketing Kit For Dummies* by Alexander Hiam (both published by Wiley).

What Is Marketing?

Marketing is about creating — and then keeping! — a relationship with your customers or clients. In this chapter, we give marketing its broadest possible definition, and we walk you through the marketing process from A to Z. More to the point, we take you through the following steps:

1. Developing a product or service while keeping potential customers or clients firmly in mind

2. Finding a route to let your product or services reach your target customers or clients

3. Pricing your product or service so it will sell

4. Locating customers or clients — or helping them to locate you

5. Selling your product or service

There's some good news about small business here: small businesses are pretty good at maintaining customer relationships, because they can know most of their customers quite well.

Let's hit the telescopes now and observe the marketing process.

Developing Your Product or Service with a Market in Mind

To start a business, you need a product or service to sell. And it needs to be something that customers or clients want to buy.

Product or service development is going to require quite a chunk of your time and energy, and it will require you to take on some tasks that may seem kind of challenging, such as researching potential customers and existing competition. We'd better get started right away, before we all lose our nerve for the enterprise.

Eureka!

To start at the very beginning, where do ideas for products or services come from in the first place? Very innocent entrepreneurs believe that the stork brings ideas, or that they're found in the garden under cabbage leaves. But entrepreneurs who've been introduced to the facts of life know that ideas really come from the following sources:

- **Potential customers:** If you're not even in business yet you don't have customers, but you're probably already in contact with people who would be glad to be your customers if only you'd provide a product or service they need. Keep your ears open in your current job — maybe your employer or your employer's competitors or your employer's customers or suppliers are making wistful comments about not being able to find Product X, or Person Y to perform Service Z.

- **Trade shows, trade journals — even the daily newspaper or a TV program:** There may already be a great idea out there. It just needs you to develop it.

- **Your fertile imagination:** You may have had a real *eureka!* moment, when you thought up a solution to a problem, or you created an invention, that people have been desperately hoping for — or that they don't even know they need yet.

Sober second thoughts

Once the *eureka!* moment has passed and your heart rate has returned to normal, you need to rationally evaluate the idea. Love at first sight can cost you a lot in business (just like in real life), so you have to make sure that this is the idea for you to get hitched up with. In this section we look at deciding whether:

- This is the right idea for you and your business personality.

- There's a market for the product or service you envision.

- You can compete successfully.

- The idea is financially viable.

If your idea is new and innovative, you may be able to get assistance with the evaluation, for example from The Canadian Innovation Centre (CIC) (www. innovationcentre.ca) in Waterloo, Ontario, an organization that grew out of the invention commercialization activities of the University of Waterloo. Their Web site has information for inventors as well as links to other useful organizations such as the (U.S.) National Inventor Fraud Center (www. inventor fraud.com), which offers advice on how to steer away from invention marketing companies that are set up only to scam inventors.

Don't get mixed up with a company that combines high-pressure sales tactics with a low success rate.

Is this idea right for you?

Or is this a good idea at all, when you get right down to it? For example, is it legal? (And if it's legal now, will it become illegal once it takes off? Remember radar detectors for the travelling public?) Is it hands-off? The idea may already be patented (see Chapter 3) and the patent owner doesn't want to license to you. Are you legal? Some products and services can be provided only by a licensed individual or business. Is the product or service safe — or will you cause harm to someone and end up with a lawsuit on your hands? And if everything's legal, hands-on, and safe, do you have the reputation or expertise needed to develop the idea into a business and reel in customers or clients?

Does anyone want the product or service?

Your idea may seem wonderful to you, but you're going to need a slightly larger market than yourself in order to prosper. So you have to do some customer research — identify a target market for the product or service and estimate the size of the market. Here's a brief guide to doing customer research.

First, think generally about who your customers or clients might be (keep in mind that you could be wrong about this, though). For example, are they

- ✔ **Other businesses?** A whole bunch of them or just one or two? Are the businesses service providers or retailers or manufacturers?

- ✔ **Individuals?** Do the individuals live in a particular neighbourhood or geographic area, or do they live all over the country or around the world? Are they men only? Women only? The young? Older people? The well-to-do, or just anyone with a buck to spend?

Once you've identified a starting point, you can proceed with your customer/client research to find out if anybody would want your product or service. Different research methods exist, and you'll probably want to try a combination of them. From the least expensive to most expensive, here they are:

- ✔ **Direct observation of potential customers or clients:** You can use your own personal knowledge of a business you're in or have followed, you can visit stores and trade shows, or you can attend presentations and conferences.

- ✔ **Review of publicly available information:** This includes TV programs, newspapers, trade journals, newsletters, and market analysis materials from the business reference section of a public or university library.

✔ **Interviews with people already in the field or with potential customers or clients:** This isn't as hard to do as you think. If you start with people you know and ask for names of other people who wouldn't mind talking to you, if you just ask for an opinion or advice and don't try to sell anything, and if you keep the interview polite and brief, you'll be surprised how many people will agree to give you 20 minutes or half an hour of their time. Try to meet face-to-face if you can — the interviewee will remember you better if it later turns out that she needs the product or service you want to provide.

✔ **Focus groups:** See if you can lure groups of potential customers or clients together to talk about the product or service. The lure should be something significant, like a free meal or a chance to win a prize. Unless you can find friends and acquaintances who'll participate in a focus group, you may be better off hiring a market analysis firm to run focus groups than trying to corner strangers on your own.

✔ **Surveys and questionnaires:** These are short written or telephone interviews distributed or conducted on a large scale. You'll have to come up with the right questions to ask, and pay for printing and distribution of written materials, find your nerve to make calls or hire trained interviewers to phone people at dinnertime, and then you'll have to analyze the results . . . if anyone answers the questions (a lot of paper surveys will be considered garbage and thrown out, and a lot of people won't answer telephone interviewers). Doing door-to-door surveys in a neighbourhood, or approaching people on the street in a business or shopping area, will probably earn you a lot of suspicion and brush-offs. As with focus groups, you may prefer to have a professional market analysis firm handle a survey. (Surveys and questionnaires are easier to handle yourself if you've already got an established customer base.)

At the conclusion of your market research, ideally you should have an idea about whether the product or service is attractive to some target group or groups, and you should also be able to estimate roughly the size of your market. Your market is the number of customers you'll win times the number of sales per customer.

Who's the competition?

And what are they up to? This information is known as "competitive intelligence." Your competitors may already have claimed all of the customers or clients you identified by doing your market research. Or they may not. But now's the time to find out by assessing your potential market share.

To start with the question we just asked (Who's the competition?), your competition is made up of the following:

✔ **Direct competitors** — who offer exactly the same product or service

✔ **Indirect competitors** — who offer an alternative product that more or less meets the same need as your product

✔ **Who-was-that-masked-man? competitors** — who offer something completely different that potential customers will spend their money on instead of on your product or a similar product, much to your regret and amazement

✔ **Inertia** — the tendency of customers and clients to do nothing at all when brought face-to-face with your wonderful product or service

As an example, if you want to offer a service tutoring children in math or reading, your direct competition is other private tutoring services, your indirect competition is the public and private schools in the area (they may be doing a fine job of teaching, in which case your services won't be required); your who-was-that-masked-man? competition is computer games and skateboards; and inertia is parents letting their kids sink or swim through school on their own.

Look carefully at your direct and indirect competitors and see if you can find out whether

✔ They've cornered the market and are doing such a good job at such a good price that you haven't much hope of taking market share away from them. Or whether you should be able to relieve them of market share because you can offer better value — for example, a lower price, a higher-quality product or service, a more convenient location, greater expertise, friendlier service, and so on. Sometimes the first competitor into the market may just have collected and educated your potential clients for you!

✔ Their business is profitable — are they growing or shrinking?

✔ They're big enough and mean enough to run you out of town if you show your face on the street (have you noticed how small airlines regularly get eaten?).

How much money can you put behind this idea?

It's unlikely that you can get your idea off the ground for free. So the last sober second-thought involves figuring out

✔ **Approximately how much it will cost to get your business launched.** This involves adding up your start-up costs plus bridge financing for your operating expenses until your business is generating income. We cover start-up costs for equipment in Chapter 6, for premises in Chapter 7, and for purchase of an existing business in Chapter 9. We look at operating costs in Chapter 10.

✔ **Approximately how much money is available to you for a business start-up.** The cash you have on hand or can raise through family contributions may be enough to get your particular business up and running; or you may need a bank loan for a larger amount; or you may need a significant investment from an angel investor or venture capital firm. (See Chapter 10 for sources of start-up money.) How much you'll be able to raise (especially from outsiders) is linked to the likely return on investment for your idea. So just because it will take $1 million to build a plant to produce your product doesn't mean you should scrap the idea. It could be full steam ahead if an investor believes that your business could generate profits of $2 million annually after a couple of years or that the business might be worth $50 million in five years.

Tinker with your idea

After you've had all these second thoughts, you have to decide whether to forget your idea altogether or rework it in light of what you've discovered about your target market and your competition. If you decide to keep going with your idea, you may now be thinking about things like

✔ How you can redesign or add value to the product or service so that it appeals more to your target market

✔ How you can provide the product or service more efficiently than the competition or at a price that potential customers or clients will find more attractive

✔ How you can redesign or reposition your product or service so that it doesn't meet a powerful competitor head-on

✔ How you can redesign or present the product or service so that it appeals to a potential investor

After you've tinkered, you may need to reevaluate.

Finding a Route to the Target Market

Okay, so you think you've got a product or service that can go the distance. Now you have to figure out how you want to get it from you to the person who will actually use it — so you have to decide on one or more distribution channels. You have two basic choices:

✔ **Distribute directly:** The product or service goes from your business to your buyer (most services and products take this route); or

✔ **Distribute indirectly:** The product or service goes from your business to another business to the buyer. Although your target market is the buyer, your customer is the "middleman" business.

Business to buyer

If you choose direct distribution, you can deal with customers or clients in two ways:

✔ **Face-to-face:** in your retail store or your office; or

✔ **Facelessly:** through an order system that uses mail, phone, fax, or a Web site. If you choose this option, remember that you'll need a place to keep your inventory, such as a room in a warehouse, and you'll need a delivery system, such as mail or courier. (Certain kinds of services provided this way — such as essays or horoscopes or advice for the lovelorn — may be deliverable electronically.)

Business to business to buyer

If your customer is a middleman, you'll probably need fewer customers in order to make a go of your business. However, a middleman may be more demanding about low prices, so your profit margin may be lower.

Middlemen include

✔ **Retailers**

✔ **Wholesalers or distributors** — who in turn sell to retailers, and sometimes to the general public

✔ **Repackagers** — who also sell to retailers after — you guessed it — repackaging the products they buy from you

You may be able to or may want to sell directly to the middleman yourself, or you may want to employ a manufacturer's agent or representative to do the selling for you (on commission). First you'll have to choose an agent who sells to the kind of middleman you want in the regions you want, and then you'll have to persuade the agent to carry your line and talk it up to customers.

Pricing Your Product or Service

You can make a profit in different ways — for example, by combining a small profit on each item or service provided with high sales volume, or by combining a low sales volume with a big profit on each transaction. (Best, of course, is high profit on each unit and high sales volume, but not many businesses are that lucky.) But if you underprice, you'll lose money on every sale even if you sell a gazillion units; if you overprice, no one will buy at all. How do you figure this whole thing out? In this section, we talk about how to settle on the right price to charge.

Deciding on the minimum price you can charge

Minimum price is not all that difficult to figure out. As a rule you don't want to charge less for your product or service than it costs to produce. (An exception to the rule is offering the product or service as a loss leader, to lure customers in — but you can't keep that up for very long, and certainly not on an important part of your line.) The formula that tells you, as the owner of a start-up business, your cost to produce (your break-even cost) is

$$\frac{\text{Total direct and indirect costs over a given period (say, one to three months)}}{\text{Total number of products or services that it would be reasonable for you to provide over the given period}} = \text{Your break-even cost for that period}$$

Your break-even cost for the period is the amount you need to charge for each unit of your product or service in order to pay your direct and indirect costs. (See the sidebar, "A sample break-even chart.")

Direct costs, also known as variable costs, include

- ✔ Materials required to manufacture the product, and cost of shipping the materials to your site
- ✔ Lease payments for factory space or storage space
- ✔ Energy (or other utility) costs of production (for example, electricity, water)
- ✔ Wages paid to subcontractors or employees to produce the product or service
- ✔ Cost of delivering the product or service to your customer

Indirect costs, also known as fixed costs or overhead, include administrative expenses such as:

- ✔ Wages for office staff
- ✔ Electricity, telephone, and other office utilities

  ✔ Office supplies

  ✔ Advertising expenses

  ✔ Rent on your office space

If your business involves supplying a service rather than manufacturing a product, you'll probably have higher indirect costs than direct costs.

Deciding on the maximum price you can charge

Now over to the other end of the price scale. Here, the ceiling for your price is the value of your product or service to the customer or client. Value is what the customer perceives that he or she is getting in exchange for the cost of the product, and includes things such as quality and reliability of the product or service, image or prestige associated with the product or service, uniqueness of the product or service, backup from your business such as support and guarantees, convenience of dealing with your business (such things as good location or inexpensive delivery or the helpfulness of your staff), and incentives such as rebates (money back following a purchase), discounts (money off the purchase price), and other freebies.

If a customer believes that your price is greater than the value of your product or service, the customer won't buy from you.

A sample break-even chart

At what sales volume will your business break even?

Direct or variable cost per month of producing total number of units you think it would be reasonable to produce and sell in a month (let's say 1,000, at $10 per unit)	$10,000
PLUS	
Indirect or fixed cost per month of producing the units	$5,000
EQUALS	
Total cost per month of producing the units	$15,000

DIVIDED BY

Number of units of product or service produced and sold per month	1,000
EQUALS	
Break-even cost, or the minimum price you need to charge per unit	$15

You can fiddle with the figures in the different boxes, increasing or decreasing the numbers in them to see how your break-even cost is affected by changes. For example, if your direct cost is $12,000 instead of $10,000, your break-even cost becomes $17. Or if the number of units produced and sold is 800 instead of 1,000, your break-even cost becomes $18.75 instead of $15.

Form 4-1 on the CD-ROM is a sample break-even chart (like the one we show in the sidebar, "A sample break-even chart") that you can use to calculate the sales volume at which you'll break even.

Setting your price

Setting a price all comes down to supply and demand. If a product is essential or useful and it's hard to find, the price can be higher and the product will still sell (until people run out of money). If a product is not a must-have or is readily available, the price has to be lower if you want to sell. Higher or lower than what? The competition's price.

So see what your competition is charging. Once you know that, then you can implement one of the following three strategies:

- ✔ **Charge more than the competition.** This will work only if your product is seen as more valuable than the competition's. You can increase the value of the same product or service offered by the competition by (for example) creating a higher-end image for your business or by trading on your reputation as an expert.

- ✔ **Charge the same as the competition.** But you still need to increase the value of your product over the competition's. You could do this, for example, by offering a more convenient location to your target customers.

- ✔ **Charge less than the competition.** Just be careful not to undercut your own cost of production, and keep in mind that you'll acquire a "reputation." Whether it's true or not, customers and clients will tend to associate lower prices with lower value. It's only in rare cases that they'll think they've made a Marvellous Discovery of a business that carries exactly the same product as the competition but at a lower price.

Finding Customers or Clients

Now that you've settled on a price, you'd like to find someone who'll pay it! So the next step is to locate potential customers and clients and tell them that you're open for business.

You can announce your presence in three different ways:

- ✔ Promotion
- ✔ Advertising
- ✔ Publicity

Promotion

In business circles, the word promotion gets tossed around quite a bit and is used to mean various things. We use it to mean activities that say "I'm here!" but that are neither paid advertising nor media-provided publicity. Promotion is sometimes considered a form of free advertising, but it isn't really "free" — there's always a cost to anything you do . . . at a minimum, your time and a new tie.

You can promote your business in lots of different ways. Whatever way you choose, although you may not look as if you're soliciting business, finding customers or clients is your aim.

Here are some promotional activities:

- **Networking:** Getting out and meeting people who may become clients themselves or who may refer clients to you. You can network practically anywhere, but typical places to network include business meetings; social, professional, or trade events; clubs; groups associated with your church, synagogue, or mosque or with your ethnic or cultural roots; conventions; conferences; trade shows; neighbourhood events; and school reunions.

- **Providing useful information in a public forum:** Teaching a course, giving a talk or presentation to a community group or at a conference, writing a column or article for a newspaper or magazine, writing a book, putting out your own newsletter for clients or potential clients, creating your own informative Web site or contributing to someone else's (for preference, that someone else should be better known than you or have a more popular Web site).

Whenever you engage in a promotional activity, make sure you provide a "take-away" for potential clients: a business card if you're networking, a business card or brochure if you're giving a talk, contact information (such as an e-mail address) if you're writing for a newspaper or magazine. On your Web site, consider including a toll-free phone number in case a potential but distant customer wants to talk after seeing the information you've provided.

Advertising

You can advertise in many different ways (and they all cost money. Some cost a lot more money than others). After you figure out what message you want to send about your business, you can send it via

- Direct mail — mailing, faxing, or e-mailing a brochure or flyer to the unsuspecting public. You can buy mailing lists of potential customers. However, many potential customers hate direct mail. (One of the authors makes a point of calling up businesses that send advertisements to her home fax machine in the middle of the night and wishing commercial disaster on them.)

✔ Telephone solicitation — calling strangers up and telling them about your business and asking if they're interested in receiving more information or in buying something

✔ Print ads — put one in the Yellow Pages if you have a local clientele in mind, or in local, regional, or national newspapers or magazines

✔ Ads on other businesses' Web sites — although, most Web surfers are now adept at ignoring ads

✔ Flyers, handbills (delivered by hand or by Canada Post's direct mail service), and street posters, or posters in other businesses' stores or offices (if they'll let you put them up)

✔ Business cards or brochures left on display at other businesses, community centres, and so on, if they don't mind

✔ Billboards and busboards

✔ Radio

✔ TV

✔ Product placement in a movie or on a TV show

As with promotion, make sure your ad contains contact information for your business.

Publicity

We're all looking for our 15 minutes of fame, but publicity is harder to come by than promotion or advertising because you have no real control over it. You can't force the media to be interested in you — okay, so you can probably snap reporters' pointy little heads around if you do something extreme like rob a bank and hand out your business card to the terrified tellers and customers as you depart, or if you announce that you're going to be the area's first nude retail store — but that would be getting carried away. Try to keep a cool business head when you're seeking publicity.

To pique media interest, you don't need to do something that will be front-page news tomorrow morning. You do need to do something that's unusual or innovative, or that is of local interest (to a local paper or TV station) or of human interest. This is your "hook" for the media. Here are some things to try:

✔ Issue a press release about the opening of your (interesting and innovative) business or about some significant activity you're undertaking or some event you're planning.

> ✔ Contact an appropriate editor or journalist and issue an invitation to an event you're staging, or ask if they're interested in writing about something you're doing (the answer is probably no . . .).
>
> ✔ Contact an appropriate editor or journalist to let him or her know you're available to be interviewed as an expert on a particular subject (if you are). When a story breaks, newspapers and TV stations often hunt down experts for quotable comments.

Unless it's a slow news day or you and your business are absolutely fascinating, don't expect too much from a publicity initiative. And certainly don't expect constant publicity if you do happen to get a nibble or two.

Professional help

You can find individuals (freelancers) or firms who will help you create and display ads or who can help you with publicity. They're advertising agencies, publicists, and public relations firms. If you want this kind of help, investigate before you hire. Watch for ads you like or PR you are impressed by, and then contact the firm or individual responsible for creating it. Ask for a detailed explanation about what the freelancer or firm can do for you, and how much it will cost.

Don't get depressed

In some cases, you'll have to cast your net far and wide to accumulate customers or clients. Don't expect to acquire a large number of clients from every activity you undertake (maybe not right away, maybe never). General contact methods such as the ones we've described above often have a pretty low success rate — if your "I'm here!" announcement reaches 100 people, you may get a response from as few as 10 people or only 1 person (or even nobody at all). Try different methods and see if there's something that seems to work for your particular business.

If nothing works, it could mean that you came up with a bad business idea . . . but you should have figured that out at the evaluation stage.

Now Get Out There and Sell!

Talking to you in this chapter about how to sell your product or service is a bit premature, but we thought we'd close the loop while we're here and discussing the marketing process.

So look into your future. You've attracted an enquiry from a potential customer or client who wants to know more about your product or service. (It's pleasant but a little unusual for someone just to walk into your premises or call you up and say "Gimme a dozen of those, here's my cash.") How do you get from the enquiry to the sale? Here are some tips for landing your customer or client:

✔ **Know your product or service inside out.** And make sure your associates or employees do too, so that all of you can answer any question about it, such as

- What is it?

- How much does it cost?

- What if I buy it and it doesn't work? (What support do you provide, and what warranties or guarantees?)

- What do you know about it? (That is, what expertise does your business have?)

- Does anybody else like it? (Can you provide references from people who've dealt with you?)

- How will you get it to me, and when? (What's your delivery method and timing?)

✔ **Know the customer or client.** This may mean doing some research (for example, on a potential business customer's Web site) and/or simply listening to the customer you're dealing with to find out what he or she really wants (or needs — the two may be different). So don't spend your precious customer contact time doing all the talking. You won't learn anything about the customer with your mouth open and your ears shut.

You also have to figure out your potential customer or client's business style so that you can adapt to meet it. For example, you'll know more about how to keep the potential customer interested in buying if you can find out whether the customer

- Is most interested in low price or high quality or reliability or speed . . . or (commonly but unrealistically) in all four

- Wants to close a deal quickly or needs time to think privately and consult with others

- Wants a prepackaged product or wants to pick and choose the components

- Prefers you to take charge or simply wants you there as support for his or her own decision

✔ **Make a presentation geared toward the potential customer's needs and business style.** This doesn't have to be a massive undertaking — and it can start as simply as "May I show you our product/tell you about our service?"

✔ **Make a proposal for a deal that you think will suit the potential customer.** For example, "Would you like to buy one of these to try?" If the potential customer starts to wiggle and squirm, he or she may not be really interested right now, or maybe you need to go back to point two, Know your customer.

✔ **Close the deal if the customer is willing.** Closing may take a few tries, even with an interested customer.

✔ **Keep the door open if there's no close.** If the closing doesn't happen, suggest reasons for you to contact the potential customer within a short time. ("Shall I find out if we can order it in another colour, and call you?" "Shall I call you on Tuesday to see if we can arrange another meeting?")

✔ **Get feedback — from customers who close and from customers who don't.** It doesn't take much to give someone an opening to tell you if they're unhappy about something. (If you have a Web site and contact e-mail, encourage users to let you know what they think about your business.)

✔ **Act on the feedback.** Unless it really seems totally loony.

Part II
Blast Off into Business

The 5th Wave   By Rich Tennant

"I appreciate you sharing your dreams and wishes for starting your own pool and spa business, but maybe I should explain more fully what we at the Make-A-Wish Foundation are all about."

In this part . . .

We help you make sure that your business launch doesn't fizzle. We explain the legal side of setting up a business, take you shopping for the basic equipment your business will require, help you decide where your business will be located (including in cyberspace), tell you about buying an existing business in case you don't want to start a business from scratch, and give you the lowdown on getting money to finance your enterprise.

Chapter 5

A Vehicle for Your Business

In This Chapter

▶ Owning your business alone or with an associate

▶ Thinking about incorporating

▶ Looking at sole proprietorship

▶ Examining partnerships

▶ Finding out about government requirements such as licensing and registration

*N*ow you're ready to blast off into business . . . but you need a vehicle. A vehicle for carrying on business is called a "form of business" or a "business organization." There are only a few forms of business, and we take you around to each one of them and help you kick the tires. After you've looked at all of them, and thought about your own business circumstances, you'll be able to decide which one is right for you.

Should You Go Alone or Take on a Co-pilot?

You'll get asked a lot "What's your business?" But right now we're going to ask, "Who's your business?" Is your business you and only you? Is it you and a pal? You and a group?

If your new business is a team effort, you can skip down to "Should You Incorporate?" now. We'll meet you there in a minute. If your new business is a one-person show, stick around and read this section. We're going to sit you down and have a little chat with you about travelling alone.

Certainly being the only owner of a business has its advantages. Here are just a few of them:

✔ The profits of the business will be yours alone. (When you've accumulated some profits you can sit on the floor and rub $50 bills all over your body, shouting "Mine, mine, all mine!" Obviously this kind of behaviour would be out of bounds if you had a co-owner.)

- ✔ You have the only say in what the business does and you don't need anyone else's agreement to do what you want to do. So there.

- ✔ Setting up a business with just one owner is usually easier, faster, and cheaper.

But there are reasons that you might want to, or have to, have a co-owner:

- ✔ You may want someone else to share the financial risks of the business with you.

- ✔ You may want company — being in business all by yourself can be lonely.

- ✔ You may need someone else to provide skills or knowledge that you don't have.

- ✔ You may want someone to share the workload.

If we've now got you considering sharing ownership of your business with someone else, you should ask yourself these questions:

- ✔ Are you capable of working well with a co-owner (and especially with any particular co-owner you have in mind)?

- ✔ Is the business likely to be able to generate enough revenue to support two (or more) owners?

- ✔ Does the business have roles for two (or more) owners to play?

- ✔ Does your potential co-owner have skills and knowledge that will add to yours (instead of having no useful skills and knowledge, or having the same skills and knowledge as you)?

The reason you decide, finally, to go on alone or take a co-pilot with you should be that it will give your business a better chance of success.

Should You Incorporate?

Are we all together again now? Then, let's proceed.

"Should I incorporate?" is a very common first question asked by entrepreneurs, whether they're working alone or in a team. But it's not the right first question. It can't be answered in a vacuum. And before you even ask the question you need to know about the alternatives to incorporation.

What are your options?

When you ask whether or not you should incorporate, what you're really asking is "What form of business organization should I choose?" You have choices, and the choices available to you depend on whether your business will have only one owner, or two or more owners.

If you will be the only owner of the business, your choices are

- ✔ To operate as a sole proprietor
- ✔ To operate as a corporation that is owned by you

If two or more people will own the business, your choices are

- ✔ To operate as a partnership
- ✔ To operate as a corporation that is owned by you and your co-owner(s)

What's the difference?

The main distinction between a business that's incorporated and one that's not is that an incorporated business is a legal being separate from the owner of the business. So if you incorporate your business, your personal assets (property owned by you personally) and the assets of the corporation (property owned by the business) are separate. Your personal debts (money owed by you personally) and the debts of the corporation (money owed by the business) are also separate. In theory then, your personal assets can't be seized to pay the debts of the business.

What many people don't know is that, in practice, it's not always possible to keep the business debts of your corporation away from your personal assets. (We tell you more about this under the heading "What's a Corporation?") They are also unaware that there are other ways to protect your personal assets without incorporating your business. (For more about this, see the heading "Protecting Your Assets without Incorporating.")

The two other main differences between an incorporated and an unincorporated business are:

- ✔ The profits of a corporation are taxed differently than the profits of a business operated as a sole proprietorship or partnership.
- ✔ The amount of paperwork increases greatly when you're setting up and running a corporation.

We talk about all of these distinctions in more detail later in this chapter. As you will see, incorporation should not be an automatic step, because it may or may not make sense for you.

The Corporation — a Form of Business with a Life All Its Own

A corporation is probably as close as most people will get to an alien life form, barring abduction by extraterrestrial biological entities (EBEs) for bizarre medical experiments. And we're not kidding when we call a corporation a "life form."

Understanding corporations

A corporation is a legal being that is created by the process of incorporation, and that has a separate legal identity from that of the individuals who create it and own it as shareholders.

Even though a corporation is not human, it has many of the legal powers, rights, and duties of a Canadian resident. But because it is not human, it must act through its human directors and officers.

Corporations can be public or private. A public corporation, or offering corporation, can sell its shares to the public. A private, or non-offering, corporation is very limited in its rights to sell its shares. Whether you know it or not, if you're thinking about incorporating a new business, you're thinking about a private corporation. When we talk about corporations in this chapter, we're talking about private corporations. In Chapter 19, we talk about the process, if you're curious, of taking a corporation public. Very few private corporations ever become public.

Who owns a corporation?

The shareholders of a corporation own the corporation through their ownership of shares in the corporation. The shareholders acquire their shares for a set price and they pay for them by giving money, goods, or services to the corporation. (The money and goods become the property of the corporation. Shareholders are not the legal owners of the corporation's property.) If the corporation is a failure, the shares will go down in value — maybe even down to zero — and the shareholders' investment will diminish and disappear. But the shareholders will not usually lose more than what they already gave in exchange for the shares, because they are not ordinarily responsible for paying any debts the corporation has.

A corporation can have several classes of shares, each of which has different rights. Common shares usually give a shareholder the right to elect directors, receive a portion of the corporation's profits in the form of dividends, and receive a share of the corporation's property if the corporation closes down. Preferred shares (also called preference or special shares) always have the right to receive dividends before the common shares do, and can have other special privileges attached to them.

Who runs a corporation?

Every private corporation must have at least one director, whose role it is to manage the affairs of the corporation. There's no upper limit on the number of directors a corporation can have, but even big public corporations don't usually have more than 10 or 20. A director has a duty to be reasonably careful in running the corporation's affairs, to act in the best interests of the corporation, and to carry out his or her duties honestly and in good faith. If a director doesn't fulfill these duties, the shareholders can take the director to court.

A director must be at least 18 years old, of sound mind, and not bankrupt. In federal corporations and in most provincial corporations, a majority of the directors must be Canadian citizens who reside in Canada; and in some provinces at least one director must also be a resident of the province.

In many corporations, the director(s) and shareholder(s) will be the same people, so the people who own the corporation also run the corporation.

Setting up a corporation

You incorporate a business by filling out and filing incorporating documents with the government and paying government fees. You can incorporate your business as a federal corporation (in which case you file with the federal government) or as a provincial corporation (in which case you file with your provincial government). Incorporating documents vary a little, but they usually include the following:

- ✔ **The name of the corporation:** For more about naming a corporation, have a look at Chapter 3.

- ✔ **The address of the corporation:** Although the business does not actually have to be carried on at the registered address, a federally incorporated business must have a registered office somewhere in Canada, and a provincially incorporated business must have a registered office somewhere within that province.

- ✔ **The number of shares the corporation can create:** (The maximum number of shares can be limited or unlimited.) Also, the rights and conditions different classes of shares will have, and any restrictions on the shareholders' rights to sell or give away their shares.

- ✔ **The director(s) of the corporation:** A corporation must have at least one director.

- ✔ **The type of business the corporation may carry on:** Federal and most provincial corporations can carry on any kind of business unless the incorporating document sets limits.

- ✔ **The powers of the corporation:** Federal and most provincial corporations have the same legal powers as a human being, but it's possible to limit their powers — for example, their power to borrow money.

In most provinces the incorporation forms are available on the government Web site, and the forms themselves look relatively simple to fill out. You don't legally need a lawyer to incorporate your business, but if you do it yourself you may make mistakes that will be difficult to correct later. We strongly suggest that you use a lawyer.

Once the documents are filed and the fees paid, the government will issue a certificate of incorporation or, in Prince Edward Island and Quebec, a charter by letters patent. This is the moment when your corporation is "born." Before it can actually start to carry on business, though, it has to have a first directors' meeting. At this meeting, the first directors pass the corporation's by-laws — the rules about how the corporation will be run — and make resolutions appointing officers of the corporation (such as the president, treasurer, and secretary, who will run the corporation day-to-day according to the directors' orders), among other things. You can buy standard printed by-laws and standard forms for the first directors' resolutions if you don't have a lawyer help you with the incorporation and this initial organization.

Running a corporation

You can't be spontaneous and freewheeling when you're running a corporation. You need to follow certain procedures for making decisions and keeping records and telling the government what you've been up to. You must

- ✔ Hold directors' meetings as necessary to make decisions, in the form of resolutions passed by a simple majority of the directors, about the affairs of the corporation — although meetings can be bypassed if all the directors agree in writing to a resolution. (**Note:** After you've been running your corporation for about 10 minutes, you may be convinced that the majority of the directors are indeed simple. But a "simple majority" means 51 percent.)

✔ Hold annual shareholders' meetings to elect directors, appoint (or dispense with) an auditor to examine the corporation's finances, and review the corporation's financial statements. Most shareholders' decisions are made by a simple majority vote. (Again, meetings can be bypassed if all the shareholders agree in writing to resolutions making the decisions.)

✔ Keep complete corporate records, including the incorporating documents, corporate by-laws, minutes of (a written report about what happened at) directors' and shareholders' meetings, and resolutions in writing.

✔ File required documents with the government, such as notices about changes that have occurred in the corporation. And if you don't file as required, the government can dissolve the corporation. (Watch in horror as your corporation disappears before your eyes and screams, "I'm melting, I'm melting!")

Advantages of incorporation . . . at least in theory

The two main — theoretical — advantages of incorporating a business are

✔ Limited liability

✔ Tax advantages

Limited liability

The main reason most people incorporate is to limit their personal liability to pay debts of the business, in case the business fails.

Here's how limited liability works in theory. The corporation is a separate legal being. If it borrows money and can't pay it back, the lender can sue only the corporation, not its owners the shareholders, and can collect on its debt by taking only the assets of the corporation, not the assets of its shareholders. Similarly, if the corporation injures someone in carrying on its business, only the corporation can be sued.

Here's how limited liability works — or doesn't work — in reality. The corporation applies to a bank to borrow money. The bank realizes that the corporation doesn't have a lot of assets for the bank to take if the corporation doesn't pay back the loan. So the bank tells the corporation's directors that it won't lend money to the corporation unless the directors and/or shareholders give a personal guarantee to repay the loan if the corporation can't repay. If the corporation doesn't pay the loan, the bank can sue the directors and/or shareholders personally. Other businesses such as landlords and suppliers that enter into big contracts with the corporation may also require personal guarantees from the directors and/or shareholders.

In other words, incorporating does not mean that you will escape personal liability for the debts of your business. You may not be liable as a shareholder, but there's a good chance you'll be liable as a guarantor.

Taxes

Corporations are taxed differently from human beings (who are known as individuals in tax jargon), and the taxes an incorporated business pays can be lower than those of an unincorporated business.

All taxpayers, whether individuals or corporations, pay both federal and provincial income taxes. Taxes are calculated as a percentage of income. Corporations are taxed on their profits at a flat rate — the percentage stays the same no matter how high the profits. The rate of tax an individual pays, on the other hand, goes up in steps as the person's taxable income goes up — the higher a person's income, the bigger the percentage paid in tax. The federal corporate and personal tax rates are the same throughout the country, but the provincial tax rates vary from province to province.

The highest flat rate for corporate taxes (provincial and federal combined) is about 39 percent. However, there is a federal Small Business Deduction for Canadian Controlled Private Corporations that may reduce the tax rate to between about 15 and 22 percent on the first $300,000 to $450,000 of taxable income (depending on the province).

The lowest personal tax rate (provincial and federal combined) is zero for a person whose taxable income is less than about $8,150. The highest combined personal tax rate is about 49 percent on income over approximately $116,000.

Let's put this all together. If you do not incorporate your business, all of the profits of the business will be taxed in your hands personally, and the rate of tax will depend on your total taxable income, perhaps to as high as about 49 percent. On the other hand, if you do incorporate your business (assuming your business qualifies for the Small Business Deduction and has a taxable income of less than $300,000 to $450,000, depending on your province) the corporation will pay tax on its profits at between 15 and 22 percent. But that's not the whole picture! At this point, the money is sitting in the corporation's hands, not yours. When you take money out of the corporation, that money will be taxed in your hands.

If as an employee you are paid a salary by the corporation, the amount of the salary will be deducted from the corporation's taxable income (and the amount of taxes the corporation has to pay will be reduced), but it will be taxed in your hands at your personal rate. If as a shareholder you are paid a dividend from the profits of the corporation, the dividend is taxed in your hands at your personal tax rate. However, it's taxed to a maximum of only about 24 to 37 percent (again depending on your province) because the profits were previously taxed in the hands of the corporation.

If your business makes only a small profit — which is what often happens in the first year or two of business — you may pay less tax if your business is not incorporated.

If your business loses money — which also often happens in the first year or two of business — you're almost certainly better off from a tax standpoint if your business is not incorporated, because you will be able to deduct the business's losses from any other income that you have. You don't get this deduction if your business is incorporated.

To decide whether incorporating your business offers you a tax advantage, you must compare the taxes you think you'd pay if your business were incorporated with the taxes you think you'd pay if your business were not incorporated. Tax planning for your business is extremely important, and you should consult an accountant and/or tax lawyer about whether it makes sense for you to incorporate.

Advantages of incorporation, continued

There can be advantages to incorporation besides the ones we discussed with so little enthusiasm in the last section:

- ✔ Your potential customers or clients may be more impressed by an incorporated business.
- ✔ The shareholders of a corporation are not responsible for each other's acts in the course of business so it's easier to avoid being held financially responsible for the acts of your business associates.

Disadvantages of incorporation

You've seen that some of the "advantages" of incorporation can turn out to be a disadvantage for your business. Incorporation also has its disadvantages:

- ✔ Corporations are expensive to set up — the government fees alone are several hundred dollars, and if you use a lawyer you will have to pay his or her fees as well.
- ✔ Corporations are expensive to run because of the requirements to maintain corporate records, hold meetings, and file documents with the government.
- ✔ The residency requirements for directors can be a problem if a majority of the people who run the business are not Canadian, or if all of the directors live outside the province.

Protecting Your Assets without Incorporating

Most people incorporate to protect their personal assets in case their business has debts that it can't pay — but that strategy doesn't always work. And we've shown you that incorporating may not be right for you in any event. But all is not lost, because there are ways to protect your assets without incorporating.

The classic method for protecting personal assets from business debts is to put those assets in the name of a spouse or other family member who is not an owner of the business. That means

- Legally registering the title to your home, cottage, or other real estate in the other person's name.

- Legally registering the ownership of your car, boat, or other vehicles in the other person's name.

- Changing your personal bank accounts or investment accounts so that they are in the other person's name only.

For this method to work, you must change ownership before your business runs into trouble. If you wait until your business starts to encounter financial problems, transferring your property to another person is considered a form of fraud, and anyone trying to collect money from you is entitled to have the property transfer set aside.

Once you put property into someone else's name, the property belongs to that other person. So there's a risk to this approach. If your marriage or relationship with your family member vanishes down a wormhole, your property may disappear with the relationship. You have to decide what you're more worried about financially — the failure of your business or the failure of your relationship.

You can also protect yourself from certain financial liabilities through business insurance. See Chapter 12 for more on that subject.

Your Choices If You're the Only Owner

Now, having shown you a corporation, we can go back to helping you decide what form of business to choose if you're going it alone. To recap, your choices are carrying on business as a sole proprietorship or as a solely owned corporation.

Sole proprietorship

If you decide to carry on business as a sole proprietor (your business is then called a sole proprietorship) there is no legal distinction between you and your business:

✔ The property of the business belongs to you.

✔ The debts and liabilities of the business belong to you — you can be forced to use your personal, non-business, assets to pay the debts of your business.

✔ The profits of your business are personal income and are taxed at your personal tax rate, and any business losses can be deducted from your personal income.

Setting up a sole proprietorship

You don't have to do very much to set up a sole proprietorship. In fact, if you start doing business all by yourself right this very minute, without taking any further steps, you are a sole proprietor. Because it happens automatically, sole proprietorship is a very easy and inexpensive form of business to set up. You don't need the help of a lawyer. In most provinces you have to register your business name with the provincial government, but that's just about the only formal requirement you'll have.

Running a sole proprietorship

There are no formal requirements about how to run a sole proprietorship. You can make it up as you go along. However, your accountant will probably tell you to set up a separate business bank account and keep track of your business income and expenses separately from your personal income and expenses — even though there's legally no difference between your personal and business income and expenses. Separating the two will make it easier for you to prepare the statement of income and expenses that as a sole proprietor you have to file with your income tax return.

Reviewing the advantages and disadvantages of a sole proprietorship

The advantages of a sole proprietorship are

✔ Simplicity of setting up and running the business.

✔ Low cost of setting up and running the business.

✔ A tax advantage if your business is losing money — you can deduct its losses from your other income.

✔ A tax advantage if your business profits are low — the rate of tax you pay on your business income will also be low.

The disadvantages of a sole proprietorship are

✔ The income of the business is taxable at personal rates, which go higher than corporate rates — if your business does really well, and your income is higher than $100,000, then the tax rate is between 39 and 49 percent.

✔ Your personal assets can be seized to pay the debts of your business, if the business can't pay them.

A solely owned corporation

If you decide to incorporate, you will be the only shareholder of the corporation and the only director. But a corporation with only one shareholder or director is still a corporation. You have to follow all the usual steps to incorporate, organize, and run your corporation.

Setting up a solely owned corporation

The incorporation process for a solely owned corporation is the same as for any corporation. You don't have to do anything extra, and you can't leave anything out, either.

Running a solely owned corporation

Even though your corporation is just you, you must still fulfill all the requirements for director's and shareholder's meetings and resolutions. You can either meet with yourself over drinks, or simply make all of your director's and shareholder's resolutions in writing. Unless you're really conflicted, you shouldn't have any trouble getting unanimous approval for anything you propose.

Your Choices If There Are Two or More Owners

If you're going to be in business with an associate, your options, you may recall, lie between carrying on business as a partnership and as a multi-shareholder corporation.

Partnership

If you start to carry on business with another person and do not incorporate your business, you will automatically be partners under provincial law.

If your business is a partnership (just as with a sole proprietorship), there is no legal distinction between you and your business:

- ✔ Your share of the partnership property belongs to you personally.

- ✔ The debts and liabilities of the partnership belong to you personally — you can be forced to use your personal, non-business, assets to pay the debts of the partnership.

- ✔ Your share of the partnership profits is personal income and is taxed at your personal tax rate, and any losses of the partnership can be deducted from your other income.

You can let the relationship between you and your partners be defined by the statute law of your province, or you can define the relationship yourself in a partnership agreement. If you stick with provincial law, in most provinces:

- ✔ All partners have an equal say in management of the partnership business.

- ✔ All partners are entitled to an equal share of partnership assets.

- ✔ All partners share equally in the profits of the partnership.

- ✔ All partners are equally responsible for the debts of the partnership.

- ✔ If one partner dies, goes bankrupt, or withdraws from the partnership, the partnership is at an end, even if there are more than two partners.

- ✔ All existing partners must consent before a new partner can be admitted to the partnership.

You can and should enter into a partnership agreement with your partner(s) if you wish to change any of these terms. You should know, however, that statute law sets two terms about partnership that you can't change through a partnership agreement — because they involve the responsibility of partners toward people and businesses outside the partnership:

- ✔ All partners are themselves individually responsible for the wrongful acts (in the course of business) of the other partners.

- ✔ All partners are bound by contracts entered into by any partner in the ordinary course of business.

Most partnerships need a partnership agreement because the terms set by the provincial statutes usually do not reflect the way partners want their partnership to work. See the sidebar "You need a partnership agreement if . . ."

You need a partnership agreement if . . .

You need a partnership agreement if you want to:

- ✔ Own the partnership property unequally.

- ✔ Define how the work will be divided among the partners.

- ✔ Define what partnership income is.

- ✔ Divide the partnership profits unequally.

- ✔ Give yourself and your partner(s) the right to draw an advance (salary) against your share of the profits.

- ✔ Divide responsibility for partnership debts unequally between the partners.

- ✔ Have the partnership continue even if one partner leaves, goes bankrupt, or dies.

- ✔ Set up a method for buying back the partnership interest of a partner who leaves or dies.

- ✔ Give each partner the right to force the other partner(s) either to buy him or her out or sell their interests to him or her.

- ✔ Require life and/or disability insurance for the partners.

If you need a partnership agreement, you need a lawyer — in fact, you need more than one lawyer. Each partner should have his or her own lawyer to review the agreement. If you and your partners have agreed on a lawyer for the business, that lawyer can draft the agreement, but should direct each of you to other lawyers for independent legal advice.

Don't try to draft a partnership agreement yourself. If you can't afford a lawyer, you'll most likely be safer living with the partnership terms set by your provincial statute.

Setting up a partnership

In most provinces, you don't have to do much to set up a partnership. A partnership automatically exists under provincial law if you start to carry on business with someone else with a view to making a profit. You don't even have to prepare and sign a partnership agreement (although we strongly recommend that you do). About the only requirement is that you may have to register your partnership's business name with the provincial government.

Running a partnership

The partnership statute or your partnership agreement gives you some ideas about how to run your partnership — for example, either that every partner has an equal share in management — that's the statute — or that one partner will be the manager or that a sub-group of partners will form the management committee. Apart from the terms of the statute or agreement, make sure that you and your partner(s) have regular communication. Even if there are just two of you, it's a good idea to schedule regular partners' meetings to discuss the ongoing business of the partnership.

You must also keep track of the income and expenses of the partnership. At the end of each year, you (or the partnership's accountant) must prepare a partnership financial statement that sets out the income and expenses of the partnership and how the partnership's profit (or loss) for the year has been divided among the individual partners.

The partnership does not file a separate income tax return. Instead, you and your partners simply include your individual share of the partnership's profit or loss in your individual tax returns.

Looking at the advantages and disadvantages of a partnership

The advantages of a partnership are similar to those of a sole proprietorship. It can be easy and inexpensive to set up (if you don't have a partnership agreement) and reasonably easy to run. There can be tax advantages if your combined income from the partnership and other sources is low, or if the partnership loses money.

The disadvantages of a partnership are also similar to those of a sole proprietorship. If your combined income from the partnership and other sources is high, your tax rate may be high. At the other extreme, if your business goes down the tubes, you can be forced to use your personal assets to pay the partnership's debts. And you can personally be held financially responsible for the acts of the other partners performed in the course of partnership business (such as injuring a customer or entering into a contract that the partnership couldn't carry out).

Investigating Limited Liability Partnership (LLP)

In some provinces, members of a profession can set up their business in the form of a limited liability partnership. Unlike a general partnership (which is the kind of partnership we discussed above), in which the partners are liable for debts and liabilities arising from the acts of all partners, the partners in a limited liability partnership are not personally liable for the acts of another partner. However, assets belonging to the partnership can still be seized to pay debts.

A multi-shareholder corporation

If you and your co-owner(s) decide to incorporate your business, you will all be shareholders, and probably directors as well, of the corporation.

Setting up a multi-shareholder corporation

We've already told you about the steps involved in setting up a corporation. In a multiple-shareholder corporation, there is another step you should take in addition to the incorporation and initial organization of the corporation — the preparation of a shareholders' agreement. If you and your fellow shareholders are essentially partners, you should have an agreement that sets out your mutual rights and obligations. A shareholders' agreement can deal with matters similar to those in a partnership agreement (see the sidebar "You need a partnership agreement if . . .") as well as other matters, such as the right of a shareholder to be or to appoint a director and how to resolve voting deadlocks.

You need a lawyer to prepare a shareholders' agreement. This is not an area for do-it-yourselfers.

Shareholders' agreements are prepared separately from the incorporating documents and are not filed with the government.

Running a multi-shareholder corporation

The requirements for running a corporation include holding regular directors' meetings and annual shareholders' meetings.

If you have multiple directors, you will have to hold actual directors' meetings (which can include telephone meetings), unless you can get all of the directors to agree to and sign written resolutions. The directors will have to meet as often as required to make decisions about the corporation's affairs. You'll need a quorum (a minimum number) of directors for a meeting to be held. If your directors are all busy people, you may sometimes find it difficult to get a quorum.

If you have multiple shareholders, you'll have to hold actual shareholders' meetings to elect directors, to appoint or dispense with an auditor and to review the corporation's financial statements — again, unless you can get all of the shareholders to agree to and to sign the necessary resolutions. A quorum is required to hold a shareholders' meeting too (normally, the holders of a majority of the shares entitled to vote constitute a quorum), but a shareholder can be represented by a proxy, who doesn't have to be a shareholder himself or herself.

So How Do You Choose?

Now that you know about the three forms of business, how do you choose one? Look at the advantages and disadvantages of each form of business organization, and think about how they relate to your particular business situation.

Get advice from a lawyer and an accountant to help you make an educated choice. Once you've made it, take the necessary steps to put your choice into effect.

A fourth form of business — the partnersnit

The authors were the first to identify and name a form of business called a partnersnit. We believe that this may in fact be the most common form of business throughout the world. In a partnersnit, the individuals in the business venture devote the majority of their time and efforts to irritating the other individuals in the business venture. The individual causing the irritation is known for the duration of the irritation as the "partner" and any irritated individual is known as a "snit." In a well-organized partnersnit, the roles of partner and snit constantly shift back and forth.

Don't incorporate your business just because you think that's what everybody does. Don't let your business become a sole proprietorship or partnership simply by doing nothing. Choosing the wrong form of business can have a major financial impact.

Some Other Start-up Concerns

Other start-up concerns include interfering mothers-in-law, nosy neighbours, falling space debris, and rational and irrational fears of failure, disability, and dismemberment. However, we'll leave those to you to ponder alone. Instead we talk here about some incredibly boring topics like permits and licences, payroll taxes, getting a business number, and registering for GST.

Investigating permits, licences, and other government requirements

The odds are very good that some regulatory scheme, either federal, provincial, or municipal (often more than one), applies to your type of business. If that's the case, you may have to get government permission in the form of a permit or licence to carry on your business. The process for getting that permission may be short and simple (and maybe even inexpensive), or it may be long and complicated (and very expensive). But if you need government permission and operate your business without it, you may face a fine or risk having your business shut down.

You can find out whether your business requires permission to operate by consulting a lawyer, your provincial Canada Business Service Centre (CBSC), a trade or industry association, or by contacting the different levels of government directly.

Registering for payroll taxes and the GST

We tell you about taxes of all kinds in Chapter 16 (now isn't that something to look forward to!). But without going into all the gory details right here, if your business will have employees, you will have to pay payroll taxes, and if your annual sales and revenues are more than $30,000, you will have to collect GST or HST from your customers and pay it to the government.

Federal payroll taxes

Employers must withhold from their employees, and send to the federal government, a certain amount on account of the employees' income taxes as well as the employees' contributions for Canada Pension Plan and Employment Insurance. Employers must also make Canada Pension Plan and Employment Insurance contributions on behalf of their employees.

GST and HST

Briefly, the GST (Goods and Services Tax) is a tax charged by the federal government on almost all goods and services supplied in Canada. GST is charged to everyone along the production and sale chain from the supplier of the materials, through to the manufacturer, wholesaler, retailer, and consumer. (Credits and refunds are built into the system to make sure that the government keeps only the tax paid by the ultimate consumer.) Nova Scotia, New Brunswick, and Newfoundland have the HST (Harmonized Sales Tax), which is a combined GST and provincial sales tax.

Any business that provides GST-taxable goods or services and has annual sales and revenues of more than $30,000 must register for, collect, and send GST (or HST) to the federal government. If your business's annual sales and revenues are less than $30,000, you don't have to register and charge GST, but you may do so if you wish. If you don't register, you can't claim a refund of any GST you pay. Even if you expect your sales to be less than $30,000 for the foreseeable future, you might want to register for the GST so that your customers don't know that your business income is so low.

Your business number

If your business will be collecting and remitting GST to the government and/or collecting and remitting federal payroll taxes, you must register the business with the Canada Revenue Agency (originally known as Revenue Canada and more recently known as Canada Customs and Revenue Agency) and get a business number. The Canada Revenue Agency (or CRA for short) uses this number to keep track of you, and you'll put it on your invoices to show customers and clients that you are entitled to charge GST (and aren't just pocketing the money).

Chapter 6

Getting Your Gear Together

. . . .

In This Chapter

▶ Deciding what furniture and furnishings you'll need for your business

▶ Figuring out what hardware and software you'll need

▶ Substituting business service-providers and software for employees you can't afford

▶ Understanding the importance of projecting a positive image

. . . .

This chapter is essentially a list of the equipment you'll need for your expedition to the final frontier. If you love shopping, this is the chapter for you! If you hate shopping, this is also the chapter for you. After you read this chapter you'll be well on your way to knowing how much it will cost to set up your business physically. For most businesses, equipment makes up most of the start-up costs.

Setting Up Your Business Office

You may start off running your business on a shoestring, but you probably can't run it on a cast-off kitchen chair and your fingers. You're going to need something to sit on and at; some means of communicating with clients and suppliers; and some equipment to help you keep track of what's coming in and what's going out.

Choosing between functional and fancy

Let's start with your office décor.

If you have a home office, you may never invite anyone there — you'll meet instead at clients' offices, suppliers' offices, or in restaurants, or in an office rented for the duration of a meeting. Then your office only has to be functional. Whatever you can live with is fine.

But if potential investors or clients or suppliers or business associates are going to see your office — whether it's a home office or an office in commercial space — you should consider your office an important part of your business image. Even if you can't afford to look Fortune 500, you still want to look respectable and clean and well-managed.

Keep in mind that if you look too down-market, clients will go to someone who looks more successful; and if you look too upscale, clients will fret that you're overcharging them and spending the money on luxuries for yourself.

Finding furniture

We'll leave it to you to decide the quality of your office furniture. We'll also leave it to you to decide whether everyone in your office should have the same or similar furniture for a coordinated look. But whatever the quality or look, you'll need these basic items:

- ✔ Desk and chair for working (They should not only be comfortable but also ergonomically correct, or you'll end up with injuries to your back or shoulders or arms or wrists — most businesses that supply office furniture will be able to discuss ergonomics with you.)
- ✔ Table and chairs for spread-out work, group work, or meetings
- ✔ Chairs and/or sofa for client entertaining; maybe a coffee table or end table as well
- ✔ Lighting (Even if your office already has overhead lighting, you'll need "task lighting," like a desk lamp. If you try to work without proper lighting you'll end up tired and cranky.)
- ✔ Filing cabinets
- ✔ Supply cupboard
- ✔ Shelves or bookcases
- ✔ Baskets or in-boxes and out-boxes to organize your paperwork
- ✔ Wastebaskets and recycling boxes for non-confidential paper

If you're operating out of a very small space — say, the dining room or a bedroom of your home — you may not have room for even a few items of furniture. But help is at hand! You can get a hideaway office — a unit that folds up, when you're not using it, into something that looks like a cupboard. These units usually include a desk, storage space, and a desk extension so you've got room to work with or without a computer.

Many stores specialize in office furniture — they may provide mainly fancy furniture, or a range from functional to fancy. At some of these stores you can rent or lease furniture as well as buy. Often these stores sell used as well as new furniture. Check your Yellow Pages under Office Furniture and Equipment.

Large stores that sell business supplies (such as Staples or Office Depot) usually carry a certain amount of office furniture — often made of melamine or fibreboard, so it's more in the functional than fancy line. Stores that sell furniture for homes may also sell furniture suitable for an office, such as desks and shelves; some large home furnishing stores such as IKEA sell home office furniture along with everything else.

Big stores such as IKEA, Staples, and Office Depot publish catalogues and display their merchandise on their Web sites, so you don't have to trek to the store for a preliminary reconnaissance. However, you may find that the piece of furniture you're looking for isn't available on the showroom floor and has to be ordered.

You may be able to get office furniture at a low price or even for nothing from a business that is redecorating or closing down and wants to get rid of things. To find an opportunity like this, you usually have to keep tapped into your network of business acquaintances, although sometimes you'll come across an ad in the paper or on the Internet.

Finding furnishings

You may be spending a lot of time in your office, so make the place bearable. Paint it a colour that won't get on your nerves, and then add some touches that you find attractive, such as

- ✔ **Carpets, if they don't come with the territory:** If dreadful carpet comes with the territory, you can cover it (or some of it) with an area rug. If you have carpets, you'll also need chair mats to protect the carpets as chairs roll back and forth or get pushed in and out.

- ✔ **Pictures, posters, paintings, sculptures, or carvings:** You need something to look at other than the depressing view from your window or the business documents strewn over your desk and floor. Posters are an inexpensive way of getting good art.

If you want real art but can't afford it, you may be able to borrow some. The National Gallery of Canada, and some provincial and municipal and university art galleries, have corporate lending programs. (They've got art in storage and think it would be nice to let it out for some fresh air.)

In other words, you can rent a painting. Or you may be able to make a deal with a private art gallery or with an artist for the loan of a painting or sculpture, or several. The artist will get some exposure, and may end up selling work to your clients.

- ✔ **Plants and flowers, real or artificial:** If you choose real plants, don't forget to water them; if you choose artificial plants because you have a black thumb or your office doesn't get much light, don't forget to dust them occasionally.

- ✔ **An aquarium:** Fish are great if you'd like to see something alive in your office. But keep in mind that they're more work than plants.

- ✔ **Newspapers and/or magazines:** Deciding which ones can take a little thought. A daily newspaper is easy; so is a magazine or journal related to your business (you may be getting it anyway, so now you just put it out where anyone can read it). If you're setting out reading material mainly for clients or customers to look at while they're waiting for you, choose things your clients might like . . . within reason. So maybe your male clients might enjoy reading *Hustler*, but your female clients will be offended. Maybe some of your female clients might enjoy reading the *National Enquirer*, but other clients may think you're wacko. Go middle of the road with things like newsmagazines (*Time*, the *Economist*, *Newsweek*) or business magazines, or travel and geographic magazines, or a magazine specifically about your city. For a well-established look, try to find magazines that are several months, or years, old, just like in your doctor's office.

Stocking survival equipment

Now that you've got started in that direction, you might as well go on concentrating on your physical comfort. Make provisions for:

- ✔ **Necessities of life:** These include microwave, fridge, water cooler, coffeemaker, kettle, teapot, toaster oven, plates and mugs or cups, cutlery, napkins. Even if you don't have a kitchen with a sink in your office (use the bathroom sink), you can fit small appliances into a corner of the office somewhere . . . perhaps inside a cupboard so your clients don't think you spend all your time eating instead of working.

- ✔ **Housekeeping supplies:** You don't want clients and customers to be disgusted by your dirty office, and even if you've made arrangements for cleaners to come regularly, they're not at your beck and call every time someone spills a mug of coffee or tramples cracker crumbs all over the floor. So keep on hand a vacuum (even a small one, like a Dustbuster); a mop or broom and dustpan; dishwashing liquid and a sponge or dishcloth; dishtowels; paper towels; and all-purpose cleaning fluid.

Getting low-tech hardware

You probably don't need much hardware, but you might want

- ✔ **A sign or nameplate for your door:** Sign companies can provide all kinds of things, from discreet brass nameplates to awnings to banners to illuminated signs to neon signs to billboards. If you're just looking for something very small and unambitious, you may be able to get it, or order it, from a hardware store.

- ✔ **A postage meter:** This will come in handy if you expect to send a lot of mail.

- ✔ **A fireproof safe:** They're not very expensive, and they're available at many hardware stores and at stores that specialize in business equipment (such as Staples and Office Depot). If you store valuable documents on your premises you may find this a good investment.

Getting high-tech hardware

Now your office is beautified, with a desk and chairs and pictures and plants and whatnot. Next you have to add the things that make it useful.

There's a lot of sophisticated computer hardware out there that seems to be essential for an office. At least prices for these things have dropped considerably over the past decade, and many kinds of equipment have shrunk in size or combined with others so that they don't take up too much room.

If you're going to be on the road a fair amount, you may need two offices — a head office and a portable office. Some people find that they can get along pretty well with just the portable office, even when they're working in head office.

Head office

You can probably count on needing the following:

- ✔ **A phone and phone line:** Actually, if you've got a computer, an Internet connection, and a microphone, you can get along without the phone — you can make phone calls through your computer with MSN Messenger Service or AOL Instant Messenger, or by using a VoIP (short for Voice over Internet Protocol) service provider. Skype (www.skype.com) offers free computer-to-computer calling worldwide, and calls to regular telephones (landlines or mobiles) for a fee. If you're on the phone a lot, a hands-free headset is also a good idea.

✔ **A fax machine:** Or a fax program on your computer (which saves money on paper and ink). You can have a separate fax line; or you can have automatic phone-fax switching (arranged through your telephone service provider with a special number and ring for the fax). Don't use phone-fax switching that isn't automatic: it looks unprofessional.

✔ **A photocopier:** Even the cheapest fax machines come with a copying feature, so that you can photocopy documents as well as fax them; but if you want to be able to photocopy flat (books, magazines) or copy large items, then you need a more expensive photocopier.

✔ **A scanner:** You'll need this to scan documents into your computer so that you can manipulate text . . . or pursue the dream of a paperless office (there's also a business card scanner for people who do a lot of networking — it reads business cards and creates an address card for each one on your computer).

✔ **A combined fax machine, printer, photocopier, and scanner:** All in one unit — if you prefer (but you may find that they're pigs when it comes to using up ink).

✔ **A desktop personal computer (PC) or Macintosh computer:** The majority of people have a PC, and it can be difficult to open e-mail attachments between PCs and Macs. However, Mac users generally swear by their computers, whereas PC users frequently swear at their computers. Get a big screen (17-inch or 19-inch) if you're going to use the computer a lot. Spring for a flat-screen LCD monitor. While slightly more expensive than an old-fashioned CRT monitor (which can take up half your desk), it will provide far better image quality and will take up far less room on your desk. The computer should have a CD (and/or DVD) writer (known to computer geeks as a "CD burner") for backing up your data. (You can also back up your data on a USB flash drive — a small, portable flash memory card that plugs into a computer's USB port and functions as a portable hard drive with up to 2GB of storage capacity.)

✔ **A surge protector:** So your computer doesn't get fried if there's a power surge.

✔ **A document shredder:** If you're throwing away documents that contain sensitive information (the kind of stuff you don't want scattered all over the street if a raccoon gets into your garbage . . . or scattered all over the newspaper if an investigative journalist gets into your garbage), you need to make it unreadable before you send it off. Burning papers in a wastebasket will probably cause a fire, and shredding paper by hand is inefficient and tiring, although it can be a satisfying alternative to grinding your teeth or pounding your fist on a desk.

Portable office

With a portable office you can work from almost anywhere. The key to a portable office is wireless technology (or other people's phone or cable lines) and batteries (or other people's electricity). With a wireless-enabled computer, you can get access to the Internet and pick up your e-mail wherever a wireless network signal is available. You can purchase your own monthly wireless access to the Internet, find a free WiFi (short for wireless fidelity) hotspot, or, if you're lucky, even tap into someone else's unsecured wireless network. Even if your computer is not wireless-enabled, you can plug into any available phone line to get access to the Internet and check your e-mail. Satellite technology will let you pick up e-mail in places where no local area network (LAN) can be found, even the Mongolian Desert and the Moon, but it's considerably more expensive than wireless technology.

For an up-to-date portable office you'll need

- ✔ **A laptop or notebook computer:** You can use a laptop or notebook as your main computer at head office, and carry it around with you on your travels. (They can be heavy, though, and many people find the keyboard uncomfortable to use or the screen too small. Using a plug-in mouse will help when you're on the road, and if you're at head office you can also plug in an ordinary keyboard.) Keep in mind that a laptop is easier to steal than a desktop. If you use your laptop or notebook for everything, be fanatical about backing up documents! And also keep in mind that someone who steals your computer will have access to your confidential information — so lock your files!

- ✔ **A cell phone:** You can even use it as your only phone if you want to. You buy the phone itself from the service provider; there may be special discounts available which make the phones very inexpensive (the providers make their money on the service plan you buy).

- ✔ **A personal digital assistant (PDA), such as a Palm Pilot:** You can use a PDA to keep track of

  - Your schedule and your time — including alarm clock reminders

  - Addresses and contact information

  - To-do lists and memos

  Some PDAs can load a modified version of Windows word processing software or spreadsheet software so that you can use them as portable computers (if you're going to word process, you'll need to buy a fold-up keyboard to go with the PDA). The newest versions let you dial up the Internet and download e-mail, and even have add-ons that can turn the PDA into a telephone, camera, bar-code reader, or Global Positioning System locator. Future versions may let you get access to your office computer. Someday all you may need for your portable office is a PDA!

- ✔ **Wireless e-mail:** For example Research in Motion's "Blackberry," which can also perform many PDA functions.

- ✔ **A pager:** Pagers predate cell phones, but they're still useful for some purposes because they can operate in areas where cell phones aren't allowed (like hospitals) or are frowned on (like conference rooms, concert halls, theatres, and restaurants). And it's always amusing for others to watch a person whose vibrating pager has just gone off, because the pagee looks as if he or she has just been bitten in an unmentionable place by a flea.

✔ **GPS (Global Positioning System) device:** It could come in handy in case you get lost on a road trip and discover that you are no tracker, and can't figure out your location by looking at the stars or moss on the north side of trees.

Where do you buy computer hardware?

If your needs are more than very basic, you should consult with a computer expert to find out what you require before you go on a buying spree. Although in some stores you may find very knowledgeable staff who will help you decide what's best and what's a good price, in others you may find staff who haven't even bothered to read what's written on the packages.

Nowadays there seems to be a computer store on every block, not to mention on the Internet. You probably want to buy at the best possible price, so shop around and compare prices on the same models and on similar models. You can start by checking the Web sites of some of the larger suppliers, such as:

✔ Dell at www.dell.ca

✔ Future Shop at www.futureshop.ca

✔ Office Depot at www.officedepot.ca

✔ Staples at www.staples.ca

✔ Tiger Direct at www.tigerdirect.ca

But we recommend that you not try to scrimp on your computer purchase by buying low-end or secondhand or reconditioned equipment. A good recent-model computer is a good investment for your business, and will make your business life easier.

Getting software and services

Your hardware won't work very well without some software and some services.

Software

Computers usually come loaded with basic software packages, but you may want to upgrade the standard package or buy additional software. Some software can actually almost replace employees or outside contract workers if you can't afford to hire help (such as a secretary or bookkeeper) yet. Here's some of the ordinary software you'll want (some of which we've included in the CD-ROM for this book — check out the Appendix for more information):

- ✔ **Word processing:** The tools incorporated into the software can help you format business letters and print envelopes, among many other things. Most common are Microsoft Word and WordPerfect.

- ✔ **Desktop Publishing:** This software allows you to get a bit fancier than you can with word processing software in creating documents such as newsletters, brochures, business forms, letterhead, and business cards. Microsoft Publisher and CorelDraw are examples.

- ✔ **Spreadsheets:** These help you crunch numbers to your heart's content (Microsoft Excel, Corel's Quattro Pro).

- ✔ **An accounting package:** Check with your accountant (if you have one) before buying, to see which package he or she recommends. Most common are MYOB, Simply Accounting, and QuickBooks. (We've included a limited-use version of QuickBooks Pro on the CD-ROM.)

- ✔ **Security software:** To protect your computer system against viruses, spyware, spam, and hackers.

- ✔ **A business contact management system:** To keep track of customer contacts and activity. Maximizer is an example.

- ✔ **Acrobat Reader:** So you'll be able to read PDF files. (Acrobat Reader is available free over the Internet.)

- ✔ **Presentation software:** PowerPoint is an example.

- ✔ **Videoconferencing software:** Windows NetMeeting, for example, which allows you to set up a videoconference through your computer.

- ✔ **Website software:** You can design and create your own Web site using software such as Microsoft FrontPage and Macromedia Dreamweaver.

- ✔ **WinZip:** To condense files so that you can store more in less space on your hard drive.

- ✔ **Voice recognition software:** A little out of the ordinary, it will allow you to dictate to your computer instead of typing in text. However, it takes quite a while for the program to get used to your voice and to become accurate in taking down your remarks, and even then, the process is slower than typing if you can type at a reasonable speed.

Services

The kinds of services you'll need include the following:

- ✔ **For your office phone:**

    - **Call forwarding or call answering:** You can arrange for call forwarding to your cell phone when you're out of the office; you can have an answering machine or call answer service provided by

Bell. Then there's also call waiting, so you never miss a call. As a businessperson, you should use call waiting VERY sparingly! No client likes to think he's less important than the totally unknown person who's beeping to get in. And there's Caller ID, so you'll know who's calling (and then either pick up immediately or totally ignore the phone).

- **Special long-distance rate packages:** Or a toll-free phone number if you want customers to call from outside the local area (try to get a 1-800 number — people are less suspicious of dialing 1-800 than 1-888) or if you're going to make a lot of long-distance calls.

- **Interactive Voice Response (IVR) technology:** If you want your business to a have the telephone presence of a large (and some might say, irritating) organization, this may be for you. IVR technology is what is behind the automated telephone reception systems that route calls by having the caller press a number on a telephone keypad or, when coupled with speech recognition technology, by speaking simple answers, such as "yes" and "no" in answer to voice prompts. A number of companies provide this service off-site, so you don't have to purchase your own equipment and software. Check out Angel.com (`www.angel.com`) or Contact Automation (`www.contactautomation.com`) for example, or search for "IVR" on the Internet.

✔ **For your cell phone:**

- **A time plan:** You can get various time plans from the service providers (Rogers and Bell Mobility) — for a flat fee you can make calls for up to a specified number of minutes per month.

- **Special long-distance rate packages:** If you use your cell phone to make long-distance calls, see if your service provider has a long-distance package.

✔ **For your computer:**

- **An Internet service provider (ISP) and connection:** You can connect to the Internet by dial-up, using your telephone to connect to an ISP. (In the not-so-distant past, this was the only way to connect to the Internet.) This is the cheapest way to connect to the Internet, but download times are very slow, and, unless you have two phone lines, you won't be able to talk on the phone and have Internet or e-mail access at the same time. For a higher cost, in many parts of Canada you can get high-speed (or broadband) Internet access through your TV cable company or through Bell's Sympatico High Speed access (`www.sympatico.ca`). In rural and remote areas that do not have access to wired broadband service, it is now possible to get high-speed Internet via satellite through, for example Telesat Canada (`www.telesat.ca`) or Direcway (`www.direcway.com`).

- **E-mail:** It's a great form of long-distance communication because no long-distance rates apply, and unlike a phone call, e-mail gives people a chance to look into a matter before answering you (just like letters used to). Even better, you can e-mail anytime and don't have to worry about waking a customer up in the middle of the night (although they may think something's wrong with you and your business because you were writing e-mails at 3:00 in the morning). If you've already got Internet access, your ISP can probably provide e-mail, but you don't necessarily have to go with your ISP.

- **Computer technical support:** You can get support through your software manufacturer (if you don't mind waiting on a phone line forever) or hardware manufacturer (if you don't mind returning the hardware for service). If you want in-home service, you may be able to arrange a service contract through the manufacturer or the retailer. Or if you live near a university or community college with a computer science department, enquire whether a student, or even a moonlighting technical employee, can be your tech support person.

✔ **Unified messaging:** You can get voice messages, faxes, and e-mail all directed to a single point (a phone or computer).

✔ **A courier account:** Unless you have an account, the courier won't pick up from you. Set it up before you need it, or you'll find you don't have it exactly when you're desperate for it.

And while you're thinking about business service-providers, consider a cleaning service for your business if you're not going to do it yourself and it doesn't come with your leased premises. If you're going to generate a lot of garbage, also think about a private waste removal company.

Establishing a Web presence

Although the dot-com revolution has kind of fizzled, every business is expected to have its own Web site these days. You don't have to do business through your Web site — but potential customers like to be able to look up information about you without having to call you during business hours. The first step is to get your own domain name, which is your Internet address.

Domain name

You can purchase a domain name through a Web host company or Internet service provider that sells a monthly hosting package, or you can buy a name independently through an authorized domain name seller (such as GetMyName.com). For more about choosing a domain name, go to Chapter 3 on using ideas in your business, and for more about purchasing a domain name, have a look at Chapter 8.

Web site

Once you have a domain name, you have to put some content at the Web address. That's your Web site. If you're over the age of 15 and don't sleep with your computer mouse under your pillow, the thought of creating your own Web site can be a little daunting. But it's easy to get help. Earlier in this chapter, we mention that you can buy Web site set-up packages that take you through the process step-by-step. Or you can use a business that will help you design and set up a Web site. For a basic Web site you might expect to pay around $500. For recommendations, ask business acquaintances who did their Web sites.

As an alternative to doing it yourself or paying for professional assistance, you may be able to get a computer science student to create a Web site for you. If you live near a university or community college with a computer science department, advertise for a student. Sometimes students are already running their own businesses as Web site designers. They'll be delighted to help you, they'll do good work (but ask to see some of their work before you hire them), and they won't charge very much.

See Chapter 8 for a more complete discussion of Web sites.

Specific Equipment for Your Business

So far we've talked about only what you'll need to get a general-purpose office set up. But every business is individual and may need special equipment, as well. If you need to visit customers or make deliveries or transport supplies, you may need a car or van. If you're a dentist you'll need the chair and the drill and the instrument sterilizer and the x-ray machine and so on. If you're a gardener you'll need a lawn mower and a leaf-blower and a hedge-clipper. If you're manufacturing something, you'll need a system for creating your product, and depending on what your business is, this could be anything from a set of chisels or a couple of sewing machines to a smelter or a laboratory. If you're setting up a retail business, you'll probably need a cash register or other cash-tracking equipment, systems for accepting credit cards or debit cards, inventory-control systems to prevent shoplifting, and display stands, cases, and cupboards. You'll also need initial inventory (the stock you're going to sell).

There are too many possibilities for specific equipment for us to address here. Just don't forget to take your special equipment into account when you're making your shopping list for gear.

Buying Equipment versus Leasing Equipment

If you don't already have your business furniture, hardware, and other equipment lying about, you'll need to acquire it. You can usually acquire these things in two ways (three if you include illegal activity) — buying and leasing. Each can have advantages and disadvantages.

You should consider checking with your accountant before you make a decision about buying versus leasing, because there could be tax implications for your business. The deductibility of a purchase is different from the deductibility of lease payments is different from the deductibility of loan payments. We talk about taxes in Chapter 16.

Buying

You can make purchases in the following ways:

- ✔ **Paying with your own cash:** Then you're the owner, no strings attached, as soon as you make the purchase.

- ✔ **Paying with your own credit card:** Again, you're the owner, no strings attached, as soon as you make the purchase. Then it's merely a question of being able to pay off your credit card.

Interest rates for credit cards are much higher than interest rates if you borrow money from a bank. So if you need to borrow to buy equipment, borrowing from the credit card company isn't the best idea. The only advantage is that it's easier than filling out forms at a bank and waiting to be approved. If you think we've just insulted credit-card buyers by suggesting that they're irrational, lazy, and addicted to instant gratification, you may be right. Credit-card buyers who are also masochistic can find additional abuse in Chapter 10.

✔ **Paying with money borrowed from a bank or other outside lender:** If the purchase is for an expensive item (say, for several thousand dollars), the lender will want you to repay the loan according to a schedule and may also want you to give back a chattel mortgage as security for the loan. If you give a chattel mortgage, you're the owner of the item, but the lender has the right to seize it if you don't repay the loan on time.

✔ **Paying with money borrowed from the seller (assuming the seller is willing to lend):** If you borrow from the seller, the seller will want to be repaid on a regular schedule and will also want security, just like an outside lender. (The seller will probably also want a down payment, so this isn't necessarily a no-cash option.) The security will probably take the form of a conditional sales agreement. If you buy via a conditional sales agreement, you won't own the equipment until you make the final payment; until then the seller owns the equipment, and can seize it if you don't make your payments. However, it will be up to you to maintain and repair and insure the equipment from the time you get it.

Leasing

A lease allows you to commit less cash or equity to acquiring equipment.

If you lease, you become a lessee. You may feel belittled by that term and would prefer to be a moree, but no such thing exists . . . only morons . . . which is what we're starting to sound like. Let's stick to business. The person or company that leases it to you is called the lessor. The lessor owns the equipment throughout the term of the lease, and you make lease payments throughout the term of the lease.

Besides being required to insure the leased item, you may be required to enter into a separate maintenance contract, so you'll have to make regular payments for maintenance as well as for the equipment. But if you have problems with your leased equipment, you can't complain to the lessor. You have to complain to the manufacturer. And you have to make your lease payments whether the equipment works or not.

If you don't make your lease payments, the lessor can usually take back (repossess) the item and then demand that you pay whatever balance is still owing under the lease to the end of the term, minus the amount that the lessor can get by selling the item or leasing it to someone else.

Two main types of lease are available:

✔ **Simple lease:** No down payment is required and the regularly scheduled, equal payments are usually calculated so that you've paid the full value of the item (plus interest) by the end of the lease. When the lease ends, the item has to be returned to the lessor. So you've paid for the item and the lessor gets it. But cheer up! In a simple lease the term usually lasts as long as the useful life of the item, and by the end of the lease it has no value anymore. However, some leases make you guarantee that the item is worth a stated amount at the end of the term, and if the lessor sells it and gets less than the guaranteed amount, the difference comes out of your pocket.

✔ **Lease with an option to purchase:** A down payment may or may not be required, but regular equal payments are certainly required. (If you make a down payment, the regular payments will be lower.) When the lease ends you can return the item to the lessor, or you can choose to purchase it by paying an amount that's stated in the lease. If you decide to buy, the regular payments you've made plus the extra amount you've paid to buy are calculated to give the lessor the full value of the item (plus interest). So leasing and then purchasing is much the same thing as borrowing to purchase.

If you're thinking of taking a lease with an option to purchase, you should check to see if it would cost less just to borrow the money and buy the item. (But check with your accountant too, to make sure you take into account the possible tax benefits of leasing.) However, each lease payment may be lower than each loan repayment because leases often have longer terms than loans.

A lease with an option to purchase may make sense if you don't want to buy equipment because it will be obsolete in a short time. When the lease ends, instead of buying the equipment, you'll take out another lease on a new model of the equipment. But, as with some simple leases, you may be required to guarantee that the equipment has a stated value at the end of the term. If you don't buy and the lessor sells the equipment to someone else, you're required to pay the difference between the value you've guaranteed and the price the lessor actually gets. (But if the lessor gets more than you've guaranteed, you don't get a refund for taking such great care of the equipment.)

Looking for help?

On the Government of Canada's Strategis site (under Sources of Financing) you'll find a Lease or Buy calculator (`www.strategis.ic.gc.ca/epic/ internet/insof-sdf.nsf/en/h_so03331e.html`). It can help you decide whether it makes more financial sense to buy or lease a piece of equipment.

Getting Business Stationery and Printed Materials

When you're not around to make a personal impression on potential customers, investors, suppliers, and media types, your materials are doing it for you. So you want to be sure that your materials are making the right impression. You might consider getting help from a graphic designer, who will help you create a logo and a look, and make sure that all your materials are consistent. Your printed materials include your

- ✔ Letterhead
- ✔ Envelopes
- ✔ Business card
- ✔ Brochure
- ✔ Catalogue (if a brochure isn't enough)
- ✔ Newsletter
- ✔ Cover or presentation materials
- ✔ Event or trade show signs and posters
- ✔ Invoices, estimates, standard contracts, and purchase orders

What's the impression you're aiming for? No matter how conservative or how wacky your business's product or service, you want your business itself to project the image of being

- ✔ Well-managed
- ✔ Successful (or at least poised to be successful)

Well-managed

One way of creating an image of good management is to make sure that all your materials are consistent with each other. Consistency shows that someone's in charge, making a plan, and thinking through all the details.

Your materials should all send the same clear message about your business:

- ✔ Your logo and slogan should give some idea about what your business does; they should be the same colour and style each time (although you can have versions of them, such as black on white, white on black, and colour on white).

✔ Your stationery should all be the same colour and finish and quality of material; but it's okay for the weight of the paper to differ between letterhead and business card.

✔ Printing should all be in the same font (see below under "Letterhead").

In addition, your materials include the following things, which should also be consistent with your printed materials:

✔ Packaging materials, package labels

✔ Business sign

✔ Web site (Your Web site will actually replace a lot of printed materials. Use the standard colours and logo of your business, and make sure your logo or business name appears on every page.)

✔ Window displays and decoration of office or store

✔ PowerPoint presentations, slides and videos

✔ Giveaways and specialty items, such as mugs, T-shirts or sweatshirts, baseball caps, pens

And don't forget these matters:

✔ Letters should be in the same format whoever writes them, and should end with the same closing salutation.

✔ E-mail signature should be common on all communications (name of your business, slogan, "visit our Web site" and the Web site address, street address, phone number, and fax number).

✔ The voice message on your phone should identify the business, sound professional (not too long or folksy), promise (truthfully) a quick return of the call, and not send callers into a voice-mail jail of automated options. Change your message as needed, to give your clients useful information.

Successful

One way of looking successful is to have materials that are of good quality and are in good taste.

For paper, good quality is usually associated with a heavier weight, a raised finish on the paper, and a watermark. For a business card, you'll want paper of a heavier weight than for your letterhead and envelopes, but you can still have the same finish and colour.

Good taste in paper is associated with a conservative colour (white, ivory, cream, and pale grey are all pretty safe) and the absence of too much decoration. Yes, it's possible to get paper with rainbows or forest scenes printed on it . . . but don't. Most customers and investors will feel more comfortable if your paper is not exuberant.

Letterhead

All your business correspondence will be written on your letterhead. Look at other businesses' letterhead, and then experiment with your computer and printer to see what looks best, or hire a graphic designer for help.

Whether or not you come up with your own design, you may want to get your letterhead professionally printed, especially if you want to incorporate a logo your computer printer can't handle or you want to use colours other than black. Some printers offer graphic design services. If you have your letterhead professionally printed, make sure you get the template so that you can put it into your own computer. And don't order a huge amount of letterhead, because your business will probably undergo changes before you use it all up.

Your Page 1 letterhead should show two pieces of information:

- **Name of your business**
- **Contact information:** The street address, phone and fax numbers, e-mail address, Web site address. Some people put all the information at the top, or all at the bottom. It can be split up between top and bottom, or it can even be put at the side.

Your Page 2 (and following) letterhead only needs to show the name of your business, and the name can be in a smaller font than on Page 1.

You should also have a fax form in the same style as your letterhead. Keep a template in your computer, and also keep some printed forms handy for scribbling quick fax messages.

The printing on your letterhead is also going to send a message about how successful you are or will be. A serif font looks more conservative than a sans serif font. (Sans serif fonts look more modern because they don't have extra little thingies — serifs — dangling from the letters.) Here are some examples of standard fonts for business that won't make your customers or investors or suppliers nervous:

Serif:

This font is Times New Roman.

This font is Courier.

This font is Book Antiqua.

Sans serif:

This font is Arial.

This font is Antique Olive.

This font is Futura.

Your font should normally be 12 points, so that it can be read easily but doesn't shout at the reader.

One of the authors wanted to add "You would be wise to avoid using fonts like Comic," (this font is Comic) but the other author said, "Exactly what is wrong with Comic?", a comment that the first author felt was only partially explained by the fact that the second author has teenaged sons. To avoid getting to know each other's peculiarities any better than they already do, the authors decided to leave out the stuff about Comic.

Business card

It's possible to print your own business cards with your computer and printer — but don't even think about it. The paper is of a light weight, so it ends up looking cheap and it isn't especially durable; plus, the perforations on the edge where the cards are separated from the sheet are visible. And you have very limited choices about the design of the card.

Your business card should be professionally printed on heavy paper, the same colour and finish as your letterhead. The ink on the card can be flat or it can be raised. The card should create a positive, interesting impression and should include

- ✔ Your name and your business's name
- ✔ Your logo and slogan, if any
- ✔ Your contact information — street address, phone and fax numbers, cell phone or pager number, e-mail address, and Web site address

Don't clutter up your business card with extra information. Its design rather than extra information should be what creates the good impression. You have a lot of freedom to design your own business card — although there are standard formats, you can ask your printer to do almost anything. Collect business cards and think about what design and format create the strongest (good) impression before you start working on your own. Your printer will also have a catalogue with lots of examples of cards that you can imitate or modify.

You can also have printing or a design on the back of your business card. If you decide to do that, be careful not to overwhelm the front of your card, or cancel out its impression.

Printing and graphic services can be quite expensive, so shop around. Some companies do offer lower-cost services. Search the Internet for "Printing" or "Graphic Design" or "Logos," because you may find it cheaper to use a service in a remote location. For example:

✓ **GotLogos.com:** A company located in Texas, they will design a logo for your business within four to five business days. The cost is $25 U.S. for a format suitable for use on a Web site, and $100 U.S. for a format that will allow you to print and use the logo on any media and at any size and resolution, such as letterhead, business cards, or signs.

✓ **VistaPrint:** A high-volume printing company with Web sites in the United States, Canada, a number of European countries, and Japan, offers low-price printing and free graphic design services (although logo design falls outside of their free design service).

Putting It All Together

Take a look at Table 6-1 here (and reproduced on the CD-ROM). This table shows you how all the items we discuss in this chapter can be tallied up. Use it to calculate your costs as they occur and to keep a close eye on your spending.

Table 6-1	Start-up Plan — Expenses for Equipment
List individual items such as	*Cost of individual items*
Furniture and furnishings	**Total cost $**
Desk	$
Chairs	$
Light fixtures, etc.	$

List individual items such as	*Cost of individual items*
Computer hardware and software	Total cost $
	$
	$
Web site design	$
Business stationery (graphic design, materials, and printing)	Total cost $
Special equipment for your business	Total cost $
Vehicles	$
Machinery	$
Cost of initial inventory (for a retail business)	$

Chapter 7

Your Business Coordinates

In This Chapter

▶ Thinking about working from home

▶ Looking at space-sharing arrangements

▶ Learning about rental of business premises

▶ Considering the purchase of business premises

*I*n the previous two chapters we talk about choosing a form of business and buying the equipment you'll need to run the business. The next step is to find a location for your business.

As someone who's just starting a small business, your main goal when you choose your business premises should be to spend as little as possible while making sure that your place of business satisfies the needs of your newly launched enterprise.

Working from Home

There's no doubt about it — working from home is the cheapest way to go. It's very popular too. According the United States Small Business Administration, 53 percent of all businesses in the United States are run from home, and over two-thirds of sole proprietorships, partnerships, and small corporations are home-based. In fact, both authors of this book work from home. (Although they both have the "home" part down, one of them is better at the "working" part than the other.) With computers, high-quality printers, e-mail, fax, and voice mail, a home-based business doesn't have to look like an amateur operation. And the Internet allows even the smallest company to have worldwide exposure. You can project a big business image even if your head office is the kitchen table.

There are other advantages, in addition to cost, to working from home:

- ✔ You'll be able to claim an income tax deduction for a portion of the expenses of running your home, even though you would have to pay these expenses anyway (see the sidebar entitled "The home business deduction" for more details).

- ✔ You won't have the cost, irritation, and wasted time involved in commuting to and from work.

- ✔ You'll have more flexibility to deal with your children, aging parents, or pets.

There are disadvantages as well, though:

- ✔ You may have little, if any, room for expansion as your business grows.

- ✔ You may find it hard to accommodate employees.

- ✔ You may find that you need facilities and services that you can't have at home.

- ✔ You may feel isolated from business associates.

- ✔ You may find yourself not isolated enough from family and friends!

But you can overcome most of these disadvantages (see below under the heading "Tips for working at home successfully"), and so our advice to you is to operate your business from home if at all possible, at least in the beginning.

Should you have a home-based business?

It may or may not be wise, or even possible, for you to run your business from home, depending on:

- ✔ The amount of space your business will need

- ✔ The type of business you will be running

- ✔ The legal restrictions you may face

- ✔ The insurance you may need and your ability to get it

- ✔ The demands of your family

- ✔ The nature of your personality

The home business deduction

If you run your business out of your home, you will be allowed an income tax deduction for the business use of your home. You will be able to deduct a percentage (based on how much of your home your business occupies) of the following expenses:

✔ The interest portion of your mortgage payments (if you own your home) or your monthly rent (if you rent your home)

✔ Property taxes (if you own your home)

✔ Utilities — heat, water, and electricity

✔ Repairs and maintenance

✔ Home insurance

To calculate your deduction, start by adding up all of these expenses. Then calculate what percentage of your home you use for your business by dividing either the number of rooms used by your business by the total number of rooms in your home, or the number of square feet occupied by your business by the total number of square feet in your home. Multiply the percentage by your expenses. You will be allowed to deduct that amount of your home expenses as a business expense.

Space considerations

In Chapter 6, we show you how to make a list of the equipment your business will need. How much space will the necessary equipment take up? Will you be able to fit your business into your home and still have a home to live in? If not, are you willing to let your business take over your home so that you're actually living in your "office"? If you need more space than you actually have to run your business, a home operation may not be possible for you.

Do you need to hire employees to help you run your business? If so, do your municipality's by-laws permit you to do so? And do you have enough room for them and their equipment — not only enough to satisfy you, but enough to satisfy any provincial occupational health and safety requirements? Even if you go around with a measuring tape and determine that there's physically room for everyone, how will you feel about sharing your home with your employees?

The nature of your business

Does the type of business you will be operating lend itself to a home-based location? The answer is probably no if

✔ Your business requires a lot of heavy equipment, because your home probably lacks the necessary infrastructure, such as reinforced floors, special ventilation or electrical capacity, to run the equipment.

✔ Your business is dangerous in any way, for example if it produces toxic fumes or waste, or uses dangerous substances or equipment.

✔ Your business relies on a walk-in trade — because let's face it, you're not going to have high-volume pedestrian traffic on a residential street or down the corridor of your apartment building.

✔ Your business involves frequent meetings on the premises with clients who expect you to have professional office space. On the other hand, working out of your home is quite feasible if your business field is so informal that a home office meets your clients' expectations. A home office is also fine if your clients don't come to you at all — you call on them.

Legal restrictions

Before you decide to set up shop in your home, make sure that there are no legal reasons that will make it difficult (or impossible) to operate your business from home:

✔ If you live in rented premises, check to see whether your lease prohibits you from carrying on a business in your home.

✔ If you live in a condominium, find out whether the condominium by-laws forbid home-based businesses.

✔ Even if you own your own home, municipal by-laws may limit your ability to work from home. Investigate whether your municipality prohibits some or all kinds of business operations in your area; or prohibits employees; or requires a permit before you can run a business from your home.

Many landlords, condominiums, and municipalities turn a blind eye to in-home businesses unless someone complains. Maybe you can't imagine that anyone would complain, but your neighbours will get testy if your business brings extra traffic to the area, or creates noise or smells.

Insurance considerations

Don't assume that your home insurance policy will automatically cover your home business. You will almost certainly need to make changes to your insurance coverage and limits to adequately protect your business, so be sure to contact your insurance company or agent. You may even have to switch insurance companies, because some companies won't provide home insurance if a business is carried on in the home.

You may invalidate your home insurance policy if you don't advise your insurance company about your home-based business.

See Chapter 12 for a more detailed look at insuring your business.

Family considerations

Your family and friends may think that because you're working from home, you're not really working at all:

- ✔ Your children may barge into your office at will, whether or not you're on the phone or meeting with clients. Or perhaps they'll be capable of understanding that you aren't to be interrupted while dealing with others, but won't allow you to complete so much as a thought if you appear to be alone. (This describes the plight of one of the authors of this book.)

- ✔ Your spouse may believe that you can now deal with every home repair, school meeting, or children's medical appointment. Your siblings may believe that you can manage any crisis involving your aging parents. Your pets may believe that you're ready and willing to provide treats and entertainment all day long. After all, since you're at home you must have lots of free time on your hands — in fact you're probably looking for things to do so you won't be bored.

- ✔ Your friends and relations and neighbours may think you're now available for baby-sitting, dog-sitting, and other neighbourly chores, or are free to chat on the phone at any time of the day. (While working on this single section of this single chapter, one of the authors had three phone calls from family and friends.)

Do you have the moral fibre to set boundaries? Will you be able to tell your family, friends, and neighbours — firmly — that your work is important and that you are not available to them during your working hours? (Unless it's an emergency. Or unless it's not an emergency but it's really important. Or unless it's not an emergency and it's not that important, but it's something that you'd like to hear about. Or that they'd really like to tell you about. Do you see what a slippery slope this can be?) They're more likely to go along with you if you don't work 24 hours a day.

If boundary-setting doesn't work too well and family, pets, and friends bother you no matter what you say to them (and how loudly you say it), do you have the discipline not to be distracted by the interruptions?

Personality considerations

Perhaps you don't need outside interruptions, because (like one of the authors) you can interrupt yourself without any help from others. Of course, a person with a tremendous talent for being distracted can be thrown off task even when working in a stern and quiet office with a boss hovering like an avenging angel, but there are so many more fun things to distract you at home — the television, the refrigerator, even cleaning the bathrooms if you're trying to avoid a particularly unpleasant piece of work. It takes discipline to get on task and to stay there.

Or perhaps you are the opposite personality type. Getting down to work is not your problem, getting away from work is. You would stay at your desk 24 hours a day, seven days a week, 365 days a year if you could. When you work in an office with other people, sooner or later they'll make you go home . . . if only to take a shower and change your clothes. When you're already home, no one will throw you out, so you must be able to limit your work hours on your own.

Even if you have the discipline to work by yourself without working yourself to death, think about how you will like working without having any colleagues around. Will you feel isolated? Are you likely to stay in your pajamas all day and stop combing your hair until you look like a poster-child for clinical depression? You'll have to make sure that you get out regularly and maintain contact with the outside world (see the "Tips for working at home success-fully" section for some helpful hints). Still, you have to be able to stand a certain amount of solitude to work at home successfully.

Tips for working at home successfully

Here are 10 tips for working at home successfully.

Keep your business separate from your family

Have a space in your home that is dedicated to your business, whether it's the basement, the attic, a spare bedroom, or a corner of your dining room. Use it only for working. That way your family will know (and so will you) that when you're in your workspace you're no longer "home," you're at work.

If your workspace has a door, keep it closed when you're at work.

If your kids aren't old enough to be left alone, or disciplined enough to leave you alone, think about hiring a babysitter, at least part-time. Use that baby-sitter time to make your business telephone calls.

Keep your business telephone separate from your family telephone

Unless you live alone, have a separate business telephone line if at all possible. That way your clients won't be plagued by busy signals while your spouse or children are chatting on the phone. And you won't have to worry about sullen teenagers rudely answering your business calls or taking messages that have about as much chance of reaching you as a message in a bottle tossed into the sea.

Get an answering machine, or better yet get the call-answer service from the telephone company, to make sure that your clients can leave a message for you if you're not there. (Call-answer is better than an answering machine because it will also take messages if you're on another call. This is preferable to call-waiting, which is very annoying to the client whose call is interrupted.) Make sure that the outgoing message your clients will hear is professional in tone, and updated on a daily basis. And be certain to pick up and return your messages promptly.

If you send or receive a lot of faxes, or are on the Internet constantly and don't have high-speed Internet service, consider getting at least one additional line, so that your clients can always get through to you on the phone. Call-answer is useful, but it's even better if your clients can reach you in person if you're in your office.

Run your business like a business

Just because you're running your business from home doesn't mean it shouldn't be a professional operation.

Don't be lazy, cut corners or take shortcuts. Make sure that you comply with all legal requirements for your business, that you have proper insurance and all the equipment you need.

Have appropriate stationery and business cards. Make sure that your business correspondence is neat, spelled properly, and grammatically correct.

Be organized. Keep track of your appointments and deadlines. Have a proper filing system so that you don't lose important documents.

Keep your work in the office and your food in your kitchen so that you don't have to worry about grease stains on your correspondence or coffee spills on your computer keyboard.

Have set work hours (even if they're odd hours)

One reason to work at home is so that you can be flexible in your work hours. But you should still have set hours. And if you're someone who tries to avoid working, setting fixed work hours will help you make sure that you actually do work. If you're a workaholic, setting fixed work hours will make sure that you don't work all the time.

Having regular business hours makes it easier for your clients to find you. If you must go out during your set hours, make sure that your answering machine or call-answer service is set to take messages, and that you check for and return your calls promptly when you get back.

To reinforce the sense that you are "at work," dress in your work clothes during your business day. And be sure to take normal breaks, including lunch.

Create a comfortable working environment

Don't run a sweatshop operation. Treat yourself as well as an employer would in creating your work environment. Get a comfortable chair. Make sure that you have a large enough work surface. If you use a computer, make sure that the keyboard is properly positioned so that you avoid wrist injuries, and that you have a computer monitor that is easy on your eyes. Make sure you have adequate lighting and proper ventilation. Have plants, put up pictures, and play pleasant music (unless, of course, you hate plants, pictures, and music).

Avoid social isolation

Take advantage of being at home to spend some time with your family during the working day. Make a point of going out for lunch with friends or colleagues or customers or clients at least once a week. Get out of the house for a bit every day, even if it's just for a walk.

A number of home business associations, many of them local, are out there. Join one, attend meetings, and take advantage of their information-sharing and networking opportunities.

Don't lose touch with your field

It's important to stay current in your field and to make and maintain professional connections. Join a trade association or professional organization. Consider joining a local business association, as well. Subscribe to at least one trade publication. Use the Internet to check in regularly on relevant Web sites. Stay current with developments in your field by attending trade shows, conventions and conferences, and by taking professional development courses in your field.

Make use of outside business support services

Your business may need facilities and services that you can't have in your home, but that doesn't mean you can't have them at all. A wide variety of business support services are available such as:

- ✔ Printing and photocopying services
- ✔ Couriers
- ✔ Packing and shipping services
- ✔ Research materials (at libraries or through the Internet)
- ✔ "Corporate identity" services that will answer your telephone calls and give you a business mailing address on a major street while forwarding your mail to your actual location

✔ Office centres that rent out office and/or meeting space on a part-time or occasional basis

✔ Freelance help such as secretaries and bookkeepers who work from their own business premises

✔ Virtual assistants who provide administrative, creative, and/or technical services on a contractual basis from their own business premises

Don't annoy your neighbours

As we mentioned, even if your municipality, landlord, or condominium corporation doesn't want you running a business out of your home, they're not likely to do anything about it unless someone complains. So don't give your neighbours any reason to complain. Don't make too much noise. Don't let litter escape from your premises. Don't stink up the neighbourhood. Make sure that your clients or customers don't arrive at your door at odd hours, or block your neighbours' driveways or park in their parking spots.

Know when it's time for your business to leave home

A home office is a great way to start your business. And depending on the nature of your business, it may grow in revenue without ever outgrowing the space you have in your home. But look for signs that it may be time for your business to leave home and get a place of its own.

Working from Real Business Premises

If you can't work from your home, you'll have to look for business premises elsewhere.

Premises available, apply within

Different types of premises are available, and the type you choose will depend on the nature of your business:

✔ **Retail:** If your business involves selling directly to the public, you need retail space. You can find retail space in a variety of locations, such as indoor shopping centres, outdoor strip malls, free-standing buildings, airports, train stations, hotel lobbies, office buildings, and theatres. You may also be able to set up a retail operation in an industrial plaza (see below).

 ✔ **Office:** You can find office space in downtown or local office buildings, business parks, above stores on streets with retail character, or in suburban shopping malls.

 ✔ **Industrial:** If your business involves manufacturing or large-scale distributing, you'll need industrial space for your manufacturing plant or warehouse facility. Industrial parks or plazas offer space designed for light manufacturing operations and for businesses that need showroom as well as manufacturing facilities.

Space-sharing arrangements

If you can't work from home, it doesn't mean that you have to rent and equip your own retail store, suite of offices, or industrial space. There are other options that give you premises that may be of modest size, and cheap to rent and equip, and that may be available on a short-term basis.

 ✔ If you need office space, you may be able to sublet a single office from another business, or rent an office in a business centre or executive suite — the landlord provides reception services and use of a boardroom and office equipment (as part of your monthly rent) and access to secretarial and other support services (usually for an additional fee).

 ✔ If you need retail space, you may be able to operate from a booth or cart in a shopping mall or in a pedestrian area. If your goods are seasonal, this may allow you to operate on a seasonal basis. It's also a good way to test your product before investing in a traditional store.

 ✔ If you need industrial space, you may be able to use a self-storage unit for your warehousing needs and maybe even for some light manufacturing or assembly of merchandise.

If you need space for your business, you should see if a business incubator is right for you. These mentoring facilities usually provide flexible rental space and flexible leases for start-up businesses accepted into their programs. See Chapter 2 for more information about business incubators.

Form 7-1 on the CD-ROM is a checklist of questions (like the one we show here) to ask before entering into a space-sharing agreement.

When you look for shared space, make sure that the premises meet the needs of your business. Find out:

 ✔ What the premises will cost up front — besides the first month's rent, will you have to pay last month's rent or a damage deposit?

 ✔ What the premises will cost on an ongoing basis — will you be paying a flat monthly rental fee that includes all utilities and services, or will there be extra charges for such things as secretarial, reception, or cleaning services?

✔ What kind of access there is — will you be able to get into and out of your premises whenever you want to?

✔ What limitations are placed on your use of the premises — will you be able to carry on all of the necessary activities of your business?

✔ What kind of security there is — will you be safe when you're on the premises and will your premises be safe against break-ins when you're not?

After you finalize arrangements for the space, you will be entering into a contract. Make sure that the contract is in writing, that you understand it, and that it sets out all the terms that are important to you.

Renting Business Premises

Most small businesses that need permanent retail, office, or industrial space rent the space (rather than buy). You should consider a number of things before you rent space.

Knowing what you're looking for

Before you start to look for rental premises, stop and think about your business needs:

✔ What kind of space are you looking for — retail, office, or industrial?

✔ What kind of image are you trying to project for your business — upscale, middle of the road, economy, grunge?

✔ What location is most accessible to your potential clients or customers and employees?

✔ What kind of parking do you need for yourself, your employees, and your clients or customers?

✔ Is it best to locate near competing businesses or away from them?

✔ How much space do you need now? How much are you likely to need in the future?

✔ What kind of layout or floor plan do you need?

✔ What are your electrical and plumbing requirements?

✔ Will your suppliers need special access to make deliveries to you?

✔ Are you willing to pay for improvements to the property you rent?

✔ How long do you want to rent these premises for?

✔ How much rent are you willing and able to pay?

Finding what you're looking for

To find commercial rental space, you can look at classified ads in the newspaper under the headings Commercial, Industrial Space, or Office, Business Space or Stores for Rent and so on. Or you can drive around areas that seem suitable and look for For Rent signs. But your best bet is probably to use a real estate or leasing agent who specializes in industrial, commercial, and investment properties.

An agent will know what space is available and can save you time by weeding out properties that don't suit your needs or meet your budget, and by taking you to see only those properties that might be appropriate. If you find a property you're interested in, the agent can help you negotiate the deal.

Usually the real estate or leasing agent is paid a commission by the landlord if you enter into a lease. If the landlord's agent shows you a property, the agent is legally the landlord's agent, not yours. A landlord's agent still has a legal and ethical duty to answer your questions accurately and honestly, and can:

✔ Help you decide how much you can afford to spend

✔ Help you screen and look at properties

✔ Identify and estimate the costs involved in the transaction

✔ Prepare offers or counteroffers on your instructions and present them to the landlord

However, a landlord's agent cannot:

✔ Recommend a price to you other than that set by the landlord

✔ Negotiate on your behalf

✔ Tell you the landlord's bottom line price

✔ Disclose any confidential information about the landlord

If you're working with the landlord's agent, you shouldn't tell him or her anything that you would not say directly to the landlord.

If you'd rather work with an agent who represents only your interests, you can hire and pay for your own agent.

Look around before you choose your space, even if you think you know just the location you want or you've had your eye on some particular building for years. It may turn out that other premises actually suit your needs better or come at a better price.

Determining the cost of your space

The rent charged for business space varies widely based on the economy, the area of the country, the type of space, and the specific location. That's one of the reasons it's important to look around before you choose your space. A real estate or leasing agent will be able to give you information about the costs of comparable space.

If you're looking for office space, the cost will depend not only on the location of the building, but also on the "class" of the building. A new, tall and luxurious skyscraper can cost quite a lot more than the perfectly respectable but older and smaller building just across the street. Be sure to look at a range of buildings in several locations.

You may be able to find space in a building you're interested in at a lower rent than that offered by the landlord if you can find an existing tenant who wants to sublet the premises or assign the lease. You'll deal with the tenant rather than the landlord, and the tenant may have had a much better deal from the landlord than what the landlord would offer you as a new tenant.

If you're looking for retail space, the rent will vary by shopping area — so be sure to look at stores in a number of locations. You may be able to get the same type and volume of clientele in several different areas in town. When you find an area you like, be sure to compare the price of similar space in the same location.

Exploring commercial leases

When you rent business space, you enter into a contractual relationship with the landlord called a commercial tenancy, and you'll sign a contract called a commercial lease. Commercial tenancies are very different from residential tenancies. Commercial tenants don't have the legal protection from their landlords that residential tenants have. In Chapter 18, we tell you about some of the trouble you can get into with your landlord (and what to do about it).

Finding the right premises

As you look at different premises, and before you start negotiating with a landlord, focus on the following matters:

- ✓ **Size of the space:** What's the square footage of the space you're getting? This is important because the rent will probably be calculated by the square foot. Is all the space actually usable? Will you be able to rent additional space if your business expands?

- ✓ **Cost of the space:** What is the basic or flat rent? In addition to basic rent, will you have to pay for anything else such as utilities, or a share of the landlord's taxes, or maintenance or operating costs? Make sure you know what the total cost is before you sign anything.

- ✓ **Leasehold improvements:** What renovations or decorating are needed to get the premises into shape? Will the landlord pay anything for them, or will you have to pay for them yourself? Will the landlord require you to spend a minimum amount of money on renovations or decorating, even if you're happy with the space the way it is?

- ✓ **Insurance coverage:** The landlord may have insurance coverage for some things and will certainly require you to provide coverage for other things. Sort out who's covering what, so that no insurance risk is missed . . . or covered twice at your expense.

- ✓ **Term of the lease:** How long does the lease run? If the term is long, you could be in trouble if your business outgrows the premises and you want to move, or if the business fails and you don't need premises anywhere anymore. If the term is short, you may find yourself forced to move too soon from a location that has become key to your business's success. When the term ends, is there a right to renew the lease? If so, how will the new rent be determined?

- ✓ **Your right to terminate the lease before the term is up:** If you have to or want to move before the lease ends, will you be able to get out of the lease, or will you be on the hook for the entire term of the lease? In most leases, it's the latter. Often the best you can do is get the right to assign (transfer) the lease to someone else or sublet the premises to someone else — but you'll almost certainly have to get the landlord's consent to do that.

- ✓ **Date the premises will be available:** When do you want to be able to move in, and when does the landlord say the premises will be available? If they turn out not to be available on the date promised, what will the landlord do for you (offer temporary space elsewhere, offer a reduction in the first month's rent, agree to terminate the lease so you can find something else)?

- ✔ **Use of the space:** Can the space be used for all the activities your business needs to carry out?

- ✔ **Protection against competition:** If you're leasing retail premises, will the landlord agree to prevent other tenants from competing with you?

- ✔ **Hours of business:** Will you be able to get access to the premises whenever you need to (and have heat or air-conditioning and electricity when you're there)? If it's retail space, will you be forced to be open during hours (such as the evening) or on days (such as Sunday and holidays) that you'd rather be closed?

- ✔ **Facilities:** Does the building have elevators, and security, cleaning, and other services?

- ✔ **Unforeseen problems with the premises:** What happens if the building suffers major damage or undergoes extensive repairs? Will you be expected to go on paying rent at the usual rate, or to stay open for business? Or will the landlord reduce your rent and/or let you close up shop either temporarily or permanently?

Form 7-2 on the CD-ROM is a checklist of the questions you need to have answered before you begin negotiating a lease.

Negotiating a lease

When you've found premises that seem to meet your needs and that you'd like to take, you will negotiate the terms of the lease with the landlord, by discussing some or all of the matters set out in the previous section. You may negotiate with the landlord directly or through a leasing agent, and you may negotiate with or without help from a lawyer. Once you and the landlord reach an agreement in principle, you will be asked to sign one or more legal documents.

You may be given a standard form lease to sign right away, or the landlord may ask you to sign a written offer in which you agree to sign the landlord's standard form lease at a later time.

Don't sign an offer agreeing to sign the landlord's standard form lease unless you have seen the lease itself and are in fact willing to sign it and be bound by its terms. Once you sign the offer, you're legally obligated to go through with signing the lease.

The landlord's standard form lease will be long, difficult to understand, and written to benefit the landlord. Most commercial landlords are not willing to make many, if any, changes to their standard form lease.

Because commercial leases are so long and complicated, you should have a lawyer look at the lease and explain it to you before you sign it. But don't spend a lot of money to have the lawyer try to negotiate changes for you, because the landlord is likely to tell you and your lawyer to "take it or leave it."

You should also go over the lease with your insurance agent or broker before you sign it so you're sure about the coverage you'll need and what it will cost.

The lease itself

Commercial leases fall into different categories based on how the rent is calculated. Here are common leases:

- ✔ **Gross lease:** Sets out a fixed amount of rent, and nothing is added to it.

- ✔ **Base year lease:** Sets out a fixed amount of rent for the first year of the lease. In the following year(s), in addition to the fixed rent the tenant also pays a share of any year-over-year increase in the landlord's operating costs.

- ✔ **Net lease:** Sets out a fixed amount of rent plus additional rent to cover the tenant's share of all of the landlord's operating costs for the coming year (based on the landlord's estimate of what those expenses will be). At the end of the year the landlord gives the tenant a statement of the actual operating costs. If the additional rent payments did not cover the tenant's share of the actual costs, the tenant has to make up the difference.

Some retail leases may also include a requirement to pay the landlord a percentage of the business's sales or profits.

Commercial lease documents are l-o-n-g — they can be 50 pages or more. Most commercial leases deal with all the matters we listed in "Finding the right premises" . . . only at considerably greater length and in language you won't understand, even if you could keep your eyes open long enough to read a page or two.

Buying Business Premises

Buying a home is a much bigger decision than renting an apartment, and likewise buying business premises is a much bigger decision than renting space.

If you buy property you will have to come up with a down payment and then, on an ongoing basis, you will have to make the mortgage payments and pay for property taxes, utilities, insurance, maintenance, and repairs. Most start-up businesses can't afford to buy their premises. Compare the cost of ownership with the cost of renting before you decide to buy business premises.

The choice between buying and renting has tax implications, so speak to an accountant before you make up your mind.

Aside from cost, it's not usually a good idea for a start-up business to buy business premises (unless it's absolutely necessary for the type of business you'll be operating — for example, a bed-and-breakfast business), because you have less flexibility to walk away if your business outgrows the premises . . . or fails.

If you're thinking about buying, you should look at business properties with the help of a real estate agent who specializes in industrial, commercial, or investment properties.

If you find something you want to buy, you will have to make an offer to purchase the property. You very definitely should have a lawyer review any offer you make before you submit it to the seller, because if the seller accepts the offer, you will have a legally binding agreement and you'll have to go through with the purchase. You'll have to have a lawyer (or, in British Columbia and Quebec, a notary) act for you to complete the deal, anyway.

Tell your lawyer how you intend to use the property. The lawyer will make sure that the offer promises that the property is appropriately zoned to allow the use you have in mind, and then will check with the municipality to make sure that the zoning by-laws permit that use.

Chapter 8

Attention: Now Entering Cyberspace

In This Chapter

▶ Finding information online that is useful to your business

▶ Communicating via the Internet

▶ Using the Internet to free your office from the constraints of time and space

▶ Setting up a Web site

*A*re you ready to engage cyberdrive? Well, then, make it so! Better strap yourself in for this chapter, because you may experience some weight-lessness — not very surprising considering that once you get into cyber-space, you have no physical existence. You and your business are about to become a bunch of bits and bytes, but we think you'll find that leading a vir-tual existence can be very productive!

Once you get yourself and your business into cyberspace, you can be any-where and everywhere. It's almost like having your very own wormhole in space so that you and your business can be two places — or a thousand places — at once. (And nobody will know that you're on a white sand beach beside a turquoise sea, instead of here in the Canadian snow where you belong.)

What Is This Cyberspace Place Anyway?

By cyberspace we mean the world of the *Internet*, which is an enormous com-puter network made up of millions of computers around the world that are linked together and able to exchange data using a number of Internet lan-guages, called "protocols." Your computer can become one of them!

Most people think of the World Wide Web (or Web) when they think of the Internet, but they are not the same thing. The Internet is the network through which computers communicate. The Web is just one way of getting access to information over the Internet, and uses HTTP (HyperText Transport Protocol) to send data. The Internet is also used to exchange information through

- ✔ **E-mail,** which uses SMTP (Simple Mail Transfer Protocol) to send data
- ✔ **Instant messaging,** which allows two computer users to communicate in real time using text
- ✔ **File transfers,** which use FTP (File Transfer Protocol) to exchange files, for example, by downloading a file from a server
- ✔ **Voice over the Internet,** which uses the Internet for telephone calls by using VoIP (Voice over Internet Protocol) to transmit voice data
- ✔ **Usenet,** a bulletin board system that contains thousands of newsgroups on a variety of topics

Using the Internet in your business

You can use the Internet, and the technology behind it, in your business in a number of ways. By using the Internet you will be able to

- ✔ Get access to untold masses of information that will help you set up and run your business.
- ✔ Send and receive mail at light speed.
- ✔ Have your office and your business at your fingertips, no matter where you are physically located in the world.
- ✔ Have as many people working with or for you in your business as you need or want, and never have to worry about finding desk space for them on your premises (and also without ever having to listen to any squabbling about whose turn it is to make the coffee).
- ✔ Be available to your customers or clients 24/7 . . . and they'll be as quiet as mice — you won't even notice them except when you want to.

Getting to the Internet

Before we tell you anything more about what you can do on, with, or through the Internet, we pause a moment and tell you how to get there.

You connect your computer to the Internet through a telephone connection or a cable connection and an Internet service provider (ISP). A dial-up telephone connection is the cheapest way to connect to the Internet (about $25 per month for unlimited use). For a higher cost, about $50 per month, getting high-speed (or broadband) Internet access is possible in many parts of Canada via either cable modem from your TV cable company, or DSL (short for Digital Subscriber Line) over your telephone line from your telephone company. In rural and remote areas that do not have access to wired broadband service, high-speed Internet is available via satellite. Monthly fees range from about $55 to $180, depending on the speed of the connection, and you also have to spend several hundred dollars to buy and install satellite equipment. As you might guess, high-speed access is faster than dial-up access — a lot faster. Web pages load so slowly via dial-up access that it's really not practical for small business use. High-speed access is definitely worth the extra cost.

Two very commonly used ISPs are Bell Canada's Sympatico (telephone connection) and Rogers (cable connection). You can find out more about them respectively at www.bell.ca and www.rogers.com. Satellite Internet is available from Xplornet Internet Services at www.xplornet.ca.

Avoiding cyberspace hazards

You can pick up some very dangerous hitchhikers while you travel through cyberspace if you're not careful. Be sure to have a look at Chapter 12 where we tell you about some of the risks that come with being online, and the ways you can protect yourself.

Surfing the Web on Business

After you get your Internet access set up, you can start wasting incredible amounts of time searching for arcane information about little-known medical conditions you suspect you have, gambling sites, and cute pictures of animals and movie stars . . . er, that is, you can get down to business. The Web is a wonderful tool for getting the information you need for just about every stage of your business.

> ✔ **When you're in the planning stage,** you can search the Web for information about business in general and your own field of business in particular. You can also use the Web to track down the training you need to be successful, and to search for a lawyer, an accountant, an insurance agent, and the other professional help you will need to get your business

off the ground. (See Chapter 2 for a discussion of some of the Web sites you may find useful.)

✔ **As you get your business underway,** you can use the Web to find furniture, equipment, and supplies for it (see Chapters 6 and 13), to help you locate business premises (see Chapter 7), and perhaps even to find a business for sale (see Chapter 9). All of these things cost money — but no problem! — you can find sources of financing on the Web (see Chapter 10) and the necessary skills to help you persuade lenders to actually give you some money (see Chapter 11).

✔ **Once your business is up and running,** you can search the Web for potential customers and for information about them that will help you make the sale (see Chapters 4 and 13). You can research potential suppliers (see Chapter 14). You can visit government Web sites to learn about your responsibilities as an employer (see Chapter 15) and about your tax obligations (see Chapter 16). At that point, you will probably go back to the medical Web sites to dwell on the little-known disease you suspect you have.

Communicating Over the Internet

Many people alive today don't even remember the good old days of the postal system. Businesses used to operate by writing things on a piece of paper, putting the paper in an envelope with the recipient's address on it, pasting a stamp on the envelope, and dropping the whole thing into a post box. A few days later, the letter would arrive at the recipient's address. The recipient would reply using the same method. Turnaround time for correspondence carried out in this fashion was typically a week or ten days — no wonder we now call the postal system "snail mail."

Now we have

✔ **E-mail,** which is a method of sending data over the Internet

✔ **Instant (text) messaging,** which allows two computer users to communicate in writing via the Internet in real time

We also have a kind of retro use of the Internet, which is Voice over Internet (also known as VoIP), which uses the Internet for telephone calls (lands sakes, Martha, what will they think of next?).

E-mail

E-mail is the oldest and most widely used Internet service. It uses the SMTP (Simple Mail Transfer Protocol) to send and receive data.

E-mailboxes and e-mail software

To send and receive e-mail you need an Internet mail address or mailbox. If you've already got Internet access, you probably also have one or more mailboxes with your Internet service provider (ISP), as part of your service. Also, a number of Web sites provide free mailboxes, such as Hotmail (`www.hotmail.com`) or Yahoo Mail (`http://mail.yahoo.com`).

However, everyone knows these days which e-mail addresses are free, and it looks kind of cheap and cheesy to be running a business on a free e-mail address. Make the big investment and get paid-for e-mail; and better yet, get an e-mail address that uses your own domain name (see "A domain name").

Unless you're using a Web-based e-mail address, you also need an e-mail program to read, send, address, and file your e-mails. The most popular e-mail programs are Outlook Express, which is included for free as part of the Microsoft Windows program, and Netscape Messenger, which is part of the Netscape Communicator Web browser program and can be downloaded free of charge from `www.netscape.com`. Outlook Express, because it is widely used, may tend to come under attack more often from cyber-hooligans.

Things to do with e-mail

You can use e-mail to correspond with customers, suppliers, lenders, employees, and colleagues . . . and even your family if you're oblivious to everything but your business computer. You can enter into binding contracts via e-mail — even contracts that are required by law to be in writing. Unlike a phone call, e-mail gives people a chance to look into a matter before answering you (as long as they don't take more than 30 seconds), and it provides a written record of what was said. You can also send e-mail attachments, which are files separate from the e-mail message itself, such as:

- ✔ Word-processor and spreadsheet documents
- ✔ Pictures in image files
- ✔ Sounds in audio files
- ✔ Movies in video files

Don't delete important e-mail messages. Treat them like important letters. Print them and file them in hard copy, or else file them electronically.

E-mail etiquette

When you're in business, your e-mails should be businesslike. That means you have to

- ✔ **Clearly describe the subject matter of your e-mail in the "subject" line.** People are inundated with e-mail. A clear subject line will help the recipient distinguish your e-mail from junk e-mail and to relocate it quickly if it gets filed or stored.

✔ **Use salutations ("Dear Mr. Smith") and complimentary closings ("Yours very sincerely") when you begin an e-mail exchange.** Start off the e-mail exchange with customers and clients with a certain amount of formality. Because an e-mail exchange becomes more like a conversation than a letter as it goes on, these formalities become optional later on.

✔ **Organize your e-mail.** Start with what you want the reader to know, and then give background information or an explanation if necessary. Use short, single-spaced paragraphs. Long paragraphs are hard to read on a computer screen.

✔ **Use proper spelling and grammar.** Also follow the standard rules of capitalization. Edit and proofread your e-mail before you hit Send.

✔ **Use a businesslike and polite tone.** Don't be overly informal or familiar, sarcastic or rude. Avoid capitalizing entire words because that's considered yelling in e-mailese. (An entire phrase, or worse an entire sentence, in capitals would come across as maniacal rage or a tantrum.) The best rule to follow with e-mail is: Don't write anything in an e-mail that you wouldn't want to read aloud in front of your mother . . . or a judge. If your mother is a judge, be doubly circumspect.

✔ **Use an electronic signature.** It sets out your name, your business's name, your position, telephone number, and fax number. You may also want to include your business mailing address.

✔ **Take care when using e-mail for confidential correspondence.** E-mail can be misdirected and/or read by someone other than the intended recipient. Check your addresses once then twice before you hit the send button, and be sure to include a confidentiality warning at the bottom of the e-mail, like the one we offer in Chapter 12.

✔ **Don't send files with huge attachments.** They can take so long to download that they can cause the recipient's e-mail program to freeze.

✔ **Don't be a spammer.** *Spam* is the term used to describe unsolicited mass e-mails, and they are a nuisance. If you send out mass e-mails, they are likely to be deleted without being read.

Instant messaging

Instant messaging (or IM) is an Internet service that allows you to create a private chat room and communicate in real time. It's like a telephone conversation except it's text-based instead of voice-based, so it's silent. It's great for communicating confidentially with your colleagues and clients when you're in a boring meeting or a public place, or for communicating with your teenaged children. Seriously though, IM is becoming more popular in the business world, because it allows employees to have instant access to managers and co-workers in different offices without having to place phone calls.

Instant message lingo

Text messaging uses a lot of abbreviations to keep things moving fast on a small screen. To make sure you're hip to the lingo before you start messaging, you can look at a list of standard text messaging abbreviations on Webopedia at `www.webopedia.com/quick_ref/textmessageabbreviations.asp`.

Abbreviation	What it means
BAU	Business as usual
BRB	Be right back
F2T	Free to talk
FOMCL	Falling off my chair laughing
GB	Goodbye
INAL	I'm not a lawyer
LOL	Laughing out loud
TTYL	Talk to you later
WOMBAT	Waste of money, brains, and time
YBS	You'll be sorry
:(	Sad or frown smiley
>-)	Evil grin
:@	Exclamation "What???"

The most popular instant messaging applications are MSN Messenger (`www.messenger.msn.com`), AOL Instant Messenger (`www.aim.com`), and Yahoo! Messenger (`www.messenger.yahoo.com`), all available by free download.

VoIP

VoIP is a service that uses the Internet to transmit voice information in digital form, using the Voice over Internet Protocol. The difference between using VoIP and making a regular telephone call is that no long distance charges apply if you're calling outside your local area. Plus it's considerably trendier to VoIP someone than just to phone them. On the downside,

- ✔ Internet connections are not as reliable as telephone lines, and if your connection goes down, you lose your telephone connection.
- ✔ Voice quality can be poor unless you upgrade the bandwidth on your existing Internet connection.
- ✔ VoIP may be subject to hackers, viruses, and voice mail spam.

Hardware-based VoIP phone services (your phone is fitted with an adapter that connects to your high-speed Internet connection) and software-based VoIP phone services (a microphone headset is plugged into your computer and your calls are routed through your cable modem by using the keyboard) are available. VoIP can also be run over a virtual private network (VPN), which we talk about later in this chapter.

Vonage Canada (`www.vonage.ca`), which connects your phone to the Internet, offers monthly packages starting at about $20. Skype (`www.skype.com`) offers free computer-to-computer calling worldwide, and calls to regular telephones (landlines or mobiles) for a fee.

Using the Internet to Get Access to Your Office . . .

. . . no matter where you are! Whatever you may have heard to the contrary, you *can* take it with you! Well, you can take your office into cyberspace at any rate. (We don't know about your worldly possessions into the next life, we're still looking into that and will update you in the third edition of this book.)

The key is to establish an Internet connection even if you're not sitting at your office computer. If you travel with a laptop or notebook computer, and your computer is wireless enabled, you can get access to the Internet in several ways:

- ✔ **Purchase your own monthly wireless access to the Internet.** Your ISP will give you a modem with an antenna that will allow you access to its wireless network, as long as you're in their coverage area. To find a wireless ISP, conduct a Web search for "broadband wireless ISP Canada."

- ✔ **Locate a WiFi hotspot.** WiFi is short for wireless fidelity, and a hotspot is a location that provides public, although not necessarily free, access to wireless broadband network services. You can often find hotspots in coffee shops, hotels, and airports. Starbucks, for example, has teamed up with Bell to provide hotspots in 400 of its locations throughout Canada, and an alliance of four major wireless carriers — Bell, Fido, Rogers and Telus — have set up many hotspot locations (in hotels, airports, conference centers, restaurants, and coffee shops across Canada) that are available to their subscribers. Use a directory such as Wi-FiHot SpotList.com at `www.wi-fihotspotlist.com` to find a hotspot in your location.

- ✔ **If you're lucky, tap into someone else's wireless network.** If someone in the vicinity has an unsecured wireless network, your computer may pick it up and give you wireless access to the Internet for free.

Even if your computer is not wireless enabled, you can use whatever Internet connection is available — cable, DSL, or dial-up — where you are staying.

Remote access to your e-mail

As long as you have access to the Internet, you can read and send e-mail from your laptop or notebook computer, or anyone else's computer for that matter. Just go to your ISP's Web site and you'll be put in touch with the e-mail that's still on the server. With most ISPs, you have access to your e-mail from anywhere in the world because your e-mail sits on the ISP server until you download it to your computer.

You can also get access to your e-mail via handheld wireless devices like BlackBerry and Palm. These personal digital assistants receive your incoming e-mail and send outgoing e-mail through a wireless network. They also include software for synchronizing address books and schedules with your desktop computer. You can find more information about Palm devices at `www.palm.com/ca`, and about BlackBerry devices at `www.blackberry.com`.

Remote access to your data

You can get access to your e-mail almost wherever you are, but what if you have to get some information from your computer in your hometown and you're miles away?

It is possible to have access to you business computer from remote locations using a *virtual private network* (VPN) — a secure, encrypted connection over the Internet connecting a computer or network at one end with a personal computer at the other. VPN technology can take a variety of forms: software installed on a personal computer and/or the network server, or a device that controls traffic flowing in and out of the network, or a combination of the two. Don't even think about using this technology if you don't have a high-speed Internet connection.

Until quite recently, VPN technology cost at least $2,000 U.S. — too expensive for most small businesses. But now you can get it for a lot less.

Some of the devices available are

- ✔ Symantec Corp. (`www.symantec.com`) offers the Gateway Security 300 Series ranging in price from $475 to $850 U.S.

- ✔ Check Point Software Technologies Ltd. (`www.checkpoint.com`) has the Safe@Office 500 Unified Threat Management appliance starting at about $300 U.S.

If you'd rather go the software route, you can purchase remote access software such as PCAnywhere from Symantec Corp., which costs about $800 U.S. for five users. Or you can subscribe to 01 Communique Inc.'s (www.01.com) I'm In Touch service for about $100 per year. The subscription includes software for installation on your office computer (the remote computers don't need any special software). You then have access to your office computer from any other computer, through 01 Communique's secure Web site.

Cisco System's Linksys division's Linksys Quick VPN product combines software with a device (a VPN router). The cost ranges from about $200 to $550 U.S.

Running a VPN does have a downside, however: You have to leave your computer running in order to get this kind of remote access. That gives hackers a greater opportunity to break in. If you decide to install remote access software, make sure that you have good security for your computer.

An alternative to remote access on your own computer is to store and transfer data through a password-protected area of your own Web site using the File Transfer Protocol (FTP). We're getting a little ahead of ourselves here because we haven't told you how to get a Web site yet, but we'll come to that shortly. You can decide what data is available for transfer, and who has access to it, and how much access they have. You could allow some password holders to make changes to the data, whereas others might only be allowed read-only access.

Only some Web hosts (see "Getting a Web Site of Your Own") offer FTP hosting, for example Internet Light and Power (www.ilap.com) or B2B2C (www.b2b2c.ca). For more providers, do an Internet search for "FTP providers."

Linking Up with Your Colleagues

What if your business has more than one location, or employees or associates who travel or live in another city (or province or country), and you and they need to exchange data and information? File Transfer Protocol (FTP) via a secure Web site is one way of sharing files with the other people involved in your business (check out "Remote access to your data" in this chapter).

You can also try "peer-to-peer" sharing. With file sharing, the data isn't stored on a central server or Web site, but instead it's placed in shared workspaces, copies of which exist on each of the computers. Whenever one user updates information in the shared workspace, the updates are copied to each of the other computers. A remote user can work off-line, but as soon as he or she logs onto the Internet, his or her updated files will be copied to all of the other computers. This is the same type of software that your kids may use to share (perhaps illegally) music over the Internet.

File sharing software costs up to about $250.00. Some examples of file-sharing software are

- ✔ Groove Virtual Office by Groove Networks, a subsidiary of Microsoft (`www.groove.net`).
- ✔ Qnext by Qnext Corp (`www.qnext.com`). (This software can be downloaded for free.)
- ✔ ShareDirect by Laplink Software Inc. (`www.laplink.com`), which is available on a subscription basis. (A free trial version of the software is available on Laplink's Web site.)

Getting a Web Site of Your Own

According to the Canadian Federation of Independent Business, about three-quarters of Canadian small businesses have their own Web sites, and your business should probably be one of them.

Entire books have been written about business Web sites, and we only touch on some of the main points in this chapter. For more information, we recommend *Starting an Online Business For Dummies* by Greg Holden (published by Wiley).

Why do you need a Web site?

You might use a Web site in your business in a variety of ways. We've already told you about using a Web site to store data where you and others with a password can get access to it from anywhere in the world. Besides that, you might want a Web site because

- ✔ **Everyone else has one.** People expect certain things of a business — to have a phone number and e-mail address and fax number and maybe even a street address. People also commonly expect a business to have a Web site, and if it doesn't they may wonder whether you really are serious about being in business!
- ✔ **It lets the world know you're there** (even though in cyberspace there's no "there" there). You don't have to do business through your Web site,

but potential customers like to be able to look up information without having to call you during business hours. More and more Canadians are connected to the Internet, and many of them begin their research about businesses not in the Yellow Pages, but on the Web. A Web site can describe your products and/or services, hours of business, location (including directions and a map if you'd like), and contact information such as telephone and fax numbers and e-mail addresses.

✔ **It provides service to your existing customers.** You can post answers to your customers' or clients' most frequently asked questions (FAQs), allowing them to get answers on their own whenever they want, without bothering you. An online FAQ can save you time in dealing with simple, repetitive questions. Your Web site can also provide a point of e-mail contact for your customers, especially if for some reason you don't want to give out your e-mail address to every passing stranger. You can have a "contact us" section on the e-mail that allows customers to write to you without you actually having to show your e-mail address. Thus you can avoid being spammed by everyone.

✔ **It allows you to carry on your business.** You can use your Web site to actually sell your goods and services to the world, 24 hours a day, seven days a week.

A Web server or a Web host

No one will be able to find your Web site unless you have a *Web server*, a computer that is connected to the Internet all of the time and delivers (or serves up) Web pages. Any computer can be turned into a Web server by installing server software. The Web server stores all of the files needed to display the pages of your Web site when someone connects to your site using a Web browser. Many Web server software applications are available, such as Internet Information Service (IIS), available for purchase from Microsoft (www.microsoft.com), and Apache HTTP Server, available free of charge from the Apache Software Foundation (www.apache.org). Of course you'll still need an ISP to connect your Web server to the Internet.

Does all of this sound too technical for you? If you don't have the technical expertise, and don't want your own Web server, you can use a *Web host*, a business that provides space on its server. You can check with your Internet service provider to see if it offers a monthly hosting package (you may even be entitled to free Web space as part of your existing Internet package), or you can find Web hosting services by searching on the Web for "Web hosting." Your choice of Web host will affect which software you use to create your Web pages, and may affect your Web address and the appearance of your site.

A domain name

The first step to setting up a Web site is to register your own domain name or URL. When you register a domain name, you're inserting an entry into a directory of all the domain names and their corresponding computers on the Internet.

Understanding domain names

A domain name has two parts. The first part identifies the site's name, and comes before the dot. The second part, which comes after the dot, is the top-level domain — one of the primary categories into which Internet addresses are divided. The most common top-level domain name is .com. In Canada, a Web site may be able to use the country code top-level domain name .ca.

The Internet's Domain Name System (DNS) allows a Web site to use a domain name instead of a long, complicated string of numbers (which is what an Internet Protocol [IP] address is). The DNS is administered by the Internet Corporation for Assigned Names and Numbers (ICANN), an internationally organized, non-profit corporation that oversees the distribution of domain names.

You have to be a little more special to register a domain name ending with .ca than with .com. You must meet certain Canadian presence requirements. For example you must be

✔ A Canadian citizen

✔ A permanent resident of Canada

✔ A legally recognized Canadian organization

✔ A foreign resident of Canada who holds a registered Canadian trademark

Choosing a domain name

You have to come up with a unique domain name. Check initially whether your name is going to be the same as, or confusingly similar to, another business's trademark or name or trade name by entering your potential domain name as a Web search.

If you want to use a domain name that someone else is already using, see if you can buy it from the owner. Check for contact information on their Web site. If it isn't on the site, you may be able to find contact information by going to www.register.com and typing in the domain name. You can also find Web sites where people offer to sell their domain names (try www.great domains.com or www.register.com).

Registering your domain name

Once you decide on a domain name, you register your name by buying it through a registrar. Check the ICANN Web site (www.icann.org) for a list of ICANN accredited registrars and their Web addresses, or, if you're interested in a name ending in .ca, the CIRA Web site (www.cira.ca/en/home.html) for a CIRA certified registrar. You can also arrange to buy a domain name through a Web hosting company or an Internet service provider that provides hosting services. The transaction is completed online, and will include a search to ensure that the name is in fact available to buy.

When you buy a domain name, you're actually getting a subscription to use that name for a set period of time, usually from one to ten years. Your domain registrar will send you a reminder 30 to 45 days before the subscription runs out, but if you don't renew it within 60 days, the name may be released to the public.

Make sure that your domain registrar has an up-to-date e-mail contact address so that the renewal notice doesn't disappear into cyberspace.

What to put on your Web site

Once you have a domain name, you have to put some content at the Web address — and that becomes your Web site.

Content

No matter what your business, every Web site should contain certain things:

✔ A description of your products and/or services, including your background and areas of expertise

✔ Your hours of business and, if you have a physical business and want people to come to it in person, your location (including directions and a map)

✔ Contact information such as telephone and fax numbers and e-mail addresses (or if not an e-mail address, a contact form)

✔ Information that new and existing customers will find useful and that adds value to your Web site and your business, such as:

  • Frequently asked questions about your business or service or products (and of course some intelligent answers)

  • Informative and/or how-to articles

  • Links to other helpful Web sites

✔ A Terms of Use Agreement containing

- A Web site information disclaimer regarding the accuracy of the information contained on your site (see the sidebar about disclaimers)

- A copyright notice claiming copyright in the content of the Web site. In Canada, a copyright notice isn't actually necessary to obtain copyright protection, but it might make Web surfers think twice before pilfering your frequently given answers and informative articles (see Chapter 3 for more about copyright).

- Your privacy policy, if your site collects any personal information from your customers (see Chapter 13)

- A hyperlink disclaimer, if your site contains links to other Web sites, stating that you don't guarantee or endorse the linked sites (see the sidebar about disclaimers)

Sample disclaimers

Accuracy of content disclaimer

The Web site and all content are provided as is. By accessing and using the Web site you acknowledge and agree that use of the Web site and the content is entirely at your own risk. We make no representations or warranties regarding the Web site and the content, including, without limitation, no representation or warranty (1) that the Web site and/or content will be accurate, complete, reliable, suitable or timely; (2) that any content, including, without limitation, any information, data, software, product or service contained in or made available through the Web site will be of merchantable quality or fit for a particular purpose; (3) that the operation of the Web site will be uninterrupted or error free; (4) that defects or errors in the Web site will be corrected; (5) that the Web site will be free from viruses or harmful components; and (6) that communications to or from the Web site will be secure or not intercepted.

Hyperlink disclaimer

The Web site contains links to third-party Web sites. These links are provided solely as a convenience to you and are not endorsements of the contents of such third-party Web sites. We are not responsible for the content of any third-party Web site, nor do we make any representation or warranty of any kind regarding any third-party Web site including, without limitation (1) any representation or warranty regarding the legality, accuracy, reliability, completeness, timeliness, or suitability of any content on any third-party Web site; (2) any representation or warranty regarding the merchantability or fitness for a particular purpose of any material, content, software, goods, or services located at or made available through such third-party Web sites; or (3) any representation or warranty that the operation of the third-party Web sites will be uninterrupted or error free, that defects or errors in such third-party Web sites will be corrected or that such third-party Web sites will be free from viruses or other harmful components.

If you sell goods or services on your Web site, your Terms of Use Agreement should set out the terms of your usual contract for the sale of goods or provision of services, as the case may be (see Chapter 13).

Design

Once you know what you want to say on your Web site, you've got to make sure that it says it. You may find the prospect of designing your own Web site a bit overwhelming, but getting help is easy. Web site creation software packages such as Microsoft FrontPage, which costs about $200 U.S. (www.microsoft.com) and Macromedia Dreamweaver, which costs about $400 U.S. (www.macromedia.com) take you through the process step-by-step. You can also find businesses that will help you design and set up a Web site. For a basic Web site, you might pay around $500. Search the Web to find a Web designer whose portfolio (and price range) appeals to you, or get business acquaintances to recommend their Web site designers.

Many Internet service providers offer help with the entire process from domain name selection through Web hosting to Web site creation.

The design of your Web site should suit your business. If you're setting up an accounting firm, you might like your site to look conservative and responsible with other people's money. If you're running a rent-a-clown business, you might want to have a little more splash and colour. Whatever the look of your site, it should be

- ✔ **Fast:** Your Web pages should load quickly (avoiding animated content helps).

- ✔ **Legible:** Use easy-to-read fonts, and make sure that your text and background are in contrasting colours. For example, don't use navy blue text on a black background, or pale pink text on a white background.

- ✔ **Understandable:** Your written content should be clear and concise.

- ✔ **Secure:** If your site collects any personal information from your customers, especially credit card information, your site must use technology that encrypts (or encodes) your customers' information. Secure Socket Layer (SSL) technology is the most commonly used. You must also comply with the privacy provisions of Canada's *Personal Information and Electronic Documents Act* (PIPEDA). See Chapter 13.

Attracting visitors

Many of your potential customers will do a Web search to find businesses that offer products or services such as yours. So you want to make sure that your business will show up in the search results of the major search engines such as Google and Yahoo.

You can list your Web site with individual search engines by going to the search engine's Web site. You will be asked to submit your URL (Uniform Resource Locator — your domain name) and information about your business. If you don't want to do the work yourself, you can use a paid submission service such as Microsoft bCentral's Submit It (www.submit-it.com) or Add Me (www.addme.com) starting at about $50 U.S.

Getting your Web site listed with a search engine is only a start. You also want to try to get it ranked as highly as possible in the search engine results. Do this by identifying the keywords most likely to be used in a Web search for your type of business, and repeat those words as often as possible on your home page.

Getting Paid Online

Just as an afterthought, since you're probably in business for the purpose (or at least the hope) of making money . . . if you'll be selling goods through your Web site, you should have a way to get paid before you process your customer's order. You can either set up a credit card merchant account with a credit card company, or you can use a third-party credit card processing company.

Merchant account

Setting up a merchant account valid for accepting online credit card payments can be very expensive, because the risk of fraud is higher when you process credit card payments without seeing either the credit card or the purchaser. The application fee alone can be several hundred dollars. In addition, you'll have to pay a monthly charge *and* a percentage commission on each transaction. You can get information about setting up a merchant account with Visa at www.visa.ca/en/merchant, and with MasterCard at www.mastercard.com/canada/business/merchant/.

Third party processor

When you use a *third-party processor*, your customer is directed to the processor's Web site to complete his or her payment. In return, you pay a transaction fee plus a commission to the processor for each payment processed.

PayPal (www.paypal.com) is one of the most popular third-party processors for small businesses (established in 1998 in California, it was acquired by eBay in 2002). You might also want to investigate Canadian-based third-party processors such as InternetSecure Inc. (www.internetsecure.com) based in Oakville, Ontario, Payment Services Interactive Gateway Corp. (www.psigate.com) based in Mississauga, Ontario, and Beanstream Internet Commerce Inc. (www.beanstream.com) based in Victoria, British Columbia.

If you use a third-party processor, you are not responsible for the security of your customers' credit card information, but you must still comply with the privacy provisions of PIPEDA, by making sure via a written contract that the third-party processor complies with PIPEDA.

Chapter 9

Custom-Made Business — or Off-the-Shelf?

In This Chapter

▶ Thinking about buying a business instead of building your own business

▶ Finding a business to buy

▶ Knowing what to look for when you're buying a business

▶ Placing a value on an existing business

▶ Putting together the deal to buy a business

▶ Contemplating a franchise

*B*uilding your own business is a lot of work. In addition to coming up with a business concept, you have to

✔ Find a good location, and prepare your business premises.

✔ Buy equipment.

✔ Find clients or customers.

✔ Set up management operations.

✔ Expand the business through your own efforts.

And when you custom-build your business, you have no one to give you on-the-job training, or to pass on wisdom gained from experience about what works and what doesn't.

But custom-building a business is not the only way to go into business. You can buy an existing business instead.

Why Buy an Existing Business?

You might want to buy an existing business for a number of reasons:

✔ You already know of a business that you want to own. Perhaps you're an employee and the owner wants to sell, or the owner is a relative or friend, who is retiring and looking for a successor, or you've been a customer or a client of the business and you know the owner would look favourably on an offer to buy.

✔ You'll be able to eliminate a lot of the difficult, early work involved in building a business. If you buy an established business you may not have to find a location or buy equipment or hunt for customers or hire employees or develop a new marketing plan.

✔ You may be able to tap into a source of advice about how to run a business because the original owner of the business may be willing to stay on with you for a while.

✔ You may be able avoid some of the risks of starting a new business:

   • When you buy a successful business you know that there's a market for the product or service you will be offering.

   • When you buy an existing business your immediate money situation may be better — you may find it easier to borrow money because banks know that the risks of failure are lower for an established business than for a start-up. And you may need less money than you would for a new business if the business has an established income stream.

✔ You may be able to get rights you couldn't otherwise get — buying a business may be the only way to get the right to distribute a specific product in a particular area, or the licence to manufacture a particular item.

But before you go rushing off to buy a business, you should know that buying a business has its disadvantages, as well:

✔ You won't be able to buy a successful business cheap. (A business that's in trouble will be less expensive to buy, but you have to be very realistic about your chances of turning the business around.) And on top of the price for the business itself, you'll have to pay professional fees — for an accountant and a lawyer at least, and maybe for others, as well.

✔ There's no guarantee that a successful business will continue to be successful for you. The success may have been based on the personality and/or skill of the current owner. When he leaves he may take the success with him. Or the business, although it pays the current owner well, may not generate enough income to give you a reasonable return on your investment (if you pay cash) or to be profitable after you make your loan payments (if you borrow money to buy the business).

✔ You'll inherit any problems the business has. Even successful businesses have problems, such as difficult employees, inefficient business practices, unreliable suppliers, or troublesome clients or customers. The previous owner may have learned to live with these problems, but they may drive you crazy — and your efforts at reform may cause resentment among employees, suppliers, or clients.

Where Do You Shop for a Business?

If you don't already have your eye on a particular business, where do you look for one that's for sale?

✔ **Read the ads:** Look in the classified section of your newspaper under Business Opportunities or Businesses for Sale. Check ads in industry journals, newsletters, and magazines.

✔ **Search the Internet:** Find Web sites that list Canadian businesses for sale. You can search for Canadian sites on Google Canada or Yahoo Canada by using the search terms "buy business Canada."

✔ **Place an ad:** Consider advertising in your local newspaper or in industry publications under Businesses Wanted.

✔ **Visit trade shows and conventions:** The program may contain ads for businesses for sale, or exhibitors may know of some. Tell people that you meet that you're looking for a business to buy. Word may reach someone who's looking to sell.

✔ **Tell business professionals that you're interested in buying:** Speak to any lawyers, accountants, financial advisors, consultants, or bank managers that you know. One of them may work with a business owner who's looking for a buyer.

✔ **Ask a business owner if he or she wants to sell:** If you know of a business that interests you, consider asking the owner if she's interested in selling. Just because a business isn't for sale doesn't mean that the owner won't consider an offer.

✔ **Use a business broker:** Business brokers help business owners sell their businesses and so will be able to tell you about the businesses for sale by their clients. If you work with a broker, keep in mind that he's interested in making a sale so he can earn a commission, and that it's his job to make his clients' businesses look as attractive as possible to a prospective buyer.

I'd Like to Have a Look at That One, Please

Before the owner agrees to answer your questions, show you around the business premises, and let you see documents, he or she may ask you to sign a *confidential disclosure agreement*. By signing the agreement you agree not to tell anyone else what you find out about the business, and usually you also agree not to use the information for any purpose but assessing the business for a possible purchase. The information and the business are protected if you decide you don't want to buy, because the owner can sue you if you don't honour the agreement.

Take a very careful, even cynical, look at any business before you make a decision to buy. Below we set out some questions to guide your examination of a business that's up for sale.

Why is the owner selling the business?

This may be the most important question to ask. There are many reasons for selling a business, but from the buyer's point of view some are better than others.

These reasons shouldn't set off alarm bells for you:

- ✔ The owner is retiring because he or she no longer needs to work, or because of age or ill-health (. . . as long as the ill-health wasn't caused by the business).
- ✔ The owner wants to pursue a different career or business opportunity (unless that desire is triggered by a problem with this business).
- ✔ The owner is having marital problems.

These reasons may signal trouble:

- ✔ The business is not profitable.
- ✔ The owner cannot raise enough money to finance the business.
- ✔ Competition for the business is heating up.
- ✔ Markets for the business's product or service are drying up.
- ✔ The hours of work are too long and/or the work is unpleasant.

The owner may be very forthcoming about her reasons for selling, or she may be reluctant to talk. Even if she does talk, don't just believe what she tells you. Try to get information from others in the same industry — business owners, employees, suppliers, and customers.

What is the reputation of the business?

A major reason for buying an established business is to get the benefit of its reputation. You hope that it has a base of loyal customers and suppliers who will be willing to continue to deal with you. Speak to the business's customers and suppliers to find out what they think of the business. Contact the Better Business Bureau, industry associations, and any licensing bodies to see if there have been any complaints made against the business.

What is the reason for the success of the business?

You want to make sure that the reason the business has been successful is a lasting one. So here are some things to check out:

- ✔ Does the business have a great product or service — or was it built on a fad that's now fading?
- ✔ If the business was built on a small number of enthusiastic clients or customers, are they likely to stay on with you?
- ✔ If the business was built on exports, what's the economic and political outlook for the countries where the exports go?
- ✔ If the business has done well because it had little competition, is competition likely to increase in the future?

How's the neighbourhood?

Perhaps your main reason for buying the business is that it has a wonderful location that draws customers like a magnet or it's perfectly placed for delivery of supplies and shipment out of products. If that's the case, be sure to check the terms of the lease for the location:

- ✔ Is the rent reasonable?
- ✔ How much time is left to run on the lease — and does the lease contain any rights to renew?

✔ If the business is located in a mall, does the lease protect you from competition by other tenants?

✔ Does the lease affect the hours you can or have to work? Some retail mall leases require storeowners to operate whenever the mall is open, and that may include evening and weekend hours you do not wish to work. Access to office, industrial, or warehouse space may be restricted to certain hours, and even if you can get in, the power, light, heat, air-conditioning, and elevators may not be operational.

If the location of the business is not the main reason you want the business, make sure, on the other hand, that the location is not a reason you'll come to regret your purchase:

✔ If this business has been at its location for only a short while, what happened to the business that was there before? Does this location have a history of failed businesses? You want to be sure that the past success of the business wasn't tied to its previous location.

✔ Does the municipality or landlord have any plans for the property that will affect traffic, parking, or access to the property? A major renovation of the building or major road construction or anything else that limits customer or supplier access could be bad news for you.

What do the financial statements tell you?

When you're looking over a business, you should ask to see its financial statements for the preceding three to five years.

The financial statements of a business contain information that will be very useful to you in deciding whether the business is worth buying at all, and, if it is, in deciding on the price you should pay. But you have to be able to understand them. We talk about financial statements in Chapter 17, and if you don't know very much — or anything — about financial statements, you should probably go to Chapter 17 now and read about them before continuing.

Have a professional accountant or business evaluator review the financial statements before you make a final decision to buy — even if you think you've got the business's financials all figured out yourself.

In the following sections, we tell you what to look for in two of types of statements: the *income statement* and the *balance sheet*.

The income statement

The income statement, also called a profit and loss statement, sets out a business's income and expenses over a stated period of time (a month, quarter, or year). The income (also called the revenues) is the money paid by customers or clients for products or services. The expenses are the costs of doing business. A business's profit equals income minus expenses.

Look at the revenues of the business, and ask

✔ **How profitable is the business?** Don't look at just the total dollar amount of the profit. Look at the *profit margin* (profit divided by revenues times 100 gives you the percentage that is the profit margin). If it's low for this kind of business (see the section "Sources of information for valuing a business" for help with questions like this), that may indicate that the business is not efficiently run.

✔ **Have revenues increased over the past while?** If they have, that's certainly good news, but try to get a sense of why it happened. You want to see an increase in the amount of business, not simply an increase in the price the business has charged for its goods or services.

✔ **Will the profits give you a reasonable return on your investment?** Compare the profits to the price you'd be willing to pay for the business. If you invested the price in something else, would the profit you see in these financial statements be a reasonable return on your investment?

Look at the expenses, and ask

✔ **Have expenses as a percentage of revenues gone up, remained steady, or gone down over the past while?** If expenses have gone up, is there a particular category of expenses that seems to be getting out of control?

✔ **Are there expenses you'll be able to cut? Are there expenses you'll want to increase?** Some expenses may be discretionary (typically entertainment, travel, car expenses, and club memberships), and if you can cut expenses, you'll be able to increase the profits of the business. But if you increase expenses, the profits will go down.

✔ **How much has the owner been paying himself or herself?** How does that salary compare to what you intend to take? The business may show a profit only because the owner has been taking little or no salary. On the other hand, if the owner has been taking a higher salary than you need, you'll be able to increase the profits of the business by taking a lower salary.

The balance sheet

The balance sheet lists and shows a value for everything a business owns (its *assets*) and everything it owes (its *liabilities*) as of a specified date, usually the last day of the company's *fiscal* year. (This is called its year-end. A fiscal year has 365 days in it, but it doesn't have to match up with the calendar year. March 31 and June 30 are common fiscal year-ends.)

Assets fall into two categories, *current assets* and *fixed assets*. Current assets are cash, and assets that are intended to be and can be turned into cash easily. Fixed assets are assets the business intends to hold onto for a long period of time.

With the balance sheet in one hand and the income statement in the other, have a look at the business's assets to find out more about the financial shape the business is in:

- ✔ One current asset is *accounts receivable* — amounts billed out to customers or clients but not yet paid. Is the accounts receivable, over time, becoming a larger percentage of the business's revenue? High accounts receivable are a sign of problems. Perhaps the customers or clients have no money. (You don't want to buy a business that has deadbeat customers.) Or maybe the customers aren't paying because they're not happy with the business's product or service. (You don't want to buy a business that has a poor reputation.)

- ✔ Another current asset, in a retail or manufacturing business, is *inventory* (unsold goods). (The balance sheet will not list the inventory in detail, but will show how much the unsold inventory cost to buy.) Have inventory levels been going up or down over the past years? You should be concerned if the inventory levels are going up more than revenues. Too much inventory may be a sign that business isn't good because nobody's buying the product. Even if the business is not in trouble, with high levels of inventory, some of the inventory may be out-of-date and therefore not worth as much as more recent inventory. Actually go and look over the inventory.

- ✔ Fixed assets include equipment. The value shown on the balance sheet for fixed assets is known as *book value*. Book value reflects the purchase price of the assets less *depreciation* (reduction in the value of the assets year by year to take into account their age), but doesn't necessarily reflect the true value of the assets. Look at the book value of equipment and then look at the equipment itself. Does it appear to be worth its book value? You don't want to overpay for assets. Is there too much equipment? You don't want to pay for equipment you don't need (and excess equipment may be a sign that business is declining). Is there not enough equipment, or is the equipment obsolete? You may have to buy new equipment once you take over the business, adding to expenses. And anyway, you don't want to pay for something you can't use.

Liabilities, or debts owed, are categorized as *current liabilities* and *long-term liabilities*. Current liabilities are debts that will be paid within a year such as *accounts payable* (money the business owes to suppliers), current wages, current taxes, and the portion of any long-term debt that's currently payable. Long-term liabilities are debts that will not be paid off within a year.

Look at the balance sheet again and ask

✔ **Who actually owns the business — the owner or the creditors?** To find this out, divide the total amount of debt (current and long-term) by the net worth of the business. You calculate the net worth, also called the *owner's equity* in the business, by subtracting the total liabilities of the business from the total assets of the business. When you divide the debt by the net worth you get the *debt-to-equity* or *debt-to-net-worth* ratio. A ratio of 1:1 (that is, the owner owns as much of the business as the creditors do) or less is what you'd like to see.

✔ **How easy will it be to borrow money?** Lenders look at the debt-to-equity ratio to decide whether or not to cough up the cash when a business asks to borrow. If the ratio is too high (2:1 or higher), you may find it hard to persuade a lender to part with its money.

✔ **How quickly could the business get cash without borrowing, if it needed to?** Divide the business's current assets by its current liabilities to get the business's current ratio. The current ratio measures the business's *liquidity* — its ability to raise cash by disposing of assets that are fairly easy to sell. The higher the current ratio, the more liquid the business and the more easily it can come up with a fistful of dollars. A ratio of 4:1 or 5:1 is very healthy; a ratio of less than 2:1 should cause you some concern.

What is the "corporate culture"?

The employees of every business develop attitudes that govern the way they deal with management, customers, suppliers, and each other. In some businesses, management, staff, suppliers, and customers may treat each other like family. (We mean like family who like each other.) In others they may treat each other very formally and follow a rigid structure. In a few, they may be engaged in guerrilla, or even open, warfare. Do you like what you see of the corporate culture? If you don't, do you think you will be able to change the culture — and still keep the business's staff, customers, and suppliers?

I Might Be Interested . . . If the Price Is Right

If you've checked out the business and are pleased with it, don't just say, "I'll take it!" You must first decide what the business is worth and what price you're willing to pay. Buying a good business for the wrong price can be as big a mistake as buying a bad business. In this section, we tell you a little bit about different approaches to valuing businesses, and about where to find information on the value of a business.

Don't make a final decision to buy a business without getting professional help — from an accountant and/or a business evaluator and/or a lawyer — perhaps from all three.

- ✔ An accountant and/or a business evaluator can help you decide what the business is worth.
- ✔ An accountant and/or a lawyer can help you decide how to structure the deal.
- ✔ A lawyer can draft the contract to buy and complete the transaction to make sure that you get what you're supposed to.

If you're wondering how you'll actually come up with the money to buy the business, go to Chapter 10.

What's a business worth?

When you buy a business as a going concern, you're buying more than the physical assets of the business. You're also buying the business's goodwill — the likelihood that the business will be successful in the future. So in arriving at a price for a business, you have to find a price that includes both.

Valuing assets

You can value physical (or "tangible") assets in different ways, and they include:

- ✔ **Fair market value** — the price you would have to pay on the open market for equipment or inventory of the same age and condition. This is usually the best way to determine what the assets are "worth," but the owner may expect you to pay more than the fair market value of the assets in order to get the business as a going concern.

✔ **Replacement value** — the price you would have to pay for new inventory and equipment to replace what the business currently has. Generally, you would not pay replacement value when purchasing used assets. However, if the assets of the business are difficult to replace, that drives their value up.

✔ **Book value** — the value at which the assets are shown in the business's balance sheet. It may be higher or lower than the fair market value of the assets.

Another is liquidation value — the price for which the equipment and inventory could be sold if the business were *liquidated* (turned into cash), for example in a bankruptcy. However, liquidation value is not normally used when the business is a going concern, because it's lower than fair market value.

Note that if you will be taking over the debts of the company (and that's the usual scenario if you buy a going concern), to arrive at a value for the assets you have to deduct the amount of debts from the value of the assets.

Valuing goodwill

If you're buying a business as a going concern, you're not just shopping for some equipment and inventory. You also want the business's goodwill, which is an "intangible" ("untouchable") asset of the business. Goodwill is valuable because it affects the business's continuing success. Goodwill is often defined as the likelihood that customers will keep coming back.

All of the following affect a business's goodwill:

✔ The customer base it has established

✔ The business's age and reputation, including its name and any trademarks or trade names

✔ The location

✔ The exclusive rights the business might hold

✔ The quality of its employees

✔ The reliability of its suppliers

✔ The amount of competition the business faces

How do you place a value on goodwill? Most valuation methods involve an examination of the past earnings of the business as the best indicator of what future earnings are likely to be.

One valuation method that's often used is the *multiple of earnings* method. With this method, the business's earnings (its income less its expenses) over the past three to five years are averaged, and then that average is multiplied by a given number to arrive at a value for the business. The given number (known as a "multiple") varies from industry to industry. The best way to figure out the multiple for the business you're thinking of buying is to get information about recent sales of comparable businesses. (We give you some suggestions for finding that information in the "Sources of information for valuing a business" section.) Divide the price for which a business sold by its average annual earnings. That will give you a multiple to use for this particular type of business.

Once you come up with a proposed purchase price, check how reasonable it is by calculating the return you would likely get on your investment if you bought the business for that price. Take the average annual earnings of the company over the past three to five years and divide them by the proposed purchase price. That will give you the rate of return you may reasonably expect from your investment. (For example, if you're thinking about paying $250,000 for a business that has had average earnings of $15,000, the rate of return is 6 percent.) How does the rate of return compare to what you might earn on the same sum put into a different investment? Is the rate of return worth it when you take into account the work and risk involved in this particular business?

Sources of information for valuing a business

The best way to figure out what the business you're interested in is worth is to find out how much comparable businesses have sold for. Unfortunately, it's a lot harder to get sales information about businesses than it is about homes. Here are some possible sources of information about sale prices, and also about valuing businesses generally.

Trade publications

Trade publications for the industry you're interested in will probably have articles about how to value businesses within that industry, and may possibly have information about actual sales.

Businesses that you've looked at

Keep track of any businesses you've looked at but decided not to buy. If a business is sold, try to find out the price by talking to the previous owner. This is a bit of a long shot, since most businesspeople don't like to gab about their financial affairs.

Accountants, lawyers, and consultants

Speak to accountants, lawyers, and consultants who work with business buyers and sellers. They may have information on comparable sales if they have been involved in sales of businesses similar to the one you're thinking of buying.

Business brokers

If you've been looking at businesses with a business broker (see the "I Might Be Interested . . . If the Price Is Right" section) he or she should have information about sales of similar businesses — at least those sold through the broker's office. Keep in mind that the broker is working on commission for the seller and the commission is based on the price you agree to pay for the business — so the broker has an interest in getting you to pay the highest possible price.

A professional business appraiser

This is probably your best bet. If you've reached the point where you're ready to make an offer, you should seriously consider hiring a professional business appraiser or business valuator, who will, for a fee, estimate the value of the business you're interested in. The amount of the fee varies with the size and complexity of the business, but may well be several thousand dollars. Your lawyer, accountant, or business consultant may be able to refer you to an appraiser or valuator. Or you can contact the Institute of Business Appraisers at `www.instbusapp.org` for a list of members in your province.

Putting the Deal Together

Once you've found a business you want to buy and you've figured out how much it's worth, it's time to negotiate a deal with the owner. If you haven't already called in your lawyer and your accountant, now's the time to do it.

We're going to give you some background on how a business purchase is structured, so that, at the very least, you'll understand why you need professional help.

Buy assets or buy shares?

The business you're interested in buying is one of the following:

- ✔ A sole proprietorship
- ✔ A partnership
- ✔ A corporation

(We tell you more about these different forms of business in Chapter 5.)

If the business is run as a sole proprietorship or as a partnership, you have to buy the business by buying the assets of the business. However, if you're buying a corporation, you have a choice between buying the assets of the business and buying the shares of the corporation.

A share purchase

Buying all the shares of a corporation makes the buyer the owner of the corporation. The corporation continues to exist just as before, and continues to own all of its assets and owe all of its debts. If the corporation was a party to any contracts, they will continue in effect. (This works in theory, at least. Some of the contracts may allow the other party to withdraw from the contract if the corporation changes ownership.)

An asset purchase

Buying all the assets of a corporation does not make the buyer the owner of the corporation. The buyer will have no relationship with the corporation itself. The corporation continues to exist. It has no assets, but it's still responsible for its debts (except for those that the buyer agrees to take over — for example, a mortgage on real property or on a piece of equipment). The buyer does not get the benefit of any of the corporation's contracts unless the corporation assigns (transfers) them to the buyer. (The consent of the other party to the contract is usually required for an assignment.)

Deciding between a share purchase and an asset purchase

If you've got the choice, how do you decide? Common wisdom is that buyers prefer asset purchases while sellers prefer share purchases. (The preference has to do with tax consequences, which we explain a bit later.) So chances are that you'll want to purchase assets and the seller will want to sell shares.

Some of the usual advantages of an asset purchase if you're the buyer are

- You can pick and choose the assets you want to buy — well, in theory, at least. The seller may refuse to sell you the assets you want to buy unless you also agree to take some or all of the other assets he or she wants to sell.

- You don't automatically take on the debts and liabilities of the business. However, you may want to take on some debts (for example, a favourable mortgage as a way to help finance the purchase of a particular asset). You may also want to take on some liabilities (for example, warranty responsibilities, so that you don't aggravate your newly acquired customers by telling them to buzz off if they previously bought faulty products from the business).

✔ You can negotiate the value assigned to each asset so as to try to get the maximum tax advantage (see the section "Allocation of the purchase price in an asset purchase").

Some disadvantages of an asset purchase if you're the buyer are

✔ You'll usually have to contend with a lot of legal paperwork in an asset purchase because each individual asset has to be identified and transferred separately, and because the purchase must comply with provincial legislation to protect creditors of the business.

✔ You'll have to pay GST and provincial retail sales tax, or HST, on the equipment you buy, and land transfer tax on the real property you buy.

✔ You'll have to go through the process of hiring any employees you want to keep. (Unfortunately, the opposite is not true — because of provincial legislation, you may find yourself stuck with some employees you don't want to keep and you'll have to pay them off to get rid of them.)

✔ You may not be able to buy certain assets without the consent of a third party. For example, the landlord's consent may be required before you can take over the lease for the business premises.

And despite the common wisdom, there can be advantages to a share purchase if you're the buyer. For example:

✔ You may face less paperwork than in an asset purchase . . . although that probably won't translate into lower professional fees because there has to be a thorough investigation of the corporation and its ownership of the assets.

✔ You likely won't have to pay GST, retail sales tax, HST or land transfer tax.

✔ You won't have to hire anyone, because the employment relationship between employees and the corporation doesn't change — although employees you'd like to keep may choose to leave because of the change in ownership (and, naturally, employees you'd like to be rid of may choose to stay).

✔ You won't have to get third-party consent to the sale, because there is no change in ownership of the assets (although some leases may contain a condition that the lease ends if there is change in ownership of the corporation).

✔ Buying the entire corporation may be the only way for you to acquire a licence or contract that by its terms cannot be transferred by the corporation to anyone else.

✔ You may be able to get a tax reduction if the business has lost money in past years — if the corporation now has a loss carryforward, it can be applied against the corporation's future profits to reduce income taxes. Of course, you have to turn the business around and generate some profits first!

Allocation of the purchase price in an asset purchase

If you proceed by way of an asset purchase, there are two parts to negotiating a price with the seller. First you have to decide what you think the business is worth as a whole and come to an agreement with the seller on an overall price. Then, you must allocate the amount of the purchase price among the various assets included in the sale (in other words, you must assign a price to each asset).

By this point, you're thoroughly sick of us telling you about all the complicated and expensive steps involved in buying a business, so you probably feel like tossing this book into a garbage can, pouring gin all over it, and lighting a match. That would be a waste of both the book and the gin — and furthermore what we have to tell you can reduce your taxes! Interested now? If so, see the sidebar "Reducing your taxes in an asset purchase."

After reading the sidebar, you may think it wouldn't have been a waste of the book and the gin if you had dropped the match.

The dear departed — can you control the former owner?

Whether you decide on a share purchase or an asset purchase, you need to cover off certain matters with the soon-to-be-ex-owner in order to increase your chance of success once you take over the business.

Non-competition agreement

When you buy a business as a going concern, you want to keep the business's customers — so the last thing you want is for the seller to set up a competing business next door. To make sure that doesn't happen you must have *a noncompetition agreement* with the seller. Without one, there's nothing to stop the vendor from competing with you and taking your customers away.

Reducing your taxes in an asset purchase

One way to reduce the tax you pay on your business income is to increase your deductions. (See Chapter 16 for more on taxes.) So when you buy the assets of a business, you want to structure the deal so that in future years your deductions from income will be as high as possible.

Many of the assets of a business are *capital property* (property with long-term value that is bought to keep). You can deduct the cost of capital property from business income, but you can't deduct the full cost of it in the year of purchase. Instead you're allowed annual deductions for capital cost allowance (which is a different name for, but pretty much the same thing as, depreciation, or decrease in value as the asset ages). Each year you can claim a deduction for *capital cost allowance* on capital property. Different rates of depreciation apply to different classes of assets. For example, the rate that applies to land is 0 percent (because land doesn't depreciate in value), to buildings 4 percent, to equipment 20 percent, and to computer hardware and systems software 30 percent. And inventory can be fully deducted as an expense in the year of purchase.

In an asset purchase, the price you allocate to each asset determines the asset's *adjusted cost base*, which is the figure used to calculate the capital cost allowance for that asset. As a buyer, you want to allocate a higher price to inventory and to assets that have a higher rate of capital cost allowance, and a lower price to assets that have a lower rate of capital cost allowance.

The seller, however, will want to allocate a lower price to assets that have a higher rate of capital cost allowance and a higher price to assets that have a lower rate of capital cost allowance. Sellers are very perverse about this, but they're not just trying to annoy buyers. They've got a reason.

The general rule in an asset sale is that the seller has to pay only *capital gains tax* on the assets sold — which means that 50 percent of the increase in value of the asset since the seller acquired it is added to the seller's income and taxed. But if the sale price allocated to an asset is higher than the depreciated value of the asset (the purchase price less the capital cost allowance claimed over the years), 100 percent of the extra amount of capital cost allowance that the seller has claimed is added to the seller's income as *recaptured capital cost allowance*. In addition, 100 percent of any amount allocated to inventory is added to the seller's income. So allocating the purchase price among assets is not going to be as easy as falling off a rocket gantry. It will be more like falling off a space station.

If you've got a non-competition agreement and the ex-owner starts competing with you, you'll have to sue to stop him or her. But a non-competition agreement will stand up in court only if it's reasonable — you'll be able to prevent the seller from setting up a similar business only for a reasonable period of time and only within a reasonable distance of your business location. What's reasonable will depend on the nature of the business (although you should always think in terms of months rather than eons and in kilometres rather than light-years). For example, it's probably reasonable to prevent the seller of a convenience store or hair salon from competing only in the immediate neighbourhood. On the other hand, it might be reasonable to prevent the seller of an advertising agency with a national clientele from competing anywhere in Canada for a period of one year.

An agreement that gives the seller a stake in the business

Another way of discouraging the seller from competing with you is to structure the deal so that the seller has a stake in the continued success of the business. The seller will have a stake in your success if you can persuade him or her to take back a mortgage or promissory note for part of the purchase price, or if part of the purchase price is made payable at a future time and is tied to the business's income.

Consulting agreement

You might like the former owner of the business to stay on at the business for a limited period of time after the sale, as a consultant. The former owner will be able to give you advice about running the business (if you think you need some help), and his or her presence may encourage customers to keep on dealing with the business while they get to know you.

A consulting contract can also be used to turn some of the purchase price into consulting fees and spread it out over the period of the contract. This has two advantages, one for you and one for the former owner. You don't have to come up with the full purchase price at the time of the sale, and the owner gets to spread taxes on the profit from the sale over two or more taxation years.

What about a Franchise?

A franchise isn't exactly an off-the-shelf business. It's more like a pre-packaged business — you add water and stir. The franchisor (the company that created and developed the original business) owns the business name and trademarks and practices and procedures; the franchisee (the buyer of the franchise) gets a licence to use them. The franchisee pays an up-front franchise fee and then also makes continuing payments (royalties) based on the franchise's earnings. The franchisee sets up his or her own business, but sets it up as if it were part of a chain with one name and with standardized products, design, service, and operations.

What are the advantages of a franchise?

Buying a franchise provides the benefits of belonging to a large organization, while still being your own boss, including

- ✔ A business concept that has been thought out, and a product or service that has been researched and developed

- A recognized business name, and centralized advertising and sophisticated marketing

- Assistance, training, and support in management and production

- Economies of scale in buying supplies and services, because purchasing is centralized

- Assistance in choosing a business location (reputable franchises check out the strength of the local market before selling a new franchise in an area)

What are the disadvantages of a franchise?

Buying a franchise can sometimes lead to trouble for the franchisee because

- Franchises are standardized operations, and standardization can be stifling to a business owner who has his or her own ideas.

- Successful franchises are expensive — and new franchises are a gamble because costs may be higher than expected and/or profits lower than expected.

- Franchise agreements are always drafted by the franchisor and they favour the franchisor over the franchisee.

- The franchisor may promise training and support, but they may not be as good or thorough as promised.

- Franchisees may be charged more than the going market rate for supplies if they have to be purchased through the franchisor or specified suppliers.

- Franchisees are often required to pay substantial amounts for advertising and they may not see that they're getting anything in return.

- Sometimes the franchisor leases premises for a franchise location and subleases them to the franchisee. Then the franchisor can use its rights as a landlord to lock the franchisee out of the premises without notice if the franchisee doesn't make all the payments required under the franchise agreement.

- If the franchisor opens too many franchises in one area, or starts distributing products through the Internet or mail-order catalogues, it can drastically reduce the profits of franchisees.

- Franchisees usually don't have special legislation to protect them against franchisors, because hardly any provinces have passed franchise statutes, although legislation is under discussion in some other provinces.

Finding a franchise

Franchises are available in just about any business area, from accounting and tax services to pet care to lawn services to funeral homes. So the first step in finding a franchise is to decide on the kind of business you want to be in. We talk about choosing your business in Chapter 1.

Once you decide on the kind of business you want to be in, find out whether there are any franchises in that kind of business, and if so, whether any franchises are being offered in the location you're interested in.

You can look for franchises that are available in Canada in a number of ways:

- **Read franchise magazines:** There are a number of magazines geared to people interested in buying a franchise, such as *Canadian Business Franchise Magazine*, and *Franchise Canada Magazine*, the official publication of the Canadian Franchise Association (CFA). These magazines contain general information and advice about franchising and contain ads for franchises for sale.

- **Check franchise directories:** Several directories list available franchises, such as the *Franchise Canada Directory* published by the Canadian Franchise Association, *Franchise Annual* published by Info Franchise News (www.infonews.com/online.html), and *Canadian Business Franchise Directory (Annual)* published by CGB Publishing.

- **Search the Internet:** Many Web sites contain information about franchises for sale. The *Canadian Business Franchise Magazine* maintains a site (www.cgb.ca/franchises.html) that lists franchises by name. The Canadian Franchise Association's Web site (www.cfa.ca) contains a "find a franchise" feature that allows you to browse franchises either by name or by category. Only CFA members in good standing are listed.

- **Visit franchise shows:** A number of franchise shows are held at various locations in Canada throughout the year, such as the National Franchise and Business Opportunities Show (www.franchiseshowinfor.com); the Franchise Show, which is organized by the Canadian Franchise Association (www.cfa.ca/events.html); and the Canadian Franchise and Investment Show (www.newbusinesscentre.com/shows.html).

- **Use a franchise advisor:** Some accounting firms, such as BDO Dunwoody, provide help in finding and evaluating potential franchises. You can also find business brokers who deal in the resale of existing franchises.

Evaluating the franchises you find

A franchise is a very expensive purchase. Many require an investment of at least $100,000. And when you buy a franchise, you're not just purchasing a product and walking away; you're entering into an ongoing relationship, somewhat like a partnership. So you should be confident that you want to go into business with the franchisor. Make a list of the franchises you find, and then investigate each of them thoroughly and carefully.

What information are you looking for?

You should know a number of things about a franchise opportunity before you buy. Form 9-1 on the CD-ROM also gives you this handy checklist of questions.

- **How does the franchisor make most if its money?** Beware of a franchisor that makes most of its money from the sale of new franchises, rather than from the profits of ongoing franchises. That's an indication that the franchisor is far more interested in selling franchises than in supporting its existing franchisees. A franchisor that is interested in the ongoing success of its franchisees will be as cautious about selling to you as you are about buying, and will want extensive information not only about your financial status, but about your personal and business background.

- **What is the franchisor's business record?** Is the franchisor well established and does it have a good business reputation? How successful is the franchisor? How successful are its franchisees?

- **How much will the franchise cost, and does the franchisor offer any financing?** Up-front costs include the franchise fee paid to the franchisor and the cost of setting up the franchise premises (construction or leasehold improvements, equipment, and initial inventory). There will also be ongoing fees such as royalties and contributions to the franchisor's advertising and marketing program. These costs are in addition to the usual ongoing costs of running the business. You may also have to pay a renewal fee at the end of the original term of your franchise agreement.

- **How much can you expect to earn?** What income will the franchise generate? And is the income enough to cover your ongoing expenses, including finances, and to provide you with a reasonable profit?

- **What is the term of the franchise agreement?** How long will your franchise rights last and is the term long enough for you to recoup your up-front investment?

✔ **Where will your franchise be located?** Will the franchisor choose your location or help you to choose? Will you be given an exclusive territory in which the franchisor agrees not to locate another franchisee? You want an exclusive territory that is large enough to protect you from competitors within the franchise, while at the same time small enough to provide wide exposure of the franchise name in your area. If your premises are leased, is the lease term at least as long as the term of the franchise agreement?

✔ **Will the franchisor train you?** Will you be given training before your franchise opens? What kind, and who pays for the training? Will you be given ongoing training and assistance once your franchise opens?

✔ **What rights do you have to sell the franchise?** Does the franchisor place unreasonable limits on your right to sell the franchise if you decide you want out?

Where can you find it?

You should get your information from several sources:

✔ **From the franchisor:** Ontario and Alberta have passed franchise legislation that requires a franchisor to give prospective franchisees a disclosure document containing, among other things, the business backgrounds of the franchise and its directors, audited financial statements and credit reports, and copies of all franchise agreements. If you live in another province, but the franchise operates in Ontario or Alberta, ask to see the disclosure document required in those provinces. Canadian Franchise Association member franchises agree to abide by a code of ethics that requires full and accurate written disclosure to prospective franchisees. Ask the franchisor to provide you with the names and contact information of existing franchisees, and of financial institutions and suppliers willing to act as references. Be very suspicious if the franchisor is less than forthcoming about any of the information you request.

✔ **From other franchisees:** Talk to several current and former franchisees either by telephone or in person. How much did they have to invest, and were there any hidden costs? How long have they been in business, and how long did it take for the business to make a profit? Did they receive adequate training and ongoing support? Has the franchisor lived up to its side of the agreement? Would they advise you to purchase a franchise?

✔ **From the Internet:** Search the franchise on Google and Yahoo, and see what turns up.

✔ **From the Better Business Bureau and trade associations:** Check to see if any complaints have been filed against the company or its products with the Better Business Bureau in your area and the area where the franchisor's head office is located. Find out the franchisor's reputation within any industry trade association and within the Canadian Franchise Association and/or the International Franchise Association.

Before you sign

Get advice from your accountant and your lawyer:

✔ Have your accountant review the franchisor's financial statements to see if they disclose any problems, and to tell you whether the financial projections are based on reasonable assumptions.

✔ Have your lawyer review the franchise agreement. At the very least, your lawyer should make sure that you understand the agreement fully. If appropriate, your lawyer should try to negotiate necessary changes to the agreement.

Well . . .

We told you that buying a business lets you eliminate a lot of the difficult, early work involved in building a business. Now you know that it gets replaced by the difficult, early work involved in buying a business. You also know now that although you can often start building your own business with a small amount of money, you'll need a reasonable amount of cash in hand to buy a business. So at the end of this chapter, you're probably still mulling over the question of a custom-made business versus an off-the-shelf business.

Chapter 10

The Money-Hunter's Guide to the Galaxy

In This Chapter

▶ Calculating how much money you need to set up your business

▶ Estimating how much first-year cash you need

▶ Forecasting your cash flow

▶ Sourcing financing for your business

▶ Looking at the risks of financing

*I*f you're hitchhiking around the galaxy, all you need is a small fish (to stick in your ear) and a good, thick towel. And maybe a guidebook. Frommer's has a very useful one.

But if you're starting a business, you need money. Maybe just a little bit, and maybe you already have it; maybe a lot and you're going to have to scout around for it. In any case, you need to know exactly how much money to hunt for, where to hunt for it, what you're going to have to do to bag it, and what it will cost you.

Your Business Needs Capital

You'll have to spend money to get your business to the point where it can begin operating. These are *start-up expenses* or *capital expenses*. In previous chapters we give you a hand in coming up with a list of the things you need to do and buy . . . and very few of them are free. You'll need money to

✔ Acquire or protect the right to use an idea in your business (see Chapter 3).

✔ Identify the nature of your business (see Chapter 4) — researching and developing your product, doing market research, and organizing initial promotional activities.

✔ Set up your business as a legal entity (see Chapter 5):

- And while we're hanging out at the lawyer's, you'll need money for any additional work your lawyer does for you, such as preparing standard documents for your business to use (see, for example, Chapters 13 and 14).

- Not to favour lawyers over accountants, you'll also need money for initial advice and assistance from an accountant about the form of your business and how best to structure it to keep accounting difficulties and taxes to a minimum (see Chapters 16 and 17).

✔ Buy equipment for your business (see Chapter 6).

✔ Locate your business in its own premises (see Chapter 7).

✔ Buy an existing business (see Chapter 9).

At the end of Chapter 6 we help you to create a table of your start-up expenses. There we focus on equipment.

In Table 10-1 below, we add up the cost of everything related to start-up. We also include this table on the CD-ROM for you to print out and fill in.

Table 10-1	Start-up Expenses for a Custom-built Business
Your Initial Capital (the money you've already got in your pocket for your business enterprise)	$
Licensing a product to manufacture or use or sell, or patenting your own invention (Chapter 3)	$
Researching and developing your product or service (Chapter 4)	$
Initial promotional activities (Chapter 4)	$
Legal and accounting fees for business set-up (Chapters 5, 16, and 17)	$
Purchase of equipment (Just put down the total figure you arrived at when you filled out the table in Chapter 6.)	$
Purchase price and legal fees if you buy property for your business premises (Chapter 7)	$
Leasehold improvements and legal fees to review the lease, if you rent business premises; or renovation costs if you set up a home office (Chapter 7)	$
Total New Capital (add up Initial Capital plus the costs you've listed)	$
Total Capital Required (subtract Initial Capital from Total New Capital): This is how much you need but don't have at the moment.	$

If you're buying a business instead of building your own, your table of start-up expenses will look like Table 10-2. (This table's on the CD-ROM, too.)

Table 10-2	Start-up Expenses If You Buy an Existing Business
Your Initial Capital (the money you've already got in your pocket to buy a business)	$
Purchase price of business	$
Professional fees (lawyer, accountant, broker, valuator, and so on) associated with the purchase	$
Total New Capital (add up Initial Capital plus the price of the business plus professional fees)	$
Total Capital Required (subtract Initial Capital from Total New Capital): This is how much you need but don't have at the moment.	$

Your Business Needs Operating Funds

Once you've figured out the capital requirements of your business, you're still not ready to carry on business . . . at least not for very long. You also have to work out how much money you'll need to run the business on a day-to-day basis (actually a month-to-month basis). These are called *operating expenses*. After your business is generating a steady income, your revenues will cover all or most of your operating expenses. But until then, you'll need to borrow money to pay for such things as:

- ✔ Salaries
- ✔ Lease or mortgage payments
- ✔ Utilities such as telephone, hydro, and water
- ✔ Insurance premiums
- ✔ Property taxes, if you own your business premises rather than rent them
- ✔ Ongoing professional fees (legal, accounting, advertising, publicity)
- ✔ Cost of running any vehicles

Projecting your expenses and revenues

For some of your operating expenses, you'll be able to write down a fairly accurate estimate from a supplier (such as a landlord or accountant or insurance agent). For others (such as utilities, and maybe salaries) you'll just have to guess.

After estimating your expenses, you have to estimate how much revenue you'll bring in to cover your expenses. This step will give you a better grasp of how much money you really need to borrow for monthly operations.

Projecting your expenses is easier than projecting your revenues. But you can make a guess at your revenues, by making some assumptions. The usual assumptions are

- ✔ The number of customers or clients you'll get
- ✔ The average amount of each sale or transaction

Multiply these two figures together to estimate sales. (Make a note to yourself about how you chose the figures you're using. You'll need to add that information as a footnote to your forecast of projected income and expenses.)

Preparing a forecast of income and expenses

The figures we discussed in the previous section get plugged into a forecast or projection of income and expenses. Take a look at Table 9-3, which is also on the CD-ROM.

Table 10-3	Forecast of Income and Expenses (For the First Year of Operation)	
Income		
Sales or revenues	$	
Other	$	
TOTAL INCOME	$	
Expenses		
Salaries		
	Owner	$
	Employee(s) (if any)	$
Lease payments	$	
Advertising	$	

Expenses		
Insurance	$	
Utilities (electricity, heat)		$
Telephone, fax, and Internet		$
Professional services		
Legal		$
Accounting		$
Vehicle operation and maintenance		$
Other	$	
TOTAL EXPENSES	**$**	
NET PROFIT (or **LOSS**) (deduct Total Expenses from Total Income)		$

After filling out this table you should have a reasonable idea of what your operating expenses will be for your first year of business, and whether you can expect that by the end of the year, your revenues will cover your expenses, or that you'll be in the hole (and how deep the hole is).

Projected cash flow

Knowing how much you need to operate your business isn't enough — you also have to know when you need the money. Income and expenses rarely match each other exactly, so you can't necessarily expect to be able to pay your expenses out of the income you're making. Your income may come in a lump once a year or a few times a year, whereas your expenses are likely to be fairly steady on a month-by-month basis. By preparing a cash flow statement, you'll know when you may need bridge financing to keep the business afloat. This is especially true during the first year or so of your business's existence, before income is steady or before you've been able to put by some profits to operate the business between infusions of income.

Many of your expenses won't change from month to month (lease or mortgage payments, for example), and others may be predictable even though they change during the course of the year (a snow removal contract during the winter months, or salaries for extra staff during a busy season). But if you had trouble estimating your total annual income, you'll have even more trouble estimating how it will come in month by month. Give it a shot, though, taking into consideration that your monthly income will probably increase over the course of the first year as your business gets established. Your business may have seasonal highs and lows, too. An accountant, for example, can probably expect a high just after income tax returns are filed and the bills go out for tax preparation; a business that sells cards and gifts can probably expect highs just before Christmas, Valentine's Day, and Mother's Day.

You'll find an example of a projected cash flow statement to use as a guide in the sample business plan, Appendix B. In Table 10-4 below, we didn't have room for all 12 months plus an annual total, so we've just used some representative months. (We highly recommend that when you prepare your cash flow statement, you fill in all 12 months. On the version of this form that's on the CD-ROM, every month is present and accounted for.)

Table 10-4	Projected Cash Flow Statement					
	Jan	Feb	March...	Nov	Dec	Year
INCOME:						
Cash sales						
Receivables						
TOTAL INCOME						
EXPENSES:						
Salaries						
Lease						
Advertising						
Insurance						
Utilities						
Telephone						
Professional						
TOTAL EXPENSES						
CASH FLOW:						

(Subtract monthly expenses from monthly income. If it comes out a negative number, put brackets around the number.)

CUMULATIVE CASH FLOW

(Move from left to right adding the previous month's cash flow to the following month. For January you will have the same number as for the January cash flow, but for February you will add the cash flow numbers for January and February together; for March you will add January, February, and March together, and so on. Again, put brackets around negative numbers.)

After filling out this table you'll have some idea of how many months of the first year you'll need a loan to pay your operating expenses (from the Cash Flow line), and at what point your revenues will start reducing your need for a loan (from the Cumulative Cash Flow line).

Locating Sources of Financing for a Start-Up Operation

Now you know, more or less, how much money you need to start up and run your business for the first year. You just don't know where you're going to find that money. Generations of businesspeople have wondered the same thing, so by now there's a standard list of sources of money. The sources include

- Personal assets
- Love money
- Borrowed money:
    - Credit card
    - Mortgage on home or vacation property
    - Commercial loans (capital and operating)
    - Micro-credit loans
- Credit:
    - Suppliers
    - Customers
- Sale of accounts receivable
- Grants and loans from government
- Investment from external sources:
    - Angel investor
    - Venture capital company

That's a respectable-looking list — somewhere among all these possibilities you should be able to find a buck or two.

The federal government site Strategis (www.strategis.gc.ca) maintains a Sources of Financing page that provides information about different types of financing and financial providers, a directory of Canadian financial providers, and a search tool that allows you to search for financing available in your province or territory. The easiest way to reach the Web page is to go to the Canada Business site (www.canadabusiness.gc.ca), and then click the link to Financing.

Mix-and-match financing

Most businesses need a combination of financing. For example, besides using personal assets and love money to get started,

✔ To get equipment, a business might need

   • A capital loan

   • A conditional sales agreement

   • A lease

✔ To get operating funds, a business might need

   • A line of credit

   • Payment in advance from customers and clients

   • Credit from suppliers

✔ To make leasehold improvements, a business might need a capital loan

So you'll likely be dealing with several sources of financing. That means you should read all of the following sections carefully.

Personal assets

Most entrepreneurs start off using at least some of their own money. Look around and see what money you have handy — or what property you could turn into cash — to finance your business start-up. Keep in mind that you still need money to live on while you're getting your business off the ground. You're not going to be a very effective CEO if you're starving or sleeping on the street.

Do you have

✔ Money in bank accounts.

✔ Bonds.

✔ Stocks — but if they've increased in value since you acquired them, you'll have to declare a capital gain on your next income tax return and could end up taking a tax hit (see Chapter 16 for more about capital gains).

✔ RRSPs — but remember that you'll have to add any amount you withdraw to your income for the year and could end up paying tax on it if you earn other income.

✔ Personal property or real property you can sell, such as vehicles, jewellery, collectibles, art, a vacation home . . . or even your real home. If property other than your real home (your principal residence) has increased in value since you acquired it, you'll have to declare a capital gain on your income tax return and may have to pay tax.

Love money

Whatever you may be thinking "love money" means, in fact it means money you can con out of your family and friends. They may be willing to lend it to you, or they may be willing to give it to you flat out. Think very carefully, however, before asking relatives and friends for money. If your business tanks and you can't repay them, they'll probably stop speaking to you. Then you'll have not only no business, but also no one to give you any sympathy either.

If you do go ahead, make a formal arrangement with the lenders, for two reasons — first, so that they can get something back if you're successful or if you go bust (a document will provide the evidence they need to make a claim against your business as a creditor); and second, so that they can't demand their money back just when you desperately need it. If the money or property is a gift, the giver should sign a document stating that the money or property is a gift and is yours absolutely to do with what you like. If the money is a loan, you should have a contract (a promissory note) with the lender setting out

✔ The amount of the loan.

✔ The rate of interest payable on the loan (if any).

✔ The amount of each payment and the dates they will be made (for example, a schedule of payments).

✔ The nature of the security, if any, the lender wants for the loan (something the lender can take in exchange if the loan isn't repaid). Security could include a mortgage against your home, or the taking of shares in your corporation, or a promise from someone else associated with you or the business that he or she will repay the loan if you don't (this is a guarantee).

Money borrowed from commercial lenders

Commercial lenders are banks, trust companies, credit unions, caisses populaires, finance companies, and insurance companies. They've got lots of money . . . if you can just get your hands on it.

Many commercial lenders can also help you get access to funds from the Business Development Bank of Canada (visit their Web site at www.bdc.ca for more information about their lending activities) and from the federal government's Canada Small Business Financing (CSBF) program. Most small businesses starting up or operating in Canada are eligible for CSBF loans, as long as their estimated annual gross revenues do not exceed $5 million during the fiscal year in which they apply for a loan. In 2002, Industry Canada started a five-year CSBF Capital Leasing Pilot Project that finances capital leases for the cost of various types of new and used business equipment. For more information about CSBF loans and leases, go to the Canada Small Business Financing Web site (part of the Strategis Web site) at strategis.ic.gc.ca/epic/ internet/incsbfp-pfpec.nsf/en/h_la00000e.html, or go to the Royal Bank Web site (www.royalbank.com) and follow the links to business banking and financing options.

Credit cards

If you need to borrow from a bank, your first thought may be to use your credit cards. It's easy — no application forms to fill out, no waiting, no business plan to prepare, no intimidating interview with a bank manager. You may even have a high enough limit on your card(s) to get as much money as you need.

Don't do it! The interest rate on credit cards is astronomical compared to the interest rate you'll pay if you borrow in a more business-like fashion — probably at least double and maybe triple. We have better suggestions here.

Mortgage on your home or vacation property

If you own real property and it isn't already mortgaged to the hilt, you can borrow against that property by taking out a mortgage. If you're thinking of mortgaging property, consider these factors:

- **What's the property worth?** Will mortgaging it get you as much money as you need? You probably won't be able to borrow its full unmortgaged value.

- **Is the property already mortgaged?** If it is, there may not be enough equity (unmortgaged value) in the property for you to get as big a loan as you need.

- **Do you need someone else's legal consent to mortgage the property?** You do if you have a co-owner. Even if you're the only owner, if you're married, in most provinces your spouse will have to give consent to the transaction before you'll get any money (sometimes even if it's not your family home that you're borrowing against).

- **Can you afford to lose the property if your business fails?** If you default on your loan (don't pay it back on time), the lender has the right to take the property — and either keep it or sell it to cover your unpaid loan. (If it's sold, you'll get the excess over the outstanding amount of the loan plus legal fees.)

Business loans

If you're borrowing because you need money to purchase capital assets for your business, you'll apply for a *capital loan*. If you're borrowing because you need money to cover the ongoing costs of running your business, you'll apply for an *operating loan*. You can go looking for either kind of loan from a commercial lender. But choose a branch that regularly handles small business clients, if you can find one — if the branch staff are only used to making deposits and withdrawals, they won't know what to do with you . . . and the easiest thing will be to show you the door.

Banks, most credit unions, and many trust, loan, and insurance companies can make a loan under the Canada Small Business Financing (CSBF) program for capital expenses including the purchase or improvement of real property, leasehold improvements and the purchase or improvement of equipment. The federal government partially guarantees CSBF loans, so lenders are more willing to lend, and owners don't have to provide personal assets as security (see the heading "Non repayment of the loan," a bit later).

The chances are good that at some point you'll want a business loan, so now we tell you about loans in detail.

Principal and interest

The amount of money the lender gives is called the *principal* or *principal amount* of the loan. The amount the borrower pays for the use of the money is called *interest*. (You're not going to find an interest-free loan if you deal with anyone other than your mother.) Interest is calculated as a percentage of the principal. If you're charged *simple interest* on the loan, you pay interest only on the principal you've borrowed. So if you borrowed $100,000 at 10 percent, you'd owe $10,000 in interest per year.

But commercial lenders charge *compound interest* on a loan if the terms of repayment stretch past the time the interest is actually due. Compound interest is interest on the principal and on the interest owing. When you're charged compound interest, you end up with a higher interest rate (the *effective interest rate*) than the rate you're quoted (the *nominal interest rate*). And the more often the interest is *compounded* or *calculated*, the higher the real interest rate.

Interest can be compounded on any basis the lender chooses — daily, weekly, monthly, semi-annually, or annually. If you borrowed $100,000 at 10 percent compounded monthly, your real interest rate would actually be 10.47 percent. And in commercial loans, unlike consumer loans, the lender doesn't have to tell the borrower the total amount of interest payable over the life of the loan (the cost of borrowing).

Repayment of the loan

You'll likely take out either a *term loan* or a *line of credit*. Capital loans are usually term loans. Operating loans usually come in the form of a line of credit. If you have a term loan, the lender sets a schedule for regular repayment of principal and interest.

If you have a line of credit, also known as *overdraft protection*, the lender (which is normally your bank) tops up your business account if you don't have enough in the account to cover a cheque. Then when you make a deposit to your business account, the money is automatically applied to pay down the loan. You may also be required to make regular payments or make a deposit to the account within a fixed period of time to cover the overdraft.

A line of credit is usually a demand loan, which means that the lender can demand payment in full at any time, not just after you've missed a payment. However, if you make your payments on time, demand will not be made — unless you do something to lead the lender to believe that your business is in trouble. The lender also usually requires you to sign blank promissory notes, which it fills in as the line of credit goes up. The promissory note provides evidence of what you owe, and the lender can also sue you on the note if you don't pay the loan.

Non-repayment of the loan

Lenders don't take it for granted that borrowers will pay up on schedule — or ever. They know they could sue the borrower for failing to pay, but they also know that suing someone is expensive and time-consuming, and even if they win the lawsuit it's often difficult to collect the money. So to make life easier for themselves, lenders usually require borrowers to give security or collateral. When a borrower gives security, he legally gives the lender the right to take specified property from the borrower if the borrower doesn't make his payments. The lender usually sells the property to pay off the loan. Typically, lenders take security on such property as

- ✔ **Real estate** — security will take the form of a *collateral mortgage* or *charge* or, in Quebec, a *hypothec*

- ✔ **Equipment and other non-land assets** — security may take the form of a *chattel mortgage*, known in some provinces as a *specific security agreement*

- ✔ **Accounts receivable, also known as *book debts*, which is money that customers or clients owe the borrower** — security can take the form of an *assignment of accounts receivable*, which gives the lender the right to collect debts owing to you if you default on your loan

- ✔ **Inventory** — the lender may be able to take security under *s. 427* of the federal *Bank Act* if you are borrowing from a chartered bank

If you have a capital loan, the lender will probably want security over the capital property (real estate or equipment) you're buying. If you have a line of credit or overdraft protection, the lender may want security over your business's accounts receivable and inventory.

Other forms of security that a lender might ask for include

- ✔ **A general security agreement:** This gives a lender security over almost all of the borrower's existing and future assets (usually excluding real property, but including equipment, vehicles, machinery, inventory, accounts receivable).

- ✔ **A debenture:** This is much like a general security agreement, except that only a corporation can give a debenture as security for a loan, and a debenture usually includes real property as well as other assets.

- ✔ **A pledge of shares (or of bonds or debentures) that are the personal property of the borrower or a guarantor:** For example, if the borrower is a corporation, the lender may want a pledge of shares of the corporation from the shareholders who have guaranteed the loan. Then, if the borrower does not repay the loan, the lender can take control of the corporation.

And lenders don't always stop at taking security. Sometimes they want (instead of or in addition to security) a *guarantee*. A guarantee is a promise by someone other than the borrower that if the borrower doesn't pay up, the *guarantor* (the person or business giving the guarantee) will repay the loan. For example, if the borrower is a corporation — especially a corporation that doesn't have much in the way of assets — the lender might ask for a guarantee from the individuals associated with the corporation, such as the shareholders or the directors. A bank can also ask for security from the guarantor, such as a *collateral mortgage* on the guarantor's home.

If the borrower does not meet the lender's criteria to receive a loan, the lender may be willing to go ahead with the loan if someone who *does* meet the criteria agrees to *co sign* the loan. Unlike a guarantor, a *co-signor* can be required to repay the loan even if the borrower is capable of repaying the loan himself.

Micro-credit funds

Micro-credit is a small loan (under $25,000, often only a few thousand dollars), available to individuals with a low income, to help them start up a very small business. (They're often targeted toward young people, or women, or new immigrants, or people with disabilities; and/or they may be targeted toward a restricted geographical area.) They can be used for capital investment or operating funds. They often offer, besides money, business courses and networking opportunities. Micro-credit may be made available by an independent operation, as part of an integrated community economic development program, or by a micro-finance program of a commercial lender.

For more information about micro-credit and especially where to find some, go to the Strategis Sources of Financing Web page (www.strategis.gc.ca) and click on <u>Micro-Credit</u>.

Credit from suppliers and clients

Maybe you didn't realize you could put your customers and suppliers to work for you as lenders.

Suppliers

If you're buying equipment or machinery, you may be able to finance the purchase through a loan from the vendor, a conditional sales agreement, or a lease. (See Chapter 6 for more about equipment, and Chapter 14 for more about suppliers.) The vendor will probably want a down payment and security (for example, a chattel mortgage if the vendor is loaning you the money), and will want to be repaid on a regular schedule, as would a commercial lender.

If you're buying inventory or supplies, you may be able to get financing through a credit arrangement. Suppliers may offer 30, 60, or 90 days to pay, with a discount if payment is made within a shorter time. (Two problems here: first, because you're a start-up without a credit history, suppliers might not want to extend credit and might instead want cash on delivery from you; and second, the effective interest rate you pay on the money you're "borrowing" by not taking the discount is high — in the range of 20 to 30 percent or more.) Suppliers might also sometimes offer a loan, or else a sale on consignment (you don't pay the supplier until a customer purchases a consigned item). If you buy inventory on credit, the supplier may want to take security in the form of a *purchase money security interest.*

Customers

You may well be able to get your clients or customers to finance the work you do for them by getting them to pay a deposit or *retainer* (that's what professionals call a deposit) and/or instalment payments as you do the work (instead of waiting to be paid when everything's finished). See Chapter 13 for more about dealing with customers.

Sale of accounts receivable

You can sell your recent accounts receivable at a discount for instant cash. This is called *factoring* and it's more expensive than borrowing — it can be a lot more expensive — but you don't have to show that your business has revenue and you don't have to put up security. The factor pays you a percentage of the value of your receivables immediately, collects the receivables, deducts fees and sends you the balance. (Depending on your arrangement with the factor, your customers needn't know they're dealing with a factor instead of with your business.)

The initial percentage you get from the factor will depend on things like the value of the receivables, number of customers and credit-worthiness of the customers — it can run anywhere from about 90 percent down to 30 percent. In "recourse" factoring, the factor can look to you to cover any bad debts, while in "non-recourse" factoring (which is, naturally, more expensive) bad debts are the factor's problem. Factoring is available from factoring companies, finance companies and some banks. It's traditionally used in the apparel, textile, carpet, and furniture industries, but it's not restricted to those industries.

Government loans and grants

You too may be able to snarf up some money from the public trough to start and run your business! You can find lots of government assistance programs — to browse, go to the Strategis Sources of Financing page (www.strategis. gc.ca) and click on Government Assistance. You can also search for government business financing available in your province. For example, you might be able to get some repayable or even non-repayable money from:

- ✔ Human Resources and Skills Development Canada, if you need to hire or train an employee

- ✔ The Industrial Research Assistance Program (IRAP) of the National Research Council, if you need to research and develop a new technological product or service

- ✔ Canada Council for the Arts, if your business involves artistic creation (like writing, painting, music, performance)

- ✔ Industry Canada, for various initiatives

Arm's-length investment

For some businesses, a start-up loan isn't much use. If you take out a loan, you have to pay it back — usually beginning right away — and your business, even though it has fantastic prospects over the next few years, won't be able to generate cash revenues for some time *and* it needs a cash infusion (perhaps a big one) to get started at all.

So maybe what you need is seed *financing* or *seed capital* from an investor such as an *angel* or a *venture capital firm*, rather than a loan from a lender.

Seed capital provides money for such things as:

- ✔ Proving that an idea or invention actually works in practice as well as it does in theory *(proof of concept)*

- ✔ Protecting intellectual property (usually through a patent — see Chapter 3)

- ✔ Completing a prototype *(working model)* of a product or invention

- ✔ Doing market research

- ✔ Creating strategic partnerships with other businesses or with potential customers

- ✔ Hiring experienced managers for the business

- ✔ Creating a business plan

- ✔ Hunting down even more capital that's required to start the business operating

The great majority of start-up businesses don't need seed capital for these kinds of things. And even start-ups that do aren't that likely to get outside investment in the business. Most requests for investment get rejected either because the business has limited financial prospects or because the managers of the business don't have the necessary skills to run the business successfully. But we'll go on and tell you about outside investors anyway.

Angel investors

If you go around talking about angel investors, chances are most people will think you've been out in the sun too long. You'll get the same kind of reaction as if you mentioned that aliens are broadcasting messages to you through the fillings in your teeth.

Angel investors actually do exist, however. They are individuals, often successful businesspeople, who want to invest their own money in promising new businesses, usually in the same field the angel comes from (many or most come from a high-technology background), and usually in businesses in their own geographic area.

What angels offer

Angels usually invest an amount in the range of $10,000 to $150,000, although some may go as high as $500,000 or more if they've got the money and they like the business's prospects. Besides providing money, angel investors also take an interest in the running of the business. Because they're experienced, they may be able to help you find customers and sell your product, put you in touch with suppliers and professional advisors, and prepare you and your business to hunt for the next round of financing.

What angels are looking for

Angels are looking for a good return on their investment in your business — typically 30 percent compound annual returns. Not many business owners even plan for their business to grow that aggressively, much less are capable of making it happen. Angels are also looking for *equity* in (a share in the value of) your business and the right to be involved in major decisions and to get frequent status reports.

Where to find an angel

Heaven? Sure, but maybe closer than that. Network in your own business community and ask around about angel investors. Ask your lawyer or accountant. Some business incubators help to connect client companies with angel investors. Or you can try the National Angel Organization (www.angel investor.ca). Finding one at all is a matter of luck, and if you do find an angel, he or she won't necessarily be interested in investing in your kind of business. Learn as much as you can about an angel before approaching him or her, and customize your pitch to match the angel's interests.

Venture capital

Venture capital is money that's available for risky investments with a good chance of getting a high return on the investment. Over $10 billion in venture capital is floating around in the Canadian economy at the moment, and in the past few years venture capitalists have poured well over $1 billion per year into businesses. However, that doesn't mean that you'll be able to get any of it. Venture capitalists are ridiculously fussy about whom they give their money to.

What kind of business opportunities is a VC looking for?

Venture capitalists are typically looking for three things:

- ✔ **A large market opportunity** — one that will provide very high returns within a fairly short time, about five to seven years (the majority of investments are made in technology)
- ✔ **Good managers** — or at least one good and committed manager who will be able to recruit a strong management team
- ✔ **A strategic plan about building the business** — one that includes a lucrative exit strategy (see "What a VC wants in return") for the venture capitalists

What a VC can offer

Like angel investors, venture capitalists offer money, management expertise, and connections — to other money, to professional advisors like lawyers and accountants, and to suppliers and potential customers.

What a VC wants in return

To put this section in perspective, we'll tell you that venture capitalists are also known, affectionately of course, as vulture capitalists. What they usually want is

- At least a 25 percent return on investment; and they're really thrilled at the prospect of getting a 300 to 500 percent return (a *home run*)

- Significant ownership of the business — usually 20 percent or more of the business's equity, plus their own pet director(s) on the board of directors

- A lucrative exit strategy within five to seven years. Exit strategies include the following:

  - An *initial public offering* (IPO — see Chapter 19)

  - Sale of the business to another corporation (see Chapter 20)

  - A company buy-back (the business or business owners buy back the VC's share of the corporation)

  - A write-off of the investment (as lost money) . . . although clearly this is not "lucrative"

Where to find a VC

Venture capital firms, unlike angels, are very easy to find. You can get a list of them by going to the Canadian Venture Capital Association Web site (www.cvca.ca), and from there you can link to the home Web site of each association member. You'll be able to get contact information, as well as some information about the interests and expectations of each member, from their Web site. Finding them, of course, does not necessarily mean getting money from them.

Applying for Money

Be aware that before you approach a commercial lender, a government granting agency, an angel investor, or a venture capital firm (and maybe even members of your family whom you're tapping for love money), you'll have to show what you plan to do with any money you get, and why you should be trusted with it. The more money you want, the more work you'll have to do when you apply for it. The most work you'll be asked to do is prepare a business plan. But for a loan that's not too large (say, under $35,000 to $50,000), you'll probably just be asked to fill out an application form provided by the lender. For much more about the application process, see Chapter 11.

Chapter 11

So Long and Thanks for All the Cash

In This Chapter

▶ Getting money from a commercial lender

▶ Finding out what's required — an application or a full business plan

▶ Getting help to write a business plan

▶ Learning (at tedious length) what goes into a business plan

Sometimes preparing an application to get money involves filling out a form created by the lender, and sometimes it involves preparing a business plan. Most of this chapter focuses on a formal business plan because it's a lot more difficult to prepare a business plan than to fill out an application form.

Preparing a business plan is usually looked upon as a thoroughly intimidating activity, so we wanted to give this chapter a comforting title. We could have called the chapter "DON'T PANIC!", but that might have tipped you off, and you would have bypassed the chapter completely.

Don't Panic!

All business books contain a chapter on writing a business plan. It's required. You can't get a licence to publish a business book unless you include a chapter on business plans.

However, to get you off on the right foot, we're going to start by telling you why you shouldn't panic at the thought of having to read the chapter — or of having to prepare a business plan.

First reason not to panic

You don't always have to prepare a formal business plan to get money. When you're looking for money, the first thing you should do (after identifying a source of money) is contact the source and find out what documentation they want in order to consider your request. Especially for smaller amounts of money (say, under $35,000 to $50,000), the source may want only a limited amount of information about your business. (See the heading "An Application Form.") Or the source may not need a full-strength business plan and instead be willing to settle for a mini business plan (see the section "A mini business plan").

Second reason not to panic

Most business books put the business plan chapter almost at the very beginning, where it's especially unnerving. Who knows how many people have decided not to go into business because they couldn't face writing a business plan as the first step in starting a business? And nobody's able to put together a description of their business and an analysis of the marketplace, and financial statements, before they've even thought about their product or service, their business organization, what equipment they'll need, where they'll be located, and what sources of funding are available to them.

We put our business plan way in the middle for a reason. By the time you get here, you've done a lot of the work needed to create a business plan — and you didn't even know you were doing it. Besides that, after going through Chapter 10 you're much more motivated to work to get some money.

Third reason not to panic

Here's yet another reason not to panic: Even if you have to prepare a business plan, you don't have to prepare the business plan on your own. For one thing, you can purchase business plan software, such as Business Plan Pro, or download free business plan software from CNET Download.com (www.download.com). For another, if you don't feel like doing this all by yourself — just you and the software — you can go to your accountant. Your accountant should be able to put together at least the financials for your business plan after talking to you for a couple of hours about your business and what you're planning to do with it.

There are also consultants who can write a business plan for you. (You can expect to drop several thousand dollars on a consultant.) It would probably be best to use a consultant who works in the field of your business rather than one who simply specializes in writing business plans.

You can find consultants (you can find consultants galore, most likely) by asking around among your business acquaintances, or approaching your provincial Canada Business Service Centre (CBSC) or a municipal or regional economic development office for their help or their suggestions about whom to contact. You can also get in touch with a university business school — MBA students run assistance programs and for a modest fee will work with you on a business plan.

First Step

Before you write down a word or add up two numbers, contact the source of financing you're interested in. Tell them how much you want to borrow and in what form, and then ask about the application process. If they say you just have to fill out a form, get the form. If they say you have to prepare a business plan, ask if they have any guidelines or forms to show what they want to see in the business plan. If they don't, you have to do it yourself — but in this chapter, we offer a lot of help about the form and content of a business plan.

Filling Out an Application Form

You may only need to fill out quite a short, simple application form to apply for the money you need. Typically, an application form will ask you to give information about how much money you want and what you're planning to use it for, and also about

- ✔ The business's primary financial institution (it might or might not be the institution you're requesting the loan from)
- ✔ The name, trade name, and address of your business
- ✔ The form of your business (sole proprietorship, partnership or, corporation — see Chapter 5)
- ✔ The nature of your business
- ✔ The length of time the business has been established, and the number of employees it has
- ✔ The financial problems and setbacks your business has experienced (if any), such as claims from creditors and lawsuits, and whether the business has ever been in receivership or declared bankruptcy

The application form will also ask for a summary of financial information about your business, including

- ✔ Total gross annual sales or revenues for the preceding fiscal year (if you've been in business for more than a year) or as projected for the year ahead (if you're a start-up)

- ✔ Net after-tax profit or loss (for the preceding fiscal year if you've been in business for more than a year, or as projected for the year ahead if you're a start-up)

Be prepared to provide the financial statements themselves. For information about preparing financial statements, see Chapter 17.

Finally, the application form will ask for information about the owner(s) of the business, including

- ✔ Names and addresses

- ✔ Income in the preceding year (as reported on the owner's tax return)

- ✔ A list of each owner's assets and debts (Later, in the "Preparing a Business Plan" section, we have a personal balance sheet that will show you the kind of information the lender has in mind.)

For a start-up business, the decision whether to lend will be based as much on the owner's personal financial status as on the business's, because start-up businesses normally don't have much in the way of assets.

If the owner has no assets, the lender will be very reluctant to lend the business any money. Probably the best indicator of whether you'll get the loan is if you own a home (one that's not 100 percent mortgaged already). The lender will feel much more comfortable giving you money if it can take back a mortgage as security. (See Chapter 10 for more about security for a loan.)

Preparing a Business Plan

Sometimes there's no other way . . . if you want money you'll have to prepare a business plan to submit to the lender.

A business plan sets out how much money you want and what you're going to do with it, describes your business, places it within the context of the industry it belongs to, examines the marketplace and competition and sets out a strategy for competing in the marketplace, and provides detailed financial information about your business.

A lender or investor looks at a business plan to see whether it's safe to put money into your business. If your business is well thought out, it's more likely to be successful, generate a profit, and be able to repay the lender or investor.

When you show someone a business plan, you're revealing a lot of important information (important to you, at least) about your business. If you want to impress on the potential lender or investor that this information shouldn't be broadcasted around the solar system, you may want to ask the lender or investor to sign a Confidential Disclosure Agreement before looking at the business plan. You'll find a sample of this document on the CD-ROM.

Checking Out What Goes into a Business Plan

Books and even chapters about business plans are often incredibly detailed and seem to be written for existing businesses that are looking for huge amounts of money to expand. They're intimidating, and by the time you get to the end of the book or chapter you feel like there's no point in writing a business plan because you don't have an MBA and you don't understand the marketing and accounting jargon.

Don't twist yourself into knots about writing a business plan. Although almost every book or article you read about creating a business plan will tell you a somewhat different way to set the plan up, all business plans contain, in the long run, the same — quite understandable — information.

We've also included a sample business plan on the CD-ROM.

A full-scale business plan

If a lender is looking for the whole shebang, business-plan-wise, here's the information required:

- ✔ The amount of money you want from the person who's reading the business plan and what you're going to do with it.
- ✔ A description of what your business does, and a description of the industry your business is part of.

✔ An explanation about why your business can compete successfully, and your strategy for competing (that is, for marketing your product or service).

✔ A description of how your business runs or will run on a day-to-day basis, including information about the business's managers.

✔ The financial information about your business, including projections about income and expenses (as a start-up you won't have much in the way of a financial history), and also about your personal financial status — so the lender or investor can decide whether it's safe to invest. A lender or investor will expect to be paid back out of profits of the business or (if the business doesn't generate enough profits) out of the sale of what the business owns . . . and/or what you own.

Below — actually, for the whole rest of the chapter — we go through these sections at much greater length.

A mini business plan

If the lender doesn't want to know every last detail about your business (and who can say whether the lenders who do want to know every detail actually read the business plan from cover to cover?), you need to prepare only a short version. A mini business plan would cover any given topic more briefly, and it might include only:

✔ The amount of money you want from the lender and what you'll do with it

✔ The name and address of the business, form of business, and how long it's been established

✔ The nature of your business, and what its goals are

✔ A basic analysis of your market and competition

✔ The financial statements

Stating How Much You Want (Your Objective)

You should say right up front how much money you want and what you're going to do with it. You should also say right up front how this money will increase the profits or value of the business so that the loan can be repaid or the investment can provide a return.

No, it's not rude or pushy to start by saying what you want. You'll save your potential lender or investor time and annoyance. No one with money wants to plod through pages of information without knowing beforehand why they're plodding. They'll want to assess what you want against what you have — and against what they have to offer — from the very beginning of your plan.

Describing Your Business

Next the plan describes your business, and how your business fits into the larger industry it's part of.

Your product or service

Start with what your business does — what product it manufactures or sells or what service it provides.

For example, if you're firing up a bakery operation, you'll describe the baked goods you're going to produce and your potential customers. If you're setting up a bookkeeping practice, you'll describe the services you plan to offer and to whom.

If your business has an intellectual property component — for example, if you're

- ✔ Manufacturing a product that's patented or whose design is registered as an industrial design
- ✔ Distributing or selling a product under a licence agreement or marketing a product under a trademark

then your plan should describe the status of protection of the product or service. For instance, if your product or method is patented, say so and mention its patent number, or if a patent has been applied for, say that a patent application is pending; if you're distributing a patented product, talk briefly about the licence agreement you have. For more about intellectual property and its protection, see Chapter 3.

For a business that needs money to start manufacturing a product, you should be prepared to show a potential lender or investor working drawings and designs of the product.

The goals of your business

While your immediate goal is to get your business set up, you presumably also have other goals on the way to success. An investor would like to know where you're headed. So your plan should outline

- ✔ Your short-term goals
- ✔ Your long-term plans

In the case of the bakery, for example, your short-term goal might be to produce ten dozen loaves of bread per day within a month of starting the operation and distribute them through five local independent food stores. A longer-term goal might be to produce 100 dozen loaves per day and distribute them through a grocery chain with stores around your city. Your ultimate goal (for the moment) might be to expand your baking operation to the point that it supplies bread for the grocery chain throughout the province; or it might be to franchise your bakery and sell franchises across the country.

If you think your business might attract a lot of interest from the world at large (and not just from your doting family and satisfied customers) and will need a large amount of invested money to expand and function properly, your long-term goal might be to become a publicly traded company. Publicly traded companies are able to raise money by offering their shares to the public through a stock exchange. For more about going public, see Chapter 19.

If you think your business is likely to be of great interest to one or more large corporations in the industry, and that a large corporation would show its interest via a nice fat offer to buy you out, your long-term goal might be to sell your business to a larger business. For more about selling out, see Chapter 20.

Your business within the industry

Your business won't be operating in isolation. Even if you haven't thought about it that way, it's part of some fairly large-scale industry. Your bakery is part of the baked goods industry, your bookkeeping practice is in a small corner of the accounting industry, your computer program for hunting down certain kinds of information on the Internet is part of the computer software industry. The lender or investor you approach may not know much about the industry at all and will need background information to make a decision.

So you need to write a short profile of the industry. To do this you'll have to conduct some research by contacting industry associations, or reading industry publications, or searching for newspaper and magazine articles, or going through Statistics Canada data. Chapter 2 can give you some ideas about doing your research.

Here are some of the things you should think about including in your profile:

✔ **The size of businesses in the industry:** Some businesses are mainly made up of large multinational corporations, like the pharmaceutical industry; some are mainly made up of national corporations, like the Canadian banking industry . . . although you're probably not thinking of starting up a bank; others may have a mix of large and small businesses, like the legal and accounting industries; and some mostly consist of small businesses, like the personal services industry.

✔ **The total volume of sales in the industry and the total value of sales:** You're just going to have a small piece of the pie to start with, but it's good to show that the pie is nice and big.

✔ **Any legislation, regulations, and standards that apply to the industry's products or services:** For example, the manufacture of food and drugs is heavily regulated by the federal government; travel agencies are regulated by provincial governments; cafés are regulated and inspected by municipal governments.

✔ **Trends in the industry:** It might be growing, or shrinking, or shifting its focus from certain products or services to others; or it might be facing stricter government regulation, or it might be about to be deregulated.

✔ **The main challenges and problems the industry faces:** Is it being forced to compete globally instead of nationally? Is it losing customers because it isn't meeting changing customer needs? Has it priced its goods or services out of the larger marketplace? Is it sluggish because it hasn't upgraded old infrastructure?

✔ **The future of the industry:** Will it stay much as it is but expand — or contract? Will it change significantly in response to consumer demand or new legislation?

By the way, don't make this stuff up. Making it up is easier and more fun, true, but it's a bad move. It will make you look light-minded and untrustworthy if anyone finds out.

And since you're not making it up, you should footnote facts and opinions that you state to show their source. If a lender or investor wants more information about the industry, he, she, or it should be able to locate your references.

Once you've finished your industry profile, you have to discuss how your business fits into the industry. Are you going to create a product that will revolutionize the industry . . . or even make it obsolete? Are you going to take advantage of a gap and expand your business to become a major player? Are you going to quietly but competently fill a little niche? How will industry trends affect your business's chance of success? How will your business meet the industry's challenges? How will your business fit into the industry's future that you've projected? This section is going to give you quite a mental workout! But preparing it will make you reflect on a lot of points that are important to your business success.

Why your business can compete successfully

After you've described your business world, you have to show that you can survive in it by competing successfully. In trying to figure out how well you'll be able to compete, you have to consider both the market for your product or your service, and your competition in the marketplace. In Chapter 4, we take you through the process of developing a product or service and researching its market and its competition.

Your market

You need to know a reasonable amount about the market for your product or service so that you'll be able to

- ✔ Identify your target market for the product or service.
- ✔ Identify your portion of the total target market (it's probably not going to be the total market, at least not to begin with).
- ✔ Identify marketing strategies (covering things such as prices, distribution, and business promotion).

Your target market

You can determine your target market in different ways. One is geography. Your target market may be the people (or businesses) within a geographic area. For example, if you run a retail business, you may see your target market as the people who live within walking distance or a short driving distance of your store. If you're distributing a product, you may have a distribution agreement with the manufacturer that allows you to distribute the product within your province or within a region (for example, the Atlantic provinces, or the Vancouver area, or specified towns in northern Ontario). If you're the sole manufacturer of a product that's in demand (say, a hula-hoop during a hula-hoop craze) your geographic market might be the entire country or the entire continent.

Another way of determining your target market is by the characteristics of your customers or clients — for example, sex, age, interests or needs and/or income level if your customers or clients are individuals; kind of business and/or annual sales if your customers are other businesses.

Your share of the target market

Besides figuring out who or what your target market is, you have to try to estimate what share of the target market your competitors hold and what share you can capture. This is guesswork unless you've got very few competitors. As an example, if you open a convenience store in a residential area where no other stores are located, you've got a good chance of getting a very big share of the target market (which is the inhabitants of the residential area). But — to take an example from the opposite end of the spectrum — if you're planning to sell T-shirts over the Internet (a huge total market), you may never be able to estimate your market share or a competitor's with anything approaching accuracy because many businesses are competing in a fickle market.

If you're looking for a large sum of money, it would be worth your while to have a professional marketing study done to examine in detail the size of the market, the existing competitors in the market, and the market share your business might expect to capture.

Marketing strategy

When it comes to identifying a marketing strategy, there are lots of details to take into account. They include

- ✓ **Your planned method(s) of selling and/or distributing your product or service:** Are you going to sell direct to the end user, or are you going to go through a third party (such as a manufacturer's agent or a distributor or a retailer, if you're a manufacturer)? If you already have contracts or partnerships with individuals or businesses or governments who are going to buy or distribute your product or service, mention them here.

- ✓ **Your location (if it has an impact on marketing):** Your location is important if, for example, you're a retail store or service relying on walk-in customers, or if you provide a product that can be shipped only short distances to customers, or if you need to project an image to customers that can be achieved in only a certain area. It's not particularly important if you provide a service or product without needing face-to-face contact with your customers or clients — for example, if you run a call-centre operation. Then it's fine to be in an industrial plaza in the middle of nowhere . . . as long as you can get workers to go there.

✔ **Your strategy for promoting the product:** This covers things like

- **Your business image:** How are you going to present your business? Are you going to package it around a logo or trademark? Are you going to build it around a concept (such as one-stop errand running if you're starting up a rent-a-wife business) or a special product? Are you going to promote it as an essential for your target market (such as a business-district spa for businesswomen)?

- **Your advertising message:** What's your message, and your method and budget for getting the message out? Methods might include TV and radio spots, newspaper ads, billboards and signs, flyers distributed around neighbourhoods or to local businesses — or even just word of mouth. The method should be appropriate to the target market and to the image you want your business to project.

- **Your public relations plan, if any:** Do you have a plan for approaching the media (in the hope that they'll write about you or interview you on TV news or a business program or a lifestyle show) and organizing events to attract media and/or customer attention? Media approaches might include press releases, contacts with acquaintances or friends-of-friends, or cold calls.

- **Your sales strategy:** How are you going to set your basic price? (Generally speaking, it should be high enough to cover your costs of providing the product or service and earn you a profit, and low enough that your competitors are not underpricing you. See Chapter 4 for more about pricing your product or service.) What other pricing procedures are you going to use to attract customers and clients? (Possibilities include gifts, coupons or two-for-one offers; special sales to groups; or special rates for large purchases of your product or time.)

- **Finding and keeping customers:** What's your plan for coming up with leads to find new customers and clients? (Tried-and-true methods include advertisements, arranging for other individuals and businesses to refer clients to you, buying customer lists.) Are you going to make presentations to prospective clients or customers? (What will the content of the presentation be, and how will you jazz it up to give it impact?) How are you going to satisfy the customers you do get? (Think about a returns policy, guarantees, and product service provided on the premises.)

Your competitors

You need to know your market, but you also need to know your competitors. If you can't beat them at their own game, that will be the end of you.

In this part of your business plan you'll

- ✔ **Fearlessly name your competitors.** Remember, though, you're talking about your competitors in your target market and not all the competitors in the total market. If you're starting a dog-walking business, your competitors aren't every personal-service provider in the province, or even every dog-walker in the city, just the dog-walkers in the neighbourhood you plan to service.

- ✔ **Describe the similar products or services available from the competitors.** What are the strong points about the competing products or services, and what are the weak points? What problems exist with the competition's product or services?

- ✔ **Explain why customers will buy the product or service from you instead of something similar from the competition.** Describe the strengths of your product or service.

Strong points of either the competitors' businesses or your business might include:

- ✔ Higher quality of services or product
- ✔ Innovative nature of the product or service (being the first to provide a product or service can give the provider a competitive edge — but keep in mind that the first provider isn't necessarily the best provider)
- ✔ Lower cost of services or product
- ✔ Better distribution system
- ✔ Better management
- ✔ Better customer service — efficient, fast, friendly
- ✔ Better service guarantees that accompany the product or service
- ✔ A more convenient location
- ✔ Established base of loyal customers or clients
- ✔ Loyalty of customers or clients to a particular brand
- ✔ Access to a client/customer base that hasn't been tapped yet

Weaknesses are the flip side of these matters — such as higher cost of the product, poorer quality of the service, less convenient location, and so on.

Don't overdo describing your competitors' strengths or your own weaknesses. You don't want to deep-six your business proposal by presenting the competition as unbeatable or you as a lost sheep among the coyotes. But you do want your potential investor to know that you've taken an objective look at the market and your chances of turning a good profit.

Explaining How Your Business Runs

Investors are amazingly curious about how you will run your business. Some even go so far as to say that they care less about the product or service the business provides than they do about who's in charge. Poor management can destroy even a great idea, while good management can nurture a less-than-fantastic idea along the path to success.

Business info and history

You're allowed to start with the easy stuff about your business:

- ✔ The address, telephone and fax numbers for the business, and the e-mail address
- ✔ A statement about the form of your business (sole proprietorship, partnership or corporation — see Chapter 5 for forms of business organization)
- ✔ A description or picture of any business logo, design, trademark, or trade name you're using
- ✔ A brief history of the business, including the date of business start-up

Business managers

Then you get down to the nitty-gritty: Who's running this show? Here you list key people (it may be a short list) and their titles, if any:

- ✔ **The owner(s) of the business:** The sole proprietor of a sole proprietorship, the shareholders of a corporation, the partners in a partnership.
- ✔ **The manager(s) of the business:** For example, the managing partner of a partnership, or the CEO (chief executive officer) of a corporation — and

the compensation the manager is to receive. Each manager's CV (*curriculum vitae*, or *resume*) should accompany the business plan. And it should show that the manager has relevant business experience. If you're a novice at running a business, your CV should at least show that you've got related work experience and/or that you've attended some courses or workshops on setting up and managing a business. If you're starting a complex business or one that requires a lot of money (hundreds of thousands or millions of dollars) at the outset, don't fool around playing CEO if you're not a seasoned professional. Investors won't look at your business unless you've got a professional with a track record in place.

✔ **The key employees of the business:** For example, the person responsible for sales and marketing or the person in charge of research and development.

✔ **The inventor(s) or creator(s) of the idea on which the business is based (if any):** For example, the inventor of a drug or medical device, or the designer of a product that the business is going to manufacture. If at all possible, you want the creative brain behind the business to come along with the business. Have an inventor or creator provide a CV to attach to the business plan.

✔ **The professional advisors of the business:** The lawyer, accountant, publicist, advertising firm.

✔ **The investors already on board:** These could be you (via your bank account, investments, sale of property, and so on) and your family and friends who loaned you cash or contributed equipment; or your bank that gave you a start-up loan, or some other arm's-length investor.

Business operations

If it's relevant to your business — for example, if you're a manufacturer or if you service products, you should also provide information about:

✔ Your facilities or physical plant or infrastructure

✔ Your equipment, and methods of operation

✔ Your materials and supplies, and their sources

Supplying Financial Information

In the finance section of your business plan you're going to crunch the numbers to show that you've got a good chance of making a profit, or at least of paying back the loan or generating a return on the investment. This is a spot where lenders or investors will become extremely eagle-eyed because they want to be pretty sure that they'll get their money back someday, one way or another.

You do this part of the business plan through spreadsheets (financial tables) rather than written text.

Specifically, investors will want to know

- ✔ **How much money the business needs to get up and running** (or to expand, if this isn't a start-up operation) — in other words, what the present *capital requirements* of the business are.

- ✔ **How many assets the business already has and how many liabilities it has** — how much property it owns, such as money, real estate, equipment, valuable contracts such as licence agreements and leases; how much it owes, such as mortgages, loans, and accounts payable. This is the *balance sheet*.

- ✔ **What the projected profit of the business is** — how much the business will earn and how much it will cost the business to earn that amount. Or to put it another way, what the income and operating expenses will be (this is a *statement of income and expenses*). You may also have to show when the income comes in and when payment of expenses goes out, with a *cash flow statement*.

- ✔ **What assets and liabilities the principals of the business have** — this means preparing a *personal balance sheet* for each owner of the business. A loan for your business will actually be a personal loan if your business is a sole proprietorship or a partnership. And even if your business is a corporation, there's a good chance you'll be asked to guarantee a business loan personally if your business doesn't generate enough profit and doesn't have enough assets to sell to repay the loan. If you're not a good loan risk personally, the whole deal may fall through.

If your business has been in operation for two or three years and isn't a start-up, you'll also be expected to provide *balance sheets* for the preceding years and *income* (or *profit and loss*) *statements*. See Chapter 17 for more about these statements.

Capital requirements of your business

We talk about calculating the capital requirements of your business in Chapter 10. You'll find a table there that will help you to prepare a statement of your start-up capital needs.

Assets and liabilities of your business

The assets and liabilities of your business are set out in a balance sheet. In Chapter 17, we explain balance sheets and how to prepare them.

Projected income and expenses of your business

We talk about preparing a forecast of income and expenses in Chapter 10, and we provide a table there to help you work out your forecast of income and expenses for the first year of business.

Your personal capital

The lender or investor may well be looking to you to pay up if your business can't. If so, you'll be asked to provide a *personal balance sheet*, often called a *statement of net worth*, listing your own assets and liabilities. This provides a snapshot of the financial you.

Table 11-1 shows an example of a personal balance sheet. You'll also find a copy on the CD-ROM that you can print out and fill in.

Table 11-1	Personal Balance Sheet
Assets:	
Cash	$
Investments	$
Cash-value life insurance	$
Real estate (home, cottage)	$
Vehicles	$
Personal property	$
Personal loans	$
Other	$
TOTAL ASSETS	$

(continued)

Table 11-1 *(continued)*	
Liabilities:	
Mortgages	$
Personal loans	$
Credit card balances	$
Other personal debts (for example, unpaid property taxes, unpaid income taxes, outstanding bills, child support)	$
Monthly bills	$
TOTAL LIABILITIES	$
NET WORTH (total assets minus total liabilities)	$

Providing References

You're exhausted now but you're not finished. As a final touch, a lender or investor might like to know more about your business reputation (or if you don't have a business reputation yet, your personal reputation) — but not from you. So be prepared to provide, if asked, the names of two or three people the lender or investor could speak to — for example, your bank branch manager if you've dealt with him or her for some time, or other business people you've dealt with over the years (probably best not to name your competitors here . . . or your mother). If you've never been in business for yourself before, you could name an employer or a customer or client you worked with. Ask your references for permission before you give their names. At the very least, you don't want them to be taken by surprise when a lender calls up for a chat about you.

If your business venture revolves around marketing a new technology (say, new computer software or hardware), a lender or investor would probably like to have the names of a couple of people who know the field and who can give an opinion about the commercial potential of your technology. Again, avoid giving the name of a competitor.

Pulling the Final Product Together

After you've put together a first draft of your business plan, you should ask someone with business experience whose judgment you trust to read the plan and comment on it. Then you revise the plan and polish up the prose. You can see how an entire business plan is supposed to look by going to the sample business plan on the CD-ROM. Your final version of the plan will include the following:

- Cover
- Title page
- Table of contents
- Executive summary
- The plan itself
- Financial statements

Cover

Don't get carried away with something expensive, or covered with decorations. Just buy a plain paper cover — preferably in a conservative colour.

Executive summary

If your plan is more than three or four pages long (excluding financial charts), you need to provide a summary at the beginning of the plan so that the reader can decide even more quickly whether to talk to you or simply toss your plan in the circular file. The summary should

- State the amount of money required and what you will do with it.
- Briefly describe the business.
- Describe the business's product or service.
- Summarize income projections.

Part III

On Board Your Enterprise

The 5th Wave   By Rich Tennant

©RICHTENNANT

Art's AUTO PARTS

GIFT BASKETS

Gasket Greetings | Valentine Tune Up | Spark plug Sampler

SALE
~~1/3 OFF~~
1/2 OFF

"I don't know, Art. I think you're just ahead of your time."

In this part . . .

We give you some help in running your new business. We explain how to go about managing your business risks, dealing with customers and suppliers, hiring employees, staying on the right side of tax authorities, and keeping your business accounts.

Chapter 12

Alert! Incoming Risks Detected

· ·

In This Chapter

▶ Investigating the kinds of risks a business can run

▶ Finding out how to reduce the risks

▶ Researching insurance for businesses

· ·

*A*ny business can be a risky business. Although you've got a risk-taking personality (you wouldn't be going into business for yourself if you didn't) you don't want your business to run any risks that it doesn't absolutely have to run.

Steering clear of risks isn't very exciting work, just as many aspects of running your own business aren't very exciting, but you can make it seem more interesting — and you can make yourself feel like a Big Cheese — by referring to the steps involved in staying out of trouble's way as "risk management."

Risk management is a process that involves the following:

✔ Figuring out what kind of trouble your business can run into

✔ Deciding how serious the risks are (both how frequently a risk may occur and how severe the damage would be if the risk materializes)

✔ Making your risks as small as possible

✔ Finding someone else to take over your risks

What Kind of Trouble Can a Business Run Into?

Operating a small business is no bed of roses. There are lots of troubles your business might encounter. The troubles fall broadly into three categories:

- ✔ Your business may cause injury to others.
- ✔ Your business itself may be injured.
- ✔ You and your business associates and employees may be injured.

You need to do an audit of your business (or business-to-be) to identify all your risks and then decide which ones you need to guard against. Some risks involve a small amount of damage but are likely to occur frequently, so it's worth your while to worry about them. (For example, shoplifting and pilferage if you run a retail business. Even though each incident might not involve a significant amount of financial loss to your business, over time the total loss can be significant.) Some risks involve a large amount of damage but are unlikely to occur (for example, earthquakes in most parts of Canada), so there's not much point in worrying about them. Some risks involve a lot of damage and are reasonably likely to occur (earthquakes on the West Coast) — then it's worth your while to worry about them.

Injury to others

If your business causes injury to someone outside the business (the injury could be physical harm, or damage to property, or damage to financial interests), your business is exposed to a lawsuit. Most lawsuits claim money damages to compensate the injured person or business. If your business loses the lawsuit and is ordered by a court to pay a large amount of money, you could end up losing your business — and if you're a sole proprietor or partner, you could end up losing your personal property as well, because there's no distinction in law between you personally and your business (see Chapter 5). Here are the main ways a business can harm others. Your business could

- ✔ Harm customers or clients or suppliers or even total strangers (and their property) by causing them to have an accident on your business premises (this is an area of law called *occupier's liability*). For example, a customer might fall while inside your store, or a passing pedestrian might be knocked over by your outdoor signboard on a windy day.
- ✔ Harm customers or clients because you or a person associated with your business gives careless advice or uses poor judgment in carrying out a business action (this is an area of law called *negligence*). For example,

you or an employee might cause a motor vehicle accident while on delivery, your business might manufacture a product that is defective (such as food that makes someone sick), or you or an employee might recommend a certain product for a customer's needs that turns out to be the wrong product.

✔ Harm customers or clients or suppliers or passing strangers through a deliberate wrongful act (this could be either a civil wrong, called a *tort*, or a *crime* — or it could be both). For example, an employee might steal from a client, or you or an employee might detain a person you incorrectly believe had shoplifted.

✔ Harm customers or clients or suppliers because your business fails to fulfill all its promises under a contract. For example, your business might not deliver a promised product to a customer on time, or might refuse to accept a product ordered from a supplier.

Injury to your business

Your troubles may not involve injury to an outsider but injury to your business itself. Here are the usual ways a business can be harmed:

✔ Business premises can be damaged by fire, flood, windstorm, and other natural and unnatural disasters.

✔ Property belonging to the business (office equipment, inventory, and so on) can be lost in the same sort of disaster that damages the premises. Or it can be stolen . . . or just mysteriously vanish.

✔ Records and valuable information can be lost, especially electronic records when a computer breakdown occurs.

✔ Accounts receivable (money owed to you by customers and clients) may not be paid, and you can't get anything even if you sue because the client or customer has gone bankrupt or disappeared.

✔ Business activities may be interrupted because of

- Damage to your own premises or equipment (such as computer failure, loss of power or heat, fire or flood).

- Damage to neighbouring premises (such as fire in another tenant's office or store that leads to the building being closed for days or weeks).

- Outside activities (such as the municipality tearing up the street outside your store, or a bomb threat leading to evacuation of your entire office building).

✔ The business may lose important personnel because of ill health or accident or death.

Injury to you and your business associates

In a small business, no one's expendable. Especially you. If you're injured or become ill, who's going to run the business to earn income for you? And what if you're sued personally for giving bad advice or making careless decisions? This can happen if you're a professional who is either a sole proprietor of a business or a partner in a business, or if you're a director or officer of a corporation. And then there are your employees. What if they're injured on the job?

Making Your Risks as Small as Possible

You can't make all risks associated with your business vanish, but you can try to cut them down to size.

Injury to others

To avoid lawsuits against your business by people or other businesses that have been injured . . . don't let anyone get injured in the first place! That's not as tall an order as it sounds. There are sensible precautions you can take so that your business doesn't pose too much (unintended) danger to others.

Preventing physical injuries and damage

If you own or lease business premises, take a tour of them and look for problem areas. Here are some of the most common problems and some suggestions for avoiding them.

To prevent slip-and-fall or trip-and-fall incidents:

- Clean up spills of any kind, as soon as you discover them.
- Regularly check for and mop up water and slush that accumulates inside entrances when it's raining or snowing; put mats down at entrances to soak up the water; put out "Caution: Slippery Floor" signs.
- Level off uneven flooring.
- Make sure carpets and mats can't bunch up and turn into a trip hazard.
- Close off areas where you're doing repairs or renovations.
- Clear snow and ice off sidewalks outside your premises, and keep walkways and parking areas free of snow and ice and wet leaves.
- Fill in any holes in walkways or parking areas, and call the municipality to have uneven sidewalks repaired.

✔ Don't leave things lying around where people will walk into them, whether inside your premises, or on the sidewalk or walkways, or in the parking area.

✔ Install handrails on stairs if there are three or more steps; make sure handrails on any staircase are sturdy; mark the edges of the steps to make them more visible.

✔ Make sure ramps aren't too steep and that they have rails if necessary; put non-slip material on the ramp, and mark the ramp edges.

✔ Keep your premises well lit, inside and outside; replace any burnt-out lights immediately.

To prevent people getting whacked or felled by doors, windows, signs, and so on:

✔ Mark glass doors and other large areas of glass so that people won't try to walk through them. (The alternative is to never clean glass . . . that makes it visible all right, but it doesn't do much for your business's image.)

✔ Check that outdoor seating (such as benches and chairs) is stable.

✔ Make sure that awnings and outdoor signs are securely fastened to the building or to some other firm anchorage.

✔ Trim back overhanging tree branches, especially low or rotting ones.

✔ Check roof and flashing to make sure that nothing is loose and might fall off.

To prevent injuries involving business equipment and business vehicles:

✔ Maintain all your equipment and vehicles properly.

✔ Make sure that anyone who is operating business equipment or a business vehicle is properly trained and licensed, and that they understand that safety comes first.

✔ Don't serve alcohol to your associates or employees (even at parties) and don't allow anyone to drink while at work.

To prevent injuries caused by manufacturing or selling defective products:

✔ If you're manufacturing a product, know all safety measures required and best manufacturing practices — and follow them; have quality assurance professionals review the product for potential defects that could cause injury.

✔ If you're manufacturing or selling a product, make sure that it's licensed or approved for distribution and sale by the proper government authorities.

✔ Keep informed about the potential dangers of any product you manufacture or sell, and put warning labels about the dangers on the product; notify in writing any customers who have already bought the product (you need to keep good records to do that).

To prevent deliberate injury or damage to customers or clients, hire carefully if employees are going to enter customers' or clients' homes or handle valuable property (including pets) or work with children. (As part of the interview process you may want a candidate to produce proof that he or she has no criminal record, and you certainly want to check references thoroughly.) For more on hiring see Chapter 15.

Preventing damage caused by giving careless advice

Sometimes just opening your mouth can pose a danger to others. So before anyone in your business says a word:

✔ Make sure that you and your associates and employees are properly educated and/or trained and/or licensed to give advice or recommendations in any particular area.

✔ Stay current in your field. Go to (or send employees to) continuing education seminars or industry-sponsored training sessions, and read newsletters and other materials that are meant to keep you up-to-date.

✔ Use care when you give advice. Make sure you know the facts before you form an opinion. Don't make assumptions. Don't be lazy, and don't let yourself or your associates be hurried into giving advice.

✔ Include disclaimers of liability in the documents you provide to customers and clients. A disclaimer says that you won't be responsible for certain kinds of damage (or even for all damage) that result from your carelessness. Disclaimers aren't always successful in providing protection, but they're worth a try. For more about disclaimers, see Chapter 13.

✔ Keep detailed documents showing exactly what information your clients or customers have provided, what advice you have given, and what work you have done.

Preventing damage caused by not fulfilling a contract

Contracts are the daily stuff of business. Take your contracts seriously.

✔ Read and understand every contract you enter into — before you enter into it! That's not easy if you're not a lawyer (and even lawyers don't always understand contracts, especially if the contracts are in an unfamiliar field, or if they're badly written). Don't just sign a contract and assume everything will be all right. Get advice from a knowledgeable lawyer about the contract's meaning and its consequences for you.

✔ Make careful note of all the things you're required to do under the contract, so that you don't accidentally fall short of the requirements.

✔ Set up a "tickler" system to remind you in plenty of time about contract deadlines, so that you don't miss them. (For more about tickler systems see Chapter 19.)

✔ If you think you may not be able to fulfill a contract, speak to your lawyer right away. It may be possible to build a bridge, legally speaking, to keep you from falling into a pit.

Injury to your business

If your business is damaged through someone else's fault, you may be able to sue for financial compensation. But that could be a long time in coming — so it's better to protect your business than to count on getting paid for any trouble you suffer. And anyway, the damage might be inflicted by you, or by someone you can't sue.

Damage to premises

There are steps you can take to safeguard your premises against damage.

Here's how to prevent fire:

✔ Install approved fire alarms and fire extinguishers, and maybe even sprinkler systems and emergency lighting.

✔ Be a good housekeeper:

- Keep premises clear of paper, packing materials, and other litter; empty wastebaskets daily.

- Unplug appliances when not in use.

- Label hazardous materials and store them safely.

- Dispose of hazardous wastes properly.

- Consider a no-smoking-on-the-premises policy.

✔ Check out building maintenance:

- See that heating and electrical systems are in good condition and are properly maintained. (While you're at it, investigate the plumbing system, as well. You don't want fires, but you don't want floods, either.)

Here's how to prevent vandalism, robbery, and theft:

✔ Lock or fasten securely all doors and windows; you may even need bars or shatter-resistant glass on windows and doors.

✔ Install burglar alarms.

✔ Cut down trees and shrubs that grow around entrances and windows and could provide cover for someone who's breaking in.

✔ Keep the premises well lit outside at night; you may also want to leave interior lights on so that police patrols can see inside.

✔ Fence the premises if necessary.

✔ Consider hiring a security guard.

✔ Keep vehicles in a secure area, with doors locked. Don't leave valuable equipment inside vehicles unless it's absolutely necessary.

Register your business with your local police and fire department so that they know whom to call in an emergency.

Non-payment of accounts receivable

As a businessperson, what you'd like best is to be paid in advance for your work, or have an absolute guarantee of payment. That way you don't have to worry about clients and customers who ignore your bills.

✔ If you're a professional such as a lawyer or accountant, you can ask clients for a retainer, an advance payment that is put into a trust account. (Although you have the money safely in hand, you cannot legally touch it until the work has been done and a bill has been sent to the client.)

✔ In any business you can ask for partial payment in advance for the work you're going to do. If a job can be divided into stages, you can ask for payment in advance for each stage.

✔ In any retail business you can insist on payment in full before delivering the item you're selling.

But if you have to deal with people who can't or won't pay in advance, here are some ways to avoid being left holding the bag:

✔ Don't extend credit yourself. Make arrangements to accept certain credit cards, and tell clients they can use those cards.

✔ Make sure customers and clients understand, before you do the work or supply the product, how much it's going to cost. (If they're not taken by surprise, they're more likely to pay the bill quietly.)

✔ Do your work properly; supply good products; provide guarantees. Clients balk at paying bills if they're unsatisfied.

✔ Bill regularly if you're supplying a product or doing work on an ongoing basis. If one month's bill isn't paid, consider not doing any more work or providing any more supplies until it is. That way you'll limit the damage to your business.

✔ Send regular reminders of unpaid bills, and start collection proceedings (small claims court, or handing the matter over to a collection agency) within a reasonable time.

For more on getting paid, see Chapter 13.

Theft and embezzlement

To prevent theft and embezzlement by employees or associates, you need to have control systems for handling cash and cheques. (For example, require that all cheques bear your own signature, or the signature of two people. Don't keep large sums of cash on the premises.) You also need to hire carefully in the first place, and not allow employees (or associates) to handle money unless you're sure you trust them.

To prevent shoplifting, keep valuable items in an area where only staff have access (such as locked glass cupboards); install a security system that sets off an alarm if goods that haven't been deactivated are taken past the exit; have enough salespeople on the job and make sure they stay alert (nobody can effectively prevent shoplifting while chatting with pals).

Loss of paper records

To avoid losing your important paper records — even temporarily — take these precautions to keep paper records safe: Store written records in fire-proof filing cabinets, store valuable written documents in a safety deposit box in a bank, or in a fireproof safe on your premises. Keep photocopies of your most valuable paper documents off-site, or scan them into your computer and store them off-site on a CD or DVD.

Computer and Internet hazards

To avoid losing or sending astray electronic data, take the following precautions:

- ✔ Maintain your computer equipment properly, and protect it from harm — with surge protectors and humidity control, for example. Remember that computers need to be well ventilated, so don't stick yours right up against a wall or cover it with papers, boxes, and so forth. Computers collect dust and need to be vacuumed every now and then — but by a computer professional, not by you with your Hoover! If you (like most small business owners, 'cause there are only 24 hours in a day) eat while you work, be careful not to spill liquids on your keyboard.

- ✔ Protect against sudden power failures by installing a UPS (uninterrupted power supply — a battery backup system). The system will give you a grace period if the power goes off — your computer will go on running normally long enough for you to shut down without losing unsaved data.

- ✔ Don't let untrained or unauthorized people mess around with your computer systems. If you can't keep your computer in a locked room, you can password protect it. However, the ability to password protect depends on your operating system plus the specific programs you're using. Be aware that some operating systems or programs claim to have password protection . . . but for practical purposes they really don't, because any kid with ten spare minutes on his or her hands may be able to crack it.

If you need password security for your computer, you should make a point of asking a computer professional for advice.

✔ Take extra precautions with your laptop. Laptops require more security than desktop computers, because someone has to break into your office or home to steal your desktop. Laptops are already out in public, just waiting to be put down for an unguarded moment in an airport or left behind in a coffee shop. So you really want to be sure that your laptop has proper password protection.

✔ Guard against viruses and worms and whatever else hackers can come up with: Start with a good security package for your computer (Norton and McAfee are probably the best known, but there are others too). Security products are constantly changing, and what worked best last year may not be as good as something else this year. So don't become emotionally locked in to your security system. When your annual renewal notice appears on the computer screen, ask for your computer professional's advice, or take time to comparison shop — check Internet chat sites to find out what people are saying about their experiences with different products.

✔ Don't leave your computer (or one of your networked computers) running and hooked up to the Internet 24 hours a day unless you have to — it gives hackers who are fishing for a computer more opportunity to find *yours*. If you're using your computer as a server with constant Internet access, maybe you should consider going to a third party provider that will look after the security issues better than you can.

✔ Don't download programs from the Internet, especially screen savers, which are known to be loaded with malicious content such as viruses, Trojan horses, back doors, and keyloggers. Don't allow programs to be installed without verifying what they are — automatic updates to your software should be okay, but otherwise take care and don't download anything from Web sites you aren't sure are safe.

✔ Don't open e-mails from sources you don't know, and especially be careful about opening attachments. Your security program may give you warnings about major new viruses circulating via e-mail, and sometimes the morning news even runs an alert.

✔ Back up your computer files frequently, and store the backup in a fireproof safe in your office, or in a safe place off-site. Get a good backup program, and use it. Backing up your data is a nuisance, but you should do it once a day if you can face it. Check your backup copies regularly to make sure that they don't contain corrupt data. (Or even no data at all . . . one author religiously backed up data using a well-known product and discovered after several years that no data had ever reached the backup disks!)

✔ Stop and think before you hit the send button on your e-mail: Check and then recheck the addressee(s). Unfortunately, it's very easy to send an e-mail, even one containing confidential information, to the wrong person or (oh-oh!) a total stranger. As a second-line precaution, if your e-mail contains any sensitive information, either in the body of the e-mail or in an attachment, add a confidentiality notice below your signature, letting recipients know that if the e-mail is not intended for them they should not read it. See the sidebar "For their eyes only" for some wording for a confidentiality notice.

Business interruption by outside forces of evil

It may be tough to second-guess what others are up to that will interfere with your business. But you can give it shot. Before you lease or buy business premises:

✔ Check what other tenants in the building or businesses in neighbouring buildings are doing. Avoid doing silly things like sharing premises with a fireworks manufacturer or locating next door to an abandoned industrial site (there may very well be toxic materials on the site, which could cause a fire or pollute neighbouring properties).

✔ Check what plans the landlord has for the building or the municipality has for the street. The landlord may be about to start a major renovation that will put off walk-in customers; or the municipality may be planning to spend several months digging up the street and installing new sewer lines, so that traffic will be restricted or banned.

And once you're in your premises, keep an eye on others in your building and on your neighbours, and be prepared to complain to the landlord or even to the police or fire department if you think they're creating a fire or any other hazard.

Outside forces of evil can include foreign governments as well as municipal. If your business involves doing something that is illegal under the laws of another country, be very careful about travelling to that country! You could find yourself arrested and detained at the border or airport. You don't even need to be selling marijuana over the Internet or running a terrorist training camp to get into trouble this way; you could be doing something perfectly legal in Canada, such as trading with Cuba (which is illegal in the United States). In the recent past the United States has taken issue with Canadian citizens residing in Canada who were violating U.S. federal law — and don't assume that the United States is the only country that might act this way.

For their eyes only

We recommend adding this postscript to your e-mails:

NOTICE: This communication is intended only for the use of the person(s) to whom it is addressed. As its content, including any attachment, may be confidential, any distribution, copying, or other use by anyone else is prohibited. If you have received this communication in error, please notify the sender immediately and delete the copy you received without reading, copying, or forwarding it to anyone.

Death or departure of a key person

If you're the one who dies or leaves, you may not care that much about what happens to the business. But if it's a partner or business associate who dies or leaves, that's a different matter. How are you going to get along without them — especially if they were storing important information in their heads? And what if the person (if alive) or the person's family (if dead) is demanding the return of an investment in the business?

If you want to keep key personnel healthy and happy in the first place, make sure everyone takes care of himself or herself. Hard work is necessary, but so is time off. Take vacations and get others to do the same. Encourage your associates to take things easier if they're turning grey and getting dark circles under the eyes, or becoming fat and wheezy.

Don't let any one person be the only person with access to essential business information. Make sure important information is written down and stored carefully. Have key personnel "cross-train" so that two or more people have at least some familiarity with essential operations. Or have an associate or employee act as an "understudy" for each key person. Take your cue from high-ranking politicians (like prime ministers and deputy prime ministers, or presidents and vice-presidents), and have key personnel travel in different cars and airplanes.

If you want to avoid destroying the business when someone leaves or dies and a big payment is demanded, start a fund that can be used to buy out a partner's or shareholder's interest. Add to the fund yearly.

Duh

We bet you can't believe you paid money for some of this advice! An awful lot of it's just common sense.

Getting Somebody Else to Take Over Your Risks

You can't eliminate every possible risk, even if you try. So you also need to pass at least some of your risks off to somebody else. Who's going to be stupid enough to take over your risks? In case you hadn't already guessed — an insurance company.

Most people think insurance is boring. But it's really quite exciting. Once you start thinking of all the dreadful things that can happen to your business and you and the people you deal with, you'll feel as though you're living in an adventure serial! You'll realize that you're constantly surrounded by danger, and that a wily mind and constant vigilance are your only protection.

Not only that, but insurance has a whiff of sin about it. It's actually gambling! Okay, so taking out insurance is not exactly like hitting the casinos. Actually, it's not even close. But here's how the insurance gamble works. When you take out an insurance policy, you're betting the insurance company that you're going to have trouble during the period the policy covers. The insurance company is betting that you're not. If you do have trouble, you win and the insurance company pays up. If nothing happens, the insurance company gets to keep its money (including the stake that you put down — the premium that you paid to buy the policy).

Have you already got insurance?

You may think you've already got enough insurance to cover your business, but you probably don't. For example, if you're going to run your business out of your home, your home insurance probably doesn't cover your business. Most home insurance policies exclude or limit coverage for business activities. If you're going to use your car as a business delivery vehicle, your existing car insurance probably doesn't cover that kind of business use. Key people in your business may already have life insurance — but the beneficiary is unlikely to be your business: it's probably their family members or their estate. Canada Pension Plan provides disability benefits if key people in your business are unable to work, but the benefits are not that easy to get, they don't amount to much, and generally they're not suited to helping your business through a difficult time.

Do you really need insurance?

Some businesses need certain kinds of insurance, whether they want it or not, because they're required to be insured under legislation governing their field, or under a contract they've entered into. (Commercial leases typically require the tenant to have insurance.)

But if you don't have to have insurance, do you need to have insurance? You don't need insurance against every risk. But it makes a lot of sense to insure against certain risks. Take these examples:

- ✔ If your business involves giving advice, you should have insurance against giving bad advice.
- ✔ If your business involves manufacturing a product, you should have insurance against defective products.
- ✔ If your business involves having customers or clients come onto your premises, you should have insurance against injuries that occur there.

Having insurance protects you from going out of business if you're sued and the court rules against you. And it also ensures that anyone you injure receives compensation for the damage you've caused.

For risks that are unlikely to materialize or that won't cause big losses, you can consider self-insuring. That means bearing the risk yourself. Sometimes a risk is so remote, or the loss is so small, that you're throwing away money taking out insurance against it. You're also self-insuring in a way if you choose a high insurance deductible. Until your loss is higher than the deductible amount of your policy, you can't make a claim. (A higher deductible means a lower premium.)

You need to talk to an insurance agent or broker (agents work for just one company, brokers deal with several companies) about your business's needs. An agent or broker will help you evaluate the risks in your business and suggest what insurance coverage you need and in what amount.

Choose someone who is knowledgeable about the kind of business you carry on. Ask business associates for recommendations, and then make an appointment to talk to two or three of the agents or brokers recommended, before choosing one who seems best able to give you advice and find the coverage you need. Make sure the one you choose has errors and omissions insurance. Then, if the agent or broker makes a mistake in getting the right coverage, you'll be able to sue for compensation for any damage you suffer as a result.

You may need different insurance from year to year, so you should review your coverage annually with your agent or broker.

Insurance Policies

Various kinds of insurance policies are available. You can often get a package policy geared to your particular kind of business. For a home-based business you may be able to get a home business insurance package that provides coverage for things such as your business property (inventory, samples, supplies, filing cabinets, computers and software, tools, customers' goods) on and off the premises, loss of cash, business interruption if your home is uninhabitable, legal liability (for products or services, or business-related accidents on the premises). Alternatively, you may be able to get an extension of your existing home insurance policy to cover your business. You may also be able to find packages for retail businesses, skilled trades, manufacturing, day care, or office-based businesses.

Below we discuss the separate kinds of coverage that come in packages or that can be purchased on their own.

You should be aware that since the events of September 11, 2001, insurance has become harder to get and more expensive to buy. Insurance companies have less appetite for risk than they did before 9/11.

Insurance in case your business causes damage

Here are the standard forms of insurance protection for damage by your business to others.

Liability insurance

Liability insurance covers your business if the *negligence* (carelessness) of a person in the business causes injury to a customer, client or consumer, or innocent bystander. This kind of insurance will pay the cost of defending a lawsuit brought against your business and will pay the judgment awarded by a court or the settlement negotiated with the injured party. You may be used to thinking of insurance as a fund that pays something to you if you run into trouble. The usual rule with liability insurance, however, is that payments go to the injured party, not to you or your business.

Commercial general liability insurance can provide coverage for a range of problems — for example, physical injury, property damage, financial loss and liability under a contract. Some policies may also cover civil wrongs (torts) like libel and slander (collectively, defamation) and false imprisonment. A commercial insurance package might also cover some of the following things, or you might have to arrange separate coverage for each:

- **Product liability insurance** — which covers third parties who are injured or suffer a loss because of a defect in a product you manufacture.

- **Errors and omissions insurance** — which covers third parties who suffer loss and injury caused by your careless advice or careless work.

- **Tenant's liability** — which covers loss and injury caused by your business to other tenants of the building your business is in. If you rent commercial premises, be sure to show the lease to your agent or broker, to make sure you get all the coverage you're required to have under the terms of the lease.

- **Limited pollution liability** — which covers loss and injury to third parties caused by an unexpected or unintentional discharge of pollutants from your business.

Automobile insurance covers loss and injury to third parties caused by your business's vehicles. This is not normally included in general commercial policies but has to be arranged separately.

Surety bonds, performance bonds, and guarantee bonds

Instead of getting insurance for liability you might have under a contract, you might be able to take out (through an insurance company) a bond that will be paid to the other party to the contract if you don't perform your obligations under the contract. (Bonds are commonly used in the construction industry.)

Fidelity bonds

You may want to have employees bonded (through an insurance company or a bonding company) if your business involves handling valuable property or working in other people's homes. If a bonded employee steals from a customer who makes a legal claim against the business, the bonding company compensates the business if the claim is successful. (A fidelity bond will also compensate the business if the employee steals from the business itself.)

Insurance against damage to your business

Here's insurance that makes a payment to your business if the business suffers damage.

Property insurance

Property insurance usually covers damage to or loss of

- The building, if you own the building where your business is located
- Leasehold improvements (tenant's renovations), if you rent space for your business
- Contents such as equipment, furniture, and inventory
- Business property (such as business tools, like a laptop; but not usually vehicles or cell phones or mobile phones) that isn't on the premises
- Employees' personal property that is on the premises
- Accounts receivable (money owing by customers and clients)
- Valuable papers, but not money or cheques for more than a few hundred dollars, or documents that prove ownership (like the title documents to a property) or debt (like an IOU)

You can insure against only a few risks or against a wide range of risks. The full range of risks includes fire, lightning, gas explosion, smoke, wind, vandalism, some kinds of water damage, impact by a vehicle, burglary, and theft. If you buy an all risks policy, you get paid if any of the risks listed here occur and you suffer damage as a result; if you buy fire and extended coverage, you're covered for most of the risks except burglary and theft, and most kinds of water damage; if you buy just fire coverage, you're covered only against fire, lightning, and gas explosion.

Even all risks policies usually refuse to cover you against damage caused by (among other things) water seepage and leaks, mechanical or electrical breakdown, changes in temperature and humidity, wear and tear, defects in purchased equipment or products, and war.

You can pay extra to get a rider to your property insurance policy to cover your business if it suffers damage as a result of rather boring perils like the cost of complying with municipal building bylaws passed since the building was originally constructed, if the building has to be rebuilt or repaired . . . or of quite exciting perils like explosion of boilers, floods, earthquakes, and pollution of your property by others.

Business interruption insurance

Business interruption insurance pays you money if you cannot carry on your business and lose income because your business premises are damaged as a result of a risk against which you're insured. The risks you can insure against are usually the same ones you can insure your property against (see the previous heading, "Property insurance"), and in fact business interruption insurance is often an extension of property insurance coverage. You'll get paid by your insurance company until your business reopens (but only for up to a year, as a rule) for loss of earnings, loss of profits, and extra expenses incurred in order to keep customers. Business interruption insurance often also covers you if you lose business not because your own business was damaged, but because another business in your building was damaged.

Electronic data processing (EDP) insurance

Property insurance doesn't always cover or fully cover computers and data processing equipment and the valuable information they contain. Some insurance companies offer additional or separate coverage for loss of income and extra expenses due to damage to data processing equipment. And with EDP insurance it may be possible to insure against risks that you can't normally insure against, such as mechanical breakdown, electrical arcing, and changes in temperature.

Crime or theft insurance

Crime or theft insurance covers losses to a business that are caused by employee dishonesty, forgery of cheques, loss of money on the business premises, robbery, burglary, and break-and-enter.

Credit insurance

Credit insurance protects accounts receivable if a customer goes bankrupt or refuses for a long time (or ever) to pay an account. It's often used by importers and exporters. (It can also cover against changes in import/export regulations, and war.)

Tenant's legal liability insurance

Tenant's legal liability insurance covers the tenant if the tenant's own premises are damaged and the landlord's insurer refuses to pay to repair the tenant's premises, on the grounds that the damage was caused by the tenant's negligence.

Overhead expense insurance or disability insurance

Either overhead expense insurance or disability insurance can cover the fixed expenses of your business if you get sick or are injured and can't work for a time.

Business life insurance and disability insurance

There are insurance policies to help your business deal with the loss (due to death or ill-health) of a partner or shareholder and the resulting demand from the former associate or the associate's family for return of the investment made in the business.

The business can take out life insurance, under various names such as *key person insurance*, *partnership insurance*, *business continuation insurance*, or *buy-sell insurance*. They all do the same thing — if the partner or shareholder dies, the insured business can use the insurance proceeds to buy the deceased person's partnership interest or shares from his or her estate. A business may also be able to take out *disability insurance* or *critical illness insurance* on a partner or shareholder. The insurance payment would let the business buy out the partnership interest or shares if the partner or shareholder were unable to come back to the business.

Insurance to protect the people working in your business

Insurance to protect the people in your business may be payable to the individual, or may be payable to a person harmed by the individual.

Errors and omissions insurance

Professionals who give advice to customers or clients need errors and omissions insurance or professional negligence insurance. (In some cases, the insurance can be purchased through a commercial general liability policy; but professionals sometimes have to be insured through a specific insurer. Most medical doctors, for example, are insured through the Canadian Medical Protective Association; lawyers are insured through their provincial law society or an affiliated insurer.) The insurance will pay the cost of defending a lawsuit if a claim is brought by a client or customer, and will pay the injured person if a court makes an award or if a settlement can be negotiated between the parties.

Directors' and officers' liability

Directors and officers of corporations can be sued by the shareholders, creditors, and employees of the corporation, or by members of the general public, if they've been harmed by a director's or officer's carelessness (but not dishonesty) in making decisions about what a corporation should do. A corporation can buy directors' and officers' *(D & O)* insurance that will pay the director's or officer's costs of defending a lawsuit and of paying an award ordered by a court judgment or negotiated in an out-of-court settlement. Alternatively, if the corporation has an arrangement to pay back *(indemnify)* directors and officers if they're sued, the policy can pay back the corporation for payments it makes to a director or officer.

Disability insurance

If you can't work, you won't have any money. But you can take out some income replacement insurance (*disability insurance* or *critical illness insurance*) to help you financially while you're out of commission.

Workers' compensation

Workers' compensation is insurance coverage provided by your provincial government, for employees who are injured on the job.

If you've got employees (in some provinces, if you have no employees but you've incorporated), workers' compensation insurance is mandatory. You have to register your business with the provincial Workers' Compensation Board and you have to pay insurance premiums. Workers' Comp pays the medical bills and replaces income while the worker is off the job. Under this plan, employees lose the right to sue the employer for job-related injuries.

Employers' liability

Employers' liability insurance covers injury to employees caused by your business and its employees. Coverage is restricted to injuries not covered by workers' compensation.

Chapter 13

Co-existing with Other Life Forms I: Customers and Clients

In This Chapter

▶ Knowing what you want from your customers and what they want from you

▶ Examining a standard business transaction

▶ Being clear on expectations

▶ Keeping your clients happy

▶ Getting paid for the work you do

▶ Learning about customer privacy

▶ Encouraging repeat business and referrals

▶ Protecting yourself if problems arise

*Y*ou are not alone in the universe. Or if you are, you're not doing any business so this book isn't for you. Even as a sole proprietor or as the sole owner of a corporation, you're going to have to deal with customers or clients in order to provide your product or service. Customers and clients need special handling. On the one hand, you have to satisfy them — by providing good quality products or services and by treating them well in your dealings. On the other hand, you have to get them to satisfy you — principally by paying you in full and in good time.

In this chapter, we talk about managing your relationship with your customers or clients so that you'll both be satisfied.

Recognizing What You Want from Your Customers or Clients

The first thing you want is for customers or clients to show up at your door enquiring about your product or service.

If instead of saying "Take me to your product" they say "Take me to your leader," you could be receiving an advance delegation from an alien empire that will promise to show earthlings how to build way cool anti-gravity skateboards and scooters, but whose secret goal is total domination of the Earth. But that's okay, because even alien invaders need toothpaste and bookkeeping services. (We talk about marketing to attract customers in Chapter 4, although we mostly stick to customers residing on this planet.)

But arrival is just the beginning. Once you have your customers inside the door, you want them to do several key things:

✔ Take the plunge and actually agree to buy your product or service.

✔ Allow you to make a profit by paying a reasonable price for your goods or services (including delivery).

✔ Pay you promptly.

✔ Come back for more and refer other customers to you. (If you can get repeat customers and referrals, you won't have to go to the trouble and expense of rounding up new customers all the time.)

Reviewing What Happens in the Usual Business Transaction

Now that you know what you want from your customers, you have to think about how to get it. Your business transactions should be designed with this in mind. Here's what you want to happen:

✔ You get the customer in the door and make your pitch.

✔ You close the deal.

✔ You document your agreement.

✔ You perform your work and/or deliver your product.

✔ You invoice (bill) your customer.

- ✔ You get paid.
- ✔ Your customer comes back again and/or refers other customers.

Getting Your Customers in the Door

Creating knowledge of and interest in your product or services is called marketing. We tell you about marketing in Chapter 4.

Your potential customers must know that you exist, what you have to offer, and where to find you. They must also be interested enough in you and your product or service to seek you out — in person, by telephone, or on your Web site — or (if you have to seek them out instead) to sit through your sales pitch.

Making the Sale

Don't make the mistake of thinking that once a customer is interested in you and your product or service, you've already made the sale. You've still got some work to do.

The pitch and the close

We talk about the actual process of making a sale in Chapter 4. Briefly, here's what you or your staff should do:

- ✔ Know your product or service thoroughly so that you're prepared to answer all questions about it and not have to give lame answers like "That's a good question," or "I can look that up for you," or "That's the first time anyone has ever asked me whether Betelgeusan *gk*ushsu* is compatible with this product/service."

- ✔ Listen to the customer or client so you know what he or she really wants, and gear your sales pitch to the customer's needs.

- ✔ Propose a deal that you think will meet the customer's needs (and yours too, of course), and close the deal if the customer is willing to accept the offered terms. (And try again if the customer isn't willing.)

When your customer agrees to buy the product or service you're offering, you have entered into a contract. Once you have a contract, you have a legal obligation to deliver your product or service, and your customer has a legal obligation to pay you for it.

Customer service, part 1 — first impressions

Customer service is an important part of any business and of every stage of contact with your customers or clients. (For more about customer service than we can cover in this chapter, check out *Customer Service For Dummies*, written by Karen Leland and Keith Bailey and published by Wiley.)

Your customers will get the first taste of your customer service when they make contact with your business and while you're making your pitch. Treat them properly. Don't keep them waiting. Greet them politely, and then pay attention to them. They do not want to be ignored in favour of other customers or, even worse, your personal business. (Aliens bent on total domination of the Earth are particularly sensitive about phone calls with friends and family, and merry socializing among the staff.) Listen to their concerns, and show that you're interested in solving their problems rather than in simply making a sale. If customers or clients come to your place of business, make sure your premises are always clean, organized, and well maintained.

Customer service doesn't end once the customer agrees to buy your product or service. You may still lose the sale if you take your customer for granted while processing the sale — for example, by taking too long to complete the paperwork or by failing to be attentive to the customer while he or she is waiting.

Documenting Your Agreement

One of the keys to good customer relations is to make sure that both you and your customer or client have a clear expectation of exactly what each of you is to do. What goods or services must you provide and when? What is the customer to pay? Does the customer have to do anything to enable you to do your work and/or deliver your product (for example, remove the old kitchen cabinets so that you can install the new ones, or provide certain documents for you to review), or does he just sit back until it's time to pay you?

The way to ensure clear expectations on both sides is to have a contract that both of you understand and are reasonably happy with. A contract doesn't have to be a pages-long document filled with small print and incomprehensible language. Contract documents and their contents vary from business to business. (In fact, a contract doesn't have to be in writing at all.) We're going to tell you about the things you should be aware of, no matter what form your contracts take.

Contracts for the sale of goods

You may be a manufacturer who sells your goods to wholesale or retail businesses, or you may have a retail business in which you sell goods to other businesses or directly to consumers. Every time you make a sale, you and your customer are entering into a contract for the sale of goods.

The terms of the contract

When you and your customer enter into a contract, you come to terms on many matters. All contracts for the sale of goods involve agreement about the following things, whether or not the contract is reduced to writing:

- **The parties to the contract:** One party (you) agrees to provide the goods and the other (your customer) agrees to pay for the goods. Your customer may be an individual, a partnership, or a corporation. If it's a partnership or a corporation, you want to make sure you're dealing with a person who has the legal authority to contract on behalf of the partnership or corporation. Be suspicious of someone who wants to sign but is not an officer of the corporation (for example, Vice President is a much more comforting title than Administrative Assistant), and ask for confirmation from a corporate officer that the person has authority to bind the corporation.

- **The goods being sold:** Include quantity, brand name, and model number, if that's important.

- **The price the buyer is to pay for the goods:** Any amounts for GST and PST, or HST, should also be shown, but separately from the basic purchase price.

- **The date(s) payment(s) is to be made:** If your contract doesn't address this question, provincial sale of goods legislation says that the buyer must pay at the time of delivery. If you agree to accept payment after delivery of the goods, your contract should set out the amount and date of each payment, and the interest rate being charged.

- **The quality of the goods:** If your contract says nothing about the quality of the goods, provincial sale of goods legislation implies a promise on your part that the goods are of reasonable quality. If the goods turn out not to be of reasonable quality, the customer can return them and get his money back. If you want to limit your responsibility and the customer's right to return the goods, your contract needs to say something. For example, it might say that you will replace or repair the goods free of charge within 90 days after the sale if there is a defect in materials or workmanship. Or (if you are not the manufacturer) it might state that the buyer must deal with the manufacturer rather than you if there is anything wrong with the goods.

Note that if you are selling goods to a consumer (rather than to another business), provincial consumer protection legislation will not allow you to limit your responsibility for the quality of your goods.

✔ **The place and date that the goods are to be delivered:** If your contract doesn't address the place, provincial sale of goods legislation says that your customer must pick up the goods at your place of business. If your contract addresses the place but not the date, the legislation says that the goods must be delivered within a reasonable period of time.

✔ **The right of the buyer to return the goods:** In the absence of a problem with the quality of the goods, a buyer has no right to return the goods unless the seller agrees to give that right. Your business should have a returns policy and it should be set out in the contract — for example, no returns; or returns for exchange or credit only; or full returns, no questions asked.

If your goods will be shipped to your customer, your agreement must also deal with

✔ How the goods are shipped

✔ Who pays for shipping

✔ Who bears the risk of damage or loss to the goods during shipping

Consider the customer relations aspects of your contracts:

✔ Think about how your customers will feel about your contract terms before you finally decide on them. (For example, having a strict no-returns policy may cost you business.)

✔ Make sure that your customers are aware of your contract terms (whatever they are) when they enter into the contract. (You may lose repeat business from a customer who doesn't notice that you don't take returns until the customer is standing in your store asking for his or her money back.)

Visible contracts

If your business involves selling products to other businesses, you will probably have a written contract of some type:

✔ **A sales order form or invoice created by you:** If your customer orders your products by telephone or over the Internet and doesn't set any terms for the contract, the terms will be governed by the wording on the invoice or sales order form you include with the shipment.

✔ **A purchase order form created by your customer:** If your customer orders goods by sending you a purchase order form setting out the terms on which the customer is willing to buy your goods, and you fill the purchase order, then the terms of your contract will be governed by the purchase order.

✔ **A formal written contract signed by both parties:** If the contract involves a large amount of money, or a custom-made item, you and the buyer may have to negotiate a contract that deals specifically with this transaction.

Invisible contracts

If you own a retail store, you'll be entering into a contract for the sale of goods every time you ring up a sale at the cash register. You won't have a written document for these sales — you may have nothing more than a cash register receipt. But you've still got a contract. If you don't say or do anything to change the terms imposed by provincial law, the basic terms of the contract will be

✔ The customer must pay for the goods in full on or before delivery.

✔ The customer must take the goods away with him or her.

✔ You are responsible to the customer if the goods are not of reasonable quality.

✔ Unless there is a problem with the quality of the goods, the customer has no right to return or exchange the goods.

You can change or narrow these terms by printing different terms on your sales receipts, or by placing signs at your cash register, or by telling your customers at the time of sale — in fact, you'd probably be wise to use all three methods. (Remember that if you're dealing with consumers, you can't change the term that you're responsible for the quality of the goods.) For example, you might want to inform customers that you don't accept personal cheques (or any form of currency not issued by a government on this planet, including Betelgeusan 10,000-credit *shmats*) as a method of payment, or that you will allow returns but only within ten days.

Contracts for services

If your business is providing services to other businesses or consumers, you will be entering into a contract every time you agree to do work for your client.

Written contracts

All of your contracts should be in writing, and the more complicated the deal, the more detail you will want in the contract. By putting the contract in writing, you and your client are forced to define the details of your agreement — and that's how you'll be sure that you really are in agreement. As you perform your services, your agreement will serve as a checklist of the work you are supposed to do. And, if a dispute occurs later on, a detailed written contract serves as evidence of what was in fact agreed to.

Make sure each party has an original signed contract. (Especially make sure that *you* have an original signed contract and that you keep it in a safe place. Clients may lose theirs, or turn them into a small pile of smoking atoms with an ultra-laser pistol, and then come up with all kinds of wild fantasies about what was in them in the first place.)

The terms of the contract

Whatever kind of services you are providing, your contracts with your clients should always deal with the following things:

- ✔ **Who the parties to the contract are:** One party (you) agrees to provide the services and the other (your client) agrees to pay for the services. Your client may be an individual, a partnership, or a corporation. If it's a partnership or a corporation, you want to make sure you're dealing with a person who has the legal authority to contract on behalf of the partnership or corporation.

- ✔ **What services are to be performed:** The contract should state in detail the nature of the services and (if appropriate) the standard of quality they must meet.

- ✔ **What the services will cost:** The cost could be fixed, or based on the amount of time you spend doing the work. Any amounts for GST or HST should also be shown, but separately from the basic price for the services.

- ✔ **How payment is to be made:** Will you be paid in full at the beginning, or paid in full at the end, or paid in instalments as you do your work or after you complete the work? If you will be paid in instalments as you provide the services, try to schedule the payments so that your costs are covered as you incur them and you are paid some of your profit as you go. If you agree to accept payment over time after you've finished providing the services, the contract should set out the amount and date of the payments, and the interest rate being charged.

- ✔ **When the services are to be performed:** The contract should give a starting date, and perhaps an end date — especially if it's important to the customer that you finish by a certain date.

- ✔ **What rights the parties have to change or end the contract:** You may want to give yourself the right to end the contract for certain reasons, and you may want to limit the customer's right to end the contract due to some sort of wrongdoing on your part. You may also want to give yourself the right to change the contract in certain circumstances — for example, the right to raise the agreed price if the cost of materials rises.

- ✔ **What happens if you don't perform the services properly:** You may want to offer a *warranty*, under which you agree to remedy problems for a fixed period of time after your service has been performed. And/or you may want to limit what you have to do if a problem occurs — for example, reduce the agreed payment by a fixed maximum amount.

✔ **What happens if you cause injury to someone or cause damage to property:** You may want to include in your contract an exemption or *exculpatory clause* that limits your liability if you cause damage or injury. (With or without an exemption clause, you should make sure that you have proper insurance in place — see Chapter 12.)

Speak to your lawyer

Before you open for business, have your lawyer prepare your standard documents, such as sales order forms and invoices, and standard form contracts.

If a customer presents you with a purchase order form or standard form contract that you don't understand clearly and agree with fully, have it reviewed by your lawyer before you fill the order. Ditto if a customer wants to make a change to your standard sales order form or standard form contract. If the terms of the customer or client are unfavourable to you, you may be able to negotiate changes.

You may also want to consult your lawyer if you are negotiating a contract that involves a lot of money or a long-term commitment.

Doing the Work

Once you enter into a contract with a customer, you have to do what the contract says you will do. If you don't carry out your promises, even if you don't get sued, you won't stay in business very long.

Do the work

This part is simple. Read the contract. Do what you agreed to do.

Customer service, part 2 — happy customers

However, just doing the work isn't enough if you want to be paid promptly and to get repeat business and referrals from your customers. You must also keep an eye on customer service:

✔ **Don't make promises you can't keep:** Don't promise to do something unless you are sure you can do it. Don't promise that you will have an item in stock by a specific date unless you know for certain that it will have been delivered to you by then.

✔ **Keep the promises you make:** This is the corollary of "Don't make promises you can't keep." If you say you'll order in a particular product, order it. If you say you'll be finished the work on the 30th, be finished on the 30th. If you're serious about making your business a success, you just have to ignore the fleets of invading alien warships filling the skies on the 28th and 29th.

✔ **Document changes:** If your customer asks for changes to your original contract, write down the changes and make sure that both parties sign to show that they are aware of and agree to the changes. That way you will both be clear about what now has to be done, and what the additional cost, if any, will be.

✔ **Communicate:** Make sure your customer knows what is going on. If she ordered a product that is not available, tell her when it will be available. If it hasn't arrived when you expect it, call her to let her know you're experiencing a delay. Call her again when the product finally comes in.

If your customer can't see the work as you are doing it, keep him or her advised of your progress. Don't wait for your customer to call to ask you how you're doing, and when you'll be finished. Provide progress reports, either by phone or e-mail or letter.

✔ **If you make a mistake or miss a deadline, deal with it:** Say you are sorry, fix the problem, and do something to try to make it up to the customer. For example, send a small gift or offer a discount on future products or services, give a free product or service, or promise preferred service in the future. Be careful about admitting that you did something wrong. Try saying, "Sorry for the inconvenience," instead of "Sorry that we screwed up and didn't do your work on time."

Especially don't admit in writing that you did something wrong. Your words could come back to haunt you if you get sued over the mistake.

Customer service, part 3 — unhappy customers

In "Customer service, part 2," we told you how to keep customers happy. In part 3, we tell you what to do with customers who are unhappy or who may in fact be downright difficult.

Even if you do everything right, you're still going to encounter unhappy customers. Sometimes things go wrong, and sometimes it's not even your fault. Sometimes you'll have a customer who is simply impossible to please. You must be able to deal with complaints, whether or not they're justified.

Here are the keys to dealing with a difficult customer:

✔ **Listen to what the customer has to say:** That's the only way that you'll learn what the problem is. Also, your customer may not be able to think about any kind of solution to his problem until he's had a chance to let off some steam (or other substance . . . stand back but not offensively far back). Show that you're listening by maintaining eye contact, nodding your head and making encouraging sounds like "uh-huh."

✔ **Show that you understand the customer's problem:** Say things like

  • I understand.

  • This must be very upsetting.

  • I can see how frustrating this must be.

  • I can sympathize with the way you feel.

  • I'm sorry.

✔ **Try to solve the customer's problem:** Before you come up with a solution, ask the customer what solution he or she would propose. See if you can do what the customer wants. If it involves performing an unnatural physical act on yourself, politely ask the customer for a different solution.

Even if you decide that you never want to have anything to do with a particular customer again, and you think it highly unlikely that the customer will ever refer any business to you, try not to send the customer away angry. You don't want him or her badmouthing you to potential customers.

Getting Paid

Often you won't get paid until after you do your work or deliver your goods, but that doesn't mean that you should put off thinking about payment until then. In fact, it's essential to lay the groundwork at the time you and your customer make your deal.

Planning to get paid

The best way to make sure that you get paid is to avoid situations in which you risk not getting paid.

✔ **Turn some customers away:** No, our brains aren't addled by cosmic rays. If you don't have the time or ability to do a job well, it's better for you to refer the customer elsewhere. If you can't do the job, you not only risk not getting paid, you also run the risk of gaining a bad reputation or getting sued. You run the same risk with a customer who has unrealistic expectations about what you can do. You should also avoid doing work for a customer who can't really afford to pay for your services, because he or she probably won't.

✔ **Make sure your agreements are fair to your customers:** You shouldn't enter into a contract that's totally one-sided in your favour, even if you have the bargaining power to do it. A customer who feels he has been treated unfairly is far less likely to pay than a customer who is happy with the deal he has made.

✔ **Get paid up front if you can:** Try to structure your deals so that you get paid before you deliver any goods or provide any services. It's reasonably common for goods to be paid for before delivery. It is less common for customers to pay in advance for services. If your customers won't agree to pay you in full before you deliver your services, unless you're 100 percent positive you'll get paid after you deliver, you should structure your deal so that you're paid in instalments as you go.

✔ **Don't be sneaky when you bill customers:** Your bill (or any part of it) should not come as a surprise to your customers. Don't include any charge you haven't discussed with a customer beforehand — your customer will think you're a sleazebag, and possibly dishonest.

✔ **Don't extend credit:** If your customers are consumers (rather than other businesses or aliens bent on total domination of the Earth), don't extend credit. Ask them to use a credit card instead. In some industries, it's customary for a business to extend credit to its business customers, but don't do so lightly.

✔ **Protect yourself if you do extend credit:** If you're planning to enter into a long-term relationship with a customer and the customer would like a credit arrangement as part of the relationship, have your customer apply for credit as he would apply for a loan at the bank. Design a credit application form (get one from one of your suppliers to use as a sample). Check your customer's credit history (to see if he has a history of non-payment of debts) and credit references (to find out whether other businesses consider him a good credit risk). If your customer is a business,

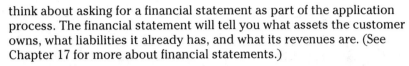

think about asking for a financial statement as part of the application process. The financial statement will tell you what assets the customer owns, what liabilities it already has, and what its revenues are. (See Chapter 17 for more about financial statements.)

You may want your accountant to help you assess the creditworthiness of a customer.

In the credit agreement, make sure that you establish terms for payment, including the amount and date of the payments, and the interest rate being charged.

If you are extending credit to a corporation that does not have significant assets, think about asking for *personal guarantees* from the shareholders and/or directors. That way, if the corporation doesn't pay you, you can demand payment from the guarantors. See Chapter 10 for information about guarantees.

If you decide to ask for a guarantee, get your lawyer to prepare the document.

If you are selling goods on credit, think about taking a security interest in the goods until they are fully paid for (for example, sell the goods under a conditional sales contract). A security interest allows you to take back and sell the goods if you are not paid. (See Chapter 10 for more about security.) If you take a security interest, you will have to register it under your province's *Personal Property Security Act*. If you take security, get your lawyer to prepare the documents and register the interest. (Do not waste your time taking security on vehicles that can move faster than light-speed.)

✔ **Do what you promised to do:** A satisfied customer is far more likely to pay for your goods and services than a dissatisfied one.

Collecting your accounts receivable

Your accounts receivable are money owed to you by your customers. It's often necessary to make a concerted effort to collect them. Nobody's keen on paying bills.

You (or your bookkeeper) have to establish a method for keeping track of and collecting what your business is owed. That includes the following:

✔ Your outstanding receivables should be *aged* at least once a month. Calculate the number of days that every unpaid invoice has been outstanding (typically 30, 60, 90, 120 days).

✔ Have a policy about what to do with unpaid accounts when they have been outstanding for periods of time — for example: add interest after 30 days (if your contract doesn't prevent that); send a reminder invoice requesting immediate payment (with interest) after 30 and 60 days; write a polite letter and make a follow-up phone call after 90 days; threaten legal proceedings after 120 days.

✔ Cut off customers who don't pay within a certain time. Do not continue to ship goods or provide services to a customer who has not paid a bill already owing, or else insist on payment before delivery.

If you are assertive in collecting an account, you may lose the customer. But keep in mind that a customer who doesn't pay is not the kind of customer you want.

Customer service, part 4 — customer privacy

In the good old days, you could keep extensive files about your customers' birthdays, wedding anniversaries, and tastes in scotch and lingerie. You could harass your customers by cold-calling their homes at dinner time, sell your customer lists to another business so *it* could harass your customers at dinner time, and much more — all without asking your customers' permission or risking more than a telephone receiver being slammed down. Alas, the good old days ended on January 1, 2004, which was the date that the federal *Personal Information Protection and Electronic Documents Act (PIPEDA)* came into force across Canada for all commercial activities.

As of January 1, 2004, if you want to collect, and keep and use or disclose any personal (factual or subjective) information about an identifiable individual, you have to get that individual's consent beforehand, and even then you can only use the information for the purpose for which consent was given. And *even then* you can only collect, use, or disclose the information for purposes that a reasonable person would consider appropriate in the circumstances. So, for example, if your customers are not reasonable people and have gladly consented for you to pass on their address, age, and weight to the organizers of the alien annual "Lottery Barbeque," you should think carefully before hitting the send button on your e-mail. That's because the customer can call the Privacy Commissioner of Canada on you if you violate PIPEDA. (However, the Commish isn't necessarily a heavy; he or she will work toward finding a solution to privacy problems and complaints, rather than immediately throwing you in jail . . . even if you probably should be thrown in jail.)

Personal information includes

- ✔ Name, address, phone numbers, identification numbers (like a social insurance number or a driver's licence number)
- ✔ Age, social status, ethnic origin, medical information and records
- ✔ Income, or credit or loan records
- ✔ Existence of a dispute between a customer and a business
- ✔ Opinions, intentions, and comments (even the printable ones)

(We'll throw you a crumb here — personal information does not include the name, title, business address, or business telephone number of an employee of an organization.)

Individuals have a right to look at the personal information that your business holds about them, and to correct any inaccuracies.

And it doesn't end here! A whole pile of responsibilities goes with PIPEDA. For a little light reading, we have included all of Schedule 1 of PIPEDA on the CD-ROM, so just see Form 13-1 for more information. But to give you a quick summary, Schedule 1 says that you have to observe ten principles about personal information:

1. **Be accountable:** Protect the information you collect (see principle 7). Develop and implement PIPEDA-compliant policies and practices for your business, and appoint someone to be responsible for your business's compliance with PIPEDA.

2. **Identify your purposes:** Before or at the time you collect personal information, for example at the cash register, or in application forms, questionnaires, or surveys, explain why you're collecting and how you will use the information (and if your reasons later change, go back to the client and explain how they have changed).

3. **Get consent:** Get the individual's consent to collect and use his or her personal information before or at the time of collection, and get consent again if you come up with a new use for the information.

4. **Limit your collection:** Don't go around collecting personal information without good reason, and don't mislead an individual about why you're collecting his or her information.

5. **Limit your use, disclosure, and retention**: Use or disclose personal information only for the purpose for which the individual agreed it could be used or disclosed, and keep the information only as long as necessary to satisfy that purpose. Create guidelines and procedures for keeping and for destroying the information (that includes keeping information

used to make a decision for a reasonable time, so that the individual involved can get the information from you), and destroy or erase or make anonymous any information no longer required for the purpose (unless you're required by law to keep it).

6. **Be accurate:** Do your best to make sure that the information is correct, whenever you make a decision based on it or disclose it outside your business.

7. **Use safeguards**: Protect the information against loss, theft, unauthorized access, copying, modification, and disclosure outside your business. For example, don't bring up personal information on a computer screen that's in public view and then wander away from the computer.

8. **Be open:** Tell your customers and clients about the policies and practices you created (see principle 5), and make them available and easy to understand. (Don't forget to tell your employees that you have policies and practices, and that the customers are entitled to know about them!)

9. **Provide answers and access:** If customers ask, tell them what personal information you're keeping about them (let them see it if they want to, and give them a copy of it; and correct anything in it that customers say is inaccurate).

10. **Provide recourse:** Develop easy-to-use complaint procedures, and let your customers know about them and about other available complaint procedures — such as those of the Privacy Commissioner, industry or professional associations, or regulatory authorities. Investigate any complaint promptly, and correct your own practices and f they seem to be falling short.

Note that PIPEDA doesn't apply in your province — don't jump for joy yet, there's a stinger in the tail here — if the province has enacted legislation that the federal government has deemed "substantially similar" to PIPEDA. (In other words, this means that you may not have to comply with PIPEDA itself . . . just with PIPEDA under another name . . .).

For quite a lot of useful information about privacy in the commercial sector, and how a business goes about complying with PIPEDA, go to the Privacy Commissioner of Canada's Web site at www.privcom.gc.ca. Or you can call 1-800-282-1376. And no, this is not the Privacy Commissioner's home phone number.

Getting Repeat Business and Referrals

If you want your customer to use your business again and refer other customers to you, first of all you've got to do your work right. But your relationship with your customers isn't over just because you've done your work and you've been paid. You have to go on paying attention to your customers.

Customer service, part 5 — the aftermath

Your customers may have questions or problems that come up days or weeks after you've provided the product or service, and even at that point it's still important to give them good service. If your customers think that you don't care about them once you've got their money, they're less likely to deal with you again or refer other customers to you.

And if your customer doesn't contact you, you should contact him or her. After delivering a product or performing a service, call to say thank you for the business and to ask whether he or she is happy with your work or product. As time goes by, contact your customers about new products or developments in your field that may be of interest to them. (Of course, you can do all of this only if you have permission to use a customer's contact information for these purposes! See "Customer service, part 4.") Send holiday greeting cards, and, depending on how personal your relationship with your customers or clients is, perhaps birthday and anniversary cards as well (but only if you have collected birth dates and anniversary dates with consent, naturally); or, to alien invaders, a congratulations card when they have achieved total domination of the Earth.

When Peaceful Coexistence Is Shattered

Your relationship with your customers and clients will not be undiluted sweetness and light. In particular, two nasty things could happen:

- ✔ You could be fired, without having done anything wrong.
- ✔ You could totally screw up (and very likely get fired).

This is the end of the business relationship. But it may not be the end of the entire relationship — you could run into the customer or client again . . . in court.

If you get fired for no good reason

It's one thing never to get any repeat business or referrals from an unhappy customer. But it's another to be told you're through while you're in the process of providing services or goods. No doubt the customer or client has reasons for booting you off the job. Some may have something to do with you, and others may not have a thing to do with you (the client's nephew's girlfriend just set up a competing business and the client wants to patronize it instead).

Customer satisfaction survey

If you think that you won't find out what customers really think about your business just by chatting with them, then offer them a customer satisfaction survey to fill out. Below is a survey that can be used for pretty well any business (it's available on the CD-ROM, too) — or you can adapt the survey for your own business. Be sure to explain on the form that you will use the survey only internally for the purpose of improving service, and that you will not retain the forms once the anonymous answers have been added to your survey tabulation.

1. If you called our company, were you happy with the way your call was handled?

    _ YES _ NO

    Comments:
    _____
    _____

2. If you've visited our place of business, did you find the premises pleasant?

    _ YES _ NO

    Comments:
    _____
    _____

3. When you dealt with our staff, did you find them courteous, knowledgeable, and helpful?

    _ YES _ NO

    Comments:
    _____
    _____

4. Are you satisfied with the quality of the product/service we have provided to you?

    _ YES _ NO

    Comments:
    _____
    _____

5. If you've had any complaints or questions, have they been handled quickly and properly?

    _ YES _ NO

    Comments:
    _____
    _____

6. Do you plan to deal with our business again in the future?

    _ YES _ NO

    Comments:
    _____
    _____

7. Would you recommend our business to others?

    _ YES _ NO

    Comments:
    _____
    _____

If your agreement with the customer or client gives him or her the right to terminate the agreement for no reason (usually on a few days' or weeks' notice), then you just have to put up with this injustice.

If your agreement doesn't give the customer or client the right to terminate for no reason (or for the reason that the client has stated), then you may be entitled to sue the customer or client for the full amount that's still outstanding under the contract. If the outstanding amount is a large sum, you may look upon this as an attractive idea. On the other hand, you may be concerned about what suing a customer or client will do to your business's image and reputation.

Talk the situation over with your lawyer before you make a decision to sue or not to sue. For more about deciding to sue, see Chapter 18.

If you really screw up

It's always desirable, but it's not always possible, to avoid making mistakes. Sometimes fixing a mistake can inspire as much customer loyalty as doing it right in the first place. But that's not the kind of mistake we're talking about here. We're talking about forgetting to fill up the gas tank before sending a customer off on a run beyond the orbit of Pluto. This is not a situation where a simple apology and a small gift are going to get you off the hook. You've got an excellent chance of being fired and a pretty good chance of being sued.

You can be sued if

✔ **You don't finish your work (on time or at all), or you do the work poorly.** You can be sued for the return of money that was paid for work that was not done or not done properly, and for the extra costs of having someone else finish or redo the work. In addition, you can be sued for any loss the customer or client suffers because the work wasn't done, including a business opportunity the customer or client lost.

✔ **You don't deliver the goods, or deliver the goods late.** If you don't deliver the goods you won't get paid, and if you've already been paid you can be sued for return of the money. You could also be sued for any loss the buyer suffers because the goods weren't delivered. If you deliver the goods late, in most cases you can still insist on being paid (but you can be sued for losses caused by late delivery).

✔ **You provide damaged or defective goods.** You won't get paid, or you can be sued for return of money already paid, and you can be sued for any extra loss the customer suffers because of the condition of the goods.

✔ **You injure someone or damage their property, either directly or by providing defective goods.** If you injure someone, you can be sued for (among other things) the cost of their medical treatment, their pain and suffering, any wages they lost while they couldn't work, and for income they'll lose in the future if the injury affects their ability to work. If you damage property, you can be sued for the cost of repairing or replacing the property, and also for costs that result from the property damage (for example, lost business if the damage causes the business's premises to close for a few days).

Don't screw up in the first place

It's a little late to tell you not to make the mistake, but we're going to do it anyway. This is our way of saying "I told you so." If you don't want to make mistakes that could end up being very costly,

✔ **Do your work . . . on time.** Don't take on a job that you don't have time to do, and make sure that you structure payments so that you can afford to finish the job.

✔ **Do the work well.** Don't take on a job that you can't do properly, and focus on the work once you start it.

✔ **Deliver the goods . . . on time.** Don't promise to deliver goods that you don't already have in your possession or that you're not sure of getting.

✔ **Don't deliver goods that are damaged or defective.** If you're the manufacturer, inspect goods before they leave your premises. If you're a retailer, inspect goods before you pass them on to customers, if possible. If you receive a warning from the manufacturer or a government authority that one of your products is dangerous, stop selling it immediately, until you can be sure that any problem has been corrected. If you're shipping goods, pack them carefully and use a careful shipper.

✔ **Don't let anyone get injured, or anyone's property get damaged.** This is kind of a tall order. Read Chapter 12 about risk management strategies.

Anticipate screwing up — and protect yourself beforehand

If it's too late to tell you not to screw up, it's also too late to tell you to protect yourself. But you've seen that we're not to be deterred.

One way of protecting yourself is to put an exemption or exculpatory clause in your contract. (We talked about this earlier in the chapter. An exemption clause may work with business customers, but may not work with consumers or alien invaders.) This clause limits your responsibility if you do a bad job. You could have a clause, for example, that says that

✔ You are not responsible at all (for a particular kind of loss such as non-delivery, or for any kind of loss, period).

> ✔ You're responsible only for correcting the mistake, or repairing or replacing the goods.
>
> ✔ You're responsible only to the extent of reducing the contract price by a fixed maximum amount, or of refunding the amount the customer or client paid.

The most important way of protecting yourself is to have third-party liability insurance. Your insurance company will defend the lawsuit and pay any compensation you are required to pay. (See Chapter 12 for more about insurance.) You can't insure against deliberate screw-ups, only careless screw-ups.

But if you aren't protected . . .

So. You couldn't or didn't prevent the screw-up from happening. And you either didn't get insurance for this kind of risk, or you can't get insurance for this kind of risk.

But all is not lost. Just because you screwed up doesn't mean you'll get sued. The larger the amount of money involved or the madder the client or customer, the more likely it is that you'll get sued. If the customer hasn't suffered a big financial loss because of your mistake, it probably won't be worth his or her while to sue you.

Suppose, though, that you do get sued. If you have insurance coverage, your insurer will defend the lawsuit on your behalf, and will pay compensation on your behalf. Notify your insurer as soon as you realize you have a problem (even before you get served with legal documents, if possible). They'll let you know whether you're covered.

Keep in mind that if you make a claim against your insurance, your premiums will rise.

If you don't have insurance coverage, speak to your lawyer right away so you can take the proper steps to defend the lawsuit.

And just because you get sued doesn't mean you'll have to pay a lot of money, or even any money . . . even if you have no insurance. The person who suffered the loss has to prove the loss and has to *mitigate damages* (take reasonable steps to reduce the loss). Sometimes people mitigate their damages right out of existence. For example, if you failed to deliver a computer system that a customer had ordered, but the customer was able to get a very similar one from another business immediately and for less money, the customer may not have suffered any damages at all. And if the customer didn't bother to try to get a computer system to replace the one you didn't deliver but just let her business go to pot, a court won't award her compensation to cover all the losses she suffered — it will order compensation only for the loss she would have suffered if she had bought a computer system from someone else.

In addition, even if you get sued there may be someone who's more responsible than you. For example, if as a retailer you sold defective goods, you can sue the manufacturer in your turn. You may not have to pay any money or may get reimbursed for the money that the court orders you to pay.

Chapter 14

Co-existing with Other Life Forms II: Suppliers and Advisors

. . . .

In This Chapter

▶ Figuring out what goods and services you will need

▶ Finding and choosing suppliers

▶ Establishing credit with your suppliers

▶ Entering into contracts with suppliers

▶ Building a good relationship with suppliers

▶ Handling problems with suppliers

▶ Working with professional advisors

. . . .

In Chapter 13, we tell you how to deal with your customers when you're providing your goods or services. But your own business needs goods and services too. So in this chapter, we tell you how to be a customer, and get the most out of your relationship with your suppliers.

As you'd guess, this chapter goes over a lot of matters that we cover in Chapter 13, only this time from the opposite point of view. We take you into the mirror-image universe of suppliers. (In a mirror-image universe, everything looks pretty much the same except it's reversed. So you write from the right edge of a page to the left, and put the forks on the right side of the plate and the knives and spoons on the left side. Lefties think mirror-image universes are great, until they get there, and realize that they're now right-handed.) But don't be alarmed. If you can handle customers — a life form from another planet — then you can handle suppliers, a life form from another universe. Stick with us and we tell you how.

So Now You're the Customer

Maybe after reading Chapter 13 you think that customers and clients aren't all that much fun to deal with, although they are admittedly essential to your business. But now the tables are turned — you're somebody else's customer!

Unfortunately, when you're in business, being a customer doesn't give you a licence to be demanding, snarky, and unreasonable (even if you see these as the defining characteristics of your own customers). Although you can indulge yourself occasionally, for the most part you're going to want to concentrate on building good relationships with your suppliers. Most businesses need suppliers as much as they need customers.

In this section, we ease you into the supplier universe. We talk about deciding what products or services you need from providers, how to make up a list of providers of those products or services, and how to choose a suitable provider from your list.

Determining what goods and services you need

Some of the purchases you make for your business simply support your business — for example, furniture for your office or office supplies or courier services. When you buy these goods and services you're essentially a consumer, and you'll make your purchases the way you'd make any consumer purchase, such as groceries or an oil change — looking for a supplier with the best combination of price, selection, quality, service, and convenience. If you're not happy with the supplier, it's fairly easy to go to someone else the next time you need to make a similar purchase.

But your business may (also) need specialized products, and their providers may be choosy about the businesses they deal with or the terms on which they deal with them. They may also not be easy to find.

Essential goods and services

Goods and services that don't just support your business but almost are your business are

- *Inventory* (the things you sell), such as shoes for a shoe store, greeting cards and wrapping paper for a card store, ready-made desserts for a food shop

- Parts and materials you use to make your product, such as the leather for making shoes if you're a shoe manufacturer, the paper for printing cards if you run a printing shop, fresh fruit and baking supplies if you have a dessert bakery

✔ Ongoing services you need for your business operations, such as an Internet service provider for a Web-based business, a pest-control service for a restaurant, or a window display service for an upscale clothing store

How do you know what you need?

Before you decide on what your particular business needs, do some research to find out what businesses in your field generally need. You can get help from the following sources:

✔ **Trade associations:** Find the trade association for your industry using Strategis, or use a search engine such as Yahoo! (www.yahoo.com) or Google Web Directory (www.google.com) to locate the association's Web site. The Web site may have useful information, or contact information if you want to speak directly to someone at the association. Many trade associations hold seminars and workshops. Contact the association to find out if they have seminars on necessary supplies and services.

✔ **Trade publications:** Many trade associations publish journals and/or newsletters with current information about the industry. These publications contain advertisements for equipment and supplies used by businesses in the field, and may contain articles from time to time about useful products and services.

✔ **Trade shows:** Most trade associations hold an industry-wide trade show at least once a year. They are a good place to make contacts in the industry and learn about the latest trends in the field.

See Chapter 2 for more about using your computer to research your business. Strategis (www.strategis.ic.gc.ca), a Web site maintained by the federal government's Industry Canada, contains information on a wide variety of businesses organized by sector. Each type of business has its own page with links to major trade associations, trade shows, and publications in the field.

Finding suppliers

Once you have an idea of what goods and services you need, you have to find a business that offers them.

Finding good suppliers in our own universe is perfectly possible. But some businesses fall into the trap of dealing with suppliers from a parallel alternate universe. A parallel alternate universe is where your keys have vanished to when you can't find them in the exact place you set them down. Oddly, keys from parallel alternate universes rarely show up in our universe. Instead, we get other universes' 3-cents-a-page photocopy shops and deep-discount computer stores. This is why, when you find a supplier who's too good to be true, you can never find it again the next time you need it. It's skylarked back to its own universe.

If you want to deal with suppliers from our own universe, you can locate them in a number of ways.

- ✔ **Speak to colleagues in your field.** Ask for the names of the suppliers they use and would recommend. (You may discover that your colleagues don't want to share their suppliers with you, though, because a good supplier gives a business a competitive advantage. They'll be so evasive about who their supplier is that you'll suspect they're dealing with one of the parallel alternate universe businesses.)

- ✔ **Contact your trade association.** Ask for a directory of industry suppliers.

- ✔ **Read trade publications.** They contain advertisements for suppliers who provide products and services to the industry, and may contain articles discussing and recommending suppliers.

- ✔ **Go to trade shows and conventions.** Look for displays by suppliers of products and services. Speak to their representatives and pick up their catalogues and other sales information.

- ✔ **Use a searchable Internet database.** For example, ThomasNet is an industrial search engine that brings together industrial buyers and suppliers and provides a single source for finding the products, services, or suppliers you're looking for (`www.ThomasNet.com`). The database includes over 650,000 distributors, manufacturers, and service companies within more than 67,000 searchable categories. Canadian Company Capabilities (`www.strategis.ic.gc.ca/sc_coinf/ccc/engdoc/homepage.html www.strategis.gc.ca/cdncc`), a database maintained by Industry Canada of 50,000 Canadian companies organized by category, contains the name, address, contacts, products, and services of each company, and provides a direct link to companies' Web sites.

- ✔ **Search the Internet with a search engine.** The Web sites of major suppliers have online catalogues setting out details of various types of supplies and equipment, including pricing and shipping information.

- ✔ **Look in the Yellow Pages.** Find the locations and telephone numbers of suppliers in your local area.

Gather the names of a number of suppliers and make a list.

Choosing a supplier

Next, you have to narrow your list of suppliers down to the supplier who's right for you. Take care, because this is a supplier with whom you'll be dealing on a regular basis and on whom you'll depend to keep your business in business.

If you rely on a single supplier for any of your important needs, you can run into serious problems if deliveries are interrupted for any reason. Sometimes you may have no choice about whom you deal with because there is only one supplier who has what you need. Other times, you may be seduced into making a commitment to a supplier because you're offered very good terms if you agree to deal with that supplier exclusively.

If you do deal with just one supplier, try to stay informed about other available suppliers, just in case you need them.

Inventory and parts suppliers

When you're deciding on a supplier of inventory or parts for your business, be sure to consider all of the following:

- ✔ Does the supplier have the full range and selection of products that you need?

- ✔ How competitive are the supplier's prices? Does the supplier ever offer any specials? Are there discounts for large or standing orders?

- ✔ How reliable is the supplier? What is the supplier's track record for filling orders completely and on time?

- ✔ What is the supplier's delivery time from the date an order is received until the date it's shipped? How are goods shipped? Who pays for shipping?

- ✔ Will you be able to return or exchange defective, damaged, non-selling, or overstocked merchandise? If so, who pays for shipping, and will you have to pay a restocking charge?

- ✔ Does the supplier provide good customer service? Will the supplier give reliable advice about what you should purchase? If you're buying complicated equipment, either for your own use or for resale to your own customers, does the supplier offer training in the operation of the equipment to you and your employees or to the customer? Does the supplier have a good reputation for responding to customer complaints?

- ✔ Does the supplier extend credit? What do you have to do to establish credit? Once you're granted credit, will you be given a discount for cash payments on delivery or for early payment?

- ✔ If you're buying goods for resale, does the supplier offer any advertising support?

Consider asking the suppliers you investigate for names of customers you can contact for references.

Service suppliers

With some service suppliers you may have a close working relationship — that might be the case with a pest control company or a security firm or a window dresser. But some of your service suppliers may almost end up living in your back pocket — they'll be more like employees of your business than independent businesses themselves. If you hire a business that provides secretarial or bookkeeping services or provides support for your hardware and software, you may be dealing with your supplier on an almost daily basis.

Take special care in choosing a supplier who will become an integral part of your business. You run the danger of getting mixed up with a supplier from an anti-universe. An anti-universe looks much like an ordinary universe, but instead of being made up of matter (like our universe), it's made up of anti-matter. When anti-matter comes into contact with matter — well, the results aren't pretty, for either side. (You might wonder why suppliers from an anti-universe risk doing business here. It's because of the very favourable exchange rate.)

To avoid unpleasantness, when you're deciding on a supplier of services for your business, you'll want to consider the following:

- ✔ **Does the supplier offer the services that you need?** Is the supplier able to provide services of the quality you want? Does the supplier have the necessary qualifications or licence to provide the services?

- ✔ **How competitive are the supplier's prices?** Check around and compare prices with those of the supplier's competitors.

- ✔ **How reliable is the supplier?** What's the supplier's record for doing good work on time and on budget?

- ✔ **Does the supplier stand behind his or her work?** How well does the supplier deal with customer complaints?

- ✔ **Will it always be the same individuals performing the work?** Will the principals of the business do the work, or will they delegate the work to less skillful employees? If the service providers are going to be on your premises a lot or in constant communication with you, do you feel comfortable working with them? Or do they make your hair stand on end?

- ✔ **Does the supplier extend credit?** What do you have to do to establish credit? Are there discounts for cash payments on delivery or for early payment?

Ask for names of customers you can contact for references. Although you can now dial direct to an anti-universe, be sure to hold the phone well away from your ear in case of accidents if you decide to contact an anti-reference.

Establishing Credit with Your Suppliers

Most businesses like to have some flexibility when it comes to paying their bills. When you're the supplier, cash on delivery is very nice. But when you're the customer, you'd much rather have time to make your payments. You may need the time to collect your own accounts receivable (some of which will have wandered off into a parallel alternate universe) so that you'll have money in the bank when the supplier goes to cash your cheque.

As a new customer, you may not be able to get credit from a supplier immediately. You may have to put up with being a COD (cash on delivery . . . and you already knew that, so stop making fish noises) customer until the supplier has had a chance to look you over and decide that you won't take the goods or services and then skip the universe without paying. Once the supplier stops being suspicious of you, you may be granted a line of credit so you no longer have to pay on delivery. The supplier may first ask for financial statements and credit references. (If your business is just starting, you'll show your supplier your projected statements and you'll offer personal credit references instead of references for your business.)

After you've got credit, the supplier will still invoice you for the product when it's delivered or for the services when they are provided. But you'll be allowed a grace period (usually 30 days) in which to pay the bill without interest being charged. If you pay the bill before the 30 days are up, you may be given a discount. Suppliers commonly give a discount of 2 percent if a customer pays within ten days.

When you first get your credit, make sure that you pay your bills on time. (Just like when you first get the keys to your parents' car you make sure that you don't crash it.) Then you'll be able to use the supplier as a credit reference for new suppliers. Over time, you'll acquire a good credit rating and suppliers will be able to get credit information about you from credit rating agencies instead of from your suppliers.

Entering Into Contracts with Your Suppliers

Every time you agree to buy goods or get services from a supplier, you are entering into a contract. In theory at least, your contracts with your suppliers will be the product of give and take on both sides, so that you negotiate an agreement that both of you are equally happy with. (In actual fact, you may not have a great deal of negotiating power, especially when your business is new and small and your suppliers are large and powerful.)

Once both sides have agreed to the contract (whether or not they're blissfully happy with it), both sides have to do what the contract says. It is important that you and your supplier understand clearly what you are to do. If one party doesn't do what the contract says, the other party may have the right to sue and/or end the contract.

Contracts for goods

Unless you're making a purchase at a retail store, you should have some form of written contract with a supplier of goods. The contract may be

- ✔ **A sales order form or invoice created by your supplier:** If you order your products by telephone and don't set any terms for the contract, the terms will be governed by the wording on the invoice or sales order form that your supplier includes with the shipment, so you should have a copy of the invoice faxed to you before you place your order.

- ✔ **A purchase order form created by you:** If you order goods by sending a purchase order form setting out the terms on which you're willing to buy the goods and your supplier fills the purchase order, the terms of your contract will be governed by the purchase order.

- ✔ **A formal written contract signed by both parties:** If the contract involves a large sale, or a custom-made item, you and the supplier may have to negotiate a contract that deals specifically with this transaction.

Whatever the form of your contract, it will involve agreement about the following things:

- ✔ **The parties to the contract:** The supplier agrees to provide the goods and you agree to pay for the goods.

  If your business is a corporation, you should be sure it's clearly stated in the contract that you're signing only as an officer of the corporation and not personally — so your signature will go over your name, plus your corporate title and the name of your corporation.

- ✔ **The goods being sold:** Include quantity, brand name, and model number (if that's important).

- ✔ **The quality of the goods:** If the contract doesn't say anything about the quality of the goods, provincial sale of goods legislation implies certain promises that the goods are of reasonable quality. Your supplier (especially if it doesn't have a parallel alternate universe to withdraw to) will probably try to limit its responsibility or state that it has no responsibility at all. If the contract you sign limits the supplier's responsibility, as a business customer you will not be entitled to any protection under provincial consumer protection legislation — so you'll have no one to complain to about the goods.

✔ **The cost of the goods:** GST and PST, or HST, should be shown too. Shipping and insurance should also be noted if you're paying for them. If you're responsible for the cost of shipping, find out what the cost will be — before you make the purchase — because the shipping costs can be quite substantial (even within our own universe . . . and the cost of shipping from an anti-universe is out of this world). You may want to request a less expensive method of shipping, or ask if your supplier will cover all or part of the shipping cost if you place an order over a minimum dollar amount.

✔ **The date you must pay for the goods:** If your contract does not specify the date, by provincial sale of goods legislation you must pay at the time of delivery of the goods. If your supplier agrees to accept payment sometime after the date of delivery, the contract should set out the terms for payment, including the amount and date of the payments, and the interest rate being charged.

✔ **The date and place that the goods are to be delivered:** If your contract does not address these matters, provincial sale of goods legislation says that you must pick up the goods from the supplier, and that the goods must be available within a reasonable period of time. If you have other plans, the contract should state where the goods are to be delivered and when. If the goods are to be shipped to you, the contract should state how they are to be shipped, who is to pay for the shipping, and who is responsible for the loss if the goods are damaged, destroyed, lost, or stolen during shipping.

✔ **Your right to return the goods:** Unless there's a problem with the quality of the goods (and the supplier has not refused to accept responsibility for quality), you have no right to return the goods unless the supplier agrees to give you that right. So if you need or want to be able to return the goods even if nothing is physically wrong with them, try to get a clause to that effect in the contract — for example, that you have the right to return them (unused) within ten days.

Contracts for services

Any time you get services for your business you should have a written contract. The more complex the arrangement for services, the more detail you'll want in the contract. By putting the contract in writing, you and your supplier are forced to define the details of your agreement, and that's how you'll be sure that one of you isn't bargaining from a mirror-image universe and that you really are in agreement. As the supplier performs its services, your contract will serve as a checklist of the work your supplier is supposed to do. And, if a dispute occurs later on, a detailed written contract also serves as evidence of what was actually agreed to.

Whatever kind of services you're getting, the contract with your supplier should always deal with the following:

- ✔ **Who the parties to the contract are:** The supplier agrees to provide the services and you agree to pay for them. (Again, make it clear that you're contracting as an officer and not personally if your business is a corporation.)

  If you want a specific individual to do the work, the contract should name the individual. Otherwise the supplier's representative who deals with you or signs the contract doesn't have to do the actual work — the supplier can assign the work to an employee or even delegate the work to another business (unless the supplier is an individual himself or herself and this is a contract for personal services). However, the supplier who is the party to the contract is still responsible for making sure that the work is done and done properly.

- ✔ **What services are to be performed:** The contract should set out in detail the nature of the services, and state the standard of quality the services must meet.

- ✔ **When the services are to be performed:** The contract should state a starting date, and perhaps an end date if you want to be sure that the services are fully performed by a certain time.

- ✔ **What the services will cost:** Is the cost fixed or is it based on time spent?

  If you're paying by the hour, protect yourself from having to pay more than you expect to pay by setting a ceiling on the number of hours that your supplier can spend on the job or by getting a firm estimate of how many hours will be spent. That way, if the job takes longer than expected, you'll be entitled to a reasonable explanation before you have to pay anything extra.

- ✔ **How payment is to be made:** Will you have to pay in full at the beginning? At the end? Or will you pay in instalments as your supplier does the work?

  If you'll be paying in instalments, try to match the amount of the instalments to the value of the work performed, so that it's not in the supplier's interest to quit in the middle of the job because he or she has already been fully paid.

- ✔ **What rights the parties have to end the contract or extend the contract:** One of the parties may want to end the contract before the services have all been performed, or to extend the contract to include additional services. If you have a contract for the supplier to provide regular services over a period of time, you may want to provide for early termination in case you're not happy with the services. Or you may want to include a right to renew the contract if you're happy with the services.

✔ **What licences and/or permits are required:** If your supplier is required by law to be properly qualified or licensed, the contract should state that the supplier has the necessary qualifications or licence. If a permit is required for the particular job, the contract should state who will get it and pay for it.

✔ **What happens if the services are not performed properly:** The contract should say what your rights are if the quality of the work is unsatisfactory. The supplier may offer a *warranty* — promising, for example, that it will remedy any problems for a fixed period of time after the service has been performed.

✔ **What happens if your supplier causes injury to you or causes damage to your property:** Your supplier may want an *exemption* or *exculpatory clause* in the contract that limits the supplier's liability for causing damage or injury, and you may have trouble getting your supplier to take the clause out. You may want the supplier to agree to maintain insurance in case it causes any damage or injury. (You should have insurance too, in case someone is injured while working on your business premises. See Chapter 12 for more about insurance, or, better yet, contact your insurance agent or broker.)

We've included a sample contract for the provision of services on the CD-ROM.

Speak to your lawyer

You should get advice from your lawyer about the contracts you enter into with suppliers.

✔ Have your lawyer prepare a standard purchase order form for you to use if you order goods on a regular basis.

✔ Have your lawyer review invoices or contracts for goods before you agree to them if you don't understand them and the supplier cannot explain them to your satisfaction If different terms need to be negotiated, your lawyer may be able to do a better job at negotiations than you can. (This is because your lawyer probably comes from a different universe, just like the supplier. See under "Using Suppliers of Professional Services.")

✔ Consult a lawyer if you're negotiating a contract that involves a lot of money or a long-term commitment.

Establishing a Good Relationship with Your Suppliers

When you find suppliers you're happy with, you want to make sure that you do what you can to establish a good working relationship. Here are some tips:

✔ Be clear about what you need and when you need it every time you place an order. Confirm that the supplier has or can get what you're ordering and can deliver on your schedule.

✔ Communicate with your supplier. If you have a minor problem, let your supplier know. Don't wait until you accumulate many minor problems or until a minor problem becomes a major problem. It's better to let your supplier know sooner rather than later, because that increases the chance that the supplier will be able do something to correct the problem.

✔ Don't squabble over every invoice, or try to get price reductions on everything you buy. Your supplier will get sick of you, and call you unpleasant names behind your back (for example, if the supplier is from a mirror-image universe it might call you an *etakspaehc*), and won't be in a big hurry to offer you discounts or other freebies that come along.

✔ Pay your bills promptly. If you know that you're going to have a problem paying on time, let your supplier know, especially if it's a temporary problem that you'll be able to fix.

✔ Treat the supplier's sales and service representatives courteously, even if you have a complaint. And even if you think they've been calling you an *etakspaehc* behind your back.

✔ Ask for special service only when you need it. Don't ask for last-minute deliveries or extra goods or services unless you're in an unusual situation. (For example, your inventory has been destroyed by a matter–anti-matter collision.)

In return, you expect quality goods or services, reliably delivered. Over time, as a valued customer you should expect some extra service. You would like to be

✔ Told of new products that become available

✔ Told of available discounts and rebates or other special deals on products you often buy, or that might be of interest to you

✔ Advised of any possible delays in delivery before they happen

✔ Helped out if you occasionally need extra inventory or immediate delivery

✔ Shown some flexibility if you have an occasional problem paying a bill on time

As a new, and perhaps small and rather insignificant, customer, you can't immediately expect the same kind of service a long-standing customer would get. It takes time to build that kind of relationship, so be patient.

You may also want to keep in mind that your Canadian suppliers are required to follow personal privacy legislation (PIPEDA) just like you are — go to Chapter 13 for a look at PIPEDA from the other side of the mirror-image universe. That means your suppliers cannot collect personal information about you and your staff without explaining why they're doing it, getting your consent, and then going through the same whole rigmarole about protecting your information and showing it to you on request and so on. So although you can still expect mail and phone calls and faxes to come to your business address and numbers, even in the middle of the night, you don't have to put up with any more personal communication from a supplier that you haven't agreed to beforehand.

If a supplier does not meet your expectations of quality, price, service, and reliability, you shouldn't fume, you shouldn't fight, you should find another supplier. Keep your bases covered — even if things are going well with your suppliers, try to stay informed about other suppliers in case you need them one day.

If you ditch a supplier you've had a long-term or important relationship with, it's good business etiquette to inform the supplier — just like it's good business etiquette for your customers or clients to let you know when they're moving on.

Problems with Suppliers

When you're the supplier, you run into problems with your customers. So it only stands to reason that as a customer you'll run into problems with your suppliers. If you're about to complain that in a mirror-image universe you shouldn't have to have problems with your suppliers as well as your customers, all we can say is: That's quantum physics for you.

Try to avoid problems in the first place

The best way to deal with problems is not to have them in the first place. So may we suggest you take the following steps:

- **Choose your suppliers wisely.** Your best protection against problems is to deal with a supplier with a good (and deserved) reputation.

- **If you're buying goods, choose the product carefully.** Even if you're in the process of building a long-term relationship with one supplier, compare the price and quality of goods available from other suppliers. If your supplier is offering an inferior product or higher prices on the same product available elsewhere, bring that to the supplier's attention. You may be able to negotiate a better deal with your supplier . . . or you may decide to go elsewhere for this item (as long as your contract doesn't prohibit you from playing the field).

- **Don't automatically accept your supplier's contract terms.** You may be presented with a pre-printed, standard form contract. If you're dealing with a large company and you're a small customer, your supplier will probably refuse to make any changes. But you may be able to get changes if you're dealing with a smaller supplier and you're giving it a lot of business.

- **Try to arrive at an agreement that's fair to both sides (even if you're the one with the bargaining muscle).** If you enter into a deal that is totally one-sided in your favour, your supplier may simply walk away from the contract, figuring it's no worse financially to be sued by you than to perform the contract. Or the supplier may perform the contract, but never want to deal with you again.

- **Put your deal in writing.** Unless you're making a purchase from a retail store, the key terms of your agreement should be in writing.

- **See a lawyer if you need to.** Have a lawyer draft or review contracts that involve a lot of money or a long-term commitment, or that you don't understand fully.

Some problems that can arise

Even if you do everything right, problems can still arise. Here are some typical problems, and some solutions.

Contracts for services

- **The supplier doesn't finish the work.** You'll have to find someone else to finish the work. Before you hire someone else, notify the first provider in writing that you consider your contract to be at an end. If you've arranged to pay when the work is done, or in instalments as it's performed and you've calculated your instalments properly, you won't have paid more than the value of the work, so you won't lose too much money. If you've overpaid for the work that was done, you'll probably have to sue to get the overpayment back. (Good luck on collecting any money a judge awards you!)

✔ **The supplier does the work badly.** If you realize that the work isn't satisfactory as the services are being provided, ask the service provider to correct the problems. If the supplier does not correct the problems, you may have the right to end the contract and refuse to pay (speak to a lawyer before you do anything, though). If you've already paid something, you'll probably have to sue to get it back. If the supplier really messed up, you may want to sue for additional compensation to cover losses you've suffered as a result.

✔ **The supplier injures you (or your associate or employee) or damages your property.** The injured person or the property owner can sue for compensation for personal injury or property damage. If the supplier has third-party liability insurance, the insurance should cover the damages. If the supplier doesn't have insurance, it may not have much property either, and you'll be up the wormhole when it comes to collecting any money a court awards you.

You may have noticed that we talked about services before goods this time. That's only because we're trying to confuse you, and not because you accidentally entered a mirror-image universe.

Contracts for goods

✔ **The supplier doesn't deliver the goods.** Don't pay for goods that are not delivered. To protect yourself, try to keep the amount you pay before delivery as low as possible. If you have already paid some or all of the purchase price, you'll probably have to sue to get it back. You can also sue the supplier for compensation for any loss you suffer because of non-delivery, such as profits you lost because you didn't receive the goods.

✔ **The supplier delivers the goods late.** Unless your contract states that "time is of the essence," you have to accept late delivery and pay for the goods in full. You may, however, be able to sue the supplier for compensation for any loss you suffer because the goods were not delivered on time.

✔ **The supplier delivers the wrong or damaged goods.** You do not have to accept or pay for wrong or damaged goods. Inspect your shipments upon receipt and refuse to accept them if you spot a problem. You may also be able to sue for compensation for any loss you suffer because of defective goods. However, the supplier may have limited its responsibility by an exculpatory clause in the contract. Then you're up the wormhole again.

If you suffer loss or damage because of your supplier

If your supplier breaches its contract with you (doesn't perform the contract as promised — for example, by not delivering the goods you ordered), you can sue the supplier for damages, which we've been referring to as "compensation" for losses you've suffered. If you win your lawsuit, the court will order the supplier to pay you money for your losses. The amount you receive in damages is supposed to put you in the position you would have been in if your supplier had performed the contract properly (and your business affairs had therefore sailed on smoothly).

If you suffer loss or damage, you can't just sit back and let your losses pile up. You have a legal obligation to *mitigate* your damages — that is, to take all reasonable steps to keep your losses as low as possible. For example, if a supplier fails to deliver parts that you need to manufacture your product, you have to try to find an alternative supply of the parts. If you don't take steps to mitigate your damages, the court will not give you an award for your total loss, only for what you would have lost if you had made an effort to reduce your losses.

Consult a lawyer immediately if your supplier didn't do what it promised under the contract and you have suffered a loss as a result. Your lawyer can give you advice about steps you should take immediately to improve your chances of recovering damages from the supplier.

Using Suppliers of Professional Services

Suppliers of professional services — that is, professional advisors — come from a somewhat different universe than other suppliers. So you have to approach them a bit differently.

In the way of professional advisors, you'll need a lawyer, an accountant, and an insurance agent or broker. Depending on the nature of your business, you may also want help from one or more of the following individuals:

✔ **A publicist or media relations expert** — to help you get publicity for your business

✔ **A marketing consultant** — to help you identify the market for your product or services and determine how best to reach that market

✔ **An interior designer** — to help you set up your business premises

- ✔ **A graphic designer** — to help you design a business logo and the look of your business cards and letterhead

- ✔ **A computer systems consultant** — to help you choose and set up your computer equipment and choose and install your software

- ✔ **A management consultant** — if you need help with management skills

- ✔ **A human resources specialist (also known as a headhunter)** — to help you hire staff

- ✔ **Business coaches** — to help you with things such as management skills, presentation skills, dress code, and social skills

Finding professional help

You'll be looking for professional advisors with experience in small business matters, with whom you'll feel comfortable working, and who will charge you a reasonable fee. To find professionals, you're going to have to venture into their universe. In hiring any kind of professional help, you should:

- ✔ **Get recommendations.** Ask your friends, relatives, or business associates for the names of lawyers, accountants, insurance brokers, and other consultants who have done similar work for them.

- ✔ **Do some investigating.** Call the lawyer, accountant, or other business professional to find out more about his or her area of expertise. Ask how you'll be charged for his or her services. Ask if the professional will see you at your place of business. (If you'll have to go to the professional's office — as you normally will for a lawyer — you'll probably want an advisor who's in a convenient location.)

- ✔ **Interview the best candidates.** Take the top two or three candidates and set up an appointment to meet with each one in person. You not only want information about the candidate, you also want to see how you react to him or her personally. Ask about his or her experience working with small businesses, what his or her fees will likely be, and whether your work will be handled by the professional personally or by someone else in his or her office.

Entering into contracts with professional advisors

You should have a contract in writing with your professional advisors, as you would with any other service provider.

Consultants

If you're using the services of most professionals other than a lawyer or accountant, your contract should cover the matters we talked about under the heading "Contracts for services." When you're dealing with an insurance agent or broker, you probably won't have a contract and the agent or broker will be paid a commission out of your insurance premium.

Lawyers and accountants

If you're using the services of a lawyer or professional accountant (a chartered accountant or certified general accountant or certified management accountant — there's a whole universe devoted just to accountants — you probably don't want to get stranded there), you should still have a written contract. Lawyers call their contracts *retainer agreements*, and accountants call their contracts *engagement letters*. The form of these agreements is a little different from a consultant's contract. The agreement or letter should include

- A description of the work the lawyer or accountant has been retained or engaged to do.
- The name of the lawyer(s) or accountant(s) who will do the work.
- The way in which you will be charged for the work — by the hour or a flat fee are common methods of billing lawyers' and accountants' services.
- An estimate of the fee — this is easy if you're being charged a flat fee. If you're being billed at an hourly rate, the lawyer or accountant can still give an estimate of what the total fee will be, plus a promise to tell you before doing work that will take the charge beyond the estimate.
- The frequency with which you'll be billed by the lawyer or accountant. You actually want to receive bills at least monthly, so you can keep track of what the lawyer or accountant is doing and how much you owe. Every bill should include a detailed account of the work done.

Service, please!

When you're dealing with a professional advisor, you should expect good customer service. After all, professional advisors are in the service industry. Your advisor should

- Return your telephone calls within 24 hours (you'll have to allow longer for replies to e-mail messages).
- Treat you with courtesy and respect.

And your advisor should not

- Keep you waiting for appointments.
- Take phone calls or allow other interruptions during your appointments.
- Charge you for time spent on personal chit-chat with you, if it was the advisor who started the conversation.

It's not necessary to set out the standard of quality of the work, or to deal with licensing issues or insurance. That's because lawyers and professional accountants must belong to a government-recognized, self-regulating body and are bound by professional standards and a code of ethics. The regulating body can discipline its members for doing poor work or treating a client badly. These professionals are also required to have errors and omissions insurance, which will compensate a client if the lawyer or accountant makes a mistake.

Working with professional advisors

Whether you're dealing with a lawyer, accountant, or consultant, you should expect your professional service provider to do the following:

- ✔ Perform his or her services competently and promptly.

- ✔ Act honestly, and not behave in a sneaky way either with you or with the people he or she is dealing with on your behalf.

- ✔ Keep confidential any information you share with him or her about your business (or personal life, for that matter, because PIPEDA applies to these advisors too).

- ✔ Avoid any conflicts of interest (for example, not take your direct competitor on as a client).

- ✔ Keep you thoroughly and regularly advised of all work being done for you.

- ✔ Act only on your instructions, and not make his or her own decisions about what's best for you and then go ahead and carry them out without getting your permission.

Dealing with problems with professional advisors

If you've chosen your lawyer, accountant, or consultant carefully, you shouldn't run into too many problems, but here are some pointers in case you do.

If you're generally pleased with the work being done by your advisor, discuss problems as they come up. Perhaps your lawyer doesn't return your phone calls soon enough, or your accountant has sent you a bill that you don't understand. So don't work yourself into a lather — give the lawyer or accountant a call, or send a letter or e-mail, and explain your concern. You'll probably get a courteous explanation (your messages have a habit of falling into a parallel alternate universe, or the bill was accidentally prepared by a mirror-image bookkeeper) and an apology. Don't be completely stunned if you also get a bill for the time spent explaining and apologizing. That's just how professional advisors are, sometimes.

If you've lost confidence in your lawyer, accountant, or consultant, or no longer feel comfortable working with him or her, you should end your relationship. If you're going to be replacing your advisor, you may want to hire a new one before you fire the old one. The new lawyer, accountant, or consultant should be able to smooth over transitional matters.

If you don't think much of the treatment you're receiving from your advisor, look for another one.

If you have more serious concerns, such as extremely careless work that was done or behaviour that was offensive to you, contact the provincial regulatory body (if any) that governs the advisor's profession. It may have the power to discipline the advisor for unbecoming conduct, or to start you on your way to making a claim against the advisor's professional liability insurance.

Chapter 15

Beam Up the Crew

. . . .

In This Chapter

▶ Finding out what you're in for as an employer

▶ Hiring an employee

▶ Being an employer

▶ Firing an employee

. . . .

As your business grows and becomes more successful, you'll have more and more work to do. Sooner or later, you're going to need some help. You may start off using computer software and contractors who provide services, but the time will come when you need another body around on a full-time basis. In this chapter, we tell you how to go about hiring an employee and being an employer. (Eventually we even tell you how to fire an employee, which is also very useful knowledge.)

What Are You Getting Yourself Into?

Hiring an employee is not like ordering in a pizza. Before you decide to take on an employee, you'd better have some idea of what will happen when you do. As an employer, you have to do the following:

✔ Pay the employee.

✔ Give the employee time off . . . with pay!

✔ Make regular payments to the federal and provincial governments on behalf of your employee and your business.

✔ Provide a workplace that's safe, and free from discrimination and harassment.

✔ Take legal and financial responsibility for your employee's actions.

Paying wages

Once you have an employee, you have to pay the employee's wages — every payday, whether business is good or bad. Your employee gets paid before you do. (In some small businesses, especially in the start-up phase, the employees make a lot more than the owner — the owner just gets whatever's left after payroll and other expenses have been met.) You may even have to borrow money to pay your employee.

You don't simply have an obligation to pay wages, you have to pay reasonable wages. All provinces have employment standards laws that set a minimum wage (in the range of $6.30 to $8.50, depending on the province or territory) for most workers. Of course, if you're looking for an employee with skills, you'll have to pay a lot more than minimum wage to interest someone in the job.

Provincial legislation also requires you to pay your employees overtime (usually at the rate of one-and-a-half times their usual pay) if they work over a fixed maximum number of hours per week (between 40 and 48 hours, depending on the province or territory) or a fixed maximum number of hours per day (usually eight).

Providing paid vacation and statutory holidays

Not only do you have to pay your employees when they're there, sometimes you also have to pay them when they're not there.

Provincial employment standards laws set public holidays (between six and ten days per year depending on the province or territory), and employees who have worked a set minimum amount of time prior to the holiday in question are entitled to be paid their usual wages while taking these days off. An employee cannot be required to work on a public holiday without being paid overtime.

In addition, employees in every province and territory are entitled to a paid two-week vacation (in Saskatchewan it's three weeks) after completing one full year of employment. In most provinces, the length of the paid vacation goes up by an additional week for longer-term employees — most commonly after five years of employment (in Nova Scotia it's eight years, and in Saskatchewan, it's ten years). In Ontario, Prince Edward Island, and the Yukon, the length of the paid vacation never changes.

You'll be pleased to know that you're not required by law in any province to pay your employees when they're off sick. It's strictly up to you to decide whether to allow your employees a certain number of paid sick days per year. If you don't offer sick days, employees use up their paid vacation days to miss work; and once they use up their vacation days, you don't have to pay them for days they don't work.

Remitting money to the feds . . . and the provs

You're required by law to deduct income taxes, Canada Pension Plan contributions, and Employment Insurance contributions from your employees' wages, and to remit them (send them directly) to the Canada Revenue Agency (CRA). You must also remit your business's contribution toward your employees' Employment Insurance and Canada Pension Plan.

In addition, you'll have to pay premiums to your provincial workers' compensation board for coverage for your employees in case they're injured on the job. In some provinces or territories, you may also be required to pay premiums for your employees' provincial health insurance coverage.

If you don't make these required payments, you'll have to pay hefty interest and penalties (as well as be treated with scorn by government representatives).

Providing a safe workplace

As an employer, you have a duty under provincial occupational health and safety or other labour legislation to take reasonable steps to provide a safe and healthy workplace for your employees. If you don't, your employees can complain about you to the provincial government — and get you inspected, fined, and even shut down.

You also have a duty under human rights legislation to provide a workplace that is free from discrimination and harassment (see the sidebar "Don't discriminate" for details). This means that you can't discriminate against or harass any employee, and you can't allow your employees to harass or discriminate against other employees.

Don't discriminate

The federal government and every provincial government have human rights laws that prohibit discrimination on a number of grounds. The grounds vary from province to province, but usually include:

✓ Race, colour, ancestry, ethnic origin, place of origin, and citizenship

✓ Religion

✓ Sex (male or female) or sexual orientation (straight, gay, bisexual, and so on)

✓ Age (Although, strangely, it's often okay to discriminate against the young — under the age of majority — and the old — over the age of 65. Go figure.)

✓ Marital status (whether a person is married) or family status (whether a person has children or is pregnant)

✓ Physical or mental disability, including such things as alcoholism and drug addiction

✓ Political beliefs

✓ A criminal record for a provincial offence, or for a *Criminal Code* offence for which the person has been pardoned (*Criminal Code* offences are more serious than provincial offences.)

Taking responsibility for your employees' actions

If your employee causes injury to a person or damage to property while performing his or her job, you are financially responsible for your employee's acts. That means that the injured person has the right to sue you the employer (that may be you personally), and you the employer are responsible for paying any sum of money a court awards the injured person.

In addition, if part of your employee's job is to enter into contracts on behalf of your business, then you'll have to carry out whatever contracts your employee makes for your business — even if they stink.

Hiring an Employee

Feeling brave enough to go ahead and hire someone? Then we'll move to the next stage.

When you hire an employee, you want someone with the right combination of skills and personality to do the job properly and get along with you and your customers. To find this paragon, you'll go through the following steps:

1. Draft a job description and qualifications.
2. Figure out how you'll pay the employee.
3. Find candidates for the job.
4. Review the job applications.
5. Interview the most promising candidates.
6. Check the candidates out.
7. Make a job offer to the most likely candidate.

Drafting a job description and qualifications

What exactly do you want the employee to do? The answer to that question is what goes in the job description. Write it all down, and be as detailed as possible. Include

- ✔ Duties to be performed.
- ✔ Days of the week to be worked.
- ✔ Hours of the day to be worked (start and end times).
- ✔ Whether the employee will be expected to work overtime.
- ✔ Whether the employee will be required to travel and be away overnight.
- ✔ Whether the employee needs to be bonded, because the employee will be handling valuable property — belonging to your business or to your customers or clients. (A bond is a kind of insurance policy that pays if the bonded person commits a dishonest act. See Chapter 12.)
- ✔ Special physical demands, if any, such as heavy lifting, standing for long periods of time, or performing repetitive tasks like keyboarding.

You'll use the job description to find a person qualified for the job, to train your employee, to do employee performance reviews, and, at some point, to decide whether to give the employee a raise in pay.

After preparing the job description, think about what qualifications an employee needs to be able to do the job well. Consider things like:

- ✔ Level of education
- ✔ Courses or training programs required
- ✔ Licences necessary for the job
- ✔ Ability to operate particular equipment
- ✔ Ability to speak English, or French, or any other language, well

Also consider how much previous work experience you would like the employee to have.

Although it will cost you more to hire someone with experience, you'll have less training and supervising to do. And you probably don't want to add "Teacher and Supervisor" to your own job description.

Write down all the qualifications you think are necessary for the job. You'll use this information to screen and interview candidates.

Writing down a detailed job description and set of job qualifications can protect you from false accusations of discriminatory hiring practices. If an applicant complains that you were discriminating when you did not hire him or her, you can use the job description and qualifications to show that you refused to hire the applicant because he or she didn't satisfy legitimate job requirements, not because you were discriminating against someone who was female/a recent immigrant/transgendered/paraplegic, and so on.

Did that last tip make you a little nervous? If this chapter's tips and warnings eventually psych you out, forget about hiring an employee and go back to using software and service contractors.

Funding an employee

Mostly your employee's wages are going to come out of the revenues of your business, or out of business loans if you don't have enough revenues, or (worst-case scenario) out of your own personal funds. But you may be able to get government money to hire people from certain specified groups (youth, people with disabilities, and so on).

You can find information about some of these government programs from your provincial Canada Business Service Centre (CBSC). Go to the CBSC Web site at www.cbsc.org. Click on Human Resources for Employers, follow the link to Hiring Employees, and then Subsidies and Programs.

Finding job candidates

Start your quest for an employee by talking to people you know. Sometimes this is the easiest way to find qualified candidates. Speak to business colleagues, sports or hobby buddies, friends, and relatives.

You can contact the career placement office of universities, community colleges, career colleges, or vocational schools, if you're interested in hiring a recent graduate from a program that's relevant to your business. Don't be afraid that you'll be sent only applicants with no previous work experience. Many students have been working the whole time they were at school, or returned to school after working full-time.

Most schools have a career placement office, but don't stop there. Try to speak to the program coordinator who runs the course whose graduates interest you. He or she will have more personal knowledge of the students and may be able to recommend a particular person to you.

You can also find potential job candidates by:

- ✔ Placing newspaper ads
- ✔ Posting ads on Internet job sites
- ✔ Posting a sign in your window
- ✔ Advertising on a community bulletin board
- ✔ Contacting employment agencies
- ✔ Contacting your local Human Resources Development Canada office

If you place an advertisement or post a job notice, don't draft your ad or notice in a way that excludes potential applicants on the basis of any of the prohibited grounds of discrimination (have another look at the sidebar "Don't discriminate"). "Seeking straight white male under 35, no children or pets, no drug problems, to perform routine office duties" is definitely out.

When you place your ad, use your job description to provide the ad content. Instead of the "Seeking straight white male" ad, try "Seeking well-organized, reliable, and energetic individual with good computer skills and general office experience."

Reviewing the job applications

Ask job applicants to complete an application form you provide and/or to give you a resume setting out their qualifications and education and employment history. (By the way, make sure the application form doesn't contain any questions like "Where were you born?" "How old are you?" "Are you married?" "Do you have children?" "Do you have a criminal record?" Revisit the sidebar "Don't discriminate.")

Review the applications and/or resumes, and choose several applicants whose qualifications best match the qualifications you set out in your job qualifications. Arrange to interview them. Interviews normally take place at the employer's business premises.

Send a polite letter to all applicants you do not plan to interview, telling them that you cannot offer them an interview at this time. If you're softhearted, you can add that you'll keep the applicant's resume on file.

Interviewing the most promising candidates

When you interview a job candidate, you're trying to find out if the person has the skills and ability to do the job and is someone with whom you can work well. So design your interview questions to give you information about the candidate's abilities and some insight into his or her personality.

Learning from a resume or application form

Don't ask questions that the candidate's resume or application have already answered, such as, "Where did you go to school?" and "What was your last job?" Instead, focus on getting answers to questions that you had after reading the resume or application. For example, you might want to ask the candidate:

- Why he or she left each prior job
- Why he or she has changed jobs so often (if that's the case), or is thinking now about leaving an employer
- What he or she was doing during any period of time that is unaccounted for in the resume
- Why his or her references don't include someone from a past job (if that's the case)
- Whom you can call for a reference at each of the candidate's past jobs
- How and where the candidate acquired a specific skill that is mentioned in the resume
- Why he or she is interested in a job for which he or she appears to be overqualified (if that's the case)

Asking about strengths and weaknesses

Don't waste a lot of time asking questions that allow the job candidates to give you canned answers about how wonderful they are. Any candidate who's taken Job Interviews 101 should be able to go on at great length in answer to the question "What are your strengths?" But a candidate's assertion that he or she has stellar problem-solving skills or out-of-this-world conflict resolution abilities doesn't prove a thing. So put the candidate to the test. Come up with situations that you encounter in your business and ask the candidate how he or she would handle them. For example, ask, "We have a lot of elderly customers. What would you do if a customer fell and couldn't get up?"

On the other hand, it's a good idea to ask a candidate about his or her weaknesses. Everybody has weaknesses, and a strong candidate will be willing to admit his or hers, while a weak candidate may not. Likewise ask the candidate about past mistakes and what he or she learned from them.

Getting a sense of personality

Throughout the interview, keep in mind that you're trying to get a sense of the candidate's personality. Therefore, pose your questions so that the candidate does most of the talking. Keep an eye out for traits that are important to you, such as a good sense of humour, an ability to maintain eye contact, a strong, clear speaking voice, relaxed body language. (Or whatever. Your preferred candidate may be totally humourless, be afraid to meet your eyes, have a barely audible voice, and be as nervous as a cat.) Feel free to ask questions that relate directly to personality issues such as:

- ✔ **What drives you nuts about other people?** If you're always setting wet glasses and mugs down on the furniture and the candidate says, "I once took an axe to someone who left a coffee ring on my table," this would be a good time to end the interview, escort the candidate out, and bolt the door behind him or her.

- ✔ **What's your most productive time of day?** If you're a morning person and the candidate doesn't speak to anyone before noon, your productive time together will be considerably shortened.

- ✔ **What are your favourite TV shows?** Newspapers and magazines? Movies? Sports teams? A *Survivor* junkie and a *Masterpiece Theatre* devotee may not just have trouble making small talk, they may have such different personalities that they can't get along at all.

- ✔ **Do you keep a neat desk or a messy desk?** Neat desk people and messy desk people tend to think that people of the opposite persuasion aren't doing their work.

Being aware of human rights considerations

There are some questions that you're not allowed to ask at an interview because they're prohibited by human rights legislation. The legislation is designed to keep you from making assumptions about how capable or reliable an employee is based solely on things like family status, age, race, disability, or religion. (Recall from memory the sidebar "Don't discriminate." You've looked at it so many times now that you know the prohibited grounds of discrimination by heart.)

Before you go into a sulk, ask yourself why you would want to ask these questions in the first place. You probably don't have anything against women with young children or men over 50 or people who use wheelchairs. In fact, some of your best friends may be women with young children or men over 50 or people who use wheelchairs. More likely, your concern is that the candidate might not be able to do the job — and that is a perfectly legitimate concern.

You can ask questions about what you're really concerned about — whether or not the candidate can actually do the job and work the hours required. See the side bar "Don't ask" for examples of how to ask the questions you really want answers to.

If you wrongfully refuse to hire a job applicant on one of the prohibited grounds, he or she can file a complaint with the human rights commission, which will investigate the complaint. In the most extreme case, you could be ordered to pay damages to the applicant and to hire him or her and to pay wages from the date you rejected him or her.

Don't ask

To avoid getting into trouble over human rights issues when you're interviewing a job candidate, keep in mind that your real concern is whether the candidate can do the job, and not whether the candidate is green, tri-sexual, or possessed of a record for the provincial offence of parking a flying saucer in a snow removal zone in the month of January. So ask questions that address your actual concerns. Here are some examples:

If you need someone to open your business every morning . . .

Ask: Is there anything that would prevent you from arriving at work every morning by 8:00 a.m.?

Don't ask: Do you have children? What are your day care arrangements?

If you need someone to travel out of town . . .

Ask: Are you able to travel out of town and be away overnight?

Don't ask: Are you married?

If the job involves standing all day . . .

Ask: Is there anything that would prevent you from standing for long periods of time?

Don't ask: Do you have problems with your back or legs?

If you need someone who can be bonded to handle valuable goods . . .

Ask: Is there anything that would prevent you from being bonded?

Don't ask: Have you ever been convicted of an offence?

If you need someone who can drive . . .

Ask: Do you have a driver's licence?

Don't ask: Can I see your driver's licence? (It contains information about age and disability that you're not entitled to know.)

Checking the candidates out

After you finish your interviews, you may find one or more candidates who look good enough to hire. But looks can be deceiving. Just because a job candidate puts something in a resume or says something during a job interview does not mean that it's true, so it's important to delve a little further into the candidate's qualifications and employment history.

Confirming education and qualifications

You can confirm a job candidate's educational background in two ways. One is to ask to see his or her diploma or degree and/or transcripts (although people have been known to forge these documents). Another is to contact the school and ask for confirmation of the candidate's diploma or degree and grades.

If you want to get confirmation from a school, you will probably need the candidate's written permission to the school to release the information to you.

If a job candidate claims to have a licence or to be a member of a professional or trade association, contact the licensing agency or governing body for confirmation. You won't need the candidate's permission to get confirmation because this information is a matter of public record.

Checking references

You should ask every job candidate for the names of two or three people you can contact as references. But don't feel limited to contacting only those people whose names you're given. In fact, a headhunter we know doesn't bother to contact the references he's given, since he knows they'll have only nice things to say about the candidate. Instead, he contacts some or all of the candidate's past employers. Past employment behaviour is a pretty good predictor of future employment behaviour, and that's what you're most interested in.

As a matter of courtesy, don't call a candidate's current employer without the candidate's permission. The employer may not know that the candidate is looking for another job.

If you're calling a large business, ask to speak to the human resources department or personnel director. If you're calling a small business, ask the receptionist who would know about the candidate's past employment. A large business will probably have a record of the candidate's employment even if it was some time ago. A small business, on the other hand, may have no recollection of a person who worked there many years ago.

Most Canadians are neurotically polite (some would say mealy-mouthed) or so nervous about saying anything negative that they're unwilling to say anything nasty about another person. As a result, you may find it hard to get any dirt about your candidates. For help in coming up with some questions to ask, see the sidebar "Don't despair."

Making an offer

After you go through all of this work, we hope you find at least one person you'd like to hire. When you do, offer him or her a job. Here are some things to keep in mind about making a job offer.

Always hire on a trial basis

Even someone who has a good resume, a great interview, and glowing references from Zaphod Beeblebrox and Mr. Spock may not be the right person for you. And as we tell you later in this chapter, firing a permanent employee isn't easy.

Hire any employee on either a probationary or contract basis to begin with. If you hire an employee for a probationary period of a few months and the employee doesn't work out, you can let the employee go any time during or at the end of the probation period without any problem. Likewise, if you hire an employee on a short-term contract, you can decide at the end of the contract whether or not to renew the contract on either a temporary or permanent basis.

Have a written contract

Once you hire an employee, you and the employee have a contract — even if you don't put anything down in writing — with rights and duties toward each other. Some of these rights and duties are imposed by law and can't be changed. Others can be changed by agreement. (See the section "Being an Employer" for more about employment rights and duties.) Most employers and employees don't have a written contract, just an oral one that addresses only a few of the terms of employment.

It's always a better idea to have a written employment contract to make sure that both employer and employee are clear about the job title and description, wages, hours of work, and amount of vacation. And if you want to change any of the rights and duties imposed by law, or if you want to deal with matters that the law doesn't cover, a written contract is a must.

A written employment contract should include

- ✔ The job title
- ✔ The employee's work duties
- ✔ The date the job starts and how long it lasts
- ✔ The employee's hours of work
- ✔ The employee's rate of pay
- ✔ The employee's right to paid vacation days and statutory holidays
- ✔ The employee's right (if any) to paid sick days
- ✔ Any employee benefits you're providing (such as extended health care or dental care or group life insurance)
- ✔ A period of probation (often three to six months)
- ✔ Any rights of the employer to discipline the employee (for example, to dock pay or suspend the employee — without this, the employer has no rights to discipline)
- ✔ A promise by the employee to devote his or her full time and attention to the employer's business
- ✔ A promise by the employee not to reveal trade secrets or other confidential information obtained during the course of employment
- ✔ An agreement by the employee not to compete with the employer after termination of employment

Plus, if the nature of the job requires or suggests it,

- ✔ Any important representations the employee has made about his or her qualifications (for example, that he or she has a particular degree or diploma, or is licensed to do certain kinds of work)
- ✔ Any unusual equipment the employer has to provide (such as a car) or unusual action the employer has to take (such as pay professional or trade association fees) for the employee to be able to perform the job
- ✔ A statement of the employer's right to ownership of anything invented or created by the employee in the course of business

If you're going to have a written employment contract, have it prepared, or at least reviewed, by your lawyer . . . before anyone signs it.

Don't despair

When you speak to a former employer of a candidate, you have to work around their desire not to say anything negative (or, in some cases, anything at all). Here are some questions that may get you some information without causing the employer to shut up like a clam:

✔ How long was the candidate an employee? What position did he/she hold? What were his/her duties? (These questions are for confirmation of what's in the candidate's resume or application.)

✔ Did the candidate perform his/her duties well?

✔ Did the candidate show up every day and on time?

✔ Did the candidate get along well with his/her managers, fellow employees, customers, or clients?

✔ Did the candidate have a positive attitude, and was he/she well motivated?

✔ Was the candidate honest?

✔ Why did the candidate leave the job?

✔ What were the candidate's strengths?

✔ What were the candidate's weaknesses?

✔ Would you hire the candidate again?

Compare the answers to what the candidate said in the resume or application and at the interview, and listen to what's not being said as well as to what is being said. Even if the person you're speaking to is determined not to talk, the accumulated answers (or lack of answers) to these questions will tell you a certain amount about the candidate.

Don't forget the unsuccessful candidates

Contact all the job candidates whom you interviewed, but not hired, to let them know that you have hired another candidate. Sound regretful that you aren't able to offer them a job. You may find yourself hunting up an unsuccessful candidate's phone number in a month or two if your chosen candidate doesn't work out.

Being an Employer

Hiring an employee is just the beginning. Once you become an employer, you must

✔ Be a human resources manager.

✔ Comply with government requirements.

✔ Maintain records about your employees.

✔ Establish fair and reasonable policies for dealing with your employees.

Being a manager

If you have an employee, you have to give him or her work to do. That involves:

- ✔ Knowing what you want done
- ✔ Instructing the employee in how to do it
- ✔ Providing and maintaining any tools and equipment the employee needs
- ✔ Motivating the employee to do the work
- ✔ Giving constructive feedback

This stuff can be harder to do than you think, especially if you're used to doing everything yourself. It may take longer in the beginning to explain the work and to supervise its execution than to do the work yourself. But remember, you're hiring an employee because you can't do all of the work by yourself. Think of your time spent in instructing, motivating, and constructively criticizing your employee as an investment that will pay off in time saved in the future.

Complying with government requirements

We tell you about some of the responsibilities imposed by law on an employer under the heading "What Are You Getting Yourself Into?" Here's a little more detail for you.

Federal requirements

As we told you earlier, you will have to withhold from your employees, and remit to the federal government, a certain amount for the employees' income taxes, as well as the employees' and employer's contributions to the Canada Pension Plan and Employment Insurance.

You can calculate the remittance using the payroll deduction booklets that the Canada Revenue Agency (CRA) provides to employers (available online through the CRA Web site (www.cra.gc.ca). You can also subscribe to an electronic mailing list to receive up-to-date payroll deduction tables as they change. Or you can ask a CRA official to visit you at your premises. This is a service offered to new employers to give them a chance to discuss concerns they may have about recording, withholding, or reporting requirements for employee earnings, income tax, Canada Pension Plan, or Employment Insurance contributions. If you want to take advantage of this program, contact the Revenue Collections Division of your local Tax Services Office. (As if! Like you're going to invite the CRA into your life.)

To make your remittances, you must register with the CRA and get a business number, which you'll mention when you make your payments. You can get a business number online through the CRA Web site or you can telephone your local CRA Tax Services Office.

When you register for a business number with the CRA online, you can also register or apply for certain programs offered by a few provincial governments (such as Nova Scotia Workers' Comp, or Ontario Retail Sales Tax).

Provincial and territorial requirements

You have to comply with all provincial or territorial requirements, as well as federal requirements, for employers. It's the provinces and territories that make up the rules about employment standards and workers' comp and health insurance and so on, so you must find out:

- ✔ What your province's or territory's employment standards are regarding minimum wage, overtime pay, statutory holidays, and vacation pay
- ✔ What you must do to register for and make contributions to your province's or territory's workers' compensation board
- ✔ Whether you have to make provincial or territorial health insurance contributions on behalf of your employees
- ✔ What you must do to satisfy your province's or territory's occupational health and safety legislation
- ✔ What you must do to comply with your province's or territory's human rights legislation

You can get this information from your provincial or territorial government or through your provincial or territorial Canada Business Service Centre.

Maintaining records

You're required by Canadian tax laws and provincial or territorial employment standards legislation to keep records for each employee, usually including:

- ✔ **Information about the employee** — such as name, address, social insurance number, date of birth, sex, and number of dependants (yeah, now that the government wants the information instead of you, you're allowed to ask about "prohibited grounds")
- ✔ **Information about the job** — such as job title, the date employment commenced, and the date employment ended
- ✔ **Information related to pay** — such as number of hours worked per day and week, including overtime, rate of pay, actual wages paid, deductions from wages, vacations and vacation pay, statutory holidays taken, and information on pregnancy or parental leave, or sick leave

Tax records must be kept for six years after the end of the taxation year, and in some provinces employment records must be kept for up to five years after the employment ends.

While you're in the record-keeping mood, you should also set up a file for each employee that contains a record of the employee's history on the job, starting with your job description and qualifications and the employee's job application. You should make a note of things like:

✔ The employee's attendance and punctuality

✔ Any changes in responsibility or pay

✔ Any complaints about or praise for the employee (from other employees, or from customers or suppliers)

✔ Performance evaluations

You'll use this information when deciding to promote an employee, or give him or her a raise . . . or fire the employee.

Establishing policies

Maybe "establishing policies" is too highfalutin a term. But you shouldn't be making up rules for your employees as you go along. (This is especially true if you have more than one employee, because you have to treat all of your employees the same way.) You need policies on issues such as:

✔ **Performance evaluations:** On what basis will an employee be evaluated for his or her work?

✔ **Wage increases:** How frequently will you review your employee's wages and what criteria will you use to decide whether or not he or she should receive a raise?

✔ **Vacations:** How long will vacations be and how will vacations be scheduled?

✔ **Sick days:** Are any sick days with pay allowed?

✔ **Overtime:** How will overtime work be assigned?

✔ **Ongoing training:** What kind of training is required, and how will it be provided?

If this sounds time-consuming, don't worry. Now that you've got an employee to help with the work, you've freed up some of your own time to write policies! (As well as to find out about and comply with laws and regulations, train and supervise the employee, evaluate the employee's performance . . . oh, well.)

Firing an Employee

What if your business doesn't do as well as you hoped and you can no longer afford to keep on your employee? Or what if the needs of your business change, and your employee's skills don't? Or what if your employee becomes a complete pain to work with?

Well, we have good news and bad news. The good news is that you almost always have the right to get rid of an employee. The bad news is that you may have to give the employee notice or pay the employee money first.

Firing for just cause

You can fire an employee without having to give notice or to pay any money instead of giving notice if you have just cause — a reason that the law recognizes as a good one. Some examples of just cause are

- Dishonesty toward your business
- Insubordination or disobedience toward you as employer
- Continued bad behaviour toward other employees, customers, or suppliers
- Drunkenness or drug abuse that affects the employee's work
- Repeated absences or lateness without a reasonable medical or personal excuse
- Incompetence or carelessness in the performance of the job that continues in spite of warnings
- A conflict of interest with your business

In most of these situations, you must give the employee a warning about the behaviour and an opportunity to correct it before you can fire him or her. But if you catch an employee with her hand in the till, or whacking a customer over the head with a chair, you can show the employee the door immediately.

If you start to have problems with an employee, make detailed notes about the problems in the employee's file. If you decide to fire the employee, the file will help you prove in court or before a human rights tribunal (you may have fired a militant employee) that you had just cause.

Firing without just cause

You can fire an employee even if you don't have just cause — for example, if you just can't afford to pay the employee any longer, or you can't stand being in the same office with the creature. However, you must give him or her reasonable notice in writing of the termination of employment ("Your job will end in X weeks") or pay in lieu of notice ("Your job ends today. Here's a cheque for X weeks' pay.").

What is "reasonable" notice? Employment standards legislation in each province or territory sets out the minimum notice that you must give to an employee. Generally speaking, an employee who has worked for less than a given period of time (one to six months, depending on the province or territory) is not entitled to any notice. An employee who has worked at least that period of time is entitled to one or two weeks' notice (depending on the province or territory) during the first year, and then, in most provinces and territories, one week's notice for each additional year worked, up to a maximum of between two and eight weeks (again depending on the province or territory).

Courts have decided that some employees are entitled to more than the minimum notice periods set by legislation, depending on factors such as position held, salary, level of responsibility, number of years of employment, age of the employee, and the employee's chances of finding another job.

If you don't want your employee hanging around during a notice period (wreaking who knows what havoc after being told that it's all over), you can pay the employee the full wages and benefits he or she would have earned during the notice period and walk him or her off the premises.

Consult a lawyer before you fire an employee. If you fire an employee without just cause, or without reasonable notice or pay in lieu of notice, the firing is a wrongful dismissal.

Wrongful dismissal

An employee you have wrongfully dismissed can sue you for compensation, which will be an amount equal to the wages and benefits the employee would have earned during a reasonable notice period. The employee must, however, mitigate damages — take all reasonable steps to reduce his or her losses — by looking for other work and accepting any reasonable offer of employment.

An employee may also be entitled to compensation for mental distress if you fired him or her in a humiliating or embarrassing way, or for damage to the employee's reputation if you make untrue statements about him or her to other employees, customers, or business associates.

Human rights concerns

Oh, no! Not again! Yes, afraid so. Human rights legislation has an impact on your right to fire an employee. You're not allowed to fire an employee on any of the prohibited grounds we told you about in the sidebar "Don't discriminate."

You may not think you're firing your employee on one of those grounds. You may think you're firing him or her for persistent lateness or absenteeism or for an inability to do the job. However, if the underlying reason for the lateness, absenteeism, or inability to do the job is in fact one of those prohibited grounds, you must first take steps to accommodate the person. For example, an employee with young children might not be able to start work at 9:00 a.m., but could get to work by 9:30 a.m. Unless it's essential to the job that the employee be at work by 9:00 a.m., you must try to accommodate the employee by allowing her to start work later and make up the half hour later in the day. And how's this for a catch-22? Alcohol or drug abuse that affects the employee's work is a just cause for firing. But, if your employee is an alcoholic or drug addict, the addiction is considered a physical or mental disability, which you must first take steps to accommodate. You don't have to make accommodations that cause undue hardship to your business, but it would be up to you to prove to human rights officials that a particular accommodation would cause you more hardship than you should have to endure. (You can argue factors such as the size of your business, the cost of the accommodation, any safety risks involved, and the effect of the accommodation on the morale of other employees.)

If an employee believes that he or she was fired on one of the prohibited grounds, the employee can complain to the provincial human rights commission, which will investigate the complaint. In the most extreme case, you might be ordered to rehire the employee, pay wages from the original date of firing, and also pay compensation to the employee.

When Your Employee Is Gone

You must do certain things when an employee leaves, whether he or she quit, was fired, or reached the end of the term of a contract for employment:

✔ You must complete a Record of Employment Form (so that the employee can apply for Employment Insurance benefits) and mail one copy to the employee and one to Human Resources and Skills Development Canada (HRSDC) within five days after the last day of employment. (HRSDC offers help in completing the form.)

You can complete the Record of Employment Form online using HRSDC's ROE Web service, available at HRSDC's Web site (`www.hrsdc.gc.ca`).

✔ You must pay, in addition to any payment in lieu of notice, any outstanding wages and vacation pay.

✔ If you agreed to continue providing benefits such as health insurance for a time, contact the benefit provider to make sure that coverage continues.

You may be contacted about the employee by a potential employer. Many ex-employers are worried that they will be sued for defamation (slander) if they say anything negative about a former employee, but you probably can't be successfully sued as long as:

✔ You honestly believe that what you're saying is true.

✔ You have reasonable grounds to believe what you're saying.

✔ You're not saying something negative for an improper motive, such as revenge or to prevent the employee from getting another job.

Keep in mind, however, that privacy legislation prohibits you from disclosing any of your former employee's personal information without his or her consent. So be careful not to disclose personal information, such as the employee's home address or any information about his or her health. For more information about what you can't disclose, see Chapter 13 where we discuss the *Personal Information Protection and Electronic Documents Act (PIPEDA)*.

Welcome Aboard!

After reading this chapter you may decide to withdraw the welcome mat and shut down the transporter altogether. Hiring employees is a serious business with potentially serious problems involved, and you shouldn't take on an employee lightly. But when your business reaches the point where you must either hire employees or purchase a burial plot for overworked you, you don't have much choice. Act carefully.

When in doubt about an employment-related matter, get in touch with your lawyer.

Chapter 16

Tax Attacks!

In This Chapter

▶ Learning about income tax

▶ Finding out about sales taxes

▶ Revisiting payroll taxes

▶ Looking at other business taxes

*R*ed alert! The tax authorities have locked onto your business and are firing demands for money (and complex forms) at you. Prepare phasers for a counter-attack!

On second thought — hold your fire for a moment. Maybe it would be a good idea to learn something about the enemy before you start blasting back at it.

One of the unpleasant realities of being in business is that you are expected to pay taxes. Every level of government — federal, provincial, and municipal — wants something. You will have to pay

✔ **Income taxes** — to the federal and provincial governments

✔ **Sales taxes** — to the federal and provincial governments

✔ **Payroll taxes** — to the federal and provincial governments

✔ **Business taxes** — possibly to the federal and provincial governments, and more likely to your municipal government

Taxes are not only hard to dodge, they are also complicated and difficult to understand. It's impossible to explain taxes fully in just one chapter. In fact, you can still be pretty muddled (not to mention shell-shocked and bored within an inch of death) after reading whole books about taxes. So in this chapter, we give you just enough information to let you know the kinds of taxes you have to pay and when you have to pay them, and we throw in a bit of advice about keeping your income tax to a minimum.

First, Review Your Troops

Before we focus on the other side, let's take a look at your side. What's your troop strength? Are you planning to fight this battle heroically alone, or are you thinking that you could use some support?

The lone warrior

If you're strong and brave, you may believe that you can face up to the enemy all by yourself. Well, don't forget that no matter how strong and brave you are, there are a lot more of them than of you. It's hardly a fair fight. So even if you've always done your own personal income tax return, now that you're in business, doing your taxes yourself is no longer a good idea.

But if you insist on going out there on a solo mission, make sure that you know what to do.

✔ Read books on tax. *Tax Tips For Canadians For Dummies* (written by Christie Henderson, Brian Quinlan, Suzanne Schultz, and Leigh Vyn; published by Wiley) is a good start.

✔ Visit the Canada Revenue Agency (CRA) Web site at www.cra.gc.ca. You can download forms, schedules, guides, pamphlets, and Interpretation Bulletins (technical and detailed statements of the CRA's position on a variety of specific subjects). Or contact your local Tax Services Office in person or by phone to ask questions.

✔ Visit non-government Web sites that specialize in tax issues such as Ernst & Young Tax Services at www.ey.com/global/content.nsf/ Canada/Tax_-_Overview or KPMG Tax Services at www.kpmg.ca/ en/services/tax.

✔ Visit the Web site of your provincial department or ministry of finance for information about provincial taxes on business.

✔ Contact your municipality for information about municipal business taxes, or visit their Web site.

The CRA is good for general information, but don't expect them to give you advice on how to save taxes. And provincial and municipal Web sites may be more interested in encouraging businesses to set up than in providing up-front details about taxes.

Cyberhelp

A number of software programs are available to help you prepare your own income tax returns, such as TaxWiz, QuickTax, and GriffTax.

When you use a computer program, you put in the numbers and your computer does all the calculations for you. If you forget something or have to make a change, the computer will recalculate your totals. Some programs offer online help and include tax-saving suggestions.

No tax program will tell you whether your claims are reasonable or correct. You need personal advice for that kind of input. And software concentrates on income taxes, not on all the different taxes you may be required to pay.

Battle-hardened soldiers

Now that you're in business, your best bet is to hire a professional accountant with experience in small business taxation to help you with your taxes. An accountant can give you advice about a wide variety of matters relating to your tax obligations. We tell you about hiring and working with an accountant in Chapter 17.

Income Taxes

You've mustered your troops, so let's move on to an analysis of the enemy's movements.

Income taxes are the main battlefront. It's here that you'll find the massed strength.

Individuals and corporations must pay taxes on income to both the federal and provincial governments. The Canada Revenue Agency (once Revenue Canada, and more recently Canada Customs and Revenue Agency) collects both federal and provincial income tax from individuals (human beings, that is) in every province except Quebec, and from corporations in all provinces except Alberta, Ontario, and Quebec, where the provincial governments collect their own corporate income taxes.

A business can also be taxed on its *capital gains*. A capital gain is the profit made on the sale or other disposition of *capital property*. Capital property is property acquired to be held onto rather than resold right away. Examples of capital property could include commercial real estate bought for use in a business, or shares in a corporation. A start-up business isn't likely to have capital gains while it's a going concern, so we don't talk about capital gains in this chapter. But a business may have capital gains or capital losses when the business is sold or is wound up, so we do talk about capital gains and losses in Chapter 20.

What income is a business taxed on?

You will be pleased to know that you're not taxed on every cent your business earns. Your income taxes are calculated only on the *profit* your business makes. Your business's profit is its *gross income* (or *revenue* — the money the business takes in) minus its legitimate expenses (the money spent or expenses incurred in order to earn the income).

The lower your business's profit, the less tax you will have to pay. So the question is how legally to keep your profits as low as possible for tax purposes. There are only two ways to have low profits (and therefore low taxes). One is to keep your business revenues as low as possible and the other is to make your legitimate business expenses as high as possible.

Unfortunately, you can't minimize your business revenue without cheating because you are required by law to report everything your business earns. So the only way to reduce your profits and your tax payable legally is to maximize your legitimate business expenses. Over the next few pages, we tell you what is considered to be business income and what is considered to be a legitimate business expense.

Everyone wants to pay as little tax as possible. Tax *avoidance* is paying as little tax as is legally possible. Tax *evasion*, on the other hand, is failing to pay taxes that are legally owing — and it's a crime. Income tax laws are complicated and change constantly, so you need expert tax advice from an accountant and/or tax lawyer to make sure that you avoid as much tax as you can without evading any tax. You also need advice to make sure that any tax-avoidance scheme you come up with will actually work.

What is business income?

According to the CRA, business income includes money earned or valuable property received from any activity you engage in as part of your business. Business income includes

✔ Fees charged to your clients for services you provide, excluding any sales tax you charged

✔ The purchase price charged to your customers for goods you sell, excluding any sales tax you charged

We give you intelligence concerning sales taxes later in this chapter.

You are required to report to the CRA all income earned by your business during the taxation year.

What are legitimate business expenses?

The CRA allows you to deduct from business income most reasonable expenses you pay in order to earn that income. Since, as we mentioned, the only legal way to reduce your profits — and therefore your taxes — is to maximize your legitimate business expenses, knowing what your legitimate business expenses are is very important. They include

✔ Mortgage interest and property taxes on real property you own and use for your business (see the heading "Home office expenses" if you run your business out of a home you own)

✔ Rent if you lease your business premises (see "Home office expenses" if you run your business out of your rented home)

✔ The cost of labour and materials for any minor repairs or maintenance done to property you use to earn income

✔ The cost of leasing equipment used in your business

✔ The cost of buying or manufacturing the goods you sold during the year

✔ Delivery, freight, and transportation expenses

✔ Insurance premiums you pay to insure any buildings, machinery, and equipment you use in your business

✔ Utilities such as telephone, electricity, heat, and water

✔ The cost of office expenses and supplies — small items such as printer ink cartridges, stationery, pens, pencils, paper clips, and stamps

✔ Some of the expenses of running a motor vehicle that you use to earn business income (for more information see the heading "Car expenses")

✔ Interest you pay on money that you borrow to run your business

✔ Annual licence fees and levies (such as municipal business taxes) to run your business

- ✔ Annual dues or fees for membership in a trade or commercial association (but not if the main purpose of the club is dining, recreation, or sporting activities)

- ✔ Legal, accounting, and other professional fees

- ✔ Management and administration fees to operate your business, including bank charges

- ✔ Expenses for advertising your product or service

- ✔ Travel expenses to earn business income

- ✔ Fifty percent of business meals, beverages, and entertainment

- ✔ Salaries and benefits you pay to employees, as well as your portion of Canada Pension Plan and Employment Insurance premiums (see the heading "Employee salaries" for more information)

You may have noticed that in this list we mention only leased equipment, and purchased office supplies of a minor kind such as pens and paper. More important items that you purchase (rather than lease) such as a computer, phone system, fax machine or other office equipment, furniture, and larger items such as buildings or vehicles, can't be fully claimed in the year of *purchase* as business expense. That's because these items, which are capital property, will continue to be useful to your business for more than one taxation year. However, since these items *depreciate* (wear out or lose their usefulness over time), you can claim a percentage of the cost as a business expense each year over a period of several years until the entire cost has been claimed. The amount you are allowed to claim on *depreciable capital property* each year as an expense is called *capital cost allowance*, and there's a special place on the income tax form for calculating the exact amount of capital cost allowance you can claim in a given year.

Many of your business expenses are clearly only for your business, such as the cost of an ad in the newspaper or lease payments on machinery used to create the product you sell. But you may use other items both for your business and personally — for example, a cell phone, a computer, or your car. When you calculate your business expenses, you are not allowed to claim any part of the expense that relates to your personal use of the item. You can deduct only the portion of the expense that relates to your business use. For example, if you use half of your monthly airtime on your cell phone for business calls and half for personal calls, you can claim as a business expense only the amount paid for the business calls.

Home office expenses

If you operate your business from your home, you are allowed to deduct expenses for the business use of your home. This allows you to get a tax deduction for a portion of your home expenses (which you would have to pay anyway).

For the costs to be deductible, your home office must either

✔ Be your main place of business

✔ If it's not your main place of business, be used exclusively for business purposes and be used on a regular basis for meeting clients or customers in connection with the business

If your home office meets one of these two tests, you can deduct a percentage of the following costs:

✔ Mortgage interest and property taxes (if you own) or rental payments (if you rent)

✔ Utilities such as heat, electricity, and water

✔ Maintenance costs or condo fees

✔ Home insurance

To figure out the percentage you're allowed to deduct, calculate what percentage of your home you use for your business. Divide the area of your office by the total area of your home. So, for example, if your home is 1,500 square feet in area, and the room you use exclusively for business is 300 square feet in area, then you can deduct 20 percent of your home costs. Or you may divide the number of rooms occupied by your business by the total number of rooms in your home. For example, if you have four rooms in your apartment and you use one of those rooms exclusively for business, then you can deduct 25 percent of your home costs.

You can use the home office deduction to bring your business income down to zero, but not to put your business into a loss position, or to increase a loss that already exists. Once you reach zero, any home office expenses that are left over can be applied against business income in future years.

Car expenses

You are allowed to deduct the expenses of running a motor vehicle that you use to earn business income. These expenses include

✔ Fuel and oil

✔ Maintenance and repairs

✔ Insurance

✔ Licence and registration fees

✔ Leasing costs or interest paid on money borrowed to buy the vehicle (but note that if your vehicle is a passenger car, there is a limit to the amount you are allowed to claim)

✔ Capital cost allowance, if you own the motor vehicle (again, if your vehicle is a passenger car, there is a limit to the amount you are allowed to claim)

If you use your car for both business and personal purposes, only the portion of your car expenses that relate to your business activities is a legitimate business expense. Use the following formula:

$$\frac{(\text{Total car expenses} \times \text{kilometres driven for business purposes})}{\text{Total kilometres driven}} = \text{Allowable business expense}$$

Employee salaries

You can deduct the salaries you pay to your employees, as well as the portion that you pay of their Canada Pension Plan and Employment Insurance contributions. You can also deduct the cost of any benefits you provide to your employees, such as health insurance and life insurance. (For more on these matters, see Chapter 15.)

Hiring a family member may be a good way to reduce your business income taxes. By paying your spouse or child or parent a salary, you reduce profits and therefore taxes payable. Your family member will have to pay tax on the salary, but will pay less tax than you or your business would, as long as his or her tax rate is lower. By shifting some of the profit to your family, you increase your family's after-tax income even though total income remains the same.

You can employ family members in your business and deduct the salary as a legitimate business expense if

✔ You actually pay the salary.

✔ The family member actually does work that is necessary for the business.

✔ The salary you pay is reasonable in comparison to what you would pay someone else.

If you are a sole proprietor or a partner, you or your partners are not employees of the business, so you cannot deduct any salary or draw taken. In order to be employees and run the business, you have to incorporate. However, there are other tax advantages to being a sole proprietor or partner, so don't go rushing off to incorporate (see Chapter 5).

How much tax will you pay?

The amount of tax you will pay depends on the form of your business (see Chapter 5). That's because sole proprietorships and partnerships are taxed differently from corporations.

If your business is a sole proprietorship or partnership

If you carry on business as a sole proprietor, from the tax point of view the business's income is considered to be your personal income. If you carry on business in a partnership, your share of the business's income is also considered to be your personal income.

You report your (or your share of the) business's profits or loss in your personal income tax return. (See the heading "When and how do you have to pay?" for more about how this is done.) Your business does not file a separate tax return.

If your business has made a profit, the profit (or your share of the profit) is included in your personal income and is taxed as personal income. If your business has suffered a loss, the loss (or your share of the loss) is subtracted from your personal income from other sources for the year. That means that a business loss reduces your total income.

If you have a business loss but you have no other income for the year, or if the loss from your business is greater than your income from other sources, you can carry the loss back and apply it against income you earned in the past three years, or you can carry it forward and apply it against income you earn in the next seven years.

Your federal and provincial income tax is calculated as a percentage of your total personal income, including your business profits or loss. Your tax rate depends on your total income — as your income goes up, so does the percentage at which it is taxed.

Federal tax rates are the same across the country, but provincial tax rates vary from province to province. As a result, the combined rates of federal and provincial tax vary across the country. You can find exact information about the combined federal and provincial tax for your province at KPMG Tax Services at `www.kpmg.ca/en/services/tax`, but in the meantime we can give you a rough idea of what you'll have to pay. In the 2005 taxation year, depending on the province, taxpayers earning

- ✔ Less than approximately $8,150 pay no tax

- ✔ Between approximately $8,150 and $35,600 pay between about 22 percent and 33 percent on the amount

- ✔ Between approximately $35,600 and $71,200 pay between about 31 percent and 42 percent on the amount over $35,600

- ✔ Between approximately $71,200 and $115,750 pay between about 36 percent and 46 percent on the amount over $71,200

- ✔ Over $115,750 pay between about 39 percent and 49 percent on the amount over $115,750

If your business is a corporation

If your business is incorporated, the corporation is a taxpayer and has to file its own income tax return (see the heading "When and how do you have to pay?" for more about how this is done) and pay tax on its profits.

Unlike individuals, whose tax rate increases in steps or brackets with the amount of income earned, corporations are taxed at a flat rate. Depending on the province, the combined federal and provincial tax rate ranges from about 31 to 39 percent. However, the federal small business deduction reduces the tax rate to between 15 and 22 percent on the first $300,000 of business income earned by a Canadian-controlled private corporation. (A Canadian-controlled private corporation is exactly what it sounds like — a private corporation controlled by Canadian shareholders.) In some provinces, the tax rate on a Canadian-controlled private corporation's business income over $300,000, up to between $350,000 and $450,000 (depending on the province) continues to be reduced, and ranges between 24 and 28 percent (again depending on the province).

The small business deduction generally does not apply to a corporation's income from interest, dividends, rents, or royalties.

If your corporation suffers a loss, the loss can be carried back and applied against profits made in the past three years, or carried forward and applied against profits made in the next seven years. (The corporation's loss cannot be applied to reduce your personal income for tax purposes.)

The tax authorities aren't finished with you after they tax your corporation. If you receive any money from the corporation in the form of salary, benefits, a bonus, or dividends, you have to report that money as income on your personal income tax return and pay tax on what you receive. (See the heading "If your business is a sole proprietorship or partnership," for tax rates.) Salary, bonus, or benefits are taxed at your personal tax rate. Dividends are also taxed at your personal tax rate, but come with a dividend tax credit that limits the tax to a maximum of about 37 percent (the figure varies by province). The tax credit recognizes the fact that dividends are a distribution of corporate profits on which the corporation has already paid taxes.

When and how do you have to pay?

Every Canadian taxpayer is required to file an income tax return each year and pay whatever taxes are owing. The type of return you file, your deadline for filing it, and the deadline for paying your taxes depend on your form of business organization.

If your business is a sole proprietorship or partnership

If you carry on business as a sole proprietor or in a partnership, your profit from the business is considered to be your personal income and is reported in your personal tax return — the standard T1-General Form. Your business does not file a separate tax return. Instead you complete a Form T2124, Statement of Business Activities (or T2032, Statement of Professional Activities, which looks much the same), and include it as part of your personal tax return. The form gives details of your business's income and expenses. You include the business's profit (or loss) as part of your income.

Individual taxpayers must file their personal income tax returns and pay any taxes owing by April 30 of the year following the taxation year. (That means, for example, filing your income tax return for 2005 by April 30, 2006.) If you are self-employed and are a sole proprietor or a partner, your tax return is not due until June 15 following the end of your business's fiscal period or taxation year (which for most partnerships and sole proprietorships must be the same as the calendar year). However, your taxes must still be paid by April 30. So even if you're not ready to prepare your income tax return, you have to estimate how much tax is owing and send that amount in by April 30 with a letter setting out your social insurance number and what the payment is for. (If you estimate wrong, you'll have to pay interest from April 30 on the amount you didn't pay but should have.)

Don't for a minute think that just because you are self-employed and not receiving a paycheque, the CRA will sit back and wait to be paid all of the taxes you owe on April 30. Self-employed taxpayers are required to pay their tax by quarterly instalments. After your first year of making a profit on which you have to pay at least $2,000 in tax, the CRA will send you an instalment notice telling you that you have to start paying taxes on a quarterly basis, and thereafter it will send you quarterly reminders to pay up. The CRA calculates your instalment payments, but you don't have to pay those amounts. You can estimate your income for the year and pay one-fourth each quarter. But if you underestimate the amount of tax you owe, you will have to pay interest on the amount by which your instalments fall short.

If you have to make quarterly instalment payments, salt away in a special bank account the amount you'll owe at the end of each quarter, so that you don't accidentally spend it.

In the first year that your sole proprietorship or partnership makes a profit, don't forget that you're a taxpayer even though you don't have to pay taxes until April 30 of the following year! Estimate (generously) how much money you'll owe in taxes on each month's income, and put that amount into an interest-earning bank account or into treasury bills or GICs so that you'll have it ready to pay on April 30 and you'll have earned some interest income on it.

If your business is a partnership with six or more partners, the partnership must also file a partnership information return — Form T5013. (An information return is not a tax return. It is not used to calculate how much tax is payable, but to give the CRA information to ensure that tax information for the partnership is being properly calculated and reported by each of the partners.) The partnership information form must be filed by March 31.

If your business is a corporation

If your business is incorporated, the corporation is a taxpayer and has to file its own income tax return — Form T2, Corporation Income Tax Return — together with information from the corporation's financial statements. (See Chapter 17 for more about financial statements.) Form T2 serves as both a federal and provincial income tax return — except in Alberta, Ontario, and Quebec, where a separate provincial corporate tax return must also be filed.

The corporation will have to file a corporate income tax return within six months after the end of the corporation's fiscal period or taxation year. Unlike a sole proprietorship or partnership, a corporation can choose any date for its year-end.

You will also have to file your personal income tax return. Your return must be filed by April 30, because you are not considered to be self-employed when you're running your business through a corporation.

A corporation must pay income tax in monthly instalments unless the tax payable for the year or the previous taxation year is $1,000 or less. (During the corporation's first taxation year, no instalment payments have to be made.) The CRA does not calculate the amount of the instalments — you must do that yourself, basing your payment on one of the following:

- ✔ An estimate of the tax payable in the current year

- ✔ The tax paid in the previous year

- ✔ A combination of the tax paid in the previous year and the year before that

If the corporation owes more income tax than it paid in its monthly instalments, it must pay the balance within two months after the end of the corporation's fiscal year (three months if the corporation is a Canadian-controlled private corporation, eligible for the small business deduction, and with an income of less than $300,000). Notice that the due date to pay the balance of the tax is earlier than the deadline for filing the corporation's income tax return.

If you've engaged in conduct unbecoming . . .

Whether your business is a sole proprietorship, partnership, or corporation, if

- You don't make your instalment payments on time
- You don't pay enough in instalment payments
- You don't pay any balance of tax owing by the due date — April 30 for individuals, and two (or three) months after the fiscal year end for a corporation

then you will have to pay interest at about 10 percent on taxes that are overdue.

You may have to pay a penalty if

- Your accumulated interest charges for any year are more than $1,000.
- You file your income tax return late.
- You fail to report income.
- You knowingly or carelessly make false statements or omissions on your tax return.

Penalties start at 5 percent of unpaid taxes . . . but they don't stop there.

What records must you keep?

Any corporation or individual who carries on a business, or is required to pay or collect income taxes, must keep books and records that allow the amount of taxes payable to be calculated and checked. You must hold onto these books and records for at least six years after the taxation year they relate to.

To make it easier to prepare your tax returns when they are due, you should keep organized books and records throughout the year as well as hang on to your invoices and receipts. You can keep actual account books, or you can use small-business bookkeeping and accounting software. We tell you more about accounting for your business in Chapter 17.

What if you're audited?

When you file your or your corporation's income tax return, it is reviewed by the CRA. When the CRA completes the review it issues a notice of assessment, which sets out the amount of tax payable for the year. The CRA has the right to reassess your return later, and can go back and reassess your returns for the past three years (or longer, if they suspect fraud) and ask you for more money. If you disagree with the CRA about the amount it says you have to pay, you (personally or through your accountant) can object to the assessment or reassessment, and try to persuade the CRA that you don't owe as much as they say by showing them documents that support your objection and even by visiting the local Tax Services Office in person to argue your case. This can go on for some time, because the CRA usually takes a while to digest any communication from a taxpayer.

A tax audit is different from (and worse than) an assessment or reassessment. In an audit, the CRA goes over all your records, including records you weren't required to send in with your tax return, to see whether you've declared all of your income and deducted only legitimate expenses.

Tax returns of corporations and self-employed taxpayers are more likely to be audited than those of taxpayers who are employees, because businesses have more opportunities to evade taxes by hiding income or inflating (or even making up) expenses.

On an audit you will have to prove all of your income and expenses by presenting receipts. So just in case you're audited, you should keep receipts that are dated and show what business activity they relate to.

If you are audited, the CRA will notify you by letter that your tax return for a stated year, or years, has been selected for review. The letter will ask you to provide specified information within 30 days (although you can ask for an extension if you need more time).

If you get an audit letter, speak to your accountant immediately. If you don't already have an accountant, this would be a good time to get one!

You can respond to the request on your own, or you can (and probably should) hire an accountant or tax lawyer.

The auditor will then arrange a face-to-face meeting (your accountant or even your lawyer can be present), during which you may be asked to justify some of your expense claims. You'll respond by showing the auditor your supporting records and receipts. You should have your records organized so that you are able to answer the auditor's questions. Be cooperative and polite, even if you're feeling cranky and angry. (There's no point in irritating a person who has the power to assess additional taxes, not to mention interest and penalties, against you.)

When the auditor is finished, he or she will send you a letter setting out proposed changes to your income tax return, and giving you time either to accept the changes or dispute them. (To dispute the proposed changes, you will have to provide new information that you didn't have for the auditor.) Then the CRA will send you a notice of reassessment setting out what you owe and when it's due.

If you accept the reassessment, you have to pay the balance by the due date. If you can't pay by the due date, you can contact the collections department of the CRA to make other arrangements for payment. You can apply to the Fairness Committee at the CRA to have any penalties or interest set aside. If you disagree with the reassessment, you can file a notice of objection with your local Tax Services Office within 90 days after the date of the reassessment.

Sales Taxes

You've had the spy-satellite overview of income taxes, so now let's move on to sales taxes.

Sound battle stations! The enemy is performing a flanking maneuver.

The federal government and every province except Alberta require sales tax to be charged when goods are sold or services are provided. The federal sales tax is the Goods and Services Tax (GST). GST and provincial sales tax (PST) are charged separately in all provinces except Nova Scotia, New Brunswick, and Newfoundland, which have combined their provincial sales taxes with the GST into a Harmonized Sales Tax (HST). Provincial sales taxes range from 7 to 10 percent, GST is 7 percent, and HST is 15 percent.

Provincial sales tax

Businesses that sell goods or provide services on which PST has to be charged are responsible for collecting the tax from the buyer of the goods or services. Businesses are required to *remit* (send) the collected taxes to the provincial government on a regular basis. In every province except Quebec (where sales tax works more like GST, see the "Goods and Services" section later), the tax is payable by the final consumer only, so businesses do not have to pay PST on goods that will be resold (although they must pay PST on goods bought for their own use).

If your business will be selling goods or providing services on which PST must be charged, you must register with your provincial government's department or ministry of finance. You will be given a registration certificate and provincial tax number. You will have to file periodic (usually monthly) returns with the ministry of finance, in which you report the amount of tax collected and remit the tax. For more information about PST in your province, check the Web site for your provincial Canada Business Service Centre or for your provincial government.

Your business must keep proper books and records to document the amount of tax collected, and you are subject to audits by the provincial government.

If you fail to file returns, collect taxes as required, or remit the taxes collected, you may be charged an interest penalty. You may even be charged with an offence and hauled into court.

Goods and Services Tax

GST applies to almost all goods sold and services supplied anywhere in Canada. Unlike PST, which is paid only by the ultimate consumer, GST is charged to everyone along the production and sale chain — from the supplier of the raw materials, through the manufacturer, wholesaler, and retailer, down to the consumer. While everyone is charged the tax, the government keeps only the tax paid by the ultimate consumer. Everyone else in the chain is allowed to claim a refund on the GST they paid (called an *input tax credit*).

You'll find plenty of information about the GST on the CRA Web site at www.cra.gc.ca.

GST categories

GST must be charged when goods and services are "supplied" — whether by sale, rental, barter, or gift. There are three categories of "supplies":

✔ Supplies that are taxable at 7 percent, which include all supplies that don't fall into the second and third categories — so chances are good that whatever goods or services you're providing are in the first category.

✔ Supplies that are taxable at 0 percent, which include prescription drugs and medical devices, basic groceries, international travel and transportation, precious metals, and farm and fishing products and equipment.

✔ Supplies that are tax-exempt, which include health care, personal care, child care, or educational services and financial services.

Are crazy people running the Goods and Services Tax department of the federal government? Why would you tax supplies at 0 percent . . . and what on earth is the difference between supplies that are taxed at 0 percent and supplies that are tax-exempt? Well, the GST people may indeed be crazy, but there's a certain method to their madness. The supplier doesn't collect GST from customers if supplies are taxed at 0 percent or if supplies are tax-exempt. But if a business provides zero-rated supplies it can still claim a refund on the GST it paid to get goods and services, whereas if a business provides tax-exempt supplies, it can't.

Registering for the GST

If your business provides GST-taxable goods and services and has annual revenues of more than $30,000, you *must* register for the GST. Otherwise you *may* register. Once you register for the GST you must charge GST to your customers and remit it to the CRA, and you can claim a refund on the GST you pay to get goods and services. If you don't register for the GST, you don't have to charge GST, but you can't claim a refund, either.

Register for the GST even if your revenues are less than $30,000. You'll be able to get back the GST paid on the goods and services your business buys. Besides, you don't really want your customers to know that your business's annual revenues are less than $30,000.

You register for the GST by applying to the CRA for a *business number*. We tell you how to go about doing that in Chapter 2.

Collecting and remitting GST

When you invoice a customer or client for goods or services you provide, you have to invoice for GST, as well. You calculate GST on the full price your customer pays, including any customs or excise duties and transportation taxes — but excluding any provincial sales tax, and not taking into account any discounts for early payment of your invoice or interest charged for late payment.

You must report the amount of GST collected and remit it to the CRA on a regular basis. How often you remit depends on your business's annual sales, as follows:

- ✓ If your annual sales are less than $500,000, you must remit GST quarterly, and you must report annually, although you can choose to report quarterly; you can also choose to report and remit monthly.

- ✓ If your annual sales are between $500,000 and $6,000,000, you must report and remit GST quarterly, although you can choose to report and remit monthly.

- ✓ If your annual sales are more than $6,000,000 (here's hoping!), you must report and remit GST monthly.

On the GST form, you show the GST your business charged on the goods and services it provided, as well as the GST your business paid on the goods and services it bought. The difference between what you charged and what you paid is the amount you must remit to the government. If you paid more than you charged, you are entitled to a GST refund.

You must keep books and records, including invoices, to document the GST collected and any refunds claimed, for six years.

If you fail to report or remit GST as required, you will be charged interest and penalties. If you willfully fail to pay, collect or remit GST, you can be charged with an offence, and if you're convicted, you can be fined or imprisoned.

Harmonized Sales Tax

Hey, what's that sound? Could it be "The Ride of the Valkyries"? Actually, it's the humming of the Harmonized Sales Tax (HST), the name given to the combined GST and provincial sales tax charged in Nova Scotia, New Brunswick, and Newfoundland.

If your business supplies goods or services in these provinces, no matter where in the country your business is actually located, you are required to collect and remit 15-percent HST to the CRA. When you register for GST, you're also registered for HST, which works the same way as GST.

Payroll Taxes

Incoming at 12 o'clock high!

Payroll taxes are taxes levied by the federal government and some provincial governments on businesses with employees. The federal payroll taxes are Employment Insurance (EI) and Canada Pension Plan (CPP). Employers must make contributions to EI and CPP on behalf of their employees, as well as withhold and remit the employees' contributions. Provincial payroll taxes include health insurance and workers' compensation premiums.

We tell you about payroll taxes in Chapter 15.

Business Taxes

Look out, they've circled around behind and are attacking from the rear!

In addition to income taxes, sales taxes, and payroll taxes, federal, provincial, and municipal governments levy other business taxes:

- ✔ The federal government levies a large corporation tax on corporations with over $10 million of taxable capital in Canada.

- ✔ Some provincial governments levy a tax on the paid-up capital of corporations. Paid-up capital is the total amount paid to the corporation for all the shares that have been issued to shareholders.

- ✔ Municipalities levy taxes on businesses. Businesses that own real estate in the municipality have to pay property taxes, but in some municipalities, even businesses that rent rather than own are required to pay taxes. These taxes may be based, for example, on the annual rental value of the property or the square footage of the premises or the value of the business's stock-in-trade.

Your accountant can tell you more about these matters, or you can contact your federal, provincial, and municipal governments or visit their Web sites.

We Surrender!

We're surrounded and outnumbered. Looks like we just can't win this battle! The only thing to do is pay up — let's just make sure not to pay more than necessary. Get professional advice and help from an accountant — or a tax lawyer — to keep your taxes to a minimum.

Chapter 17

Close Encounters with Accounting

In This Chapter

▶ Learning why accounting is important for your business

▶ Finding out what records to keep and how to keep them

▶ Learning the basics of bookkeeping

▶ Being introduced to financial statements

Don't run away in terror just because you saw the word accounting and bright lights started flashing before your eyes. We come in peace, earthling. And we bear important information.

To be successful, a small business owner has to keep track of what the business earns and what it spends, and what it owns and what it owes. That means that every small business owner has to know something about accounting. But we're not going to inflict an entire accounting course on you (we haven't got the space/time continuum) — we're just going to tell you about the absolute basics. If you find yourself yearning for more information than we provide here, you can turn to *Accounting For Dummies,* 3rd Edition by John A. Tracy (Wiley).

Close encounters are often marked by strange and mysterious changes in gravity and the magnetic field, and by episodes of "missing time." So be prepared, as you go through this chapter, to feel weighed down as though the force of gravity has increased, to feel magnetically drawn to almost any other activity — and to wonder, when you reach the end, where the last half hour of your life went.

What's Accounting and Why Is It Important?

The essence of accounting is keeping track of financial transactions. Accounting is a process that begins with the collecting and recording of information about transactions and continues with the sorting of the transactions by category and ends in the preparation of financial statements and income tax returns.

Accountants call this process the accounting cycle. Some of the steps in the accounting cycle will be carried out by you, others will be carried out by your bookkeeper and/or your computerized accounting system, and still others will be carried out by your accountant.

Accounting is important in the day-to-day operation of your business because it helps you

- ✔ Collect your accounts.
- ✔ Pay your bills.
- ✔ Pay your taxes.
- ✔ Keep track of your inventory.
- ✔ Prevent theft and fraud by your associates, employees, and customers.

Accounting is also important in the long term because it helps you

- ✔ Assess how your business is doing.
- ✔ Collect the information you need to plan and make decisions.
- ✔ Give lenders the information they want before they will lend you money.
- ✔ Give investors the information they want before they will invest in your business.
- ✔ Give a buyer the information he or she wants to see before buying your business.

Close Encounter of the First Kind: Bookkeeping

Bookkeeping is the information-gathering and record-keeping aspect of accounting. No matter how much professional or computer help you intend to have with your bookkeeping, keeping track of all the financial transactions of your business is up to you — such as making sales, buying inventory, paying salaries, and borrowing money.

Your first chore as a bookkeeper is to keep all the pieces of paper, such as invoices, sales slips, and credit card slips that document business transactions (and the more organized you are about it, the better). You should also keep a record of these transactions.

Saving pieces of paper

Every financial transaction of your business should be documented by a piece of paper

- ✔ **Whenever your business provides a service or sells a product:** You should generate an invoice. (You may have the kind of business where you prepare invoices only on a weekly or monthly basis.) Most accounting software can generate invoices. If you're in a retail business, your cash register may generate a sales slip or invoice when you ring up the sale, or you may have to write up an invoice by hand. Send or give the invoice to the customer or client, and keep a copy for your records.

- ✔ **Whenever your business incurs an expense or makes a payment:** No matter how small the payment, you should get a bill, invoice, or receipt. If it's not clear what the receipt relates to, or the date the payment was made, make a note on the receipt identifying the transaction more clearly.

  For income tax purposes you have to keep a copy of both the bill and a copy of your cheque as proof of payment.

You must save every last one of these pieces of paper, which accountants and bookkeepers refer to as *source documents*. You can just throw all of them into a file, and let your bookkeeper and/or accountant sort them out later (and charge you for the extra work), but it makes more sense for you to set up some sort of system for filing them by category. For example, you may want to set up separate files for

- ✔ Invoices you give to your customers when you provide a service or product
- ✔ Inventory purchases
- ✔ Office supply expenses
- ✔ Car expenses
- ✔ Entertainment expenses
- ✔ Accounting expenses

Recording your transactions

The next step in the bookkeeping process is to make a written record of the financial transactions, taking the information from your source documents.

Open a business bank account

If you want to keep track of and have a record of your business transactions, you should open a bank account that is just for your business. Open a separate account even if your business is a sole proprietorship or partnership. (See Chapter 5. If you're a sole proprietor or partner, your business is not legally separate from you as an individual.) You might think that it doesn't matter if your business and personal accounts get mixed up — but once we get finished with you in this chapter, you'll come around to our point of view that it's best to keep your business affairs to themselves.

The bank account should be a chequing account that gives you a monthly statement and that automatically returns your cancelled cheques. Unless you will be using a computerized accounting program that will prepare and keep track of your cheques (see later in this chapter), order cheques for your new account, and get a cheque register. (This little booklet for recording transactions in your account usually comes with your new cheques or can be wheedled out of a teller at your bank or trust company.)

Pay into and out of your business account

Whenever you receive a payment for goods or services provided by your business, deposit the entire amount immediately in your business account. Enter the payment received in your cheque register.

As much as you possibly can, make any payments for your business by cheque. If you like to make payments by credit card, consider getting one card that you use for nothing but business purposes. Always pay your monthly bill for that card out of your business account.

If you have just one credit card for both personal and business purposes, you can pay the monthly bill out of your personal account and then write a cheque to yourself on your business account for the business portion of the bill. On the cheque stub for the total repayment, make a note of the individual amounts and the supplier's name — that way your accountant (or your auditor) won't have to go through your personal records to verify your expenses. Similarly, if you happen to make a cash payment out of your personal pocket for a business expense, write yourself a cheque on your business account to repay yourself.

Whenever you make a payment, enter it in your cheque register.

If you operate this way, you automatically create a record of all your business's income and expenses. In accounting language, you are *recording* entries into a *cash receipts and cash payments journal*.

Cash accounting or accrual accounting?

When you record a business transaction in your cheque register, you are not recording the transaction until you actually make or receive a payment. This is called *cash accounting* — you record income when you actually receive it and expenses when you actually pay them.

Cash accounting is an *accounting method.* An accounting method is supposed to match up your income and expenses in a consistent way. *Accrual accounting* is another accounting method.

In accrual accounting, you record income when you earn it (when you send out an invoice for the service performed or product supplied), and you record expenses when you incur them (when you receive a service or product). You'll actually receive the income or pay the expenses at some later time.

Once you choose an accounting method, do not change back and forth.

Speak to your accountant about whether to use cash accounting or accrual accounting in your business. Service providers usually use the cash method, while retailers usually use the accrual method. You will have to report your business income on an accrual basis for income tax purposes.

If you use accrual accounting in your business, you will have to keep another set of records to record sales when you make them (called a *sales journal*) and purchases when you make them (called a *purchases journal*).

Sorting your income and expenses by category

The next step in the accounting cycle is to sort your business's financial transactions into categories. You need to know what categories your income and expenses fall into in order to prepare your income tax returns and financial statements, and in order to keep track of how your business is doing and to make decisions and plans.

Sorting your income

All money your business receives is not identical. For example, when you receive a payment from a customer or client, most of it will be payment for your product or service, but some of it will be payment of GST/HST and/or provincial sales tax.

Your business may receive other kinds of money, as well, such as:

- ✔ Advances from the bank under a loan to your business
- ✔ Refunds for goods your business has purchased and returned
- ✔ Payment from an insurance policy for losses your business has suffered
- ✔ Refund of a security deposit given when you entered into a lease
- ✔ Money you or your family invest in the business

You need to sort income by category, because different kinds of income are treated differently in preparing financial statements and for tax purposes.

Sorting your expenses and other payments

You also need to sort your expenses and other payments by category, because different kinds of expenses are treated differently in preparing financial statements and for income tax purposes. (See Chapter 16 for more about expenses and taxes.)

Here are some of the categories of expenses you will want to keep track of:

- ✔ **General expenses to run your business:** This includes things such as:
  - • Rent
  - • Interest on borrowed money
  - • Legal and accounting fees
  - • Office supplies
  - • Professional or trade association fees
  - • Wages paid to employees (including deductions)

  These operating expenses are fully deductible from income in the year the expense occurred. They are sometimes called overhead.

- ✔ **Costs incurred to produce a product you manufacture:** These costs are fully deductible from income in the year the cost occurred too, but they show up in a different place on financial statements, so you might as well stick them in a different category from the beginning.

- ✔ **Inventory:** The cost of buying inventory is also fully deductible from income, but it too has a special place on a financial statement.

- ✔ **Auto expenses:** If you use a vehicle partly for business purposes and partly for personal purposes, only the business portion is deductible. So keep auto expenses separate from other expenses so that you can calculate the deductible portion at the end of the year.

✔ **Home office expenses:** You can deduct only a portion of your home rent or mortgage and utilities if you're running your business out of your home. So keep these expenses separate from other business operating expenses.

✔ **Business entertainment:** Only 50 percent of a business entertainment expense is deductible from income, so don't just toss it into the general expense pile.

✔ **Capital purchases:** (These are purchases of capital property, which is property with a long-term value, such as equipment, vehicles, and furniture.) You can't deduct any portion of a capital purchase in the year of the purchase, and after that you can deduct only a specified percentage as capital cost allowance (also known as depreciation). So definitely don't let your capital purchases get mixed up with your operating expenses. (See Chapter 16 for more about capital cost allowance.)

✔ **GST/HST payments:** Keep track of the amount you pay for GST/HST separately, so that you can incorporate input credits into your calculation of how much you owe at the end of each quarter.

In accounting language, these categories are called *accounts*.

TECHNICAL STUFF

More accounting jargon

We've already introduced you to some accounting jargon in this chapter . . . now we're adding a sidebar for those who'd like to see more of it.

In the language of accounting, the place where you record your day-to-day transactions (whether relating to income or expenses) as they occur is called a *journal*.

In a small business, all transactions of every description could be entered into one journal called a *general journal*. As the business gets bigger and more complex, it might need several journals for different types of transactions, such as:

✔ A *sales journal* for sales on credit

✔ A *purchases journal* for purchases on credit

✔ A *cash receipts* journal for receipts of cash

✔ A *cash payments* journal for payments of cash

✔ A *payroll journal* for payroll expenses

✔ A *general journal* for special or unusual transactions

The bookkeeper *records* transactions into the appropriate journals, in the order in which the transactions occur.

The income and expenses recorded in the journal(s) are periodically sorted into categories by *posting* the transaction to the appropriate *account* for each category of expense. The accounts are recorded in *ledgers*. Ledgers classify and summarize the information taken from the journals. The ledgers will later be used to prepare the financial statements and tax returns for the business.

Record keeping

In order to sort your income and expenses by category, you need to keep separate records for the different types of income received by your business and the different types of expenses incurred by your business. (This is in addition to keeping a cheque register.) Ask your accountant about the categories your business needs to keep track of.

At a minimum, you'll need different file folders to hold the source documents for each category. But you should also keep a written record of income and expenses. At the most basic level, you could keep these records on sheets of lined paper. At a slightly more sophisticated level, you could keep the records in account books purchased from a business supply store such as Grand and Toy or Staples/Business Depot or Office Place. (Account books are specially lined.) These days, however, most businesspeople use accounting software, which creates the records automatically from the entries that you make. Whichever way you do it, the same purpose is served and the same record is created.

Handling the bookkeeping burden

As you can imagine, proper bookkeeping involves a great deal of detailed work. How are you going to get it done?

You have three options.

Keep your own books manually

This tried-and-true method is cheap and easy to set up (you can buy manual bookkeeping ledger and journal systems, with directions, from any office supply store), but difficult and time-consuming to maintain.

You have to make all of the journal entries by hand, and then post the changes to the proper *accounts* (see sidebar "More accounting jargon"). If you need to generate a summary or financial statement, you have to work it out yourself.

If you decide to go this route, you should ask your accountant to help get you started.

Keep your own books using accounting software

You can use accounting software designed primarily for personal use, such as Quicken or Microsoft Money, or a more sophisticated system designed with small businesses in mind, such as MYOB (Mind Your Own Business), QuickBooks, or Simply Accounting.

The mysteries of double-entry accounting revealed right here — and also over here

Accounting operates on the theory that every business has on the one hand *assets* (property like equipment, inventory, money) and on the other hand equal and offsetting *liabilities* (claims against the assets in the form of money borrowed from lenders or invested by the owner — all assets are either owed to the lenders, or owned by the owner). This theory is expressed in the basic business accounting equation "Assets = Liabilities."

Every financial transaction of a business affects both sides of the business accounting equation. If the assets of the business increase, so does either the claim of the owner or the claim of the lenders.

Result: invention of *double-entry accounting*. The essence of double-entry accounting is that every transaction is recorded in two places, to maintain the overall balance between the asset side and the liability side of the equation. (You'll see this in action in the financial statements covered later in this chapter.)

Double-entry accounting also recognizes the give-and-take nature of every business transaction. For example, if a business spends $1,000 to buy $1,000 worth of inventory, the total value of the business hasn't changed — but its cash-on-hand decreases as the value of its inventory increases.

The personal-use systems are basically electronic cheque registers, with the added ability to sort expenses into categories and to generate income statements and balance sheets. When you enter your business's financial transaction into the computer, the program will post the changes to the appropriate accounts automatically.

A good business system will also generate sales invoices, track and report GST/HST/PST, track and age your accounts receivable, help keep track of your inventory, and compute employee payroll.

Ask your accountant for advice on the accounting software that's best for your business. You should also consider speaking to a computer consultant to make sure that you have the computer required to support the software you want to buy, and to ensure that the software is installed properly.

Use a freelance bookkeeper

If you can't or don't want to do your bookkeeping yourself, get someone to do it for you. When you first start your business, you probably won't need . . . or be able to afford . . . to hire a full-time bookkeeper. It makes more sense to contract with a freelance bookkeeper who will work only the number of hours that your business actually needs.

Your accountant is your best source for finding a bookkeeper. In fact, your accountant probably has a bookkeeper with whom he or she works on a regular basis and who is familiar with the accountant's requirements.

Your bookkeeper and accountant can decide whether to work with a manual or a computerized bookkeeping system.

Inventory Accounting

If you're not in a pure service business, one of the things you want your accounting system to do is to keep track of your inventory so that you know when to buy replacement inventory, and also what kind and how much. You need to know what sells and what doesn't in order to know what to buy in the future.

The best way to get this information is by using inventory-tracking software. If you have a retail business, you want a point-of-sale system that makes adjustments to your inventory records when sales are entered at the cash register. As we tell you under the heading "Handling the bookkeeping burden" earlier, some computerized bookkeeping packages include inventory-tracking features. If you prefer a low-tech approach, ask your accountant to help you develop a manual inventory-tracking system.

Whatever system of inventory tracking you use, be sure to do physical counts of your inventory two to four times a year. Compare the results of your physical count with what is shown in your financial records.

Valuing your inventory

In addition to knowing what you have in your inventory, you need to know how much it's worth. This isn't easy to figure out if you bought identical inventory items at different times and prices throughout the year. (You can't just shrug this question off because it affects the Cost of Goods Sold figure in your income statement and the Inventory figure in your balance sheet. See below under "Financial Statements.")

Since it is generally impossible to identify your inventory really specifically, you address this question by using one of two accounting methods. The First In, First Out (or FIFO) method assumes that the inventory you bought earliest is sold first. Under this method you value your inventory at the most recent price you paid for it. The Last In, First Out (or LIFO) method assumes that the inventory you bought last is sold first. Under this method, the value of your inventory is based on the oldest item in it. Your accountant will advise you which method you should use. For income tax purposes, you have to use the FIFO method.

Internal Controls

Think no one associated with or working for your business will ever stick his or her hand in the till? Think again. Although shoplifting gets more attention, internal theft and fraud cost businesses far more each year. In consultation with your accountant, establish and enforce internal controls, a system of checks and balances, to discourage and detect both honest mistakes and dishonesty. Here are some examples of internal controls:

- Inspecting and counting shipments from suppliers before paying for them
- Requiring two signatures on cheques over a certain amount
- Having outsiders or employees who aren't normally involved do surprise inventories and compare them with inventory records
- Having one person record sales and collections while another person records and takes the deposits to the bank
- Requiring every associate or employee to take a vacation, during which time someone else does that person's job

Close Encounter of the Second Kind: Preparing Financial Documents

Your bookkeeping efforts will soon be put to good use. In no time at all you'll find yourself filing tax and tax-related returns and needing financial statements to track your business's activities.

Tax and related returns

Go to Chapter 16 to find out more about your tax obligations — but briefly,

- If you've registered for GST/HST, you'll have to file statements (usually quarterly), and calculate whether you have to pay GST/HST (and how much) or whether you're entitled to a rebate because you've paid out more in GST/HST when making purchases than you've taken in when charging GST on your goods and services.
- In every province except Alberta (which has no provincial sales tax) and Nova Scotia, New Brunswick, and Newfoundland (which have HST), you will have to file provincial sales tax returns (usually monthly), in which you report the amount of sales tax you have collected from your customers or clients, and remit that amount to the government.

✔ If you have employees, you must complete and file with the CRA a Current Source Deductions Remittance Voucher on a regular basis (usually monthly) in which you report your gross payroll for the remitting period, the amount that you are paying on account of income tax, Canada Pension Plan, and Employment Insurance that you have withheld from your employees, and your contribution toward your employees' Canada Pension Plan and Employment Insurance. At the end of each year you will have to file a T4 Summary form in which you report your total payroll for the year and all amounts you have previously remitted.

Depending on your province, you may also have to file returns with your provincial workers' compensation board or provincial health insurance commission, setting out the amount of your payroll.

✔ After you've been in business for a year, if you've had any kind of success at all, you'll have to pay your income tax quarterly in advance. So you need to put aside an appropriate amount out of income at the end of each week or month so that you'll have your payment ready when the quarter-day comes around (March 15, June 15, September 15, December 15).

✔ At the end of the year, your tax return will have to be prepared. If your income is all ready to add up, and your expenses are categorized so you can easily apply the proper tax treatment to them and enter them in the correct lines, preparing your return should be a breeze (either for you or your accountant).

Financial statements

Your records will also be used to prepare financial statements. Businesses use financial statements for a number of purposes:

✔ To help you track the progress of the business, and plan for the future.

✔ To provide information that may have to be included in income tax returns for the business.

✔ To show to lenders when you're trying to persuade them to lend you money. A lender will want to know how profitable your business is, and to see trends in the income and expenses of the business — and so will want to see your financial statements, over several years if possible, and your cash flow projections. A lender will also be very interested in the amount of debt your business already has.

✔ To show potential buyers when you're trying to sell your business. A prospective buyer will want to see the financial statements for your business for the past three to five years. See Chapter 9 for a discussion of what the buyer will be looking for in your financial statements.

Businesses have historical financial statements and forward-looking financial statements. Historical statements report actual results of the operation of the business after they've taken place. The income statement and balance sheet are the main types of historical financial statements. Forward-looking statements (sometimes known as *pro forma* financial statements) are used to plan for the future, and they include forecasts of income and expenses and cash flow projections.

Historical Financial Statements

The income statement and the balance sheet are the main types of historical statements. You use these statements to track the progress of your business and help you plan for the future.

Creating financial statements

The avant-garde Devils Tower Accounting Project, operating out of Wyoming, has had a certain amount of success in constructing financial statements from mounds of mashed potato, but we don't recommend this approach for those of you who do not have advanced degrees in accounting, cuisine, and sculpture.

If you have accounting software that prepares financial statements and you've faithfully recorded all your transactions, you can generate accurate financial statements by clicking a button.

It's also perfectly possible to create financial statements by hand. (In the good old days this was the only way to create them.) In the following discussions about income statements and balance sheets, we'll explain the process to you in case you want to try it yourself — but mainly so you'll have an idea of what's going on inside your computer . . . or your accountant's head.

The income statement

The *income statement*, also called a *profit and loss statement*, sets out the business's revenues (or income or sales) and expenses over a stated period of time (a specific month, quarter or year). The business's *revenues* are the money that its customers or clients pay for its products or services. Its *expenses* are the costs incurred in doing business. The business's profits equal its revenues minus its expenses.

How do you prepare it?

Table 17-1 contains our instructions for preparing an income statement. (At the end of the chapter is a completed Statement for you to look at; see Figure 17-1.)

If you are in a retail or manufacturing business, start with Gross Sales (which is all the money you took in minus GST/HST charged) and then deduct the Cost of Goods Sold, which is what you paid directly for your inventory, either to buy it or manufacture it — Gross Sales minus Cost of Goods Sold equals Gross Profit. (If you are a service business, you will not have a cost-of-goods-sold expense.) Then set out and add up all of your expenses of operating the business other than those directly related to creating or acquiring the product you sell (that's your overhead), and subtract the total from Gross Profit to find your Net Income or (Net) Profit before taxes are taken into account.

See the CD-ROM for a version of Table 17-1 that you can fill in to create a statement of income and expenses for your business.

Table 17-1	Statement of Income and Expenses		
	Prior Year (or month quarter)	*Budget (for current year or month or quarter)*	*Current Year or (or month or quarter)*
Gross Sales MINUS **Cost of the Goods Sold** EQUALS	As a start-up you won't have a prior year, month, or quarter until you've been in business for a while.	Your budget is the projected statement of income and expenses that you prepared before the start of this year. See below for forecasting income and expenses.	These are the actual figures from the records you've kept for the period.
Expenses (such as)			
Accounting/legal, Bank charges, Depreciation, Insurance, Marketing, Rent, Telephone, Wages Total Expenses			
Net Income or **Profit** (before income tax) (Subtract Total Expenses from Gross Profit)			

You prepare a budget for an upcoming period by preparing a *forecast of income and expenses*. It is meant to be a realistic prediction of the revenue you will earn and the expenses you will incur over that period. Before you start your business, your income and expense forecasts are based on a combination of research and hope. (It's a lot easier to project your expenses than your revenues before your business is actually up and running. We give you some advice in Chapter 10 about forecasting income and expenses.) After your business has been in operation for a year, you'll be able to make your forecasts based on past performance and your knowledge of trends in your field.

What can it tell you?

By comparing the current year's (month's, quarter's) Gross Sales figures to the previous year's (month's, quarter's), you can tell whether your sales are going up or down. By comparing current Expenses to previous Expenses, you can tell which of your expenses have gone up or down.

By looking at your Gross Profit and Expenses together, you'll see whether you're generating enough through sales to cover your operating costs.

By dividing your Net Income or Profit by your Gross Sales, you'll find out what your return on sales is. That gives you an idea about how efficiently your business turns a dollar's worth of sale into a profit.

By dividing your Gross Profit by total sales made to find your gross profit margin, you can see how much profit you earned on sales before taking into account your costs of selling the products and administering your business.

By dividing your Net Income or Profit by your total sales, you can find your net profit margin or profit margin. A low net profit margin may indicate that the business isn't being efficiently run.

The acceptable profit margin varies with the type of business, and you should be able to find out through your professional or trade association what a decent profit margin is for your type of business.

The balance sheet

The balance sheet lists a value for everything a business owns (its *assets*) and everything it owes (its *liabilities*) as of a specified date, usually the last date of the company's *fiscal* (financial) year, referred to as its *year-end*. It's called a balance sheet because the total assets have to equal the total liabilities (including the owner's equity). (If you come up with a balance sheet where assets don't equal liabilities, you haven't created an imbalance sheet; you've just done it wrong.)

How do you prepare it?

You create a balance sheet by setting down the value of the business's assets and liabilities in a recognized order.

Start with assets, which are categorized as *current assets* or *fixed assets*. Current assets are cash or assets that are intended to be and can be converted into cash easily. Fixed assets are assets the business intends to hold onto for a long period of time.

Then list liabilities, categorizing them as *current liabilities* or *long-term liabilities*. Current liabilities are debts that are expected be paid within a year, such as accounts payable, current wages, current taxes, and the current portion of long-term debt. Long-term liabilities are debts that will not be paid off within a year. *Owner's equity* — what a business is worth after its debts are deducted from its assets — is also considered a liability. (It's that double-entry accounting thing again.) Take a look at Table 17-2.

Use the version of Table 17-2 on the CD-ROM to create a balance sheet for your business.

Table 17-2	Balance Sheet	
Prior Year (month, quarter)	*Budget*	*Current Year (month, quarter)*
ASSETS		
Current Assets		
Cash		
Accounts receivable		
Inventory		
Total Current Assets		
Fixed Assets		
Furniture and fixtures		
Equipment		
Total Fixed Assets		
Total Assets		
LIABILITIES		
Current Liabilities		
Accounts payable		
Short-term notes payable		
Total Current Liabilities		
Long-term Liabilities		
Long-term notes payable		
Total long-term liabilities		
Total Liabilities		
Owner's Equity or Net Worth (Subtract Total Liabilities from Total Assets)		
Total Liabilities and Net Worth (Add Total Liabilities and Net Worth together)		

What can it tell you?

By dividing the Total Liabilities (the total debts of your business) by the Owner's Equity or Net Worth, you'll get the debt-to-equity ratio of your business. This ratio will tell you what percentage of the business you own and what percentage your lenders own. Generally speaking, you don't want the ratio to go above 1:1 (that is, you own as much of your business as your lenders do). If it goes above 2:1 (your lenders own twice as much as you do), you may find it difficult to borrow money because even the most optimistic lender can't be sure of getting the money back out of the business. Keep in mind, though, that if you have too little debt, you may not be realizing the full potential of your business — because you can use borrowed money to expand and improve your business and make it more profitable.

By dividing Current Assets by Current Liabilities, you'll find your *current ratio*. It tells you how *liquid* your business is — how quickly you can come up with cash if you need to. A 1:1 ratio means that your business has a dollar in current assets to cover every dollar of current liabilities. You don't want to fall below 1:1, and you'd like to stay at 2:1 or higher. By dividing the Current Assets minus Inventory (that is, only Cash and Accounts Receivable) by the Current Liabilities, you'll come up with the *quick ratio*. The quick ratio will give you an idea how quickly you can come up with cash without selling off your inventory. You want your quick ratio to be at least 1:1.

By dividing the Net Income or Profit (from the income statement) by the Net Worth of the business (from the balance sheet), you can find out what your *return on equity* or return on investment is. You'd like a return at least equal to what you'd get if you just sold the business, invested the cash, and collected interest or dividends. (But if you look at your return on equity and panic because it's low, remember to take into account any money you are getting from the business as salary.)

Case Study: E.T.&T. Telecommunications Inc.

Let's put into practice what we've just discussed and look at some completed financial statements (for E.T.&T. Telecommunications) to see what the figures tell us.

Have a look at the sample income statement shown in Figure 17-1.

You can see that E.T.&T.'s Gross Sales went up in the current year, but not as much as predicted in the budget, while the Cost of Goods Sold went up more than predicted. As a result, Gross Profits went up, but not as much as the owner had looked for. In addition, while some expenses went down, wages went up by 20 percent (the owner had predicted that they would go up by only 10 percent). (These wages included a salary for the owner of $40,000.) Overall, expenses went up at a higher rate (by over 15 percent) than sales, which went up by only about 6 percent. (Note, however, that telephone expenses hardly went up at all — is the owner really phoning home often enough or is he losing commitment to this business?) The business made a profit of $23,560 on total sales of $160,000, or about 14.75 percent. Looks like the owner of E.T.&T. should be thinking about:

✔ Increasing sales

✔ Finding a less expensive source of inventory

✔ Cutting the number of hours worked by employees other than the owner (they should be spending more time riding their bicycles, anyway)

E.T.&T. Telecommunications Inc.
Income Statement
For the year ending December 31, 2006

	Prior Year	Budget	Current Year
Sales	$150,000	$165,000	$160,000
- Cost of goods sold	50,000	52,000	55,000
- Gross profit	$100,000	$113,000	$105,000
Expenses			
Accounting/Legal	$2,000	$2,500	$2,250
Bank charges	1,500	1,500	1,500
Depreciation	1,450	1,115	1,115
Insurance	650	675	675
Marketing	1,000	1,500	1,500
Printing	750	750	500
Rent	12,000	12,600	12,600
Telephone	1,200	1,200	1,300
Wages	50,000	55,000	60,000
Total expenses	$70,550	$76,840	$81,440
Profit (before tax)	$29,450	$36,160	$23,560

Figure 17-1: Income statement.

Now look at the balance sheet for E.T.&T shown in Figure 17-2.

The Net Worth of E.T.&T. went up by $22,445. (That increase is equal to the profits for the year of $23,560, shown on the income statement, minus the amount by which the furniture, fixtures, and equipment went down in value as a result of depreciation.)

The profit of $23,560 is over 45 percent of the net worth of the business. When you consider that the owner also took a salary of $40,000, that's a healthy return on investment.

E.T.&T.'s Current Assets amount to $62,510 and its Current Liabilities to $5,500, so its current ratio is approximately 11:1 — this business can come up with cash to pay off its debts at the drop of a Reese's Piece. E.T.&T.'s debts total $15,500 compared to Owner's Equity of $50,945, a ratio of about 1:3. In other words, the owner owns over two-thirds of the business outright, compared to less than one-third owned by creditors. This is a healthy debt-to-equity ratio. Maybe a little too healthy — is the owner failing to take advantage of loans or outside investment in order to expand and become a more serious player in the field . . . or even to move into a related field, such as aerospace? (Building your own rocket is getting cheaper and cheaper, so why just phone home when you can go home?)

E.T.&T. Telecommunications Inc.
Balance Sheet
For the year ending December 31, 2006

	Prior Year	Budget	Current Year
Assets			
Current assets			
Cash	$29,450	$55,860	$24,010
Accounts receivable	1,000	0	500
Inventory	16,500	18,250	20,000
Total current assets	$46,950	$75,110	$62,510
Fixed assets			
Furniture & fixtures	$3,200	$2,560	$2,560
Equipment	1,850	1,375	1,375
Total fixed assets	$5,050	$3,935	$3,935
Total Assets	$52,000	$79,045	$66,445
Liabilities			
Current liabilities			
Accounts payable	$3,500	$500	$500
Short-term notes payable	5,000	5,000	5,000
Total current liabilities	$8,500	$5,500	$5,500
Long-term liabilities			
Long-term notes payable	$15,000	$10,000	$10,000
Total long-term liabilities	$15,000	$10,000	$10,000
Total Liabilities	$23,500	$15,500	$15,500
Owner's equity (net worth)	$28,500	$63,545	$50,945
Total Liabilities and Net Worth	$52,000	$79,056	$66,445

Figure 17-2: Balance sheet.

Cash Flow Projections

Income and expenses rarely match each other exactly. Your income may come in a few times a year, whereas your expenses are likely to be fairly steady on a month-by-month basis.

As a result, knowing how much money your business is going to earn is not enough. You must also know when you are actually going to receive it. Likewise, knowing how much money you'll need to operate your business is not enough. You also have to know when you'll need it. A cash flow projection charts not only how much money you can expect to receive and pay, but when.

You use a cash flow projection when you first start your business to help you calculate how large an operating loan you need until you can establish an income flow that more closely matches the amount and timing of your expenses.

Cash flow projections remain useful, if not essential, even after your business is established. While some of your expenses are fixed and occur on a regular basis, you have some control over the timing of other expenses. Cash flow projections help you plan, both to put off expenses you have control over until you expect to have the income to cover them, and to borrow money to cover expenses you can't put off. You should make cash flow projections for at least six months into the future, updating them every month.

If you borrow money, the lender will want to see your cash flow projections to help decide whether and when you'll be able to repay the loan.

See Chapter 10 for more about cash flow, including an explanation of how to build a cash flow table. For an example of a cash flow table, see the Sample Business Plan on the CD-ROM.

Close Encounter of the Third Kind: Hiring an Accountant

So, does your business need an accountant? If you've paid the slightest attention to anything we've said in this chapter, you'll be screaming "Yes!" Although you don't have to have an accountant as a permanent member of your staff, you need to consult an accountant on an ongoing basis:

✔ **To help you set up your bookkeeping system** — either a manual or computerized one, and to build in internal controls to help reduce errors and to prevent and detect theft and fraud

✔ **To prepare various financial statements** — such as budgets, cash flow statements, income statements, and balance sheets, based on a review and analysis of financial data

✔ **To prepare your income tax returns** — based on a review and analysis of financial data in the context of income tax law

✔ **To deal with the CRA from time to time** — if you experience difficulties arising out of your income tax returns or with respect to your GST or employer remittances

What kind of accountant?

In Canada, anyone can call himself or herself an accountant. What you want is a professional accountant. There are only three types of recognized professional accountants — chartered accountants, certified general accountants, and certified management accountants. These accountants have a professional designation and belong to government-recognized self-regulating bodies, just as lawyers do.

Chartered accountants (CAs) are regulated by provincial institutes of chartered accountants. They must have a Bachelor of Commerce or equivalent university degree, complete 30 months of supervised employment, take a series of professional courses, and pass a number of examinations, including a nationally administered Uniform Final Exam.

Certified general accountants (CGAs) are regulated by provincial associations of general accountants. They must have a university degree, take a series of distance learning courses through the Certified General Accountants Association, complete between two and three years of supervised employment, and pass a series of examinations.

Certified management accountants (CMAs) are regulated by provincial societies of management accountants. They must have a university degree, pass a CMA entrance examination, and complete a two-year program while gaining practical experience by working in a management accounting environment. Most CMAs are managers who are employed by businesses, but there are also consulting CMAs who offer strategic and financial management accounting services to the public on a fee-for-service basis.

For more information on finding and dealing with professional advisors such as accountants and lawyers, see Chapter 14.

Part IV
What Does the Future Hold?

The 5th Wave   By Rich Tennant

"It's quite a business plan, Ms. Strunt. It's the first
one I've read whose mission statement says,
'...keeps me out of trouble'."

In this part . . .

We give you a glimpse of what the future may hold for your business. We give you advice about dealing with common problems (to wit, lack of money, and disputes), some tips about how to expand your business successfully, and guidance about getting out of business.

Chapter 18

Houston, We Have a Problem

- -

In This Chapter

▶ Making a plan when you can't repay a debt

▶ Dealing with lack of funds to pay your rent or mortgage

▶ Coming up with a strategy when you can't pay your taxes

▶ Negotiating settlement of a dispute

▶ Using alternative dispute resolution to end a dispute

▶ Deciding when to start a lawsuit

- -

Oh-oh, looks like trouble ahead. When trouble arises, your first thought will probably be, Beam me up, Scotty! But get over looking for a miraculous rescue — Scotty would be the first person to tell you that the transporter is broken. (Maybe because he was always trying to fix that highly sophisticated machine — which could turn matter into energy and back into matter again — with a screwdriver.)

To avoid some of the trouble we discuss in this chapter in the first place:

✔ Don't borrow more money than you can realistically expect to repay on schedule.

✔ Do a credit check on customers before you do the work.

✔ Follow up on collections after you send a bill.

✔ Take care not to do shoddy work or provide defective products.

✔ Always have contracts in writing that you understand.

✔ Perform your contracts properly.

But when you can't avoid trouble, you have to deal with it. So this chapter is meant to help you face your problems head-on, make an objective assessment of the situation, and try to come up with a plan of action.

No Money

So your creditors are after you. They want their money and you haven't got it at the moment. Maybe

- ✔ You can't repay a loan.
- ✔ You can't pay for equipment you're buying on credit.
- ✔ You can't pay your rent.
- ✔ You can't pay off a mortgage.
- ✔ You can't pay your taxes.
- ✔ You are insolvent.
- ✔ You are about to go bankrupt.

What's going to happen and what can you do?

Even though you may be broke, consider talking to your lawyer (if your lawyer will talk to someone with as little money as you have). Borrowing and lending are subject to legal rules and you may be in a better position than your creditor thinks (and your creditor is in a worse position). Your lawyer may be able to help you negotiate an extension of the deadline for repayment, or more favourable terms of repayment.

You shouldn't put up a fight against your creditors out of sheer pig-headedness. If you lose the fight, you'll owe even more money — because creditors are usually allowed to pass on the cost of collecting their debts to you, the debtor. (And you'll still have to pay your own legal fees.)

Your business can't make a payment that's due

If you borrow money, you're expected to repay it. If you don't repay, the lender is liable to get a little exercised. But what the lender can do depends on the nature of the lender and the loan. If you end up getting sued, see the section later in this chapter on "Litigation." And, since we frequently suggest that you try to work out a deal with your creditor, you'll also find a section further along on "Negotiation of a settlement."

A payment on a loan from a non-commercial source

You got *love money* from a family member or friend to set up your business (see Chapter 10) but the lender doesn't feel so loving now — maybe he needs the cash desperately, or maybe you've ticked her off by not taking her canny business advice.

Besides giving you the cold shoulder or not inviting you over for dinner any-more, the lender can sue for return of the money. This is true whether or not there's a written contract. An *oral contract* (a contract made through conver-sation) is as valid as a contract in writing. It's just harder to prove the terms of an oral contract because no one wrote them down. Your lender is legally able to tell the court about the conversations you had when the loan was made (the terms of the loan agreement will be the lender's word against yours) and can require other people who have heard you talk about the loan to repeat in court what they heard, and can show to the court documents such as a note or letter you wrote to the lender acknowledging the loan or saying that you would pay the money back.

So don't ignore the lender or tell him to buzz off. If you have no money to pay now, try to reach some kind of agreement:

- ✔ See if the lender will agree to wait a few weeks or months until you do have the money.

- ✔ See if the lender will agree to accept smaller payments over a longer term, or smaller payments now and "balloon" payments later to make up for the smaller payments now.

- ✔ Offer something other than money in full or part payment of the loan — something you own or the business owns, or your services for free.

- ✔ Offer security for the loan, such as a mortgage on property you own; or offer a share in your business (although doing these things could create more problems for you in the long run).

Then put into writing the agreement you've reached, and sign it and have the lender sign it. Each of you should get an original of the signed agreement.

A payment on a loan from a commercial source

If you have a commercial loan, you probably agreed to pay it off in instalments, so you may think that not being able to pay one instalment is not such a big deal. You're wrong. Most commercial term loans (see Chapter 10) have an acceleration clause. That means that the lender can demand that you repay the entire loan as soon as you miss one payment by more than a few days. And if you have a line of credit (see Chapter 10), it's probably repayable on demand — so you don't even have to miss one payment before the lender has the right to tell you to repay the full amount.

If a lender makes a demand for repayment and you can't repay, the lender has the right to sue you for the outstanding amount of the loan, plus interest owing, plus the lender's costs of collecting the debt from you. If you've given security for the loan (a right against property — again, see Chapter 10), your agreement with the lender probably allows the lender to realize on the security after you miss a payment. That means that the lender, after demanding repayment of the loan and waiting a few days for payment,

- ✔ Can take property you offered as security and either keep it or sell it (or start a lawsuit for possession of the secured property if you won't let the lender have it)

- ✔ Can demand that a person who guaranteed the loan pay back the loan (plus interest)

- ✔ May be able to appoint a receiver/manager to take possession of the secured property and sell it, depending on the terms of the loan agreement

If a lender seizes secured property, you may have the right for a short period (a couple of weeks) to get the property back by paying what you owe plus interest and costs. If the lender sells the property, it has to make sure that it gets a fair price, and afterward has to account to you for the property. The lender is not allowed to keep more than it's owed (don't forget that this includes interest and the costs of taking and selling the property), and it has to pay you any surplus from a sale.

If you know that you don't have the money to make a payment, but you think that you'll have money soon to get back on track,

- ✔ First, try to find the money for the payment from another source, if you can. Unless you're on really good terms with your commercial lender and have the lender's trust and adoration, it's probably best not to let the lender know that you're in a bit of trouble. The lender might panic and pull the plug on your loan, and on any other dealings you have with that lender.

- ✔ Then, if you can't get money from another source, talk to your lender before the due date of the payment that you're going to miss. The lender may agree to overlook your default for a short time, especially if you offer some additional security (if you've got anything left that's not already being used for security, that is — if you don't, the lender might accept security from someone else, such as a personal guarantee from a relative or associate).

Be careful about borrowing more money and offering more security for a loan that you're already having trouble repaying! You may just be digging yourself deeper into a hole and in the long run you may lose more.

If you're in a really bad financial position and you don't think that a little extra money or a little extra time is going to do anything but delay bigger trouble, you should think about making a proposal to all of your creditors or even going bankrupt (see the heading "Your business is insolvent").

A payment for an asset bought on credit

If you've bought assets (such as equipment or vehicles or furniture) for your business and are paying for them over time, you've almost certainly entered into a financing agreement such as a *chattel mortgage, conditional sales agreement, purchase money security interest,* or a *lease with an option to purchase*. If you stop making your payments, the other party to the financing agreement can

- ✔ Sue you for the full amount still left to pay (plus interest)
- ✔ Seize the asset and sell it (and account to you after the sale)

See if the financer is willing to give you more time to pay (and then try to find some money) . . . that's about all you can do.

A payment under an equipment lease

If your business leased assets instead of buying them outright or on time, you're not in any better position if you stop making your regular payments. The terms of a commercial asset lease normally don't allow you to stop making your lease payments for any reason — and that includes the fact that the asset is broken or defective and the fact that you have no money. You have to make all the payments for the full term of the lease. If you miss a payment, the lessor can

- ✔ Sue you for the full amount owed under the lease
- ✔ Seize the asset (and, if you have an option to purchase, sell it and account to you)

Once again, about the only thing you can do is try to negotiate more time to pay, and look for some money to pay with.

You've personally guaranteed a debt for your business and your business can't pay

If you've given a personal guarantee for a business loan and your business can't make a payment, the lender can demand payment from you. If you don't pay, the lender can sue you for the full outstanding amount of the loan, plus interest. If you gave security (such as a mortgage on your home) as well as guaranteeing the debt, the lender can realize on the security.

If you've co-signed a loan with your business, the lender doesn't even have to wait for your business to miss a payment — it can demand that you make the payment instead, because you're equally responsible for the loan from the get-go.

Note that if you're a member of a partnership, in most provinces the partners are individually responsible for paying debts of the partnership if the partnership itself can't pay (see Chapter 5).

Your business can't pay its rent

If you can't pay the rent owing under your commercial lease, your landlord has a variety of nasty things it can do to you including

- ✔ Sue you for *arrears of rent* (rent owing) or for *damages* (money compensation) for breach of the lease, while letting you stay on under the lease.

- ✔ Retake possession of the premises and terminate the lease (in which case, although the landlord can sue for arrears of rent before termination, it can't sue for any rent due after the date of termination).

- ✔ Retake possession of the premises and terminate the lease with notice for future loss of rent. (Then the landlord can sue for arrears of rent before termination and also for damages for future loss of rent after the date of termination. If the landlord makes a reasonable effort but can't find another tenant, or another tenant who's willing to pay as much as you agreed to pay, the landlord can sue you for the entire shortfall over the rest of the term of your lease.)

- ✔ Retake possession of the premises without terminating the lease, and re-letting the premises acting as your agent (you remain responsible for the rent, minus whatever the landlord collects from the new tenant).

- ✔ *Distrain* (seize and sell your property on the premises) to satisfy arrears of rent. In most provinces, if you remove your property from the premises to keep your landlord from getting its hands on it, the landlord can seize the property wherever it is (if the landlord can find it) within the next 30 days and can make you pay a penalty for being such a sneak.

If your landlord terminates your lease, retakes possession of your premises, or distrains, consider seeing a lawyer to find out whether the landlord is within its rights. Landlords sometimes ignore the fine print of the law, and you may have some rights of your own. For example:

- ✔ A landlord cannot terminate a lease for non-payment until the rent has been unpaid for 15 days or more in most provinces (and it can't terminate for other reasons without giving you proper notice and a chance to fix whatever the landlord is complaining about).

- ✔ If the landlord terminates, you can go to court to get the termination set aside — if you can pay the arrears of rent.

- ✔ A landlord can't distrain until the day after the rent was due, and has to carry out the *distraint* (also known as a *distress*) during daylight hours.

> ✔ A landlord that distrains (in most provinces) can't seize fixtures, cash, property that belongs to others (such as inventory on consignment), or perishable goods, and it has to leave tools you use in the business up to a value of $2,000.

> ✔ The landlord has no right to distrain if it has already got a judgement for arrears of rent, or has terminated the lease or locked you out, or if you and the landlord have agreed that the lease is at an end.

Your business can't pay a mortgage on real property

If you took out a mortgage to buy real property for your business and you can't make your payments, the *mortgagee* (the lender) has the right in many provinces to *foreclose* on the mortgage (become the legal owner of the property), or to sell the property — under court supervision in a *judicial sale,* or privately under a *power of sale*.

If the mortgagee starts a legal action for foreclosure or judicial sale, you can stop it by paying off the entire mortgage, or in some cases by paying the payment(s) you missed plus a penalty. If you can't pay the entire mortgage immediately, you can ask the court for a delay (from about two to six months) in order to come up with the money. You can also stop foreclosure by asking for judicial sale. If the foreclosure goes through, in most provinces your mortgage debt is cancelled and you don't owe the mortgagee anything, even if the property is worth less than the debt you owe (but on the other hand the mortgagee doesn't owe you anything if the property is worth more than the debt you owe). If the property is sold in a judicial sale, any money left over after payment of the mortgage debt plus interest plus legal costs is yours; but if there's a shortfall, the lender can require you to make it up.

Most mortgagees prefer to act under a power of sale, if they can, because they don't have to go to court to sell the property. The lender has to notify you that it's going to exercise its power of sale, and you'll be given a short time (about a month) to stop the sale by paying off the mortgage or in some cases by making up the payment(s) you missed. As with a judicial sale, the proceeds from the sale will be used to pay the outstanding amount of the mortgage, as well as interest and costs; the mortgagee can sue you for any shortfall, but if money is left over, the mortgagee has to return it to you.

If the mortgagee wants to sell the property, see if it will let you try to sell the property yourself first. Buyers may think they can get a good deal and may offer a lower price when they see it's a judicial sale or sale under a power of sale. The more money the property sells for, the less you'll owe the mortgagee or the more you'll get to keep.

Your business can't pay its taxes

The Canada Revenue Agency (CRA) has a *statutory lien* against the personal property (as opposed to real property, or real estate) of a taxpayer who does not pay taxes or remittances that are due. This lien lets the government seize your business's personal property — which is your personal property, if you're a sole proprietor or partner — after giving 30 days notice (during the notice period you can pay up and avoid the seizure).

If you own real property in a municipality and you don't pay your property taxes, the municipality will add interest charges and penalties to your property tax bill. If you still don't pay your taxes, the municipality has the right to sell your real property. (The municipality doesn't get to keep all the money from the sale, only the amount that you owe in taxes.)

Your business is insolvent

Your business is insolvent if it owes at least $1,000 and cannot pay its debts as they become due. There's nothing wrong with being insolvent in itself (apart from the fact that you have no money), but if you're insolvent, you're in danger of being forced into bankruptcy. A creditor to whom you owe more than $1,000 and who has no security from you for the debt can petition your business into bankruptcy if your business commits an act of bankruptcy — such as not paying a debt when it's due or not complying with a court order to pay a creditor who's won a lawsuit against the business, or telling a creditor that you're not going to pay your debts, or hiding or disposing of property to avoid paying a creditor.

If you're dealing with unsecured creditors

If you're insolvent, what can you do before someone petitions you into bankruptcy? You can try to reach some kind of agreement with your creditors — for example, that they'll give you more time to pay, or accept part payment of your debt. Put any agreement into writing. By the way, your creditors won't likely be interested in cutting you some slack unless your business has decent prospects.

If your business does have prospects, it might be wise to get some advice from a lawyer who specializes in insolvency, or from a *trustee in bankruptcy* who deals with businesses (rather than with consumers). Your advisor might recommend making an informal offer to your creditors, or a formal proposal under the *Bankruptcy and Insolvency Act* (see the next paragraph).

If you're dealing with secured creditors

If you're insolvent and a secured creditor notifies you that it's going to realize on its security, you should consider making a formal proposal under the

Bankruptcy and Insolvency Act. If you do nothing at this point, your secured creditors are going to make off with the secured property, and you probably need it to keep your business running. You should get a trustee in bankruptcy to advise you and to file in bankruptcy court a *notice of intention to make a proposal.* Once the notice is filed, your business has some protection from secured and unsecured creditors for at least a month:

- Creditors can't seize any property.

- Companies that supply things such as electricity, heat, water, and telephone can't cut off service.

- Parties to contracts with your business can't terminate the contracts or invoke acceleration clauses (an acceleration clause makes a debt you're paying off in instalments come due all at once).

On the downside, you have to pay cash up front for any supplies you buy.

After you file your notice of intention, you have to file the actual proposal, and then your creditors meet within about three weeks to vote on it. Here's another downside to the proposal process: If your secured creditors reject the proposal (even if your unsecured creditors don't), they can immediately realize on their security. In addition (as if you needed an addition at this point), your business is deemed to have made an *assignment in bankruptcy* (a transfer of its property to the trustee in bankruptcy) and will be officially declared bankrupt.

You can choose to go bankrupt

You can be forced into bankruptcy, but you can also choose to go into bankruptcy by making an assignment in bankruptcy. Why would you actually want to go bankrupt? Well, once you're declared bankrupt by a court, your trustee in bankruptcy deals with your creditors. You don't have to look at their ugly faces anymore. Your trustee will make arrangements to sell the business's property to pay the debts. And you'll be able to start over again.

If you're carrying on business as a sole proprietorship or a partnership, you'll go bankrupt as an individual. If you're carrying on business as a corporation, the corporation will go bankrupt. As an individual you'll probably be discharged from bankruptcy after nine months, and if you receive an absolute discharge, almost all of your debts are cancelled. (If you receive a conditional discharge, you'll still be responsible for repaying certain debts — income taxes for example.) A corporation can't be discharged until it has paid all its debts, but you can always start up a new corporation (however, you may find that the creditors you stiffed won't be very anxious to deal with your new corporation).

See the next section for more (yum!) about bankruptcy.

Bankruptcy

Once the bankruptcy court has made an order that your business is bankrupt, it appoints a trustee in bankruptcy. The trustee becomes the legal owner of all the unsecured property that formerly belonged to your business (and to you if your business is a sole proprietorship or a partnership — see Chapter 5) and it uses the property to pay off debts. Your secured creditors keep their rights over secured property. It doesn't go to the trustee.

If you're a sole proprietor or partner and you go bankrupt, you'll be allowed to keep some personal property — about $5,000 worth (more in some provinces) of clothing, furniture, and "tools of your trade."

If your business is a corporation and you're a director, you may not escape having to make some payments personally if your business goes bankrupt. You'll be held responsible for up to six months' worth of unpaid wages for employees, for unpaid amounts owed to the CRA for income tax and GST/HST, Canada Pension Plan and Employment Insurance, and for unpaid provincial sales tax owed to your provincial department or ministry of finance. And that's on top of paying any business loans for which you gave a personal guarantee.

If your business disposed of any property to save it from creditors, you can be personally charged with a criminal offence. And your trustee in bankruptcy can sue to get his hands on property that was improperly transferred away from the business, so that it can be distributed among the creditors.

If a person or business is an undischarged bankrupt, he, she, or it can't borrow more than $500 without telling the lender about the state of bankruptcy (and not telling is an offence punishable by a fine or imprisonment). If a person is an undischarged bankrupt, he or she cannot be the director of a corporation.

Disputes

Well, that was depressing talking about money troubles. Let's talk about something more cheerful, like fighting with your customers, suppliers, and neighbours.

Somebody doesn't like what you've done (or what you've charged). Or you don't like what somebody else has done (or charged). Maybe you feel like a fight . . . maybe you don't. But you're a businessperson, not a doormat, so you have to do something.

Disputes can escalate and end up in court, but they don't have to. (On the other hand, some disputes belong in court.) In this section, we lead you gently through the mechanisms available for resolving a dispute. They range from negotiation of a settlement through mediation and arbitration, and all the way to litigation. We won't get into the messy illegal stuff like baseball bats and cement overshoes.

But before we go any further, we want to say two things about any dispute you get into:

✔ **Wrap it up in writing.** If you and the other side reach an agreement, write it down. You may need or want a formal contract or a formal release drawn up by a lawyer, or a scribbled note signed by both sides may seem like enough, or you may simply write a letter or send an e-mail to the other side confirming that you reached an agreement (and setting out the terms of the agreement). A written document will help keep the resolution from unravelling, and will be valuable evidence of the agreement if the dispute erupts again.

✔ **Learn from this experience.** Ask yourself what you can do to prevent a dispute like this from arising again. For example, you may want to make sure that in the future you have written contracts that cover all the essential details, or that you get payment in advance for part of the work you do, or that you investigate a potential customer or supplier more thoroughly before making a deal.

Negotiation of a settlement

When you find yourself in a dispute, before you start shouting "I'll see you in court!" (or before anyone else starts shouting it), consider whether the dispute can be cleared up through negotiation.

The traditional way to negotiate a settlement is for each side to state what it wants and then use whatever power it has at its disposal to persuade or force the other side to agree. The sides sometimes exaggerate what they want so they'll have maneuvering room if they're forced to make a compromise. The purpose of traditional negotiation is to win, not necessarily to solve the problem effectively.

We give you some help to learn how to be a successful negotiator without upsetting the traditional negotiation pattern too much. We do this by showing you various negotiation techniques, including how to focus not on what you want (or on what the other side wants) but on interests that you and the other side may have in common.

Preparing for negotiations

If you want to be successful in your negotiation, you can't just rush in punching as soon as the bell sounds — first, you have to prepare to negotiate. Preparation involves two steps: studying the situation, and planning your moves. When you study the situation, you will

- ✔ **Gather information about the matter in dispute.** You should know the facts backward and forward and sideways. If you've got the facts at your fingertips you'll be much more effective at arguing for the resolution you want. You would also be wise to know the law relating to the dispute, so consider speaking to your lawyer about the matter even if you plan to handle the negotiations yourself.

- ✔ **Separate your *position* in the dispute from your short-term and long-term business *interests*.** Your position, for example, might be "I want to be paid the full amount for the work I did." Your interests are a lot more various — they might include needing X dollars to keep the business running, or wanting to keep a customer (or wanting to get rid of an annoying customer without damaging your business's reputation too badly), or wanting to maintain your personal reputation for doing good work at a fair price or for never backing down when you're under pressure.

- ✔ **Think about what the other party's business interests are.** (You may already know their position or you may be waiting to hear it.) Just like you, they have lots of different interests, and you should be able to use that fact to help find a solution that gives something to both parties. You may be able to give up easily something that the other party wants badly, and vice versa.

- ✔ **Think about what your goals in this negotiation are.** Again your goals are different from a position. For example, a position would be "I want to be paid the full amount for the work I did." Your goals might be getting as much of the full amount as possible while keeping the customer, and not appearing to back down when a customer turns purple in the face and starts screeching at you. Choose some objective criteria that will allow you to decide whether an offer is acceptable and meets your goals — that way you won't give in just because you're being bullied. Objective criteria might include things like:

  - **A fair market price:** What do other businesses charge for this product/service?

  - **Legality:** Is their offer legal?

  - **Accepted standards:** Is the offer in line with the other side's own standards, or standards in the business generally, or legal standards in court decisions, or scientific standards, and so on.

- ✔ **Gather information about the other party in the dispute.** Get information about the business *and* about the individual you're going to be dealing with. Talk to people who know them or have dealt with them. Find out what their strengths and weaknesses are, and how they're likely to behave during the negotiation (and how others have handled their behaviour). You want this background in order to know what might be influencing the position the other side is taking (such as little-known financial difficulties, or generalized distrust of businesses in your field).

✔ **Think about the side problems you may encounter in the negotiating process and how you might deal with them.** For example:

- *A history of bad blood exists between you and the person you'll have to negotiate with.* If you can't find a way of negotiating with that person's associate or superior instead, you'll have to try to focus on the problem to be solved and not on the personalities involved.

- *The person you're supposed to negotiate with doesn't have authority to make a deal with you because he or she isn't high enough up in the organization.* Try to find a way to negotiate with someone who does have authority to make a deal with you.

- *The other party doesn't give a damn about you — as is sometimes the case with large businesses that haven't trained and motivated their employees properly.* You'll have to try to find a way of making the other party give a damn.

- *The other party has a lot of power over you that is not related (or not closely related) to the issue in dispute.* You'll have to try to get them to focus on the problem in dispute and set aside other power issues for the time being.

- *The time for negotiations is limited and it favours the other side, not your side.* Sometimes deadlines cut both ways, so don't automatically accept the other party's story that only you are adversely affected by the deadline. And if a deadline is being used just as a pressure tactic, it can often be extended or ignored by the party that set it.

✔ **Think about the leverage you can use to argue for your interests.** No matter how grim things look for you in the dispute, you've probably got something to use. Leverage includes things like:

- Contract wording that supports your position.

- Law (either legislation or court decisions) that supports your position.

- *Precedent* that supports your position — what you want has been done before (either by the other side or by a similar organization).

- The desire of both sides to maintain a decent relationship.

- The desire of the other side to get the matter settled quickly and quietly. You could have a lot of nuisance value if you start writing to and phoning people in the organization, or if you talk to others about the problems you're having with the person or organization, or if you drag matters on into the next budget year.

Planning

Next it's time to plan — but if you did all that preparation, the planning is easy. Here are the steps:

1. **Create a list of alternatives to the position the other side is taking or is likely to take.** Take into consideration your interests and the probable interests of the other side, and try to come up with alternatives that would satisfy at least some of the interests of both sides. Then, when they announce their position, you'll have some maneuvering room — and you'll be able to offer them some maneuvering room too.

2. **Choose your own opening position.** Make it realistic, based on the information you gathered about the issue and the analysis you made of your interests.

3. **Marshall the arguments you think you can use to persuade the other party of the strength of your position.** Use the list of leverage you made in the planning stage. Don't argue using general statements, use specific facts. (For example, "I did a lot of work for you and got as good a result as could be expected" should be ditched in favour of "Here is a list of the work I did for you, here is the problem I had to deal with, here is the result I got, and here is the less favourable result obtained when you took your work to someone else.")

Opening discussions

Don't let discussions get under way until you're ready. If you haven't finished your planning and preparation when the other side announces that it's ready to negotiate, tell them that you have to look into the matter and will be back in touch as quickly as possible. If they won't go away, encourage them to chat about the problem. If the issue is personal to the other party, this will give him or her an opportunity to blow off a little steam; and you should be able to get valuable information about the other party's position, interests, and side issues if you let the person talk and you just listen.

But once you're ready to discuss the problem via a meeting or telephone call,

✔ **Start by getting personal, if possible.** See if you can make a connection with the other individual if you don't already know (and hate) each other. Some brief preliminary remarks about the weather (always a popular and acceptable topic in Canada), or the failings of a local sports franchise, or the news, or a mutual acquaintance ("I hear you know my colleague Joe Blow quite well") help set the tone that you're both human beings.

✔ **Don't be in a hurry to state a position or describe your interests.** Let the other side go first. (Most people can't wait to open their mouths and start talking, so it's usually pretty easy to go last.) You're in a better negotiating position if you know what the other side wants before you tell what you want or are ready to give. And when you do talk, the other person will be more likely to listen to what you have to say.

✔ **Be courteous to the individual you're dealing with.** And definitely don't make any personal attacks.

✔ **Do your best not to get angry or upset.** Try to remain objective throughout the discussion.

✔ **Really listen to the other side.** Show them that you're listening and understand what they're saying (whether or not you agree with it). Asking for clarification of vague or ambiguous statements or summarizing what they've told you are two ways of showing you're listening. Get them to explain their position in detail and what they don't like about your position.

✔ **Admit that the other side has reason to be annoyed with you and/or your business, if the reason is legitimate.** Apologize if you think an apology will remove a barrier to reaching a solution.

✔ **Focus on your interests and champion them.** Don't let the other side talk you out of the interests of importance to you, and don't get sidetracked from the issue under negotiation.

✔ **Look for ways of putting your interests and their interests into the same basket.** You may or may not have interests that you actually share, but you almost certainly have interests that fit together even if they don't overlap.

✔ **Deal with solvable issues.** If the dispute is made up of several issues and some of them seem unsolvable at the moment, put those aside and deal with the solvable ones. If you can reach an agreement on some or most of the solvable issues, the previously unsolvable ones may then appear more manageable.

✔ **Avoid using threats or pressure tactics against the person or organization.** Use offers instead. (Have you ever heard the expression "You'll catch more flies with honey than with vinegar"?)

✔ **Offer the other side ways of moving from its original position toward your position.** Some of the items on your list of leverage will come in handy here — for example, "The contract seems pretty clear on this point," or "You've done this before," or "Doing this for me won't set a precedent in other cases because . . ." or "In the long run this will save you money."

Calling it quits

Quit while you're ahead. But how will you *know* when you're ahead?

✔ **Use the objective criteria you dreamed up in the planning stage.** With any offer, ask yourself whether it meets those objective criteria. If it doesn't, explain to the other party why it doesn't meet your criteria. They may not agree on the criteria you've chosen, but you may get them to agree with you that a decision should involve objective criteria and not mere pressure.

✔ **Ask yourself what your alternatives are if you don't agree to the other side's offer.** Your alternatives might include

- Further negotiations (but are they likely to lead somewhere or will they just go on forever? Your time, money, and emotional energy are not infinite)

- Accepting a less favourable offer from the other side

- Accepting a more favourable offer from a third party

- Getting outside assistance to resolve the dispute, from a mediator, an arbitrator or the courts (see the upcoming sections on "Alternative dispute resolution" and "Litigation")

- Ending the relationship between the parties (this might or might not seem like an attractive alternative)

✔ **Ask yourself whether you and/or the other side will be able to or will want to go through with the terms of the deal.** A deal that's going to be broken right away isn't a good deal. Also ask yourself about the repercussions of a particular deal. For example, will the other side pay up but say nasty things about you in the business community . . . or even vandalize your property someday?

For more information

You might like to read these books on negotiating:

✔ *Getting to YES, Negotiating Agreement Without Giving In*, by Roger Fisher and William Ury (published by Houghton Mifflin Company). This is the famous book about negotiating that grew out of the Harvard Negotiating Project and that everyone has heard about. We based a lot of our advice about negotiating on this classic. If you want to know more about the Harvard Negotiating Project, you can go to its Web site at www.pon.harvard.edu.

✔ *Swim with the Sharks Without Being Eaten Alive*, by Harvey Mackay (published by William Morrow and Company).

✔ *Negotiating For Dummies*, by Michael C. Donaldson and Mimi Donaldson (published by Wiley).

If you'd prefer something more hands-on, you can probably sign up for a negotiation workshop offered in your community.

Alternative dispute resolution (ADR)

The "alternative" in alternative dispute resolution means alternative to going to court. Litigation is expensive and usually leads to bad feelings between the parties — and just because there's a dispute doesn't mean you want to spend as much money as possible to resolve it or end up never doing business again with the other side.

The two usual forms of ADR are *mediation* and *arbitration*.

Mediation

In mediation, a neutral third person (a *mediator*) meets with the parties to try to help them reach an agreement. Mediation is negotiation with a kind of coach present. The parties choose the mediator, and they should try to get someone who has experience in the particular area of the dispute and who has good mediation skills. (Ask around for recommendations.) The mediator doesn't take sides and doesn't judge between the parties as to who's right and who's wrong, but merely tries to help the parties find a solution that meets everyone's needs. The solution can be more flexible than one the parties could get by going to court. (Courts are best at awarding money to one side, not at coming up with creative answers to problems.)

Mediation is *useful* if the parties

✔ Want to save face by not backing down on their own (a mediator will be able to point out the issues that aren't worth arguing about)

✔ Want to save time and money by not going to court

✔ Want to maintain a good business relationship

Mediation is *not useful* if

✔ One of the parties does not want mediation — the parties both have to have some desire to settle the matter and must both be willing to meet with a mediator.

✔ One of the parties has a lot more power than the other and is going to use it to impose a solution on the weaker party.

In some provinces, the parties to a lawsuit are required to go to mediation shortly after the lawsuit starts, to see if the matter can be settled without going any further through the court system.

Arbitration

Arbitration gets closer to court proceedings. In arbitration, a neutral third person (the *arbitrator*, sometimes three arbitrators are involved) is chosen by the parties to hear both sides' stories. The parties can design their own process, or they may prefer to conduct proceedings under provincial arbitration legislation. (As part of the design, the parties can agree on rights to appeal the arbitrator's decision to a judge or can agree that the decision cannot be appealed.) After listening to each side's presentation, the arbitrator makes a decision that one side or the other has won, and usually makes the kind of order that a court would make in the same circumstances. The decision can be registered with the court and enforced the same way as a judge's decision.

The advantages of arbitration are that

- ✔ Arbitration can be faster and cheaper than a lawsuit (although the bigger and more complex the dispute, the closer arbitration costs get to litigation costs).

- ✔ Parties can choose as arbitrator someone who has expertise in the area of the dispute (instead of just hoping that the judge they draw knows something about it). This can be very important in specialized areas of business.

- ✔ Arbitration proceedings are private and confidential — unlike court proceedings, which are public.

- ✔ Arbitration decisions do not set precedents (establish examples that have to be followed in later cases) the way court decisions do.

Litigation

When disputes arise, the parties often think of a lawsuit as the first option. As we discuss earlier in this chapter, a lawsuit is just one of several options and may even be the last option. In this section we talk about deciding whether a lawsuit is your best option.

Should you sue?

If you're the injured party, it's up to you to decide whether to take the dispute to court. You need to talk to a lawyer about deciding whether to sue. Your lawyer will help you make the decision, based on the following matters:

- ✔ **What are your chances of winning the lawsuit?**

  - Is the law on your side?

  - Do you have the evidence you need to persuade a judge to help you?

  - Are you in time? There's a time limit on starting any lawsuit — it varies according to what the dispute is about, and in some cases you've only got a few days to get started, although in most cases you've got several years. Only a lawyer can tell you how long you've got, and starting from when.

- ✔ **What will you get if you win?** If you want money, will the court give you enough to make the process worthwhile? If you don't want money, the court can give you other things — but none of them may be what you really want. Besides money (called *damages*) to compensate you for losses and maybe even to punish the other party, the court might be able to give you

- An *injunction* — to prevent someone from doing something; or a *mandatory injunction* — to make someone do what he or she promised to do

- An *order for specific performance* — to make the other party honour its agreement with you (such as an agreement to sell you a piece of land)

- In certain special cases, an order requiring the other party to do something such as sell property and divide the proceeds with you, or allowing the court to oversee some activity that the other party is carrying out

If what you really want is an apology, or the other party to parade naked through town carrying a sign that says "I'm evil," you won't get much satisfaction from a court.

✔ **What's this going to cost?** The short answer is . . . a lot. Litigation is very expensive — and that's if you win. The losing side is usually ordered to pay some of the winner's legal fees, but not all of them (except in rare circumstances). In the meantime, before you win (if you do) your lawyer will be asking you for payment of her fees as you go along. If you lose, you'll have to pay the amount of any judgement the court awards against you, very likely at least part of the winner's legal fees, and all of your own lawyer's fees.

✔ **Where's the lawsuit going to take place?** If the other party doesn't live in or carry on business in your province, you may have to start the lawsuit wherever that party *does* live or carry on business — maybe another province, maybe another country. Extra cost and extra uncertainty.

✔ **What are your chances of making the other party carry out the court order if you win?** For example, if the court awards damages, it's up to you to collect the money. (Court officers such as the sheriff will help but they won't do it all for you.) If the other party doesn't have any money, or is really good at hiding it, you'll probably never see a penny of it. And you can spend quite a bit of money on collection.

✔ **Will you be able to stand the litigation process?** Your lawyer won't do everything — he'll have you digging around for documents and providing information and attending meetings. And there are some things your lawyer can't do on your behalf, such as undergo questioning by the other side before trial (the *discovery* process). Even if you've got the time (and money) to carry on a lawsuit, you may not be up to coping with the emotional stress involved in preparing for trial . . . and many people are terrified at the thought of testifying in court and being cross-examined by a lawyer for the other side.

If you do decide to start a lawsuit, you'll be happy to know that most lawsuits do settle. Only a small fraction actually go to trial.

If you decide not to sue, you can still try to settle the matter through negotiation or mediation (possibly with the threat of court proceedings hanging over the head of the other side).

What should you do if you're sued?

If you are sued, your options are narrower than if you're the one deciding whether to sue. You can put in a statement of defence and then defend the action vigorously, or you can put in a statement of defence and then try to negotiate a settlement. In some cases you can put in a statement of defence and a *counterclaim* (a lawsuit against the other side) or a *third party claim* (a lawsuit against other people who were really responsible for causing the problem in the first place — hey, the more the merrier, right?). Or you can do nothing.

Doing nothing is a poor option. If you don't defend, and the other side continues with its lawsuit, the court will quickly enter judgement against you and the other side can start trying to enforce the judgment right away. However, doing nothing is a possibility if

- ✔ **Your business has nothing to lose.** If the plaintiff is looking for money and your business has no cash or other assets, defending the action is a waste of your time.

- ✔ **You have nothing to lose personally.** If your business has nothing, but you're on the hook to pay debts that your business can't pay, you should defend . . . unless you don't have any cash or assets, either. But be aware that even if you have nothing now, the plaintiff will be able to grab money or property that you get in the future.

In the no man's land between doing absolutely nothing and responding formally to the lawsuit, you could see a lawyer and try to

- ✔ Settle the matter before the deadline for putting in a defence has passed (the defendant usually has several weeks after being notified of the lawsuit to file a statement of defence, but sometimes the allowed reaction time is much shorter).

- ✔ Persuade the other side to call off the lawsuit even if the dispute can't be settled right away.

Chapter 19

The Expanding Business Universe

In This Chapter

▶ Considering what "doing more business" means to your business

▶ Knowing when not to do more business

▶ Finding more business

▶ Financing your business expansion

▶ Managing a bigger business

*Y*ou had your Big Bang when you launched your business. Now your business is expanding at the speed of light . . . or sound . . . or maybe just at the cruising speed of a jet. Or you'd like it to be. In any case, you have to have some idea of what you're getting into when your business expands, and how you can finance an expansion and manage a bigger, busier business. And for those of you who aren't expanding but want to, you have to know how to go about finding more business. So strap on your rocket-pack and let's go.

What "Doing More Business" Means

If you're thinking that "doing more business" means "making bigger profits," "having access to more opportunities," or "becoming a more important player," you're right. But that's not all it means. They say that for every action there is an equal and opposite reaction — well, in this case the reaction can seem bigger than the action! Here are some of the things that go along with doing more business:

✔ **You'll probably do even more work than you're doing now.** And it may be different work from the work you're doing now too — you may be doing less of what you think of as your business . . . and more managing. Better ask yourself if this is something you want.

✔ **You may have to travel more.** Do you enjoy business travel? Does it fit in with your current lifestyle? (Maybe you went into business so you could stay at home with the kids or the goldfish . . . or wouldn't have to do any more business commuting.)

- ✔ **You may have to create new lines of products or services to entice customers and clients to your business (or to satisfy their demands).** That may mean doing more research and development and making a new marketing plan — go to Chapter 4 if the thought of that doesn't scare you.

- ✔ **You'll probably need new accounting and bookkeeping and/or inventory control systems to handle the increased business.** Unless you planned for this expansion when you originally set up your business.

- ✔ **You'll need employees, or more employees, to help you.** (See Chapter 15 on hiring employees.) Will your customers or clients accept new people? Maybe your business and you have been very closely identified with each other up to now, and customers and clients will resist dealing with someone other than you. And you'll have to worry about finding capable people who can handle some of the important functions of your business.

- ✔ **Your employees will need training, or more training.** They'll need it to deal with the added business and the things that go along with it.

- ✔ **You'll need more equipment.** The new employees will use it, and increased production will demand it. (See Chapter 6 for information about equipping your business.)

- ✔ **You'll need more inventory if you're in the retail or wholesale business.**

- ✔ **You'll need bigger premises to hold the new employees, new equipment and increased production capacity, new product lines and increased inventory, and to provide larger areas for client meetings.** We talk about choosing a place of business in Chapter 7.

- ✔ **And last but not least, you'll need money.** You'll need it to hire the employees, buy the equipment, lease the premises, and so on. So you've got financing concerns. We deal with financing a business in Chapter 10.

Haven't we been here before? Most of these issues look strangely familiar. This lends support to the theory that the expanding universe isn't infinite but looks sort of like a hollow bagel — if you go far enough you'll end up where you started out.

Expanding a business will upset its equilibrium. You and your business will probably have trouble coping, at least in the beginning. In fact, you may never be ready to cope. Sometimes expansion is just not the best thing for you, and you and your business will be happier if things stay the way they are.

Don't Do More Business If . . .

In the previous section we aren't trying to tell you not to do more business, we're just trying to show you that more business doesn't happen in a vacuum — it has consequences, and some of them you may find unpleasant.

In this section, on the other hand, we tell you not to do more business — if doing more business would just get you into financial trouble. And in financial trouble is where you'll end up if you expand because your business isn't profitable now and you think doing more business will make it more profitable.

Lack of profitability is the result of low margins. Your margin is the price you sell your goods or services for minus the cost of providing the goods or services. Your business may have low margins for two possible reasons. One is that expenses are too high, and the other is that prices are too low.

If you expand an unprofitable business, you'll just end up with a bigger unprofitable business . . . which means you'll go down with a real thud later on. Remember the joke about the dot-com companies? "We lose on every transaction but we make it up on volume." Don't allow the glorious martyrdom of the dot-coms to have been in vain. Learn from their example: Become profitable before you think about becoming bigger.

Now we discuss lowering expenses and raising prices in order to become profitable.

Lowering expenses

Controlling expenses is a two-step process. You have to audit your business to find out whether you're spending money on things you shouldn't be spending money on, and you have to review your expenses to see whether they're higher than necessary.

Audit your business activities

Sit down with your account books and do some thinking. Ask yourself, for example:

✔ **Do you have expenses that you could pare down?** Are you over-entertaining clients or potential clients? Maybe a business meeting in the client's office would accomplish as much as or more than lunch at a good restaurant. Are you doing unnecessary travelling? Combine several activities into a single trip (on a single plane or train ticket or gasoline bill). Are you buying premium-quality equipment and supplies when ordinary quality would do the job just as well? A desktop PC may be as much as your business needs, and that top-of-the-line laptop computer is more about your love of neat gadgets. Are you spending money you can't afford on furnishings for your office or on a company car? A desk is a flat surface to work on, you don't need cherry wood with a matching credenza. A $20,000 car will get you the same places as a $40,000 car . . . and a taxi could take you to a lot of them too. Are you renting premises that are too expensive for you? Could be time to move back home.

✔ **Are you spending your time inefficiently?** Is important work not getting done (like billing) because you're too busy with other things? If you need help with accounts or inventory control or payroll, buy a software package to do the job. Or outsource the work to another business or bring in a temporary or part-time worker. If your files are disorganized, you may be wasting time hunting information down instead of using the information to do business. Spending a few hours organizing your files properly may save you dozens or hundreds of hours over the course of the year.

✔ **Are you making good use of your employees?** Are you paying someone full-time to do part-time work? Are you paying someone to do work that he or she can't or isn't doing? Don't take on employees until they'll make money for your business rather than cost money — don't hire somebody to do work that you (or software or another business) can do more cheaply.

Review how much you're spending

Even if you're sure that you need everything you're currently paying for, you need to make sure that you're getting it at the best price. Make it a habit to re-price your supplies on a continuing basis. Before you make a purchase — equipment, lease for premises, business loan, telephone services, insurance, and everything else — get three or four quotes from competing suppliers. If you find a cheaper supplier, though, make sure you'll be getting comparable quality before you make the switch.

In some businesses, you might consider becoming your own supplier of certain products if an analysis indicates that you can provide your own supplies more cheaply.

Always ask suppliers for itemized invoices, and go over them carefully for mistakes.

Raising prices

Your prices are not fixed in stone. Review them whenever you notice an increase in demand or an increase in competitors' prices. And review them annually to see whether your costs are creeping up on them.

Before you raise your prices, consider whether higher prices could translate into lower sales, as customers go elsewhere for lower prices. Are your customers with you just because of your prices, or do they take into account other factors such as your expertise or your location?

If you decide to raise prices, start with your lower-priced goods or services, or with the ones that you don't think need to be competitively priced to sell.

If you're a manufacturer, think about opening your own retail or wholesale outlet or becoming your own distributor — if you eliminate the middleman you can charge middleman prices yourself.

How Do You Find More Business?

If you're still reading at this point in the chapter, it's because you want to expand and you believe that expansion is not going to lead to disaster. So now you may want to know how to go about increasing the amount of business you do so you can get on with the expanding process.

Some enterprises are born with more business, others have more business thrust upon them. But some have to achieve more business. If you're not flooded with work but you'd like to be, there are four ways to proceed:

- ✔ Do more of what you're already doing for the customers you already have.
- ✔ Find new customers for the work you already do.
- ✔ Do new work for the customers you already have.
- ✔ Find new customers for new work.

See if you can do more of the same work for existing customers

This is the most cost-effective way to expand. You already know your product and your customers. It costs a lot less to do more for the customers you have than it does to go out and find new customers or to hunt down or create new products.

The first place to start in your quest to do more work for your customers is to review your customer turnover rate and, if it's significant, to find out why customers aren't coming back to you. Speak to non-returning customers, if you can. Ask what they like about the business they're dealing with instead of you, and if they'd be interested in doing business with you again if you made some changes. If you can't talk to the lost sheep, chat with the customers who're still with you and try to get a sense of what they like and don't like about your business. Make reasonable changes as required.

Next, go to work on the customers you've got. Try to "generate new demand" by getting them to use more of your products or services, or use the same amount but more frequently. Apart from persuading your customers or clients that they'll benefit from using more of your products or services (for example, be healthier, smell cleaner, save money), here are some moves you can try out on them:

✔ **Make sure they know everything you can do for them.** Bring their attention to your complete line of products or services by posting them on your Web site, mentioning them in conversation or in reporting letters, sending around newsletters, brochures, and special promotion letters about them, even listing them on your packaging. When an opportunity comes up for you to do something or provide something the client hasn't requested, ask directly for their business.

✔ **Reward your customers.** Offer them discounts for volume, rebates on certain items, gifts for buying a pre-set amount. Make sure they know you're handing out rewards.

✔ **Bundle your products or services.** For example, offer a service contract with the product, or complimentary products as a package (for a slightly lower price than if they were purchased separately).

✔ **Make your product or service more appealing.** For example, make it easier to use. Or make the packaging more attractive. (Customers can be pretty shallow.)

✔ **Come up with new uses for the product or service.**

✔ **Switch to autopilot.** Make your product or service more convenient to get. Automate delivery, via a monthly or annual contract. Or at the end of an appointment or meeting, set up the next one. Or send reminder letters or make reminder phone calls when it's time for the customer or client to make an appointment.

Overall, one of the most important things you can do is to develop a good relationship with your customers. Make them your friends. Listen to them — and give them lots of convenient ways of talking to you, such as voice mail, e-mail, a 1-800 number, and, if possible, regular opportunities to meet face to face. If they have complaints or concerns, respond to them. If they have suggestions, pay attention to them.

Don't waste or lose any information your clients provide you with. Keep a customer information file for each client (or at least for the best ones or up-and-coming ones) that includes notes and records of

✔ Which products or services the customer buys, how frequently the customer buys, and how much the customer spends

✔ How the customer makes the purchase and payment (and any interesting collection history) and takes delivery

✔ Any complaints the customer has made, and what you did in response

✔ Which products or services you provide that your customer buys from someone else, and why; and which products or services you provide that your customer doesn't buy at all, and why

✔ Any notes about the customer's plans (that might tie in with your goal of providing more to the customer)

✔ Any of the customer's special interests and important dates (these may not involve flogging any of your products or services; remembering them may just be good customer relations)

✔ Any ideas you have about how you might persuade the customer to buy more of your products or services

Customers and clients will be pleased that you consider them important enough to remember details of past transactions, and they'll be thrilled if you remember something about them that isn't immediately linked to making a sale.

Find more customers for the same work

If you're sure that your current customers are satisfied with the work you're doing, then you can go out and look for new customers. You can look for them in a new geographic area or in a new target group. When you go into a new area or after a new group, focus on it and make a good job of capturing it before you move on to another area or group. Don't try to expand on too many fronts at once.

You can hunt for new customers, either geographically or by group, by

✔ Creating a new marketing campaign (see Chapter 4), which might include repackaging your product or service under a new label.

✔ Acquiring customer lists from another business.

✔ Luring customers away from the competition with goodies such as rewards for switching over, or with the usual incentives (see Chapter 4) such as lower prices, better service, and so on.

✔ Getting new premises by renting in a new location or buying an existing well-located business. If you're a manufacturer, you can open a retail outlet.

✔ Going into the export business. This involves a lot more trouble because you have to assess market opportunities in the new country and comply with local laws and regulations, as well as physically deliver your goods or services. We get exhausted just thinking about it, so we won't wear ourselves out further writing about it. Check out the Infoguide on exporting at the Canada Business Service Centres site (www.cbsc.org).

Do new and additional work for existing customers

Don't go wild if this is the route you decide to take! Just because your customers love what you're doing with their stock portfolio doesn't mean they'll also be eager to buy pedicures and facials from your business. The best way to proceed here is simply to ask your customers what more they'd like from you — or even just listen to what they're saying in your regular contacts with them. You'll probably find that your customers and clients are the best source of new ideas for you.

When you bring in new products or services, consider having a testing period with free samples or with an "on approval" arrangement. This will give your customers a chance to try out the new product or service without any financial risk (to them, that is).

Find new customers for new products or services

If you're looking for new customers and new products, it almost means you're starting over again! So you'd better go back and read Chapter 4.

But steering your business off in a new direction isn't as hard as setting up a new business, because you've already got some things going for you, such as:

- ✔ Experience in product or service development and delivery, and in business management
- ✔ An understanding of how the marketplace works
- ✔ A few hard-earned skills in dealing with customers
- ✔ A name in the business community, and a history of operations

And in addition you may have some money that you've made and set aside that can fund this venture. Or your business may have more capacity than it's using right now — maybe you could produce more, or sell other products through your existing channels.

Alternatively, you may be nervous about keeping your business based on one product or service and you want to branch out as a form of insurance.

How Do You Finance Your Expansion?

Earlier in this chapter, we talk about the kinds of things you'll need money for in an expansion. Now we talk about where to get the money. Essentially, you'll go to the same sources we sent you in Chapter 10. This time it should be easier to pry money out of them — especially the commercial sources — because you've got a track record as a business.

In addition, you have some new sources of financing, including sale or sale and leaseback of assets, retained earnings, and equity investment from people inside and outside your business. We cover these next.

Sale or sale and leaseback of equipment

If you already own equipment, you can sell it to a leasing company and then lease it back. Or you can sell one thing, and then lease something else. Or you can sell and not buy anything. Whichever way you go, you free up some cash for other purposes.

Retained earnings

Retained earnings are money you've set aside out of the profits of your business. As soon as you can, you should start building a fund from your profits for unforeseen problems and for expansion . . . instead of blowing every penny that comes in on fancy office furniture or by taking all your profits as salary.

Equity investment

An equity investment is capital for your business in exchange for partial ownership of your business. (In Chapter 10 we talk about this as arm's-length investment.)

Venture capital and angel capital

You're no longer a start-up, but you're still eligible for an investment from an angel or from a venture capital firm. In fact, you may be more eligible because you've been in operation for a while and it will be easier for an investor to tell whether your business is going places (or not). Venture capitalists will probably see you as looking for "first stage financing" (to increase production) or "second stage financing" (to increase production and expand your markets). Heck, you may even be ready for "mezzanine financing" (to expand prior to an *initial public offering* — see "Investment from outside the business" — or a buyout of your business by another business).

Investment from within your business

If you bring in new people who are going to run the business with you, it's usual to ask them to buy a partnership share (if your business isn't incorporated) or to buy shares in the corporation (if it is incorporated). This gives you some fresh capital to play with. The new guy normally takes out a loan to make the purchase; the interest payable on the loan is deductible from his or her income.

If your business is incorporated, you can set up a stock plan that allows employees to buy shares in the business. This not only brings in capital, but also gives employees an incentive to work hard to make the business more profitable. However, to get much money via employee investment, you'll probably have to sell a significant percentage of shares, and even though you make sure you keep at least 51 percent of the shares, you can still end up with conflict about control of the corporation.

Investment from outside the business

Under provincial securities laws in Canada, up to 50 people who are not employees of the corporation can own shares in a private corporation. So you can go looking for a few individual investors. But if you want more money than 50 outside investors can provide, you'll have to "go public" or make an initial public offering (IPO) — in other words, become a corporation whose shares are traded on a stock exchange such as the Vancouver Stock Exchange (VSE), Toronto Stock Exchange (TSE), or Montreal Stock Exchange (MSE).

If after reading that last sentence you're already toying with the idea of taking your business public and are daydreaming about what your stock symbol will be, we've got some cold water to pour over you. An IPO is complicated and costly to set up, and there isn't necessarily a guarantee that you'll get any money out of it. As a result there aren't many IPOs in Canada. In 2000, which was a good year for IPOs, there were fewer than a hundred.

Here's how an IPO works. After collecting numerous expensive outside advisors including an *underwriter*, lawyers, accountants, auditors, and investment relations specialists, you prepare a *prospectus*, which you file with the Securities Commission in any province where you're making your offering. The prospectus provides detailed information to both the Securities

Commission and potential investors about your business, the stock to be issued, and the purpose for which the money raised will be used. It has to give full disclosure of all important information. The underwriter, after looking your business over even more carefully than a venture capitalist would, agrees to buy shares from the corporation and then resell them (taking a commission) to the public for a short period of time, usually just a few days. The price set for the shares will depend on various things, including your business's financial history, how glamorous your industry is, and current share prices of other public companies in your industry. Depending on your agreement with the underwriter, the offering may be cancelled if not enough shares are sold within a specified period.

After the IPO is completed, the shares that have been sold trade on the stock market without affecting the value of the payment your corporation received for the shares. So if the value of the shares drops dramatically, that's not good news for your business, but at least you don't have to make refunds to purchasers.

Once you become a public corporation, you're required to provide information to the Securities Commission and public on a regular basis about things you might actually prefer to keep secret, such as important changes to your business whenever they occur, quarterly and annual financial statements, the amount of compensation for senior executives, and share purchases or sales by insiders (people who have access to special knowledge of the business, particularly employees and their immediate families). And you have to worry about keeping your investors happy, or else they'll sell their shares and drive down the value of your business.

If this all sounds like a massive pain, it is. And this description of the IPO process has only scratched the surface.

How Do You Manage a Bigger Business?

The bigger a business grows, the more managing, and the more expert managing, it needs. Poor management is probably the most common reason for a business to fail.

The first thing we talk about is how to manage yourself. If you can't manage your own time and work efficiently, you're going to have a lot of trouble managing anybody else. Besides which, because you're the most important person in the business at this point, you won't have a business to manage if you can't keep it together personally.

Bring it forward

A "bring-forward" book is a binder with 31 tabbed and numbered pages in it, one for each day of the month. (You can get a set of 31 tabbed pages at your business stationer's.) Here's how to use it. You check your bring-forward book every day, looking at what you've filed under the tab for that day. If you write a letter on the 1st and expect a response by the 7th, stick a copy of your letter, with a note about what you plan to do with it (for example, make a follow-up call if no response has arrived yet), under tab 8. On the 8th of the month your bring-forward book notifies you to make a follow-up call about the letter.

Learning personal management techniques

As your business expands, you're going to have more and more to do and less and less time to do it. So you're going to have to make the time you do have go further. Here's some advice about managing your time and work.

Schedule your time wisely

Don't rely on your memory! You haven't got one anymore — it drowned in the sea of details that a business floats in. So plan ahead in writing. Plan your year, your month, your week, your day. Keep a calendar or daybook — just one, if possible! — or computer organizer. If you have a pocket organizer as well as a daybook or an organizer on your computer, make sure that they're always synchronized. Otherwise, you'll end up with two incompatible schedules. When you plan

- ✔ Include your personal as well as business commitments and intentions, so you don't end up with conflicts, or miss dental appointments.

- ✔ Don't just schedule appointments in your daybook, also schedule phone calls you intend to make and matters you intend to deal with. Make lists of to-do jobs for the day, week, or month (some calendar systems incorporate to-do lists). At the end of each day, week, or month, cross off the jobs done and carry forward the ones not done or not finished.

Schedule as efficiently as you can:

- ✔ Schedule meetings and work that require your full concentration at the time of day you're at your sharpest; schedule mindless tasks for the time of day when you're mindless.

- ✔ Schedule in the right order. For example, if a client wants to talk to you about the poor quality of a product you provided and what you're going to do about it, don't schedule that appointment before an appointment to talk to the supplier of the product.

✔ When you're on the road, plan your trips so that they cover a number of tasks. For example, if you have to travel to another city to meet a client, see whether you can also meet with other clients, or a supplier or potential investor you have in that city. Plan even short trips to accomplish several things — on a drive to meet with a local client, work in other destinations that aren't too far off your route, like the gas station, business supply store, or dry cleaner's.

✔ Combine some of your down time — lunch, golf, a hockey game — with a low-key meeting with a client, supplier, or investor.

✔ Allow yourself some flexibility in your schedule so that you don't end up running late or wasting time. Some meetings take longer than planned, others get cancelled. So don't plan important meetings back to back, and always have a Plan B if you unexpectedly find you've got some extra time on your hands.

Remind yourself what you're supposed to be doing now or next — have a *tickler system*:

✔ Your daybook or organizer may be enough of a tickler system for you. Get into the habit of glancing frequently at your tasks for the month, week, and day. Every night before you close up shop (or before you go to sleep, whichever comes first), look over your schedule and to-do list for the following day. If you don't, you'll end up missing a morning meeting or phone call.

✔ You may need a "bring-forward" book as well as a daybook. See the sidebar "Bring it forward."

Whenever you do something, keep a record of the action taken. Otherwise, a day or two later you won't remember whether or not you've done something, and what it was you did. And when a matter has been finally disposed of, put documents relating to it in your storage area, not in your active files area, so you won't be wondering if you're *still* supposed to do something.

Meetings can be terrible time wasters. So first of all make sure that a meeting is necessary, and that it can't be replaced by a phone call or an e-mail. Then make sure that you're properly prepared for the meeting . . . and that everyone else is too:

✔ In preparation, review your files, gather any additional information that's necessary, make notes about what you've done and what you want to talk about.

✔ If you're hosting the meeting, send around a detailed agenda, so everyone else knows what the meeting is about and what they should do to prepare for it. If you're not the host, request an agenda. If you don't get a response, circulate a suggested draft to the participants. If you get an inadequate agenda, send it back with suggested additions.

✔ At the end of a meeting, prepare minutes of (a summary of what was said or what happened at) the meeting or request that someone else provide minutes to be sent around to all the participants. The minutes should include an "action agenda," so that everyone knows not only what's been discussed and decided but also what the participants are supposed to do and by when.

Screen and bundle

Don't let your phone and e-mail and faxes and mail and drop-in associates or employees rule your time. Organize your day so that you have blocks of time when you give your full attention to matters that require thought and concentrated effort, and other blocks of time when you read and answer your mail and return telephone calls. Let customers or clients and suppliers know that you return phone calls and e-mails within 24 hours, but that they should not necessarily expect an instant response.

✔ Don't answer your phone every time it rings (or at least get caller ID if you're afraid of missing important calls). You've got voice-mail, let it do its job. Don't check your e-mail every ten minutes (or ten seconds). E-mail messages will wait quietly there until you reply. Don't leap up every time you hear the fax machine ring.

✔ Screen incoming voice messages and e-mail or faxes or letters according to whether they are urgent and should be dealt with immediately, or should be dealt with within your normal 24-hour period, or should be answered within 24 hours but require a longer period of time to be dealt with, or can be delegated to someone else, or can be filed without a response or even completely ignored (like junk mail).

✔ When you pick up your messages, e-mail, faxes, and letters, group them by category and deal with them by category. For example, here are some categories:

- Matters that can be dealt with by a phone call. Sit down and make all your phone calls at once.

- Matters that can be dealt with by an e-mail reply. Do all your e-mail at once.

- Matters that require a letter to be written and posted or faxed. Write all your letters at one time.

- Bookkeeping matters, such as entering expenses or writing cheques or creating bills. Enter all your expenses together, write all your cheques in a group, and put aside time to run bills.

Put off procrastinating

Putting off work that has to be done is one of the biggest thieves of your time. So no matter how much you DON'T WANT TO DO IT, start your work right away — and finish it too.

Here are some tips for the hard-core procrastinator who's looking to reform:

- **Divide up complex work into smaller segments.** It's all too easy to avoid doing something because it looks daunting — but you'll be surprised how much you can accomplish if you do a task in bites instead of trying to swallow it whole.

- **Don't avoid starting something just because you won't be able to finish it in one sitting.** If you know that a task will take six hours, don't wait until you've got six hours free. Say to yourself, "I can spend half an hour now, and tomorrow I can fit in an hour, and the next day I can do two hours" and so on.

- **Set a deadline.** If your client (or the CRA or whoever wants this work done) hasn't set you a deadline, set one yourself. Tell your client you'll have the work done by such-and-such a date, and then deliver on your promise.

- **Reward yourself.** Promise yourself that if you finish this matter, you can have a cup of coffee, or can do some work that you enjoy doing more. Yes, these are pretty feeble rewards. Maybe you can persuade yourself that if you finish this matter, one day a multinational corporation will buy you out for $100 million.

- **Get an employee or business associate or family member to nag you.** You do not want your clients or customers (or the CRA) to have to nag you.

- **Live in fear.** Keep in mind that if you don't do your work on time, your business will fail and you'll end up penniless and starving on the street, your name cursed by all who once knew and respected you.

One of the authors of this book has a little trouble with not procrastinating . . . but she's learning to say, "I'll procrastinate tomorrow! Today I'll get my work done."

Delegate

Do what you do best, and delegate the rest. If you're not a secretary and you're doing a lot of secretarial work; if you're not a bookkeeper and you're doing a lot of bookkeeping; if you're not a salesperson and you're making a lot of sales calls; if you're not an office manager and you're spending all your time marshalling employees and ordering supplies; if you're not a janitor and you're doing a lot of cleaning — it means you need to hire someone to do these tasks. Your time is better spent doing what you're expert in. Try outsourcing this work, or hiring a temp or a part-time worker, before you hire a full-time employee.

While we're on the subject of delegation, don't let people you've hired delegate to you! "Upward delegation" is a sneak attack. If someone you've delegated to isn't doing the work right, don't do it for him. Provide more training, or give guidelines for correcting the work and have the person try again until he gets it right. Otherwise you'll end up doing the work and paying someone else to do it.

Just say no

There's a lot of power in the word *no*. Sometimes you have to use it to keep other people from hijacking your time and your energy.

- ✔ **Whenever someone makes a demand on you, ask yourself what's in it for you?** What will you gain if you do it, and what will you lose if you don't? Will attending a community event or giving a presentation help you find more customers? Will turning away a potential client who wants you to perform a time-consuming low-paying service destroy your business? Will telling a supplier to check her own files before you check yours ruin your relationship?

- ✔ **Don't hold or attend useless meetings.** When someone says, "Let's have a meeting!", consider whether a meeting could be replaced by a phone call or e-mail, or a brief informal chat, or an information document that can be circulated.

- ✔ **Discourage drop-in visits from colleagues and clients.** Sure, visits are more fun than work, but you don't get paid for visits and they interfere with your carefully planned day. If a client drops by at an inconvenient time, have a short stand-up meeting and make an appointment for a real meeting later.

- ✔ **Tell your family and friends not to call you all the time to chat.** Now that you're working for yourself, everyone thinks you can spend the whole day shooting the breeze. (You can, but your business will flop.) This is especially true if you have a home office, where spouses, children, and pets will not just call but will also show up in person.

And don't forget to take care of Number One

Finally, make sure you keep yourself in good shape to run your business:

- ✔ **Take time off to refresh yourself.** Leave the office for a coffee break, go for a walk, take evenings and/or weekends off.

- ✔ **Eat properly!** Low blood sugar won't do anything for your concentration — and neither will a blood sugar high if you get tired and try to cure the problem with cookies, doughnuts, chocolate bars, and lots of caffeine.

✔ **Get enough sleep.** Lack of sleep won't help your concentration either, or your mood — or your looks.

✔ **Get regular exercise.** It's easy to let your exercise program slide when you're busy, but you need to be healthy to keep the business running. And you want to stay alive to enjoy the fruits of your labour.

Learning business management techniques

As your business expands, it's turning into an enterprise that needs professional management. You may be able to turn yourself into a professional manager, or you may need to bring managers on board. While you wait to discover whether you have what it takes to be a professional manager (management may be something you left your employed life to avoid), you can think about the issues we talk about next.

Give up control (at least a little)

Giving up control isn't something you want to hear about — unless, of course, someone's buying you out for an obscenely large amount of money. One of the reasons you went into business for yourself was so you could run things the way you wanted to! But the fact is that you can't do everything yourself, so you're going to have to share some of the responsibilities with others or even hand responsibilities over entirely.

Start off slowly, if you like:

✔ **Have brainstorming sessions to solve problems.** You may find that you come up with better solutions when you get two or three other people to help you think.

✔ **Take your time to think about important matters, and gather information and get advice before you make a decision.** Look at the matter in the context of your goals and vision for your business, rather than making it a personal decision.

✔ **Make yourself redundant.** There are many critically important areas of your business, and if an area is entrusted to just one person (even if that person is you), you're putting your business at risk. What if you get sick, or you're injured? What if you want to go on a vacation? So find yourself an understudy, or even hand over primary responsibility to someone else (who was carefully chosen by you, of course).

✔ **Set up formal systems to make business decisions.** That means bringing your associates and/or employees into the process. Maybe it's even time for you to get a board of directors for your corporation, including some experienced businesspeople from outside your business who can help you with your expansion.

Set goals

You've probably had goals all along. But do they still match the direction your business is taking? Are you following the right strategies to reach them? Review your goals, and set new ones if that makes sense. Rethink your strategies if your goals are fine but you're not making headway in reaching them.

Your goals should take into account the underlying values of your business (such as fairness, honesty, reliability) and the purpose of your business. They shouldn't focus purely on making money, or you'll find yourself going astray pretty quickly.

When setting your goals, keep in mind that they should be:

- ✔ **Realistic** — so do your homework before you set the goal.

- ✔ **Specific** — but with enough flexibility built in that you can go off course if the right opportunity arises.

- ✔ **Measurable** — use actual numbers. And build milestones into your plan so that you'll know as you go along whether you're going to meet your target.

- ✔ **Time limited** — set a deadline to meet the goals.

- ✔ **Well communicated** — so everyone knows what's being aimed for and what they're supposed to do to help the business get there.

As an example, after reviewing your profit and loss statement, you might set a goal to increase sales by 5 percent in one year, or to reduce expenses by 10 percent within six months. Your milestone #1 to increase sales might be to identify a specific number of new customers or identify customers for whom you could do more work. Milestone #1 for reducing expenses might be to perform an audit of your business activities. You'd create a document setting out your goal and the tasks involved in reaching the goal, your deadline, your milestones and milestone dates, and assigning the appropriate people to take charge of the tasks. You'd circulate the document, meet with the people in charge of the tasks, and you might also hold a general staff meeting to explain the plan for reaching the goal.

Focus on your strengths

Focus on your areas of strength. Have you heard of the "80/20" rule? It says that the most significant areas of your business (whether significant for good or bad reasons) actually make up a small percentage of your business. For example, about 20 percent of your customers give you about 80 percent of your business, about 20 percent of your products bring in about 80 percent of your revenue, and about 20 percent of your employees do about 80 percent of the work. (And about 20 percent of your clients and employees give you about 80 percent of your headaches.)

So concentrate on your best customers, your top-selling products, your best employees. If you can't move your unproductive customers into your Best Customer category, maybe you should gently try to find them another home. If you've got products that aren't moving and you can't get them moving, maybe you should drop them and free up shelf space. If you can't get more work out of an employee, maybe you should encourage the employee to depart. Don't spend a lot of your time and effort on customers, products, and employees who aren't going to generate a return on your investment.

Learn to live with change

In fact, go beyond living with change and learn to embrace it. Change brings you opportunities as well as challenges.

- ✔ **Keep your eyes open at all times.** What is the economy up to? What is the market up to? What are your customers up to?

- ✔ **Be ready to act when there's a change.** You'll need to reinvent your business, or pieces of it, constantly to keep up with the changing world you operate in. And if you get used to coping with small changes all the time, you'll be better prepared to cope with the big changes that sometimes shake an industry, or an economy.

- ✔ **Assume there will be change even when things are looking pretty stable.** For example, when you invest in new technology, leave yourself some growing room. If a technical product is just right for your business now, you may outgrow it before too long.

- ✔ **Learn from your mistakes.** Analyze what went wrong, make recommendations about how to avoid such a mistake in the future, and then implement any necessary changes.

Make good use of employees

You're the boss. If you hire people to work for you, make sure you help them do a good job.

- ✔ **Communicate clearly.** One of your duties as an employer is to tell your employees what to do (see Chapter 15). Making sure that your employees know what their jobs are and how they're supposed to perform them is also sound business practice. So tell them clearly what you want done, and give the same story to everyone — the employee, the employee's superiors, and the employee's subordinates.

- ✔ **Encourage employee input.** They know quite a lot about your business, so their input is extremely useful. And if you pay attention to their input they'll feel more commitment to carrying out their duties because they're helping to make or at least refine the plans.

✔ **Don't discourage employee output.** By output we don't mean work (although we don't want you to discourage work, either), we mean questions. Tell your employees there is no such thing as a stupid question. But there are stupid mistakes that arise from ignorance and could cost your business a lot of money.

✔ **Run a tight ship — but not too tight.** Don't let your employees treat your workplace as a social forum — they're not there to have extended non-business chats with co-workers or to take nonessential personal phone calls, or to surf the Net or play computer games. But at the same time remember that employees who aren't allowed to speak to their fellows or call home to see how a child or elderly parent is doing are going to be unhappy and unproductive because they'll be cranky and worried. And try to restrain yourself from telling your employees what they can and can't do on their lunch hour or break, even if it involves using your business's computer equipment (as long as they're not doing something that could lead to complaints from co-workers, like visiting porn Web sites).

✔ **In fact, try not to be a control freak in general.** Give your employees responsibility and make them accountable for their work. Tell them that the buck stops everywhere. Let them know in advance what the rewards for achievement are (such as a bonus). (Avoid dwelling on punishments for failure, it's bad psychology. But if you have an employee who does a lot of failing, keep notes — you'll need them when the time comes to fire him or her.) Follow up so you'll know whether they're succeeding.

✔ **Don't let the sun set on employee conflicts.** Warfare among your staff will cripple your business. It's up to you to try to resolve conflicts, and the earlier the better. Don't tell yourself that whether they get along is their business. It's *your* business.

Chapter 20

The Contracting Business Universe

In This Chapter

▶ Thinking about selling your business

▶ Learning about going out of business

▶ Contemplating being put out of business

▶ Planning for your death

*Y*ou've had your Big Bang (when you started up your business). Things didn't work out quite the way you expected . . . and now your business could be heading for the Big Crunch.

It may seem strange in a book about starting a business to talk about getting out of business. But you may have good reasons to get out of business sooner than you planned.

✔ **Someone wants to buy you out.** Your business is so hot that a buyer approaches you. Or you decide to try to find a buyer because you can make more by selling your business than by running it.

✔ **You want out.** Although business is fine, you're ready for a change. Maybe you're bored. Or maybe you hate your business. Or maybe you love your business, but hate your spouse, and have to sell your business to settle property claims in the divorce. Or maybe you love your business and your spouse, but you and your spouse are moving to another city and your business can't. Or, like one-fifth of small business owners, you're planning to retire.

✔ **You have to get out.** A lot of new businesses fail, so there's a chance that your business is not as successful as you had hoped. A buyer (if you can find one) may be able to turn the business around, or you may think it best just to put your business out of its misery. Or your creditors may take over your business to pay off the debts you owe.

> ✔ **You keel over and die.** We saved the most alarming possibility for last. Starting a business doesn't offer you any special immunity from death. (If you incorporated, your corporation theoretically has perpetual existence, but you as the shareholder don't.)

In this chapter, we tell you about what's involved in selling your business as a going concern, going out of business voluntarily, being put out of business by your creditors, and making arrangements about your business in the event of your death.

Parting from Your Business May Be a Joint Venture

What happens to your business if you want out will not be yours alone to decide unless you are in business by yourself, either as a sole proprietor or as the only shareholder of a corporation.

If you have associates, either as partners or as fellow shareholders, they will have something to say about what happens. You won't be able to sell the entire business to an outsider or hand it over to family members without their agreement. Actually, if you have associates, they're the real market for your share of the business if you want out, because outside buyers aren't likely to want a share in someone else's business. But just because you want to sell to your associates doesn't mean they have to buy — unless you have a partnership agreement or shareholders' agreement that covers this situation (see Chapter 5).

For the purposes of this chapter, we assume that you're the sole owner of your business, either as a sole proprietor or the only shareholder in your corporation, or that you have the full agreement and cooperation of your associates for your plans.

Tax Considerations When You Get Out of Business

In Chapter 16, we tell you more than you really want to know about taxes on your business. But we don't tell you everything. We deal only with the taxes on an ongoing business, and we don't talk about the special tax considerations that arise when you get out of business.

The special considerations have to do with *capital gains*.

Taxation of capital gains

When you sell your business, either by selling the assets (property) of the business or by selling your shares in the corporation that carries on the business, you are selling *capital property*, which is property with long-term value. The profit you make from selling capital property is called a *capital gain*. A capital gain is not taxed the same way as the profits you make from running your business. The entire profit you make from running your business is taxed as income. But only one-half of a capital gain is taxed. (If you have a *capital loss*, one-half of it can be used to reduce your capital gains, although it can't be used to reduce your other income.)

Calculation of capital gains

A capital gain or loss is calculated by comparing how much you get when you sell the property to how much it cost you when you bought the property. If you sell property for more than it cost you, you have a capital gain. You don't use just the raw sale price and the raw purchase price when you're making this calculation, though. You use the *adjusted sale price* — which is the sale price of the property minus the expenses associated with selling it, and the *adjusted cost base* — which is the purchase price of the property plus the expenses associated with buying it.

The calculation gets a bit more complicated (What? You thought it was already complicated?) if you sell capital property against which you have claimed *capital cost allowance* (CCA). You can't claim the full cost of capital property as a business expense in the year of purchase because its usefulness to your business lasts for more than one year. However, its usefulness doesn't last forever, so you can claim a percentage of the cost as an expense every year over a period of several years until the entire cost has been claimed. The amount you are allowed to claim on capital property each year as an expense is called capital cost allowance.

If you've claimed CCA on property that you then sell, you have to take the CCA you've claimed into account when you calculate the adjusted cost base of the capital property. If you sell the property for more than its *undepreciated capital cost* (its value on your business's books after you've claimed CCA) — and this is quite possible to do because an asset's book value is not necessarily the same as its market value — then you've claimed too much capital cost allowance, and you have to pay back the excess to the tax authorities.

The excess capital cost allowance is taxed fully as income of your business, not just one-half as a capital gain. (That's because you used the CCA as an expense to reduce the income of your business, and now the government wants to collect the tax you should have paid.) Taxing excess capital cost allowance is called a *recapture* of capital cost allowance . . . picture the tax officials chasing the capital cost allowance around with a net. On the other hand, if you sell capital property for less than its undepreciated capital cost, you did not claim enough capital cost allowance over the time the business owned the property, and you may be able to deduct the entire loss — called a *terminal loss* — as an expense from the income of the business.

And now a few words in plain English

What we've just been trying to tell you, in words of five syllables or more, is that when you sell your business — especially if it's been successful and has increased in value — you may have to pay tax on half of the money you get from the sale (and on all the excess capital cost allowance you claimed on assets purchased for your business). As if you hadn't already paid enough tax when you were running the business — see Chapter 16. So the sale proceeds aren't pure profit to you. Don't go on a spending spree until you've figured out how much belongs to the Canada Revenue Agency. We talk further along in this chapter, however, about ways of reducing the tax consequences of a sale. See the headings "Sale of assets or sale of shares," "Allocation of purchase price if you sell assets," and "Consulting agreements."

Now that we've given you a headache by talking about taxes, we turn to the actual process of parting from your business.

Selling Your Business as a Going Concern

If someone approaches you about taking over your business, or if you want someone to take over and run the business, you're looking at selling your business as a going concern.

In Chapter 9, we talk about buying an existing business. Now we hop over to the other side of the fence to look at the transaction from the seller's point of view.

Knowing what your business is worth

If you are selling your business, you need to have a good idea of what it's worth, both to set a reasonable asking price and to decide whether or not to accept any offer that a buyer might make.

When you sell your business as a going concern, its value is based not only on what its physical assets are worth, but also on the value of its *goodwill*. Goodwill, which can be defined as the likelihood that the business's customers will come back, is usually valued by looking at the business's past earnings. (See Chapter 9 for more about how assets and goodwill are valued.)

The best way to figure out what your business is worth is to find out how much comparable businesses have recently sold for. You may be able to get this information from industry publications, your accountant, lawyer or other consultants, a business broker, or a professional business appraiser.

Finding a buyer

Unless a buyer approaches you, you'll have to find a buyer. You can:

✔ Place an ad in your local newspaper or industry publication under Business Opportunities or Businesses for Sale, or on a Web site that lists businesses for sale.

✔ Read the ads in your local newspaper or industry publication under Businesses Wanted, or check the Buy a Business section of Web sites that list businesses for sale.

✔ Tell your lawyer, accountant, financial advisors, consultants, bank manager, or people in your industry that you're interested in selling.

✔ Use a business broker to find a buyer for you — but keep in mind that if you use a broker, you'll have to pay him or her a commission (a percentage of the sale price).

Dealing with prospective buyers

No one is going to just show up at your door and say "I'll take it! Show me where to sign." Any prospective buyer is going to have lots of questions about your business, and you have to be prepared to answer them.

For example, a buyer might want to

✔ Know why you are selling the business

✔ See the lease for your business premises

✔ Know whether you're aware of any plans by the municipality or landlord that will affect traffic, parking, or access to the premises

✔ See the business's financial statements for the past three to five years (See Chapter 9 for a discussion of what the buyer will be looking for in your financial statements.)

You may or may not be asked to give a lot of information about your business to a prospective buyer, but if a buyer asks you a question, you must answer it honestly. Don't make any false statements about your business. A buyer who decides to buy your business based on your false statements may be able to set the sale aside or sue you for financial compensation if he or she suffers losses after the deal goes through.

Don't agree to show a prospective buyer around your premises, answer questions about your business, or let the buyer see any business documents, unless the buyer first signs a *confidential disclosure agreement* under which he or she agrees not to tell anyone else what he or she finds out about your business and not to use the information for any purpose other than assessing the business for possible purchase. You'll find a sample confidential disclosure agreement on the CD-ROM.

Putting the deal together

If you find someone who wants to buy your business, you'll have to negotiate a deal with the buyer. That will involve deciding between a sale of assets and a sale of shares if your business is incorporated, deciding on a purchase price for individual assets if you go for an asset sale, arranging to pay off the business's debts out of the sale price, and working out the terms of a non-competition agreement and possibly a consulting agreement.

Be sure to get advice from your lawyer and accountant before entering into any agreement to sell your business.

Sale of assets or sale of shares

There are two ways of selling a business — by selling the property the business owns (the assets) or by selling ownership of the whole business.

If your business is a sole proprietorship or partnership, you have no choice — you must sell the business by selling its assets. If you sell the assets of a sole proprietorship or partnership, you personally are the seller and you personally receive the sale proceeds. The proceeds will be taxed in your hands as a capital gain (or loss). Any recapture of capital cost allowance will be taxed in your hands as income.

If your business is a corporation, you have a choice between selling the assets of the business and selling ownership of the corporation by selling the shares of the corporation:

> ✔ **If you sell all the shares of the corporation,** the buyer will become the owner of the corporation. The corporation will continue to exist, and will continue to own all its assets and owe all its debts. The corporation will continue to carry out any contracts it entered into, including any lease on business premises (unless the lease includes a "change of ownership" clause — then the landlord can decide whether to terminate the lease).

✔ **If you sell the assets of the corporation,** the buyer will be the owner of the assets, but you will continue to be the owner of the corporation because you still own the shares. The corporation will continue to exist, even though it won't have much in the way of assets (instead it will have cash from the sale of the assets) — but will still owe all its debts. The corporation will have to carry out any contracts it entered into, including any lease on business premises, unless the corporation *assigns* (transfers) the contracts to the buyer of the assets (which can be done only with the consent of the other party to the contract).

The choice between a sale of shares and a sale of assets will be based mainly on the tax consequences. Consult your lawyer and accountant to help you decide between the two and to find out how to reduce your taxes as much as possible.

If you sell the shares of your corporation, you are the seller and you receive the sale proceeds personally. The sale proceeds will be taxed in your hands as a capital gain (or loss). If you sell the assets of your corporation, the corporation, not you, is the seller. The corporation receives the sale proceeds, and pays tax on any income or capital gains resulting from the sale. You get your money from the corporation in the form of a dividend on which you will pay tax as income (subject to the dividend tax credit).

Owners of a corporation usually prefer to sell shares because

✔ The sale of shares (rather than assets) doesn't involve the recapture of capital cost allowance (CCA). Remember that recaptured CCA gets added to the seller's income and is 100 percent taxable — whereas capital gains are only 50 percent taxable.

✔ The capital gain (if any) on the sale of your shares may be tax-free up to $500,000 because of the capital gains deduction available for some small business corporations (and no equivalent deduction is available on the sale of assets).

✔ The buyer has to buy all the corporation's assets, and can't just pick and choose the assets he wants.

✔ The buyer takes over the debts and liabilities of the business.

Keep in mind, though, that the buyer may well prefer an asset sale because

✔ He'll have a better chance of rejecting assets he doesn't want.

✔ She doesn't have to take over the debts and liabilities of the business.

Allocation of the purchase price if you sell assets

If you sell the assets of your business, negotiating the price has two parts. First, you have to come to a decision on an overall price. Second, you must *allocate* the amount of the purchase price among the various assets included in the sale (in other words, you must assign a price to each asset).

The way you allocate the purchase price among the assets will affect the amount of tax you pay on the sale:

- ✔ You will want the price allocated to each asset to be less than its undepreciated capital cost (its value on your books after deducting the capital cost allowance you have claimed). If you allocate a sale price to an asset that is higher than its undepreciated capital cost, the recaptured capital cost allowance (the extra amount of CCA that you claimed over the years) will be taxed as income in your hands.

- ✔ You will also want to allocate as little of the purchase price as possible to the business's inventory. That's because 100 percent of any amount allocated to inventory will also be taxed as income.

As it turns out, the buyer will want to allocate a higher price to the very assets to which you want to allocate a lower price, because that allocation will save him or her taxes down the road (see Chapter 9).

Paying the debts of the business (if you sell assets)

When you sell all the assets of your business, your business remains responsible for its debts. Your business is you personally if it's a sole proprietorship or partnership, or your corporation if your business is incorporated.

Once a business sells off its assets, it has no way of earning money to pay off its debts. So creditors of a business can get the short end of the stick when a business sells off all or substantially all of its assets. For that reason, every province has legislation to protect creditors. This legislation — called the *Bulk Sales Act* in most provinces — requires the buyer and seller to make arrangements to pay the creditors out of the proceeds of the sale. Usually that means that the proceeds of the sale will be paid directly to the business's creditors, and the owner who sold the assets (the corporation or the sole proprietor or partner) will get only what's left over. So if your business has debts, be prepared to see the sale proceeds shrink or even vanish.

Non-competition agreements

When you sell your business as a going concern, whether by share sale or asset sale, the new owner will want to make sure that you don't set up a competing business nearby and take away all the business's customers. To keep you from doing this, the buyer (if he or she is on the ball) will want you to sign a *non-competition agreement* — an agreement not to enter into a competing business within a specified distance for a fixed period of time. A cautious buyer is likely to want an agreement that prevents you from opening a business anywhere within the orbit of Jupiter and anytime before the 23rd century.

If you sign a non-competition agreement and then start up or join a competing business, the buyer's remedy would be to sue you, either for compensation for the business he loses to your competing business, or for a court order to stop you from competing. But a court will enforce a non-competition agreement only if it's reasonable — in other words, if it keeps you from setting up a similar business for a reasonable period of time and within a reasonable distance of the business location. What's "reasonable" will depend on the nature of the business. It's usually much less than the buyer would like.

Consulting agreements

A consulting agreement keeps you on as a consultant with the business for a limited period of time after the sale, and allows you to turn some of the purchase price of the business into consulting fees spread out over the period of the contract. You'll pay tax on the part of the purchase price that's paid in consulting fees as income rather than as a capital gain — so you'll pay tax on 100 percent of the amount rather than on 50 percent — but you'll get to spread the tax payable out over two or more years.

Going Out of Business

If business is bad, you may not be able to find a buyer to take it over as a going concern. Then your only choice is to close the business down and try to sell off as many of its assets as you can. You'll need to find buyers for the business's inventory, fixtures, and equipment. If you're lucky, you'll raise enough cash to pay off the debts of the business before you close the door and turn off the lights.

Here's some advice on how to go out of business with your head held high and without leaving a bad smell behind.

Finding buyers for your business's assets

If you are in a retail business, you can have a "Going Out of Business" sale to sell off your inventory, and perhaps some of your store fixtures.

Terminating the corporation (if you sell assets)

If your business is a corporation and you sell its assets, you'll still have the corporation on your hands when the sale is completed unless you terminate its existence.

If the corporation has no assets left in it at all, you can do nothing, and eventually the government that incorporated it may *dissolve* it (end its existence) for not filing documents and/or not paying fees.

If the corporation still has assets that must be used to pay off debts of the corporation or that the shareholders want returned to them, the shareholders can vote for the *winding up* (or, in some provinces, for *voluntary dissolution*) of the corporation. When a corporation is *wound up* or *liquidated*, arrangements are made to pay its debts and distribute any remaining property to the shareholders. Then documents are filed with the incorporating jurisdiction (the federal or a provincial government — see Chapter 5) that allow the corporation to dissolve.

A provincially incorporated corporation may need the consent of the provincial department or ministry of finance before it can terminate its existence. Since the minister of revenue is no dummy, no consent will be given until all provincial corporate taxes have been paid. You don't have to have the consent of the CRA to terminate the existence of your corporation, but you should get it anyway to protect the directors and officers of the corporation from being held personally liable to pay federal taxes owing by the corporation.

Speak to your landlord and your municipality before holding any sort of liquidation sale. Most commercial leases state that the landlord's permission is required, and many municipalities require a permit or licence before a going out of business sale may be held. Also check your lease to make sure that your store fixtures don't belong to your landlord.

Also speak to your lenders before holding any sort of liquidation sale. Most commercial loan agreements state that a going out of business or liquidation sale is a breach of the loan agreement. If you hold a sale without first getting permission, your lender may demand immediate payment of all your loans. And if you have given security for the loans, the lender may seize the property that is the security (see Chapters 10 and 18).

When it comes to your machinery, computers, office furniture, office supplies, and so on, you can try offering them to business associates, or family and friends. If you don't get any takers, you can place ads in the newspaper or Internet classifieds, or try to find a dealer who buys used equipment. Businesses sometimes end up giving their assets to charity for a tax credit, or simply giving them away to anyone who's willing to remove them from the premises.

If you don't have the heart to sell off the bits and pieces of your business personally, you can hire a business liquidator to sell your inventory, equipment, and supplies for you.

Unloading leased equipment

If your business has leased equipment, you can't just return the equipment and stop paying. Your obligation to make the lease payments continues for the full term of the lease (see Chapter 6).

Speak to the lessor (the business that leased you the equipment) to find out whether you can arrange for someone to take over your lease. Perhaps the lessor knows of someone who may be interested. Or see if you can negotiate some sort of payment to terminate your lease.

Paying off your debts

If you sell all or almost all of the assets of your business, you will have to comply with your province's *Bulk Sales Act*, which is designed to protect the creditors when a business sells all or substantially all of its assets. You will have to make arrangements to pay your creditors out of the proceeds of the sale. Usually that means that the proceeds of the sale will be paid directly to the business's creditors, and the business will get only what's left over.

If nothing is left over from the sale proceeds but more debts, you're in trouble. How much trouble will depend on whether or not your business is incorporated. If your business is a sole proprietorship or partnership, your business's debts are your personal debts and you will have to use your personal assets to pay off any debts left over after you use up the assets of the business. If your business is incorporated, you won't have to use your personal assets to pay the business's debts unless you gave a personal guarantee for the debts of the business (see Chapter 10). See Chapter 18 for a fuller discussion of what happens when you can't pay your business debts.

Notifying your clients or customers

Let your customers and clients know that you are shutting down your business. If you are a service provider, finish off whatever work you are doing and send your customers a final bill. If you have property belonging to your customers in your possession, tell them to come and pick it up. As a final act of customer relations, thank your customers and clients for their business over the years, and, if possible, refer them to another business that can offer them similar goods or services.

In some professions, you must find another professional in the field to take over your clients. Speak to your professional organization to find out what your obligations are when you close down your business.

Notifying your suppliers

Tell your suppliers that you are closing down your business. Return any goods that you have on consignment. If you have purchased supplies or inventory outright, ask if your suppliers will take anything back and give you a refund.

See if your suppliers will agree to cancel any ongoing contracts for the regular delivery of goods or services. You may have to pay something to get out of these contracts.

Pay off your outstanding accounts if you are able. You may not be able to pay off your accounts until you sell off the assets of your business. In that case, let your suppliers know what you are doing to see that they are paid.

Negotiating with your landlord

If you have leased business premises, you can't just close up shop and walk away. Your obligation to pay rent continues to the end of your lease, and your landlord can sue you if you don't keep on paying. So you'd better have a chat with your landlord.

Unless your landlord is willing to let you out of your lease (which is unlikely), you will have to find someone who is willing to take over your lease. Your landlord may know of someone who is interested in your space. If not, you will have to find a new tenant yourself.

You can place a classified ad in the newspaper under the headings Commercial, Industrial Space; Office, Business Space; Stores for Rent; and so on. Or you can place a For Rent sign in your window. (Make sure you have your landlord's permission.) Or you can use a real estate or leasing agent who specializes in industrial, commercial, and investment properties — but you'll have to pay a commission.

If you find someone who wants to take over your premises, you will have to get the consent of your landlord to the *assignment* (transfer) of your lease.

Being Put Out of Business

If business is really bad, you won't be able to pay your debts. Once that happens, the decision to go out of business may be made for you by your creditors.

When you started your business you probably borrowed money. In fact you probably took out several different loans, such as:

- ✔ A capital loan to pay for your business's start-up expenses
- ✔ An operating loan, perhaps in the form of a line of credit, to help you cover the ongoing expenses of your business
- ✔ A loan to help you pay the purchase price of a particular piece of equipment

You may have other debts as well: an outstanding balance on your business's credit cards or money owing to your business's suppliers. (For more about borrowing money see Chapter 10.)

When you borrowed money (whether through a bank loan or on your credit card or by being given credit by your suppliers) you entered into a contract to repay the money. If you don't repay the money as promised, the lender has the right to take steps to collect the money that you owe. The steps that a lender can take will depend on the terms of your contract and the kind of security the lender holds. If you owe money to (and are not paying) a number of lenders, they'll probably all be taking steps to get their money back at the same time. And some of those steps may put you out of business.

In Chapter 18, we tell you about all the nasty things your lenders can do to you if you don't repay your loans. Here we tell you about only those things they can do that will put you out of business.

How your secured creditors can put you out of business

Your secured creditors are the lenders to whom you gave security (which is the right to take specified property from you if you don't repay the loan).

When you borrowed money and gave security, you may have signed a *general security agreement* or given a *debenture*, both of which give the lender security over all your business assets, including equipment, vehicles, machinery, inventory, and accounts receivable. Under a general security agreement or a debenture, the lender has the right to take possession of all this property (including the right to collect your accounts receivable) if you don't repay your loan. Many general security agreements and debentures give the lender the right to appoint a *receiver/manager* to take possession of the secured property if the loan is not repaid.

Once your lender appoints a receiver/manager, you are effectively out of business. The receiver/manager will take over your business and either liquidate it or run it for the sole purpose of taking possession of the secured property, which will then be sold to pay off your loan.

How your unsecured creditors can put you out of business

If your business can't pay its debts as they become due, and it owes at least $1,000, your business is *insolvent*. If your business is insolvent, any *unsecured creditor* (a lender who has no security from you for the debt) to whom you owe more than $1,000 can *petition* your business into *bankruptcy* if your business commits an *act of bankruptcy*. Not paying a debt when it's due is an act of bankruptcy.

If the court makes an order that your business is bankrupt, it will appoint a *trustee in bankruptcy*. The trustee becomes the legal owner of all the unsecured property that belongs to your business and will use the property to pay off your debts. Once the court appoints a trustee in bankruptcy, you are (once again) effectively out of business. The trustee will take over your business and liquidate it or run it for the sole purpose of taking possession of the unsecured property, which will then be sold to pay the business's debts. If you're a sole proprietor or partner, the trustee will take over your personal property as well as your business property (with some exceptions, so that you don't freeze to death) and sell it to pay your debts (see Chapter 18).

Dying to Get Out of Business

Thinking about dying is not very pleasant. (If it will make you more comfortable, you can think of it as "going supernova.") We cover this topic quite briefly, so you're probably not in danger of having an emotional breakdown before you get to the end of the chapter. If, however, you're keen to know more about how to arrange your business and personal affairs before you pass on, you should read *Wills and Estates for Canadians For Dummies* — also by Margaret Kerr and JoAnn Kurtz and published by Wiley.

If your business is worth anything, you'd probably like to pass its value on to your family when you die. You can do that by leaving it to family members to run or by making arrangements to sell it to someone outside the family and leaving the proceeds to your family.

The decision whether to keep your business in the family or to sell it is a complicated one. If you're thinking of keeping it in the family, you have to consider the nature of the business, the abilities and interests of your family members, and your own temperament:

- ✔ **Is your business one that can be passed successfully on to family members?** Can your business exist without you, or will it simply collapse without your personal presence? Is it worth enough to pass on? Will your estate or your family be able to pay the tax on any capital gain that results if you leave your business to family instead of selling it to an outsider? (The CRA says that there is a "deemed disposition" — a kind of pretend sale — of a taxpayer's property when the taxpayer dies, and the taxpayer's estate has to pay capital gains on any increase in value of property.)

- ✔ **Can your family run the business without running it into the ground?** Does anyone in your family have both the desire and ability to run your business?

- ✔ **Can you do whatever is necessary to ensure a smooth transfer of control of your business to your family?** Can you choose a successor? Are you willing to hand over some control to your family while you are still alive?

- ✔ **Will all hell break loose?** If you have more than one family member, can you leave the business to all of them, or only to one or two? If you leave the business to only some of your family, do you have enough other property so that everyone gets something and no one is seriously prejudiced by your arrangements?

Short-term planning versus long-term planning

You're just starting up your business at this point. Practically speaking, it will probably be some time before you really need to think about whether your family should take over and run the business or whether it should be sold to an outsider. But, again practically speaking, it's not too soon to make some sensible short-term plans about what should be done with your business if you were to die suddenly (or even if you were to become seriously ill).

Whatever your long-term plans for your business, you should have someone on tap who can step in and run your business, at least temporarily. (The best way to maintain the business's value is to keep it running; and even if it's not going to run for much longer, it still needs to be properly shut down.) That person can be your spouse, your adult child, another family member, a trusted employee, or a manager hired by the *executor* of your will (the person you name in your will to handle your estate).

The person, whoever it is, will need access to enough information about your business to be able to operate it on short notice for a period of time. If the person you have in mind is a family member or employee, you should keep him or her informed about the business's activities. You should also keep your business's books and documents in good order and together in an obvious (but secure) place.

In addition, you should consider whether you need life insurance so that you have enough money to

- ✔ Pay the debts of your business.
- ✔ Pay for someone to help your family run the business.
- ✔ Help cover the business's expenses if its income goes down because of your death.
- ✔ Pay any capital gains tax that result from your death.

Finally, you'll need a properly drafted will so that the assets of a sole proprietorship (or partnership) or the shares of a corporation are passed on to the appropriate person or people to allow the business to continue to operate or to close down in an orderly fashion. If you don't have a will, provincial legislation determines who gets your property after your death. You need to speak to your lawyer about drafting a will.

Keeping it in the family

Now back to planning for the longer term.

If you want to pass your business on to your family, you must plan how and when to do it. If you want family members to run your business successfully after you die, you may have to transfer ownership or part-ownership of your business to them while you're still alive. When the time comes, you'll have to consider whether you can afford to retire from the business and/or whether you can afford to pay the tax on any capital gain that results from a full or partial transfer of ownership. (Even if you don't take any money for handing over a share of the business, the CRA says this is another "deemed disposition" or pretend sale that triggers capital gains.) If you can't afford to transfer ownership of your business before you die, you should still give some thought to bringing your family into the business (as employees, for example), so that they can have the opportunity to learn about the business from you and to get to know your clients or customers.

There's a legal side to bringing your family on board too. For example, if you're a sole proprietor and you want to share ownership of your business during your lifetime, you'll have to transfer legal ownership of all the assets of the business jointly to yourself and to the person or people you have in mind as successor(s). If you want to hand over full ownership of your corporation, you'll have to transfer legal ownership of all the shares of the corporation to your intended successor(s). If you want your family to take things over only when you die, you will need a properly drafted will leaving the assets of the business or the shares of the corporation to your intended successor(s).

You'll need the advice of both your lawyer and your accountant about bringing your family into the business.

Selling to an outsider

If you want to sell your business to an outsider — so that when you die your family gets the proceeds of the sale of the business instead of getting the business itself — you have two choices about when to sell. You can sell while you're still alive, or you can let your executor sell after you die. If your business is worth more as a going concern than as a collection of assets, its sale value will probably be greatest while you're in the land of the living. But you may not be able to afford to retire from business, or to pay the tax on the capital gain, if you sell the business while you're alive.

If you want to sell your business during your lifetime, you'll have to find a buyer and then legally transfer ownership of all the assets of the business, or the shares of the corporation, to the buyer. (As you may recall, we talked about selling your business earlier in this chapter.) If you don't want to sell your business until you die, you will need a properly drafted will directing your executor to sell your business and then leaving the proceeds of the sale to your family. Either way, you'll need the help of your lawyer and other professionals to sell your business.

Part V

The Part of Tens

"What'll we do with all this inventory?"

In this part . . .

In three short chapters we offer you ten mottos for a successful small business, identify ten key documents a business needs, and give the addresses of ten Internet sites you may find useful.

Chapter 21

Ten Mottos for a Successful Small Business

*N*eed to motivate yourself for success? Here are ten somewhat hack-neyed mottos that sum up the characteristics of successful small busi-nesses. You can adopt one as your very own. Stay tuned for more than we promised!

Eyes on the Prize

The prize is meeting the goal that you set when you decided to go into busi-ness for yourself. Choose your goal carefully — you want a goal that

- ✔ Is in harmony with your skills
- ✔ Suits your needs
- ✔ Is reachable without superhuman efforts
- ✔ Motivates you every time you think about it

Once you've got a goal, then keep your eyes on it!

We learn something new about this business every day

The right time to stop learning about your business is . . . never. Keep thinking of ways to make your business better and more profitable, by learning about

- Your field of business
- Marketing
- Management skills
- Customer relations
- Risk management
- Law
- Finances and funding

We've even got our competitors working for us

Get ideas and feedback about running your business from every source you can think of. Listen to what your customers and suppliers have to say. Ask advice from business mentors. And don't forget to get advice from other businesses — especially from your competitors — by watching what they do. If they have new ideas, be prepared to adopt them if they're good, but let other businesses get rid of the bugs first. If other businesses are doing something wrong, analyze the problem and avoid it if you can.

By the way, don't forget that your competitors are probably watching you. If you implement a great idea, keep in mind that your competitors may react — for example, by swiping your idea, or by attacking it.

We're focused on what we do best

Concentrate on your core strengths. (How many times do you think you'll hear that over the course of your business life?)

For example, there are five important elements in dealing with consumers: price, product, service, access, and customer experience. No business can do all five well, so concentrate on one or two elements that you're sure you can do well — such as a good product plus good service, or good prices plus a wide range of products, or easy access plus a really good customer experience.

Another thing — don't waste your time and money doing things that you can have others do for you. Delegate or outsource work so that you and/or your business can focus on what you do best.

We have 80/20 vision

This motto probably needs a little explaining. It's an offshoot of focusing on what you do best.

A long time ago a guy named Vilfredo Pareto (1848–1923) came up with a theorem that says, "The significant items in a given group normally constitute a small portion of the total; the majority of items will be, in the aggregate, of minor significance." In business, this translates into the "80/20" rule. According to the 80/20 rule, roughly

- 20 percent of your customers give you 80 percent of your business.
- 20 percent of your employees produce 80 percent of your company's output.
- 20 percent of the items you stock represent 80 percent of your inventory turnover.

So if you're wise you'll identify and focus your attention and energy on the important and productive 20 percent of your business.

By the way, the corollary of this rule is that roughly

- 20 percent of your employees will give you 80 percent of your employee problems.
- 20 percent of your equipment will give you 80 percent of your equipment problems.
- 20 percent of your customers will give you 80 percent of your late payment problems.

So you should also identify the trouble-making 20 percent of your employees, equipment and customers . . . and ditch them.

We watch every penny

The way to make a profit in business is to have costs that are lower than your prices. One way to achieve this is to keep your prices high. The other way to achieve this is to keep your costs down. Guess which method makes more sense?

Our customer is our CEO

Your customer is always right — so listen to your customer when he or she tells you how your business should be run. We mean listen with both your ears open.

A 2001 study conducted by Cap Gemini Ernst & Young showed that retail businesses may be listening to what their customers are saying, but they're definitely not hearing what is being said. Customers say that they want

- **"Low" prices** — by which it seems they really mean they want honest or fair prices
- **"Good" products** — by which it seems they really do just mean "good," and not "great" or superior products
- **"Superior" service** — by which it seems they mean "the ability to return products without hassles," and respect and courtesy from the business's staff

Retailers have replied by providing customers with loyalty programs, special promotions, and ever-wider selections of products and features.

The study consultant said, "Retailers continue to plow money into frequent-shopper programs. Why not give everybody good, honest prices and put more resources into training staff so they will treat customers well?"

Here today, there tomorrow

While you're concentrating on your core strengths, you also have to remember that you're doing business in a world that's in nonstop motion. You have to be ready to change what you're doing and how you're doing it in order to meet changes in economic conditions, market demand, competitors' tactics, supplier capabilities, the law, your personal circumstances, and probably a lot of other things that we can't think of offhand. So be ready to keep reinventing your business . . . or be ready to get trampled into the dirt.

The buck stops everywhere

When you're the only person in the business, the buck stops with you. But once you have others working with you and for you, don't let them get away with doing poor work and then hiding behind you because you're the Big Dog. Let everyone know that they're a very important part of the business and that within the business they're responsible and accountable for their actions.

Make haste slowly

This motto is at least 2,000 years old, and was familiar to the Romans as *"Festina lente."* (Readers of our books have come to expect foreign, usually dead, languages in them.)

To make haste slowly, you should

- ✔ **Sleep on important decisions:** Take your time to think over a matter that will have a major impact on your business — if you make the wrong decision, at least you want it to be a well-thought-out wrong decision, and not a wing-it wrong decision.

- ✔ **Stay cool and calm:** Although it's perfectly okay for an important decision to be based in part on emotion, it's not okay to for it to be based on a wild flurry of nerves.

Ten Expressions That Sum Up Your Feelings

Okay, so we promised you ten mottos and like every successful business we strive to deliver much more than we promised. That way we are sure to keep customers coming back. One of those ten mottos should suit you to a tee. But now, as a bonus, here are ten expressions that you may feel better describe the small business experience:

- ✔ If at first you don't succeed, destroy all evidence that you tried.

- ✔ Eagles may soar, but weasels don't get sucked into jet engines.

- ✔ Experience is something you don't get until just after you need it.

- ✔ The sooner we fall behind, the more time we'll have to catch up.

- TEAMWORK . . . It means never having to take all the blame yourself.
- Aim low, avoid disappointment.
- We waste time so you don't have to.
- Indecision is the key to flexibility.
- Never put off until tomorrow what you can avoid altogether.
- Someday we'll look back on this, laugh nervously, and change the subject.

If you adopt one of these expressions as your REAL business motto, don't let your customers, suppliers, and lenders know. . . .

Added Bonus! Five Personal Mottos for You

Can you believe the freebies we're giving away with this chapter? It's because you're our most valued customer.

Here are some personal mottos — take your pick:

- It's a thankless job, but I've got a lot of Karma to burn off.
- That sounds reasonable. I must need to up my medication.
- An executive decision marks the place where I got tired of thinking.
- I can stay calm while all around me are losing their heads . . . but it usually means I haven't completely understood the seriousness of the situation.
- I'm out of my mind. Please leave a message.

Chapter 22

Ten Key Documents for a Small Business

*M*ake life easier for yourself as a business owner! Don't try to keep all the information you need in your head, or all the agreements you make in a handshake.

Marketing Plan

See Chapter 4. A marketing plan contains your master plan for selling your product and making a killing. Here's what it covers:

- ✔ Your planned method(s) of selling and/or distributing your product or service.

- ✔ Your strategy for promoting the product. This covers things like your business image, your advertising message, your public relations plan, your sales strategy, and your strategy for finding and keeping customers.

- ✔ An analysis of your competitor's strengths and weaknesses and your own strengths and weaknesses, and a strategy for competing.

Partnership agreement or shareholder agreement

See Chapter 5. These documents set out how your business is run. In most provinces, the law makes certain rules about how partnerships are run. The laws include:

✔ All partners have an equal say in management of the partnership business.

✔ All partners are entitled to an equal share of partnership assets.

✔ All partners share equally in the profits of the partnership.

✔ All partners are equally responsible for partnership debts.

✔ If one partner dies, goes bankrupt, or withdraws from the partnership, the partnership is at an end, even if the partnership has more than two partners.

✔ All existing partners must consent before a new partner can be admitted to the partnership.

If you want to customize these terms to suit your own partnership, you need a partnership agreement. It can do a number of things, including let you and your partners

✔ Own the partnership property unequally

✔ Define how the work will be divided among the partners

✔ Divide the partnership profits unequally

✔ Divide responsibility for partnership debts unequally between the partners

✔ Have the partnership continue even if one partner leaves, goes bankrupt, or dies

Similarly, if your business is a corporation, provincial statute law makes rules about how to run it. If your corporation has two or more shareholders, you may want a shareholders' agreement that sets out mutual rights and obligations. A shareholders' agreement can deal with matters similar to those in a partnership agreement as well as other matters such as the right of a shareholder to be or to appoint a director and how to resolve voting deadlocks.

Lease for your business premises

See Chapter 7. A commercial lease for your business premises will cover a whole slew of matters that are important to you, including:

- ✔ The size of the space — you need to know how much room you'll have, but you also need to know the size because rent is usually calculated by the square foot.

- ✔ The cost of the space — basic rent plus any other costs you'll be responsible for.

- ✔ Leasehold improvements — what needs to be done to renovate or decorate the premises, and who pays?

- ✔ The term of the lease — how long does the lease run?

- ✔ The use of the space — can you use the premises for all the activities your business needs to carry out?

- ✔ Protection against competition — in a shopping centre, will the landlord agree to prevent other tenants from competing with you?

- ✔ Hours of business and hours of access to the premises.

- ✔ Facilities in the building — such as elevators, and security, cleaning and other services.

- ✔ Insurance policies that the landlord requires you to take out.

- ✔ Your right to transfer the lease to someone else or sublet the premises to someone else.

Insurance policy

See Chapter 12. You need insurance to manage the risks associated with carrying on your business. Your insurance policy will tell you

- ✔ Who's insured (a corporation or individuals) — so you'll know whose problems are covered by insurance.

- ✔ What perils (risks) you're insured against, and any exclusions — depending on the kind of coverage you choose, risks might include physical injury to others, damage to your property or others' property, damage to your business's computers, your or others' financial loss, defamation, false imprisonment, the death or disability of a key member of the business — so you'll know whether a particular problem is covered by insurance.

✔ Whether you have actual value or replacement cost coverage — so you'll know how much money to expect to receive from the insurance company.

✔ What your premium is — so you'll know what you're paying per year for your coverage.

✔ What your deductible is — so you'll know how much is coming out of your own pocket if you make a claim.

Business plan

See Chapter 11. If a lender or investor is trying to decide whether to give you a lot of money, it will want to be sure before reaching into its pocket that it will get its money back. So the lender will want information about:

✔ How much you want and what you're going to do with it

✔ What your business does, and what industry your business is part of

✔ Why your business can compete successfully, and your strategy for competing

✔ How your business runs or will run on a day-to-day basis, including information about the business's managers

✔ Your business's finances, including projections about income and expenses and information about your personal financial status

This information is traditionally wrapped up in a business plan.

Loan documents

See Chapter 10. If you're borrowing money, a loan agreement sets out matters you need to know about the loan including:

✔ The principal amount of the loan

✔ The lender's obligation to continue giving you loan funds if you're receiving the loan in instalments

✔ The interest rate

✔ The repayment terms and any right you have to pay off the loan early

✔ The kind of security to be provided

✔ Any promises you make to the lender (apart from promising to repay the loan), such as a promise not to dispose of any major assets of the business or to change the nature of the business

✔ What constitutes default under the loan (and will cause the loan to be immediately due and payable), such as breaking any promises made to the lender, not making payment in full and on time, becoming insolvent or going bankrupt, or not paying your debts to other lenders as those debts become due

✔ What the lender can do if you default — such as seizing assets that you've provided as security for the loan, or appointing a receiver

Standard customer contract

See Chapter 13. Providing goods or services to customers is what your business is all about. A standard contract with your customer or client should cover

✔ The parties to the contract.

✔ A detailed description of the goods being sold or the services being provided.

✔ The quality of the goods or services, and what your responsibility is to the customer or client if the quality isn't up to snuff. A contract for goods should also cover the customer's right (or lack of right) to return the goods if there's nothing wrong with the quality.

✔ The price to be paid for the goods or services, and what the GST/PST or HST is.

✔ When and where the goods are to be delivered or the services are to be performed.

✔ When payment is to be made — before, at the time of or after delivery of the goods or performance of the services. If you agree to accept payment after the date of delivery of the goods or performance of the services, the contract should set out the terms for payment, including the amount and date of the payments and the interest rate being charged.

If you're supplying goods and they will be shipped to your customer, the contract must also deal with

- The method of shipping
- Who pays for shipping
- Who bears the risk of damage or loss to the goods during shipping

If you're performing services, the contract should also deal with

- The rights of the parties to change or end the contract before the services have been fully performed.
- What happens if you cause injury to someone or cause damage to property. You may want to limit your liability to compensate the injured person or the property owner.

As you deliver the goods or perform the services, your agreement will serve as a checklist of what you are supposed to do. And if a dispute arises later on, a detailed written contract is evidence of what you and your customer or client agreed to.

Employment contract

See Chapter 15. When you hire an employee, you want both of you to be sure what the terms of employment are. A written employment contract should include

- The job title
- The employee's work duties
- The date the job starts and how long it lasts
- The employee's hours of work
- The employee's rate of pay
- The employee's right to paid vacation days and statutory holidays
- The employee's right (if any) to paid sick days
- Any employee benefits (such as extended health care or dental care or group life insurance)
- A period of probation (a period of time, often three to six months, during which the employer can terminate employment without having to give a reason, notice, or compensation for termination)

✔ Any rights of the employer to discipline the employee (for example, to dock pay or suspend the employee)

✔ A promise by the employee to devote his or her full time and attention to the employer's business

✔ A promise by the employee not to reveal trade secrets or other confidential information obtained during the course of employment

✔ An agreement by the employee not to compete with the employer after termination of his or her employment

Confidential disclosure agreement

See Chapters 3, 11, and 15. If you need to show or tell others confidential information about your business — for example, if you're telling a potential investor about your invention, or giving financial statements or an outline of your marketing strategy to a lender, or sharing trade secrets with an employee of your business — before you make the disclosure you should have the other person (or business) sign a promise not to reveal the information to others and not to make use of it themselves for their own purposes. Otherwise you may find that someone else has made off with your ideas and information and is putting them to good (and profitable) use.

Non-competition agreement

See Chapters 9 and 15. If you buy a business as a going concern, you want to keep the business's customers — so the last thing you want is for the seller to set up a competing business next door. Similarly, if one of your associates or employees leaves your business, you don't want that person setting up his or her own shop and nabbing the customers you worked so hard to get.

To make sure that doesn't happen you must have a non-competition agreement with the seller or your colleagues and employees. Without one, there's nothing to stop the seller from competing with you and taking your customers away, and there may not be anything stopping your former associate or employee from tempting customers away, either.

A non-competition agreement will stand up in court only if it's reasonable — you'll be able to prevent the seller, colleague or employee from setting up a similar business only for a reasonable period of time and only within a reasonable distance of your business location. What's reasonable will depend on the nature of the business.

Chapter 23

Ten Internet Sites You May Find Useful

In This Chapter

▶ Bookmarking some Internet sites that could be useful for setting up and running your business

Canada Business Service Centres (www.cbsc.org)

*T*he Canada Business Service Centres (CBSCs) provide access to both government and general business information. They are designed for use by both start-up entrepreneurs and established small and medium-size businesses in any field. Every province and territory has a CBSC.

The CBSC Web sites provide information on government services, programs, and regulations pertaining to business. Each centre also has an extensive and up-to-date reference collection of general business information from government and non-government sources — topics include starting a business, writing a business plan, finding financing, marketing, exporting, and being an employer. In addition you can get products, services, publications, and referrals to experts. Here are some examples of the products the CBSCs provide:

- **Interactive Business Planner:** This software helps you work online to prepare a business plan.

- **Business Start-up Assistant:** This Web site contains information for starting up a business from federal and provincial government and other sources.

- ✓ **Online Small Business Workshop:** This Internet-based workshop gives information and techniques for developing your business idea, starting, marketing, and financing a new business, and improving an existing small business.

- ✓ **Info-Guides:** These guides on different topics provide brief overviews of services and programs.

- ✓ **"How-to" Guides:** These guides provide information about the potential license, permit, and registration requirements for specific types of businesses.

- ✓ **Fact Sheets:** These fact sheets contain information about starting and running a business and are available online.

- ✓ **Business Information System:** This searchable database contains more than 1,000 documents that describe business-related services and programs of the federal and provincial governments and other Canada Business partners. Each provincial/territorial centre has a similar collection of information about provincial/territorial programs.

Your provincial government

Each provincial and territorial government maintains a Web site. Some of the provincial sites contain good general business information, as well as information about provincial programs for small business, and laws and regulations.

- ✓ Alberta: www.gov.ab.ca

- ✓ British Columbia: www.gov.bc.ca

- ✓ Manitoba: www.gov.mb.ca

- ✓ New Brunswick: www.gov.nb.ca

- ✓ Northwest Territories: www.gov.nt.ca

- ✓ Nova Scotia: www.gov.ns.ca

- ✓ Nunavut: www.gov.nu.ca

- ✓ Ontario: www.gov.on.ca

- ✓ Prince Edward Island: www.gov.pe.ca

- ✓ Quebec: www.gouv.qu.ca

- ✓ Saskatchewan: www.gov.sk.ca

- ✓ Yukon: www.gov.yk.ca

Royal Bank (www.royalbank.com)

The Royal Bank Web site contains information about many general business topics such as starting, managing, financing, and growing a business. Each topic has articles under the headings "Things to Know" and "Business Tips and Strategies," as well as answers to frequently asked questions. You can also download "The Big Idea," software designed to guide you through the steps of developing a business plan. "The Big Idea" has sample business plans, and business tips and strategies from other small business owners and entrepreneurs.

Strategis (www.strategis.gc.ca)

This Industry Canada Web site contains information on a wide variety of businesses organized by sector. Each type of business has its own page, with more pages on a number of sub-topics. The sub-topics vary for each business category, but include things such as:

✔ **Company directories:** with links to lists of Canadian companies carrying on business in the field

✔ **Contacts:** with links to major trade associations in the field and a list of Industry Canada contacts

✔ **Events:** with links to major trade shows in the field

✔ **Regulations and standards:** with links to relevant government regulations and standards organizations

✔ **Related sites:** with links to relevant economic statistics, trade and investment information, labour unions, licences, legislation, trade periodicals, and research and technology information

✔ **Statistics:** with links to selected Canadian statistics on topics such as Canadian market, imports and exports

✔ **Trade and exporting:** with links to relevant international trade agreements and export information

Search engines (www.yahoo.com; www.google.com)

Looking for something on the Internet? Use a search engine such as Yahoo! (www.yahoo.com) or Google (www.google.com). If you use Yahoo! Canada's site (www.yahoo.ca) or Google Canada's site (www.google.ca) you can restrict your search to Canadian sites only.

You may also find it useful to keep a meta-search engine handy. A meta-search engine conducts searches through a group of ordinary search engines, so you won't likely miss anything, no matter how out-of-the-way your topic. We like one called Metacrawler (www.metacrawler.com).

The Yellow Pages (www.yellowpages.ca)

If you're looking for a business in a particular field and/or geographic area, let your fingers do the walking (across your keyboard instead of through the phone book)!

Suppliers (www.thomasnet.com; www.strategis.gc.ca/cdncc)

Thomas Register Online, an industrial search engine maintained by Thomas Industrial Network, contains over 168,000 American and Canadian companies classified by product and service category, some of which post catalogues online. Canadian Company Capabilities, a database maintained by Industry Canada of 50,000 Canadian companies organized by category, contains the name, address, contacts, products and services of each company, and provides a direct link to companies' Web sites.

Office supplies (www.staples.ca; www.officedepot.ca)

And if all you're really looking for right now is some office supplies, you can hit the Web sites of Staples/Business Depot (www.staples.ca), Office Depot (www.officedepot.com), or Grand and Toy (www.grandandtoy.com).

Business Development Bank of Canada (www.bdc.ca)

The Business Development Bank of Canada Web site has information about its lending programs and activities. Pay it a visit if you want to drool over some money.

Canada Revenue Agency (www.cra.gc.ca)

You'd hardly credit the number of fun and exciting items you'll find on the Canada Revenue Agency (CRA) Web site. Forms and information galore about income tax, tax credits, customs, and GST/HST. Visit this Web site whenever you want to get the butterflies in your stomach stirred up — or, of course, whenever you need some information about tax, GST/HST, and so on.

Appendix

What's on the CD-ROM

In This Appendix:

▶ System requirements
▶ Using the CD with Windows and Mac
▶ What you'll find on the CD
▶ Troubleshooting

System Requirements

Make sure that your computer meets the minimum system requirements shown in the following list. If your computer doesn't match up to most of these requirements, you may have problems using the software and files on the CD. For the latest and greatest information, please refer to the ReadMe file located at the root of the CD-ROM.

- ✔ A PC with a Pentium or faster processor; or a Mac OS computer with a 68040 or faster processor

- ✔ Microsoft Windows 98 or later; or Mac OS system software 7.6.1 or later

- ✔ At least 32MB of total RAM installed on your computer; for best performance, we recommend at least 64MB

- ✔ A CD-ROM drive

- ✔ A sound card for PCs; Mac OS computers have built-in sound support

- ✔ A monitor capable of displaying at least 256 colors or grayscale

- ✔ A modem with a speed of at least 14,400 bps

If you need more information on the basics, check out these books published by Wiley Publishing, Inc.: *PCs For Dummies,* by Dan Gookin; *Macs For Dummies,* by David Pogue; *iMacs For Dummies* by David Pogue; *Windows 95 For Dummies, Windows 98 For Dummies, Windows 2000 Professional For Dummies, Microsoft Windows ME Millennium Edition For Dummies,* all by Andy Rathbone.

Using the CD

To install the items from the CD to your hard drive, follow these steps.

1. **Insert the CD into your computer's CD-ROM drive. The licence agreement appears.**

   Note to Windows users: The interface won't launch if you have autorun disabled. In that case, click Start⇨Run. In the dialog box that appears, type D:\start.exe. (Replace D with the proper letter if your CD-ROM drive uses a different letter. If you don't know the letter, see how your CD-ROM drive is listed under My Computer.) Click OK.

2. **Read through the licence agreement, and then click the Accept button if you want to use the CD. After you click Accept, the Licence Agreement window won't appear again.**

3. **The CD interface appears.** The interface allows you to install the programs and run the demos with just a click of a button (or two).

What You'll Find on the CD

The following sections are arranged by category and provide a summary of the software and other goodies you'll find on the CD. If you need help with installing the items provided on the CD, refer back to the installation instructions in the preceding section.

Shareware programs are fully functional, free, trial versions of copyrighted programs. If you like particular programs, register with their authors for a nominal fee and receive licences, enhanced versions, and technical support.

Freeware programs are free, copyrighted games, applications, and utilities. You can copy them to as many PCs as you like — for free —but they offer no technical support.

GNU software is governed by its own licence, which is included inside the folder of the GNU software. There are no restrictions on distribution of GNU software. See the GNU licence at the root of the CD for more details.

Trial, demo, or *evaluation* versions of software are usually limited either by time or functionality (such as not letting you save a project after you create it).

Forms

What follows is a list of all the documents on the CD.

Form 3-1	Application for Registration of Industrial Design
Form 3-2	Confidential Disclosure Agreement
Form 3-3	Application for Registration of a Proposed Trademark
Form 3-4	Application for Registration of a Trademark in use in Canada
Form 3-5	Application for Registration of a Copyright
Form 4-1	Sample Break-Even Chart
Form 6-1	Start-up Plan: Expenses for Equipment
Form 7-1	Space-sharing Checklist
Form 7-2	Leasing Checklist
Form 8-1	Accuracy of Content Web Site Disclaimer
Form 8-2	Hyperlink Web Site Disclaimer
Form 9-1	Franchise Checklist
Form 10-1	Start-up Expenses for a Custom-Built Business
Form 10-2	Start-up Expenses for an Existing Business
Form 10-3	Forecast of Income and Expenses (for the first year of operation)
Form 10-4	Projected Cash Flow Statement
Form 11-1	Sample Business Plan
Form 11-2	Personal Balance Sheet
Form 13-1	Personal Information Protection and Electronic Documents Act
Form 13-2	Customer Satisfaction Survey
Form 14-1	Contract for Provision of Services
Form 17-1	Statement of Income and Expenses
Form 17-2	Balance Sheet

Software

What follows are descriptions of the software applications available on the CD:

Business Plan Toolkit

For Windows. Commercial product. The Business Plan Toolkit has everything you need to evaluate your business idea, test your financials, and start writing your business plan. It includes a Break-Even Calculator, a Starting Costs Calculator, and a Cash Flow Calculator to explore different financial scenarios. It also includes a free sample business plan from a successful business and links to 60 other free sample business plans. Vendor: Palo Alto Software; www.paloalto.com.

Dreamweaver 8

For Mac and Windows. Trial version. Dreamweaver 8 is the industry-leading Web development tool, enabling users to efficiently design, develop and maintain standards-based Web sites and applications. With Dreamweaver 8, web developers go from start to finish, creating and maintaining basic Web sites to advanced applications that support best practices and the latest technologies. Vendor: Adobe; www.adobe.com.

Maximizer 8

For Windows. Trial version. This powerful contact manager software allows you to manager your schedule and keep track of customers, prospects, and vendors. Also included are trial versions of Accounting Link for QuickBooks, which enables you to use Maximizer with QuickBooks Accounting and ecBuilder Pro Lite, which leads you through the steps of creating an online store, as well as a Flash demo that shows you how it all works. Vendor: Maximizer Software Inc.; www.maximizer.com.

QuickBooks 2006

For Windows. Trial version. The software contained on this CD gives you a 60 day trial of the full version of QuickBooks 2006, EasyStart, Pro or Premier version. If you decide to purchase after you try QuickBooks, you can easily unlock your choice of the three products right from the CD. Simply call **1-888-333-8580** (campaign 1300) **to order.** Vendor: Intuit; `www.intuit.ca`.

WinZip 10.0

For Windows. Shareware. With WinZip you can quickly and easily compress and decompress files, folders, and entire folder trees to save storage space and reduce e-mail-transmission time, as well as encrypt and decrypt your sensitive documents. Features include tight integration with Windows Explorer, support for most Internet file formats, and one-click zipping and e-mail. Vendor: WinZip Computing; `www.winzip.com`.

Word Viewer 2003

For Windows. Commercial Product. Word Viewer 2003 lets you open Word 2003 documents and documents created with all previous versions of Microsoft Word for Windows(r) and Microsoft Word for Macintosh. Vendor: Microsoft; `www.microsoft.com`.

Troubleshooting

We tried our best to compile programs that work on most computers with the minimum system requirements. Alas, your computer may differ, and some programs may not work properly for some reason.

The two likeliest problems are that you don't have enough memory (RAM) for the programs you want to use, or you have other programs running that are affecting installation or running of a program. If you get an error message such as `Not enough memory` or `Setup cannot continue`, try one or more of the following suggestions and then try using the software again:

- **Turn off any antivirus software running on your computer.** Installation programs sometimes mimic virus activity and may make your computer incorrectly believe that it's being infected by a virus.

- **Close all running programs.** The more programs you have running, the less memory is available to other programs. Installation programs typically update files and programs; so if you keep other programs running, installation may not work properly.

✔ **Have your local computer store add more RAM to your computer.** This is, admittedly, a drastic and somewhat expensive step. However, adding more memory can really help the speed of your computer and allow more programs to run at the same time.

If you have trouble with the CD-ROM, please call the Wiley Product Technical Support phone number at (317) 572-3994. You can also contact Wiley Product Technical Support at `http://www.wiley.com/techsupport`. John Wiley & Sons will provide technical support only for installation and other general quality control items. For technical support on the applications themselves, consult the program's vendor or author.

Index

• A •

Access Copyright, 64
accountants
  buying a business and, 172, 183
  contract with, 284
  general, 41
  hiring, 348
  problems with, 285–286
  types of, 349
  working with, 285
accounting
  cash, 333
  double-entry, 337, 344
  general, 329–330
  inventory, 338
  jargon, 335
  method, 333
  software, 111, 336
accounts payable, 169
accounts receivable
  aged, 257
  assignment of, 196
  collecting, 257–258
  general, 168
  insurance, 240
  non-payment of, 232
  sale of, 198–199
accrual accounting, 333
Acrobat Reader, 111, 436
adjusted cost base, 177
adjusted sale price, 395
advantages of small business, 10–11
advertising, 42, 78–79
agreement
  confidentiality, 13
  loan, 422–423
  noncompetition, 13
  partnership, 98, 420
  shareholder, 420
alternative dispute resolution (ADR),
    368–370
angel capital, 381–382
angel investors, 200–201
Apache HTTP Server, 154
arbitration, 369–370
arrears of rent, 358–359
The Asper Centre for
    Entrepreneurship, 35
asset purchase
  advantages, 174–175
  disadvantages, 175
  general, 174
  reducing taxes in, 177
assets
  current, 168, 345
  fixed, 168–169, 343
  personal, 192–193
  sale of, 398, 399
  valuing, 170–171
associations
  list of, 43–44
  research and, 38, 269
audit, 322–323, 375–376
auditor, 322, 323

• B •

balance sheet, 168–169, 218, 343–345
bank account. *See* business account
Bank Act, 196

bankruptcy
  act of, 406
  assignment in, 361
  general, 361
  trustee in, 360, 361, 406
Bankruptcy and Insolvency Act, 360, 361
B2B2C.ca, 152
bidding services, 45
bonds, 240
book debts, 196
bookkeeping. *See also* financial
    statements; taxes
  freelancers and, 337
  general, 321, 330–338
  manual, 336
  methods, 336–338
  recording transactions, 331–333, 336
  software, 336–337
  source documents and, 331
"bring-forward" book, 385
Bulk Sales Act, 403
Business Access Canada, 45
business account, 332
business appraiser, 173
business broker, 173
business card, 121–122
business coach, 43, 283
Business Development Bank of Canada,
    194, 431
business evaluator, 42
business incubators, 35–36
business liquidator, 402
business number, 102
business plan
  business managers and, 216–217
  business operations and, 217
  competitors and, 215–216
  executive summary, 221
  financial information and, 217–220
  general, 203–205, 422
  goals of, 210
  industry profile and, 210–212

mini, 208
  preparation, 206–221
  references and, 220
  software, 204
Business Plan Pro, 204
Business Plan Toolkit, 436
buying a business. *See also* franchise
    purchase
  corporate culture and, 169
  financial statements and, 166–169
  general, 161–184
  location and, 165–166
  negotiations for, 173–178
  reasons for, 162–163
  reputation, benefits of, 165
  value and, 164–166, 170–173
  where to look, 163

• *C* •

Canada Business Service Centre (CBSC),
    30–33, 39–40, 205, 292, 324, 379,
    427–428
Canada Business site, 191
Canada Pension Plan contributions, 289
Canada Revenue Agency (CRA), 41, 301,
    302, 310, 311, 319, 320, 322, 324, 340,
    402, 431
Canada Small Business Financing (CSBF)
    program, 194
Canadian Association of Business
    Incubators, 36
Canadian Association of Women
    Executives and Entrepreneurs
    (CAWEE), 43
Canadian Business Corporation Act, 57
Canadian Company Capabilities, 270, 430
Canadian Council for Aboriginal
    Business, 44
Canadian Gay and Lesbian Chamber of
    Commerce, 44
Canadian Innovation Centre (CIC), 69

Canadian Intellectual Property Office
(CIPO), 51, 54, 58, 63
Canadian Internet Registration Authority
(CIRA), 156
Canadian Patent Database, 55
Canadian Venture Capital
Association, 202
capital cost allowance (CCA),
177, 314, 395
capital expenses. *See* start-up costs
capital gains
calculation of, 395–396
tax, 177, 394
capital property, 177, 395
capital purchases, 335
cash accounting, 333
cash flow
projected, 189–191, 347–348
statement, 218
cash receipts and payments journal,
332, 335
CD-ROM, included
software available on, 436
system requirements, 433
troubleshooting, 437
using the, 434
what you'll find on, 434–435
CDEM Business Incubator, 35
Centre for Entrepreneurship Education
and Development Incorporated
(CEED), 35
Centre of Entrepreneurship, 35
certified general accountant (CGA), 349
certified management accountant
(CMA), 349
chartered accountant (CA), 349
Check Point Software Technologies
Ltd., 151
cheque register, 332
claim, third party, 372
clip art, 65
CNET Download.com, 204

co-signor, 197
COD (cash on delivery), 273
commercial lenders, 193–194
common shares, 89
competition
business plan and, 215–216
direct, 71
indirect, 71
prices and, 77
research, 71–72
Competition Act, 25
competitive intelligence, 71
computer. *See also* e-mail; software
hardware, where to buy, 110
Internet service provider (ISP),
112–113, 145
laptop, 109
precautions with, 233–235
technical support, 113
wireless e-mail, 109
wireless-enabled, 109, 150
computer systems consultant, 42, 283
conditional sales agreement
confidential disclosure agreement,
164, 425
consultants, 284
consulting agreement, 178, 401
continuing education courses, 40
contracts
breach of, 282
customer, 423–424
employee, 298–299
employment, 424–425
exemption or exculpatory clause,
264, 277
for goods, 274–275, 281
invisible, 251
lawyers and, 253
oral, 355
parties to the, 249
with professional advisors, 283–285
for services, 275–277, 280–281

contracts *(continued)*
  supplier, 273–277
  terms of, 249–250, 252–253
  visible, 250–251
  written, 251–252, 274, 298–299, 355
Contracts Canada, 45
copyright
  general, 62–63
  music, 66
  permission to use, 63–64
  pictures and drawings, 65–66
  theft, 64
corporate culture, 169
corporate name
  choosing, 57–58
  numbered, 57
corporations
  advantages, 91–93
  bankruptcy discharge and, 361
  directors meetings, 90, 100
  disadvantages, 93
  general, 88–89
  multi-shareholder, 99–100
  running a, 90–91
  sale of shares and, 398
  setting up, 89–90
  solely owned, 96
  taxes and, 92–93, 318
  terminating, 402
cost of goods sold, 342
costs
  direct, 75
  indirect, 75–76
courier account, 113
credit
  cards, 194
  establishing with suppliers, 273
  extending to customers, 256–257
  line of, 195, 196, 355
  non-repayment of, 405–406
  reference, 273
  repayment, 357
  supplier, 198
crime, 227

curriculum vitae (CV), 27
customer privacy, 258–260
customer service
  customer privacy and, 258–260
  general, 248
  problems, resolution of, 254–255
  repeat business and, 253–254, 260–261
  satisfaction survey, 262
customers
  closing notification and, 403
  contracts and, 423–424
  finding, 379, 380
  losing, 261, 263
  maintenance of existing, 377–379, 380
  relationships with, 245–246
  research, 44–45

damage to premises, 231–232
death
  family and, 408–409
  planning for, 407–408
  selling a business and, 406–409
debenture, 197, 405
debt repayment. *See also* guarantee
  arrears of rent, 358–359
  asset sales and, 400, 403
  commercial loan, 355–356
  on credit, 357
  equipment lease, 357
  mortgage, 359
  non-commercial loan, 354–355
  taxes, 360
delegation, 387–388
depreciation, 168
direct mail, 78–79
directors
  general, 89
  meetings, 90
disadvantages of small business
  competition, 15
  insurance, 16
  labour, 17

list of, 11–12
regulations, 15–16
start-up costs, 16
discovery process, 371
disputes
    alternative dispute resolution (ADR),
        368–370
    discussion of, 366–368
    general, 362–372
    negotiation, preparation for, 363–366
distraint, 358–359
distribution channels, 73–74
document shredder, 108
domain name
    choosing a, 61–62, 155
    e-mail address with, 147
    explained, 155
    purchasing a, 114
    registration, 61, 156
    using someone else's, 62
Domain Name System (DNS), 155
double-entry accounting, 337
Dreamweaver 8, 436
DSL (Digital Subscriber Line), 145

• *E* •

e-commerce, 13
economy, shape of, 26
education, 39–40
e-mail
    defined, 146
    etiquette, 147–148
    Internet protocol and, 144
    mailbox, 147
    office set-up, 113
    remote access to, 151–152
    screen and bundle technique and, 386
    software, 147
    spam, 148
    uses for, 147

employee benefits
    paid vacation, 288–289
    statutory holidays, 288–289
employee wages
    government funding and, 292
    paying, 288
    payroll deductions, 301–302, 312
employees. *See also* contracts; payroll
        taxes; termination of employment
    audit of, 376
    discrimination, 290
    finding, 292–293
    government standards for, 302
    hiring, 290–292
    human rights and, 295–296, 306
    interviewing candidates, 294–296
    job applications, reviewing, 293–294
    job description, 291–292
    management techniques, 391–392
    managing, 301
    offering a job to, 298–299
    personality, 295
    policies, 303
    probation, 298
    qualifications, 297
    record keeping and, 302–303
    references and, 297–298, 300
    resume review, 294
    safety, 289
    strengths and weaknesses of, 294–295
employment benefits, 11
Employment Insurance
        contributions, 289
Enterprise UNB, 35
entrepreneurship centres, 34–35
equipment. *See also* computer; phone
    buying, 115–116
    cell phone, 109
    combined, 108
    document shredder, 108
    fax machine, 108
    GPS (Global Positioning System), 110

equipment *(continued)*
  leaseback of, 381
  leasing, 116–117, 403
  pager, 109–110
  PDA (personal digital assistant), 109
  photocopier, 108
  postage meter, 107
  safe, fireproof, 107
  scanner, 108
  selling off, 402, 403
  specialty, 114–115
  surge protector, 108
  UPS (uninterrupted power supply), 233
equity investment, 381–383
Ernst & Young Tax Services, 310
errors and omissions
  defined, 239
  insurance for, 243
essential goods, 268
European Patent Office, 54
executor, 407
expansion
  achieving, 377–380
  consequences of, 373–374
  financing, 381–383
  general, 373–377
  management of, 383–392
expenses. *See also* start-up costs
  auto, 315–316, 334
  business entertainment, 335
  employee salaries, 316
  general, 341
  home office, 314–315, 335
  legitimate business, 313–314
  lowering, 375–376
  sorting, 334
extraction business, 12

• F •

factoring, 198–199
fair market price, 364

fax machine, 108
fidelity bonds, 240
financial statements. *See also*
    bookkeeping; taxes
  creating, 341
  general, 339–348
  historical, 341–347
  pro forma, 341
financing
  expansion, 381–383
  first stage, 382
  Lease or Buy calculator, 117
  mezzanine, 383
  seed, 199–202
  sources, 191–192
First In, First Out (FIFO) method, 338
first stage financing, 382
fiscal year, 168
franchise purchase
  advantages, 178–179
  disadvantages, 179
  evaluating a, 181–183
  finding a, 180
free time, loss of, 11
FTP (File Transfer Protocol), 144, 152

• G •

general journal, 335
general security agreement, 197, 405
going out of business. *See also* selling a
    business
  debt repayment and, 403
  general, 401–404
goods, essential, 268
Goods and Services Tax. *See* GST
goodwill, 171–172
Google Canada, 429
Google Web Directory, 269, 429
GotLogos.com, 122
government assistance, 199
GPS (Global Positioning System), 110

Grand and Toy, 430
graphic designer, 42, 283
GriffTax, 311
Groove Virtual Office, 153
gross profit, 342, 343
gross sales, 342, 343
GST (Goods and Services Tax)
  bankruptcy and, 362
  categories, 324–325
  collecting, 325–326
  filing returns, 339
  general, 102
  registering for, 325
  remitting, 325–326
  tracking, 335
guarantee
  general, 197
  personal, 357–358
guarantor, 197

• H •

headhunter, 43
home-based business. *See* working from
    home
hotspot, 150
HST (Harmonized Sales Tax), 102, 326,
    335, 339
HTTP (HyperText Transport
    Protocol), 144
Human Resources and Skills
    Development Canada (HRSDC), 307
human resources specialist, 43, 283

• I •

icons, explained, 4–5
ideas
  ownership, 48–49
  protection of, 49–50
  value of, 48

income
  defined, 312–313
  gross, 312
  sorting, 333–334
income statement, 167, 218, 341–343
income tax
  calculation basis, 312
  filing returns, 340
  remittance of, 309
incorporation
  alternatives to, 87, 94
  certificate, 90
  general, 87
incubation, 36
industrial design, 50–51
industrial design registration, 50–51
information
  Internet surfing for, 145–146
  searching for, 29–45
infringement, 49
injunction, 371
injury
  to business associates, 228
  to others, 226
  personal, 228
  prevention, 228–236
  types of, 226–228
insolvency, 360–361, 406
instant messaging (IM), 144, 146, 148–149
Institute of Business Appraisers, 173
insurance
  automobile, 240
  bonds and, 240
  broker, 238
  business continuation, 242
  business interruption, 241
  business life, 242
  buy-sell, 242
  commercial general liability, 239
  credit, 242
  crime or theft, 242

insurance *(continued)*
  critical illness, 242
  directors' and officers' liability, 243
  disability, 242, 243
  electronic data processing (EDP), 241
  employers' liability, 244
  errors and omissions, 239, 243
  general, 236–244
  home business, 128
  key person, 242
  liability, 239–240
  limited pollution liability, 239
  overhead expense, 242
  partnership, 242
  policies, 238–239, 421–422
  product liability, 239
  property, 240–241
  requirements, 42
  tenant liability, 239, 242
  third-party liability, 265
intellectual property, 50
Interactive Voice Response (IVR)
    technology, 112
interior designer, 42, 282
internal controls, 339
Internet. *See also* e-mail; web site
  broadband, 145
  connecting to, 144–145
  defined, 143–144
  DSL (Digital Subscriber Line), 145
  FTP (File Transfer Protocol), 144
  general, 143–156
  instant messaging, 144
  peer-to-peer sharing, 152–153
  precautions with, 233–235
  protocols, 143
  surfing for information, 145–146
  Usenet, 144
  using in your business, 144
  virtual private network (VPN), 151–152

  voice over the Internet, 144
  web host, 154
  web server, 154
  wireless access, 150
Internet Corporation for Assigned Names
    and Numbers (ICANN), 61, 155, 156
Internet Information Service (IIS), 154
Internet Light and Power, 152
Internet Protocol (IP), 155
Internet service provider (ISP),
    112–113, 145
Internet tips, 37
inventions. *See also* patent protection
  manufacturing, 51–52
  patent, using someone's, 55
  unpatented, using someone else's,
    55–56
inventory. *See also* accounting
  essential, 268
  general, 168
  liquidation value of, 171
  loan security with, 196
  selling off, 401–402
  sorting expenses, 334
  value, 338
investment. *See* equity investment
IPO (initial public offering), 202, 382, 383

• J •

job applications, 293–294
job security, 10
judicial sales, 359

• K •

Kerr & Kurtz Not-Particularly Standard
    Scale of Aptitude for Entrepreneur-
    ship, 19–23
KPMG Tax Services, 310, 317

• L •

Last In, First Out (LIFO) method, 338
lawsuits, 49, 263–264, 265, 370–372
lawyers
  buying a business and, 172, 183
  contracts, 253, 277, 284
  debt repayment and, 354
  general, 41
  problems with, 285–286
  working with, 285
lease
  base year, 140
  commercial, 137–140, 404, 421
  equipment, 357
  gross, 140
  negotiation, 138–139
  net, 140
  with purchase option, 117, 357
  simple, 116
  terms of, 138
leasehold improvements, 138, 240
ledgers, 335
letterhead, 120–122
liabilities
  current, 169, 343, 345
  general, 168
  long-term, 169, 344
  total, 345
Library of Congress, 63
licence agreement, 48
limited liability, 91
limited liability partnership (LLP), 99
litigation, 370–372. *See also* lawsuits
loans
  agreement, 422–423
  application, 205–206
  business, 195–197
  demand, 196
  government, 199
  interest on, 195

non-repayment of, 196, 405–406
principal amount of, 195
repayment of, 195–196
term, 195–196, 355
"love" money, 193, 354

• M •

Macromedia Dreamweaver, 158
management consultant, 42, 283
management techniques. *See also*
    schedules
  change and, 391
  delegation, 387–388
  employees and, 391–392
  focus on strengths and, 390–391
  giving up control and, 389
  goal setting and, 390
  procrastination, putting off, 387
  screen and bundle technique, 386
manufacturing business
  defined, 12
  product design, 50–51
market. *See also* target market
  identifying, 70
  research, 70–71
marketing
  defined, 68
  plan, 419
  process, 67–82
  strategy, 213–214
marketing consultant, 42, 282
Maximizer 8, 436
media relations, 42, 282
mediation, 369
merchant account, 159
Metacrawler, 429
mezzanine financing, 382
micro-credit funds, 197–198
Microsoft Frontpage, 158
Microsoft Money, 336

Montreal Stock Exchange (MSE), 382
mortgage
  arrears on, 359
  chattel, 196, 357
  collateral, 196, 197
  taking out a, 194
mottos for success, 413–418
multi-shareholder corporations, 99–100
multiple of earnings method, 172
MYOB (Mind Your Own Business), 336

• N •

name search, 57
National Angel Organization, 201
National Inventor Fraud Center (U.S.), 69
National Library of Canada, 63
negligence, 226–227, 239
net income, 342, 343, 345
net worth, 345
net worth statement, 219–220
networking, 78
non-competition agreement, 176–178,
  400–401, 425
Northern Alberta Business Incubator, 35
NUANS, 57, 59
NUANS "Do it yourself" Real-Time
  System (RTS), 57

• O •

occupier's liability, 226
office. *See also* equipment
  courier account, 113
  décor, 103–104
  furnishings, 105–106
  furniture, 104–105
  head, 107–108
  portable, 108–110
  setting up, 103–123
  signage, 107

stationery, 118–122
  supplies, 106
Office Depot, 430
Ontario Small Business Enterprise
  Centres, 34
operating expenses
  list of, 187
  projection of, 187–189
order for specific performance, 371
overdraft protection, 195
owner's equity, 344, 345

• P •

partnership
  advantages, 99
  agreement, 98, 420
  disadvantages, 99
  general, 96–98
  limited liability, 99
  running a, 98–99
  setting up, 98
  taxes, 317
patent protection, 53–54. *See also*
  inventions
payment, obtaining, 255–258. *See also*
  debt repayment
payroll journal, 335
payroll taxes
  defined, 326
  federal, 102
  filing returns, 340
  record keeping and, 303
  registering for, 102
  remitting, 289, 309
PDA (personal digital assistant), 109, 151
PDF (Portable Document Format), 436
peer-to-peer sharing, 152–153
*Personal Information Protection and
  Electronic Documents Act (PIPEDA),*
  158, 160, 258–260, 279, 307

Personal Property Security Act, 257
phone
    cell, 109
    equipment, 107
    long-distance rate packages, 112
    screen and bundle technique and, 386
    services, 111–112
    time plan, 112
    unified messaging, 113
    working from home and, 130–131
photocopier, 108
postage meter, 107
power of sale, 359
pre-incubation, 36
precedent, 365
preferred shares, 89
premises. *See also* lease
    buying, 140–141
    damage to, 231–232
    general, 133–141
    industrial, 134
    office, 134
    renting, 135–140
    retail, 133
    shared, 134–135
presentation, 111
prices
    raising, 376–377
    setting, 74–77
procrastination, 387
profit and loss statement. *See* income
    statement
profit margin, 15
promotion, 78
prospectus, 382
PST (provincial sales tax), 323–324
public domain ideas, 49
publicist, 282
publicity, 79–80
publicity "hook," 79
purchase money security interest
purchase order form, 274

purchase price allocation, 400
purchases journal, 333, 335

• *Q* •

Qnext, 153
qualities, entrepreneurial, 17–19
quick ratio, 345
QuickBooks, 336
QuickBooks Pro, 436
Quicken, 336
QuickTax, 311

• *R* •

recaptured capital cost allowance, 177
registration mark, 51
résumé, 294
retail business, 12
retained earnings, 381
retainer, 198
revenue, 341
risk. *See also* injury; insurance
    audit of, 226
    business interruption and, 235
    computers and, 233–235
    death and, 236
    Internet hazards and, 233–235
    loss of records and, 233
    reducing, 228–236
risk management, 225–244
Royal Bank, 194, 429
royalties, 178

• *S* •

safe, fireproof, 107
sale of business. *See* selling a business
sales. *See also* contracts
    closing, 247
    pitch, 247
    process, 246–247

sales journal, 333, 335
sales taxes. *See also* GST; HST; PST
  filing returns, 339
  general, 323–326
  remitting, 309
scanner, 108
schedules
  "bring-forward" book, 385
  tickler system and, 230, 385
  tips for, 384–386
screen and bundle technique, 386
search engines, 159, 429–430
Secure Socket Layer (SSL), 158
Securities Commission, 382, 383
seed capital, 199–202
selling a business. *See also* going out of
    business
  death and, 406–409
  general, 393–401
  partners and, 394
  prospective buyers, 397–398
  reasons to, 393–394
  tax considerations and, 394–396
  value and, 396–397
service business, 12
service mark, 58
service providers, 269
share purchase
  advantages, 175–176
  described, 174
ShareDirect, 153
shareholders
  agreement, 420
  described, 88, 89
  meetings, 91, 100
  taxes, 92
shares
  common, 89
  pledge of, 197
  preferred, 89
  sale of, 398, 399
signage, 107

Simply Accounting, 336
small business centres, 34–35
SMTP (Simple Mail Transfer
    Protocol), 144
SOCAN (The Society of Composers,
    Authors and Music Publishers of
    Canada), 66
software
  accounting, 111, 336
  bookkeeping, 336–337
  business plan, 204
  CD-ROM, available on, 436
  contact management system, 111
  desktop publishing, 111
  e-mail, 147
  income tax returns, 311
  security, 111
  spreadsheets, 111
  web site, 111, 158
  word processing, 111
sole ownership, 85–86
sole proprietorship
  advantages, 95
  bankruptcy discharge and, 361
  disadvantages, 96
  running a, 95
  setting up, 95
  taxes, 95
source documents, 331
spam, 148
specific security agreement, 196
Staples/Business Depot, 430
start-up considerations, 24–28
start-up costs, 16, 72–73, 185–187
start-up ideas, 13, 14, 15, 16
statement of net worth, 219–220
stationery, 118–122
Strategis, 36–38, 117, 191, 198, 199,
    269, 429
suppliers
  choosing, 270–272
  closing notification and, 404

credit, 198
finding, 269–270
inventory and parts, 271
problems with, 279–281
of professional services, 282–286
relationships with, 278–279
researching, 45
service, 272
web sites, 430
surge protector, 108
Symantec Corp, 151

● **T** ●

target market, 212–213
tax advantages, 11
tax avoidance, 312
tax evasion, 312
taxes. *See also* bookkeeping; financial
    statements; income tax; payroll
    taxes; sales taxes
  arrears of, 360
  audit, 322–323
  capital gains, 177, 394
  filing returns, 319–320, 339–340
  home business deductions, 127
  other business, 309, 327
  partnership, 317
  preparing for, 310–311
  property, 313, 315
  sole proprietorship, 317
TaxWiz, 311
termination of employment. *See also*
    wrongful dismissal
  general, 304–307
  human rights and, 306
  just cause, 304
  notice requirements, 307
  without cause, 305
terms of use agreement, 157–158
theft, 233

third party claim, 372
third party processor, 159–160
Thomas Register Online, 430
ThomasNet, 59, 270
tickler system, 230, 385
Toronto Business Development
    Centre, 35
Toronto Stock Exchange (TSE), 382
tort, 227
trade associations, 38
trade journals, 38
trade name, 58
trade secret, 52–53, 56
trademark
  choosing, 58–59
  defined, 58
  protection, 60
  registration, 60
  unregistered, 59
  using someone else's, 60–61
training, 39–40

● **U** ●

undepreciated capital cost, 395
underwriter, 382
United Kingdom Patent Office, 51
United States Copyright Office, 63
United States Patent and Trademark
    Office (USPTO), 51, 54, 58
UPS (uninterrupted power supply), 233
URL (Uniform Resource Locator), 159
Usenet, 144

● **V** ●

valuation method, 172
value
  book, 168, 171
  fair market, 170
  inventory, 338

value (continued)
  liquidation, 171
  replacement, 171
  selling a business and, 396–397
  sources, 172–173
Vancouver Stock Exchange (VSE), 382
venture capital, 201–202, 381–382
video conferencing, 111
virtual private network (VPN), 151–152
VistaPrint, 122
voice recognition, 111
VoIP (Voice over Internet Protocol), 107, 144, 146, 149–150

• W •

warranty, 277
web host, 154
web server, 154
web site. See also Internet
  attracting customers to, 158–159
  bank and trust company, 34
  content, 156
  design, 114, 158
  designer, 42
  disclaimer, 157
  domain name, 114
  online payments and, 159–160
  provincial/territorial government, 33–34, 428
  Royal Bank, 429
  search engines and, 159
  setting up, 113–114
  software, 111, 158
  terms of use agreement and, 157–158
  why you need a, 153–154
wholesale business, 12

WiFi (wireless fidelity), 150
Wi-FiHotSpotList.com, 150
WinZip, 111, 436
Word Viewer, 436
workers' compensation, 243–244
working from home
  advantages, 126
  disadvantages, 126
  family and, 129, 130
  general, 125–133
  hours and, 131
  income tax deduction, 127
  insurance, 128
  isolation and, 132
  legal restrictions, 128
  personality and, 129–130
  phones and, 130–131
  professionalism, 131
  space and, 127
  tips, 130–133
  work environment and, 132
World Intellectual Property Organization, 63
World Wide Web, 144
wrongful dismissal, 305–306. See also termination of employment

• Y •

Yahoo!, 269, 429
Yahoo! Canada, 429
year-end, 343
The Yellow Pages, 430
The Young Entrepreneurs Association, 43
Young Entrepreneurs Association (YEA), 43

Notes

Notes

Notes

Notes

John Wiley & Sons Canada Ltd., End-User License Agreement

READ THIS. You should carefully read these terms and conditions before opening the software packet(s) included with this book ("Book"). This is a license agreement ("Agreement") between you and John Wiley & Sons Canada, Ltd. ("Wiley Canada"). By opening the accompanying software packet(s), you acknowledge that you have read and accept the following terms and conditions. If you do not agree and do not want to be bound by such terms and conditions, promptly return the Book and the unopened software packet(s) to the place you obtained them for a full refund.

1. **Licence Grant.** Wiley Canada grants to you (either an individual or entity) a nonexclusive license to use one copy of the enclosed software program(s) (collectively, the "Software") solely for your own personal or business purposes on a single computer (whether a standard computer or a workstation component of a multiuser network). The Software is in use on a computer when it is loaded into temporary memory (RAM) or installed into permanent memory (hard disk, CD-ROM, or other storage device). Wiley Canada reserves all rights not expressly granted herein.

2. **Ownership.** Wiley Canada is the owner of all right, title, and interest, including copyright, in and to the compilation of the Software recorded on the disk(s) or CD-ROM ("Software Media"). Copyright to the individual programs recorded on the Software Media is owned by the author or other authorized copyright owner of each program. Ownership of the Software and all proprietary rights relating thereto remain with Wiley Canada and its licensers.

3. **Restrictions on Use and Transfer.**

   (a) You may only (i) make one copy of the Software for backup or archival purposes, or (ii) transfer the Software to a single hard disk, provided that you keep the original for backup or archival purposes. You may not (i) rent or lease the Software, (ii) copy or reproduce the Software through a LAN or other network system or through any computer subscriber system or bulletin-board system, or (iii) modify, adapt, or create derivative works based on the Software.

   (b) You may not reverse engineer, decompile, or disassemble the Software. You may transfer the Software and user documentation on a permanent basis, provided that the transferee agrees to accept the terms and conditions of this Agreement and you retain no copies. If the Software is an update or has been updated, any transfer must include the most recent update and all prior versions.

4. **Restrictions on Use of Individual Programs.** You must follow the individual requirements and restrictions detailed for each individual program in Appendix A, "About CD," of this Book. These limitations are also contained in the individual license agreements recorded on the Software Media. These limitations may include a requirement that after using the program for a specified period of time, the user must pay a registration fee or discontinue use. By opening the Software packet(s), you will be agreeing to abide by the licenses and restrictions for these individual programs that are detailed in the "About the CD" appendix and on the Software Media. None of the material on this Software Media or listed in this Book may ever be redistributed, in original or modified form, for commercial purposes.

5. **Limited Warranty.**

   (a) Wiley Canada warrants that the Software and Software Media are free from defects in materials and workmanship under normal use for a period of sixty (60) days from the date of purchase of this Book. If Wiley Canada receives notification within the warranty period of defects in materials or workmanship, Wiley Canada will replace the defective Software Media.

   (b) **WILEY CANADA AND THE AUTHOR OF THE BOOK DISCLAIM ALL OTHER WARRANTIES, EXPRESS OR IMPLIED, INCLUDING WITHOUT LIMITATION IMPLIED WARRANTIES OF MERCHANTABILITY AND FITNESS FOR A PARTICULAR PURPOSE, WITH RESPECT TO THE SOFTWARE, THE PROGRAMS, THE SOURCE CODE CONTAINED THEREIN, AND/OR THE TECHNIQUES DESCRIBED IN THIS BOOK. WILEY CANADA DOES NOT WARRANT THAT THE FUNCTIONS CONTAINED IN THE SOFTWARE WILL MEET YOUR REQUIREMENTS OR THAT THE OPERATION OF THE SOFTWARE WILL BE ERROR FREE.**

   (c) This limited warranty gives you specific legal rights, and you may have other rights that vary from jurisdiction to jurisdiction.

6. **Remedies.**

   (a) Wiley Canada's entire liability and your exclusive remedy for defects in materials and workmanship shall be limited to replacement of the Software Media, which may be returned with a copy of your receipt to the following address: Software Media Fulfillment Department, Attn.: Canadian Small Business Kit For Dummies, 2nd Edition, Wiley Publishing, Inc, 10475 Crosspoint Blvd, Indianapolis, Indiana 46256, or call 800-762-2974. Please allow three to four weeks for delivery. This Limited Warranty is void if failure of the Software Media has resulted from accident, abuse, or misapplication. Any replacement Software Media will be warranted for the remainder of the original warranty period or thirty (30) days, whichever is longer.

   (b) In no event shall Wiley Canada or the author be liable for any damages whatsoever (including without limitation damages for loss of business profits, business interruption, loss of business information, or any other pecuniary loss) arising from the use of or inability to use the Book or the Software, even if Wiley Canada has been advised of the possibility of such damages.

   (c) Because some jurisdictions do not allow the exclusion or limitation of liability for consequential or incidental damages, the above limitation or exclusion may not apply to you.

7. **General.** This Agreement constitutes the entire understanding of the parties and revokes and supersedes all prior agreements, oral or written, between them and may not be modified or amended except in a writing signed by both parties hereto that specifically refers to this Agreement. This Agreement shall take precedence over any other documents that may be in conflict herewith. If any one or more provisions contained in this Agreement are held by any court or tribunal to be invalid, illegal, or otherwise unenforceable, each and every other provision shall remain in full force and effect.

BUSINESS & PERSONAL FINANCE

0-470-83768-3

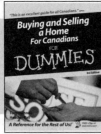

0-470-83740-3

Also available:

- Accounting For Dummies
  0-7645-5314-3
- Business Plans Kit For Dummies
  0-7645-5365-8
- Cover Letters For Dummies
  0-7645-5224-4
- Investing For Canadians For
  Dummies 0-470-83361-0
- Leadership For Dummies
  0-7645-5176-0

- Managing For Dummies
  0-7645-1771-6
- Marketing For Dummies
  0-7645-5600-2
- Money Management All-in-One Desk
  Reference For Canadians For
  Dummies 0-470-83360-2
- Resumes For Dummies
  0-7645-5471-9
- Stock Investing For Canadians For
  Dummies 0-470-83342-4

HOME & BUSINESS COMPUTER BASICS

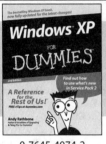

0-7645-4074-2

0-7645-3758-X

Also available:

- ACT! 6 For Dummies 0-7645-2645-6
- iLife '04 All-in-One Desk Reference
  For Dummies 0-7645-7347-0
- Macs For Dummies 0-7645-5656-8
- Microsoft Money 2004 For Dummies
  0-7645-4195-1
- Office 2003 All-in-One Desk
  Reference For Dummies
  0-7645-3883-7

- Outlook 2003 For Dummies
  0-7645-3759-8
- PCs For Dummies 0-7645-4074-2
- TiVo For Dummies 0-7645-6923-6
- Upgrading & Fixing PCs For
  Dummies 0-7645-1665-5
- Windows XP For Dummies 2/e

FOOD, HOME, GARDEN, HOBBIES, MUSIC & PETS

0-7645-9904-6

0-7645-5232-5

Also available:

- Bass Guitar For Dummies
  0-7645-2487-9
- Diabetes Cookbook For Dummies
  0-7645-5130-2
- Gardening For Canadians For
  Dummies 1-894413-37-7
- Holiday Decorating For Dummies
  0-7645-2570-0
- Home Improvement All-in-One Desk
  Reference For Dummies
  0-7645-5680-0

- Knitting For Dummies 0-7645-5395-x-
- Piano For Dummies 0-7645-5105-1
- Puppies For Dummies 0-7645-5255-4
- Scrapbooking For Dummies
  0-7645-7208-3
- Senior Dogs For Dummies
  0-7645-5818-8
- Singing For Dummies 0-7645-2475-5
- 30-Minute Meals For Dummies
  0-7645-2589-1

INTERNET & DIGITAL MEDIA

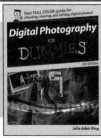

0-7645-9802-3

0-7645-6924-4

Also available:

- CD & DVD Recording For Dummies
  0-7645-5956-7
- eBay For Dummies 0-7645-5654-1
- Fighting Spam For Dummies
  0-7645-5965-6
- Genealogy Online For Dummies
  0-7645-5964-8
- Google For Dummies 0-7645-4420-9

- Home Recording For Musicians For
  Dummies 0-7645-1634-5
- The Internet For Dummies
  0-7645-4173-0
- Preventing Identity Theft For
  Dummies 0-7645-7336-5
- Roxio Easy Media Creator For
  Dummies 0-7645-7131-1

SPORTS, FITNESS, PARENTING, RELIGION & SPIRITUALITY

0-7645-5146-9

0-7645-5418-2

Also available:

- The Bible For Dummies
  0-7645-5296-1
- Buddhism For Dummies
  0-7645-5359-3
- Catholicism For Dummies
  0-7645-5391-7
- Curling For Dummies 1-894413-30x

- Pilates For Dummies 0-7645-5397-6
- Rugby For Dummies 0-470-83405-6
- Teaching Kids to Read For Dummies
  0-7645-4043-2
- Weight Training For Dummies
  0-7645-5168-x

TRAVEL

0-470-83398-x

0-7645-5453-0

Also available:
- Alaska For Dummies 0-7645-1761-9
- Cancun and the Yucatan For Dummies 0-7645-2437-2
- Cruise Vacations For Dummies 0-7645-6941-4
- Europe For Dummies 0-7645-5456-5
- Ireland For Dummies 0-7645-5455-7
- Las Vegas For Dummies 0-7645-5448-4
- London For Dummies 0-7645-4277-x
- New York City For Dummies 0-7645-6945-7
- Paris For Dummies 0-7645-5494-8
- Walt Disney World & Orlando For Dummies 0-7645-6943-0

NETWORKING, SECURITY, PROGRAMMING & DATABASES

0-7645-3910-8

0-7645-5784-x

Also available:
- A+ Certification For Dummies 0-7645-4187-0
- Access 2003 All-in-One Desk Reference For Dummies 0-7645-3988-4
- Beginning Programming For Dummies 0-7645-4997-9
- C++ For Dummies 0-7645-6852-3
- C For Dummies 0-7645-7068-4
- Firewalls For Dummies 0-7645-4048-3
- Home Networking For Dummies 0-7645-4279-6
- Network Security For Dummies 0-7645-1679-5
- Networking For Dummies 0-7645-1677-9
- TCP/IP For Dummies 0-7645-1760-0
- VBA For Dummies 0-7645-3989-2
- Wireless All-in-One Desk Reference For Dummies 0-7645-7496-5

HEALTH & SELF-HELP

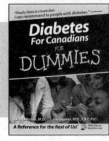

0-470-83370-x

0-7645-4149-8

Also available:
- Alzheimer's For Dummies 0-7645-3899-3
- Asthma For Dummies 0-7645-4233-8
- Controlling Cholesterol For Dummies 0-7645-5440-9
- Depression For Dummies 0-7645-3900-0
- Fertility For Dummies 0-7645-2549-2
- Fibromyalgia For Dummies 0-7645-5441-7
- Improving Your Memory For Dummies 0-7645-5435-2
- Pregnancy For Dummies 0-7645-4483-7
- Quitting Smoking For Dummies 0-7645-2629-4
- Relationships For Dummies 0-7645-5384-4
- Thyroid For Dummies 0-7645-5385-2

EDUCATION, HISTORY & REFERENCE

0-470-83656-3

0-7645-2498-4

Also available:
- Algebra For Dummies 0-7645-5325-9
- British History For Dummies 0-7645-7021-8
- English Grammar For Dummies 0-7645-5322-4
- Forensics For Dummies 0-7645-5580-4
- Italian For Dummies 0-7645-5196-5
- Latin For Dummies 0-7645-5431-x
- Science Fair Projects For Dummies 0-7645-5460-3
- Spanish For Dummies 0-7645-5194-9
- U.S. History For Dummies 0-7645-5249-x

Available wherever books are sold. For more information or to order direct: U.S. customers visit www.dummies.com or call 1-877-762-2974.
U.K. customers visit www.wileyeurope.com or call 0800 243407. Canadian customers visit www.wiley.ca or call 1-800-567-4797.

 WILEY